The Spectator. [By Joseph Addison, Richard Steele and Others]

ODI PROFANUM

Theodore Iulius Hare.

F. Hayman delin.   C. Grignion sculp.

THE

SPECTATOR.

VOLUME the THIRD.

LONDON:

Printed for J. and R. TONSON and S. DRAPER.

MDCCLIII.

To the Right Honourable

HENRY BOYLE, Efq;

SIR,

AS the profeft Defign of this Work is to enter-tain its Readers in ge-neral, without giving Offence to any particular Perfon, it would be difficult to find out fo proper

DEDICATION.

a Patron for it as Your Self, there being none whose Merit is more universally acknowledged by all Parties, and who has made himself more Friends, and fewer Enemies. Your great Abilities, and unqueftioned Integrity, in thofe high Employments which You have paffed through, would not have been able to have raifed You this general Approbation, had they not been accompanied with that Moderation in an high Fortune, and that Affability of Manners, which are fo confpicuous through all Parts of your Life. Your Averfion to any Oftentati-

ous

DEDICATION.

ous Arts of setting to Show those great Services which you have done the Publick, has not likewise a little contributed to that Universal Acknowledgment which is paid You by your Country.

THE Confideration of this Part of Your Character, is that which hinders me from enlarging on those Extraordinary Talents, which have given You so great a Figure in the *Britiſh* Senate, as well as on that Elegance and Politeneſs which appear in Your more retired Converſation. I ſhould be unpardonable, if, after what I have ſaid, I ſhould longer detain

A 2   You

DEDICATION.

You with an Address of this Nature: I cannot, however, conclude it without owning those great Obligations which You have laid upon,

S I R,

Your most obedient,

humble Servant,

The SPECTATOR.

THE

SPECTATOR.

VOL. III.

THE
SPECTATOR.

N°. 170 *Friday, September 14, 1711.*

In amore hæc omnia insunt vitia: injuriæ,
Suspiciones, inimicitiæ, induciæ,
Bellum, pax rursum —— Ter. Eun. Act 1. Sc. 1.

All these Inconveniences are incident to Love: Reproaches,
Jealousies, Quarrels, Reconcilements, War, and then
Peace.

PON looking over the Letters of my female Correspondents, I find several from
Women complaining of Jealous Husbands,
and at the same time protesting their own
Innocence; and desiring my Advice on
this Occasion. I shall therefore take this
Subject into my Consideration; and the more willingly,
because I find that the Marquis of *Hallifax*, who, in his
Advice to a Daughter, has instructed a Wife how to behave herself towards a false, an intemperate, a cholerick,
a sullen, a covetous, or a silly Husband, has not spoken
one Word of a Jealous Husband.

JEALOUSY is that Pain which a Man feels from the
Apprehension that he is not equally beloved by the Person
A 4   *whom*

whom he intirely loves. Now because our inward Paffions
and Inclinations can never make themfelves vifible, it is
impoffible for a jealous Man to be thoroughly cured of his
Sufpicions. His Thoughts hang at beft in a State of
Doubtfulnefs and Uncertainty; and are never capable of
receiving any Satisfaction on the advantageous Side; fo
that his Inquiries are moft fuccefsful when they difcover
nothing. His Pleafure arifes from his Difappointments,
and his Life is fpent in purfuit of a Secret that deftroys
his Happinefs if he chance to find it.

A N ardent Love is always a ftrong Ingredient in this
Paffion; for the fame Affection which ftirs up the jealous
Man's Defires, and gives the Party beloved fo beautiful a
Figure in his Imagination, makes him believe fhe kindles
the fame Paffion in others, and appears as amiable to all
Beholders. And as Jealoufy thus arifes from an extraordinary Love, it is of fo delicate a Nature, that it fcorns to
take up with any thing lefs than an equal Return of Love.
Not the warmeft Expreffions of Affection, the fofteft and
moft tender Hypocrify, are able to give any Satisfaction,
where we are not perfuaded that the Affection is real and
the Satisfaction mutual. For the jealous Man wifhes himfelf a kind of Deity to the Perfon he loves: He would be
the only Pleafure of her Senfes, the Employment of her
Thoughts; and is angry at every thing fhe admires, or
takes Delight in, befides himfelf.

P H Æ D R I A's Requeft to his Miftrefs, upon his
leaving her for three Days is inimitably beautiful and
natural.

Cum milite ifto præfens, abfens ut fies:
Dies noctefque me ames: me defideres:
Me fomnies: me expectes: de me cogites:
Me fperes: me te oblectes: mecum tota fis:
Meus fac fis poftremò animus, quando ego fum tuus.

Ter. Eun. Act 1. Sc. 2.

" When you are in company with that Soldier, behave
" as if you were abfent: but continue to love me by Day
" and by Night: want me; dream of me; expect me;
" think of me; wifh for me; delight in me: be wholly
" with me: in fhort, be my very Soul, as I am yours.

T H E

THE jealous Man's Difeafe is of fo malignant a Nature, that it converts all it takes into its own Nourifhment. A cool Behaviour fets him on the Rack, and is interpreted as an inftance of Averfion or Indifference ; a fond one raifes his Sufpicions, and looks too much like Diffimulation and Artifice. If the Perfon he loves be chearful, her Thoughts muft be employed on another ; and if fad, fhe is certainly thinking on himfelf. In fhort, there is no Word or Gefture fo infignificant, but it gives him new Hints, feeds his Sufpicions, and furnifhes him with frefh Matters of Difcovery : So that if we confider the Effects of this Paffion, one would rather think it proceeded from an inveterate Hatred, than an exceffive Love ; for certainly none can meet with more Difquietude and Uneafinefs than a fufpected Wife, if we except the jealous Hufband.

BUT the great Unhappinefs of this Paffion is, that it naturally tends to alienate the Affection which it is fo folicitous to ingrofs ; and that for thefe two Reafons, becaufe it lays too great a Conftraint on the Words and Actions of the fufpected Perfon, and at the fame time fhews you have no honourable Opinion of her ; both of which are ftrong Motives to Averfion.

NOR is this the worft Effect of Jealoufy ; for it often draws after it a more fatal Train of Confequences, and makes the Perfon you fufpect guilty of the very Crimes you are fo much afraid of. It is very natural for fuch who are treated ill and upbraided falfly, to find out an intimate Friend that will hear their Complaints, condole their Sufferings, and endeavour to footh and affuage their fecret Refentments. Befides, Jealoufy puts a Woman often in mind of an ill Thing that fhe would not otherwife perhaps have thought of, and fills her Imagination with fuch an unlucky Idea, as in time grows familiar, excites Defire, and lofes all the Shame and Horror which might at firft attend it. Nor is it a Wonder if fhe who fuffers wrongfully in a Man's Opinion of her, and has therefore nothing to forfeit in his Efteem, refolves to give him reafon for his Sufpicions, and to enjoy the Pleafure of the Crime, fince fhe muft undergo the Ignominy. Such probably were the Confiderations that directed the wife Man in his Advice to Hufbands ; *Be not jealous over the Wife*

A 5

of thy Bofom, and teach her not an evil Leffon againft thy-
felf. Ecclus.

AND here, among the other Torments which this
Paffion produces, we may ufually obferve that none are
greater Mourners than jealous Men, when the Perfon
who provoked their Jealoufy is taken from them. Then
it is that their Love breaks out furioufly, and throws
off all the Mixtures of Sufpicion which choked and
fmothered it before. The beautiful Parts of the Character rife uppermoft in the jealous Hufband's Memory,
and upbraid him with the ill ufage of fo divine a Creature as was once in his Poffeffion; whilft all the little
Imperfections, that were before fo uneafy to him, wear
off from his Remembrance, and fhew themfelves no
more.

WE may fee by what has been faid, that Jealoufy
takes the deepeft Root in Men of amorous Difpofitions;
and of thefe we may find three Kinds who are moft over-
run with it.

THE firft are thofe who are confcious to themfelves
of an Infirmity, whether it be Weaknefs, Old Age, Deformity, Ignorance, or the like. Thefe Men are fo well
acquainted with the unamiable Part of themfelves, that
they have not the Confidence to think they are really beloved; and are fo diftruftful of their own Merits, that
all Fondnefs towards them puts them out of Countenance, and looks like a Jeft upon their Perfons. They
grow fufpicious on their firft looking in a Glafs, and are
ftung with Jealoufy at the fight of a Wrinkle. A handfom Fellow immediately alarms them, and every thing
that looks young or gay turns their Thoughts upon their
Wives.

A Second Sort of Men, who are moft liable to this Paffion, are thofe of cunning, wary, and diftruftful Tempers.
It is a Fault very juftly found in Hiftories compofed by
Politicians, that they leave nothing to Chance or Humour,
but are ftill for deriving every Action from fome Plot and
Contrivance, for drawing up a perpetual Scheme of
Caufes and Events, and preferving a conftant Correfpondence between the Camp and the Council-Table. And
thus it happens in the Affairs of Love with Men of too
refined a Thought. They put a Conftruction on a Look,
and

and find out a Defign in a Smile; they give new Senfes and Significations to Words and Actions; and are ever tormenting themfelves with Fancies of their own raifing. They generally act in a Difguife themfelves, and therefore miftake all outward Shows and Appearances for Hypocrify in others; fo that I believe no Men fee lefs of the Truth and Reality of Things, than thefe great Refiners upon Incidents, who are fo wonderfully fubtle and over-wife in their Conceptions.

N O W what thefe Men fancy they know of Women by Reflexion, your lewd and vicious Men believe they have learned by Experience. They have feen the poor Hufband fo mifled by Tricks and Artifices, and in the midft of his Inquiries fo loft and bewilder'd in a crooked Intrigue, that they ftill fufpect an Under-Plot in every female Action; and efpecially where they fee any Refemblance in the Behaviour of two Perfons, are apt to fancy it proceeds from the fame Defign in both. Thefe Men therefore bear hard upon the fufpected Party, purfue her clofe through all her Turnings and Windings; and are too well acquainted with the Chace, to be flung off by any falfe Steps or Doubles: Befides, their Acquaintance and Converfation has lain wholly among the vicious Part of Womankind, and therefore it is no Wonder they cenfure all alike, and look upon the whole Sex as a Species of Impoftors. But if, notwithftanding their private Experience, they can get over thefe Prejudices, and entertain a favourable Opinion of fome *Women*; yet their own loofe Defires will ftir up new Sufpicions from another Side, and make them believe all *Men* fubject to the fame Inclinations with themfelves.

W H E T H E R thefe or other Motives are moft predominant, we learn from the modern Hiftories of *America*, as well as from our own Experience in this Part of the World, that Jealoufy is no Northern Paffion, but rages moft in thofe Nations that lie neareft the Influence of the Sun. It is a Misfortune for a Woman to be born between the Tropicks; for there lie the hotteft Regions of Jealoufy, which as you come Northward cools all along with the Climate, till you fcarce meet with any thing like it in the Polar Circle. Our own Nation is very temperately fituated in this refpect; and if we meet with fome few dif-
ordered

ordered with the Violence of this Paſſion, they are not the proper Growth of our Country, but are many Degrees nearer the Sun in their Conſtitutions than in their Climate.

AFTER this frightful Account of Jealouſy, and the Perſons who are moſt ſubject to it, it will be but fair to ſhew by what means the Paſſion may be beſt allay'd, and thoſe who are poſſeſſed with it ſet at Eaſe. Other Faults indeed are not under the Wife's Juriſdiction, and ſhould, if poſſible, eſcape her Obſervation ; but Jealouſy calls upon her particularly for its Cure, and deſerves all her Art and Application in the Attempt : Beſides, ſhe has this for her Encouragement, that her Endeavours will be always pleaſing, and that ſhe will ſtill find the Affection of her Huſband riſing towards her in proportion as his Doubts and Suſpicions vaniſh ; for, as we have ſeen all along, there is ſo great a Mixture of Love in Jealouſy as is well worth the ſeparating. But this ſhall be the Subject of another Paper.   L

N° 171   *Saturday, September* 15.

Credula res amor eſt ⸺   Ovid. Met. 7. v. 826.

The Man, who loves, is eaſy of Belief.

HAVING in my Yeſterday's Paper diſcovered the Nature of Jealouſy, and pointed out the Perſons who are moſt ſubject to it, I muſt here apply myſelf to my fair Correſpondents, who deſire to live well with a Jealous Huſband, and to eaſe his Mind of its unjuſt Suſpicions.

THE firſt Rule I ſhall propoſe to be obſerved is, that you never ſeem to diſlike in another what the Jealous Man is himſelf guilty of, or to admire any thing in which he himſelf does not excel. A jealous Man is very quick in his Applications, he knows how to find a double Edge in an Invective, and to draw a Satire on himſelf out of a Panegyrick on another. He does not trouble himſelf to

conſider

confider the Perfon, but to direct the Character; and is
fecretly pleafed or confounded as he finds more or lefs of
himfelf in it. The Commendation of any thing in another ftirs up his Jealoufy, as it fhews you have a Value,
for others, befides himfelf ; but the Commendation of
that, which he himfelf wants, inflames him more, as it
fhews that in fome Refpects you prefer others before him.
Jealoufy is admirably defcribed in this View by *Horace* in
his Ode to *Lydia*.

Quùm tu, Lydia, Telephi
 Cervicem rofeam, & cerea Telephi
Laudas brachia, væ meum.
 Fervens difficili bile tumet jecur:
Tunc nec mens mihi, nec color
 Certâ fede manet ; humor & in genas
Furtim labitur, arguens
 Quàm lentis penitùs macerer ignibus. Od. 13. l. 1.

When *Telephus* his youthful Charms,
His rofy Neck and winding Arms,
With endlefs Rapture you recite,
And in the pleafing Name delight ;
My Heart, inflam'd by jealous Heat
With numberlefs Refentments beats ;
From my pale Cheek the Colour flies,
And all the Man within me dies :
By Turns my hidden Grief appears
In rifing Sighs and falling Tears,
That fhew too well the warm Defires,
The filent, flow, confuming Fires,
Which on my inmoft Vitals prey,
And melt my very Soul away.

THE Jealous Man is not indeed angry if you diflike
another : but if you find thofe Faults which are to be
found in his own Character, you difcover not only your
Diflike of another, but of himfelf. In fhort, he is fo defirous of ingroffing all your Love, that he is grieved at
the want of any Charm, which he believes has Power to
raife it ; and if he finds by your Cenfures on others, that
he is not fo agreeable in your Opinion as he might be, he
naturally concludes you could love him better if he had
             other

other Qualifications, and that by Confequence your Affection does not rife fo high as he thinks it ought. If therefore his Temper be grave or fullen, you muft not be too
much pleafed with a Jeft, or tranfported with any thing
that is gay and diverting. If his Beauty be none of the
beft, you muft be a profeffed Admirer of Prudence, or,
any other Quality he is Mafter of, or at leaft vain enough
to think he is.

IN the next place, you muft be fure to be free and
open in your Converfation with him, and to let in Light
upon your Actions, to unravel all your Defigns, and difcover every Secret however trifling or indifferent. A jealous Husband has a particular Averfion to Winks and
Whifpers, and if he does not fee to the bottom of every
thing, will be fure to go beyond it in his Fears and Sufpicions. He will always expect to be your chief Confident,
and where he finds himfelf kept out of a Secret, will believe there is more in it than there fhould be. And here
it is of great Concern, that you preferve the Character of
your Sincerity uniform and of a piece: for if he once finds
a falfe Glofs put upon any fingle Action, he quickly fufpects all the reft ; his working Imagination immediately
takes a falfe Hint, and runs off with it into feveral remote Confequences, till he has proved very ingenious in
working out his own Mifery.

IF both thefe Methods fail, the beft way will be to let
him fee you are much caft down and afflicted for the ill
Opinion he entertains of you, and the Difquietudes he
himfelf fuffers for your Sake. There are many who take
a kind of barbarous Pleafure in the Jealoufy of thofe who
love them, that infult over an aking Heart, and triumph
in their Charms which are able to excite fo much Uneafinefs.

> *Ardeat ipfa licet, tormentis gaudet amantis.*
> Juv. Sat. 6. v. 2c8.

> Tho' equal Pains her Peace of Mind deftroy,
> A Lover's Torments give her fpiteful Joy.

But thefe often carry the Humour fo far, till their affected
Coldnefs and Indifference quite kills all the Fondnefs of a
Lover, and are then fure to meet in their Turn with all
the

the Contempt and Scorn that is due to so insolent a Behaviour. On the contrary, it is very probable a melancholy, dejected, Carriage, the usual Effects of injured Innocence, may soften the jealous Husband into Pity, make
him sensible of the Wrong he does you, and work out
of his Mind all those Fears and Suspicions that make you
both unhappy. At least it will have this good Effect, that
he will keep his Jealousy to himself, and repine in private, either because he is sensible it is a Weakness, and
will therefore hide it from your Knowledge, or because he
will be apt to fear some ill Effect it may produce, in cooling your Love towards him, or diverting it to another.

THERE is still another Secret that can never fail, if
you can once get it believ'd, and which is often practis'd
by Women of greater Cunning than Virtue : This is to
change Sides for a while with the jealous Man, and to turn
his own Passion upon himself; to take some Occasion of
growing jealous of him, and to follow the Example he
himself hath set you. This counterfeited Jealousy will
bring him a great deal of Pleasure, if he thinks it real;
for he knows experimentally how much Love goes along
with this Passion, and will besides feel something like the
Satisfaction of a Revenge, in seeing you undergo all his
own Tortures. But this, indeed, is an Artifice so difficult,
and at the same time so disingenuous, that it ought never to
be put in practice, but by such as have Skill enough to cover the Deceit, and Innocence to render it excusable.

I shall conclude this Essay with the Story of *Herod* and
Mariamne, as I have collected it out of *Josephus*; which
may serve almost as an Example to whatever can be said
on this Subject.

MARIAMNE had all the Charms that Beauty, Birth,
Wit and Youth could give a Woman, and *Herod* all the
Love that such Charms are able to raise in a warm and
amorous Disposition. In the midst of this his Fondness
for *Mariamne*, he put her Brother to Death, as he did her
Father not many Years after. The Barbarity of the Action was represented to *Mark Antony*, who immediately
summoned *Herod* into *Ægypt*, to answer for the Crime
that was there laid to his Charge. *Herod* attributed the
Summons to *Antony*'s Desire of *Mariamne*, whom therefore, before his Departure, he gave into the Custody of his
Uncle

Uncle *Joseph*, with private Orders to put her to Death, if any such Violence was offered to himself. This *Joseph* was much delighted with *Mariamne*'s Conversation, and endeavoured, with all his Art and Rhetorick, to set out the Excess of *Herod*'s Passion for her; but when he still found her cold and incredulous, he inconsiderately told her, as a certain Instance of her Lord's Affection, the private Orders he had left behind him, which plainly shewed, according to *Joseph*'s Interpretation, that he could neither live nor die without her. This barbarous Instance of a wild unreasonable Passion quite put out, for a Time, those little Remains of Affection she still had for her Lord : Her Thoughts were so wholly taken up with the Cruelty of his Orders, that she could not consider the Kindness that produced them, and therefore represented him in her Imagination, rather under the frightful Idea of a Murderer than a Lover. *Herod* was at length acquitted and dismissed by *Mark Antony*, when his Soul was all in Flames for his *Mariamne*; but before their Meeting, he was not a little alarm'd at the Report he had heard of his Uncle's Conversation and Familiarity with her in his Absence. This therefore was the first Discourse he entertained her with, in which she found it no easy matter to quiet his Suspicions. But at last he appeared so well satisfied of her Innocence, that from Reproaches and Wranglings he fell to Tears and Embraces. Both of them wept very tenderly at their Reconciliation, and *Herod* poured out his whole Soul to her in the warmest Protestations of Love and Constancy; when amidst all his Sighs and Languishings she asked him, whether the private Orders he left with his Uncle *Joseph* were an Instance of such an inflamed Affection. The jealous King was immediately roused at so unexpected a Question, and concluded his Uncle must have been too familiar with her, before he would have discovered such a Secret. In short, he put his Uncle to Death, and very difficultly prevailed upon himself to spare *Mariamne*.

AFTER this he was forced on a second Journey into *Ægypt*, when he committed his Lady to the Care of *Sohemus*, with the same private Orders he had before given his Uncle, if any Mischief befel himself. In the mean while *Mariamne* so won upon *Sohemus* by her Presents and obliging Conversation, that she drew all the Secret from him,

him, with which *Herod* had intrusted him; so that after his Return, when he flew to her with all the Transports of Joy and Love, she received him coldly with Sighs and Tears, and all the Marks of Indifference and Aversion. This Reception so stirred up his Indignation, that he had certainly slain her with his own Hands, had not he feared he himself should have become the greater Sufferer by it. It was not long after this, when he had another violent Return of Love upon him; *Mariamne* was therefore sent for to him, whom he endeavoured to soften and reconcile with all possible conjugal Caresses and Endearments; but she declined his Embraces, and answered all his Fondness with bitter Invectives for the Death of her Father and her Brother. This Behaviour so incensed *Herod*, that he very hardly refrained from striking her; when in the Heat of their Quarrel there came in a Witness, suborn'd by some of *Mariamne*'s Enemies, who accused her to the King of a Design to poison him. *Herod* was now prepared to hear any Thing in her Prejudice, and immediately ordered her Servant to be stretch'd upon the Rack; who in the Extremity of his Tortures confest, that his Mistress's Aversion to the King arose from something *Sohemus* had told her; but as for any Design of poisoning, he utterly disowned the least Knowledge of it. This Confession quickly proved fatal to *Sohemus*, who now lay under the same Suspicions and Sentence that *Joseph* had before him on the like Occasion. Nor would *Herod* rest here; but accused her with great Vehemence of a Design upon his Life, and by his Authority with the Judges had her publickly condemned and executed. *Herod* soon after her Death grew melancholy and dejected, retiring from the Publick Administration of Affairs into a solitary Forest, and there abandoning himself to all the black Considerations, which naturally arise from a Passion made up of Love, Remorse, Pity and Despair. He used to rave for his *Mariamne*, and to call upon her in his distracted Fits; and in all probability would soon have followed her, had not his Thoughts been seasonably called off from so sad an Object by Publick Storms, which at that Time very nearly threatned him.　　L

N° 172   *Monday, September* 17.

*Non solùm Scientia, quæ est remota à Justitia, Calliditas
potiùs quàm Sapientia est appellanda; verùm etiam Animus paratus ad periculum, si suâ cupiditate, non utilita-
te communi, impellitur, Audaciæ potiùs nomen habeat,
quàm Fortitudinis* ——   Plato apud Tull.

*As Knowledge, without Justice, ought to be called Cunning,
rather than Wisdom; so a Mind prepared to meet Danger,
if excited by its own Eagerness, and not the Publick Good,
deserves the Name of Audacity, rather than of Courage.*

THERE can be no greater Injury to human Society
than that good Talents among Men should be held
honourable to those who are endowed with them
without any Regard how they are applied. The Gifts of
Nature and Accomplishments of Art are valuable, but as
they are exerted in the Interests of Virtue, or governed
by the Rules of Honour. We ought to abstract our Minds
from the Observation of an Excellence in those we converse with, till we have taken some Notice, or received
some good Information of the Disposition of their Minds;
otherwise the Beauty of their Persons, or the Charms of
their Wit, may make us fond of those whom our Reason
and Judgment will tell us we ought to abhor.

WHEN we suffer ourselves to be thus carried away
by mere Beauty, or mere Wit, *Omniamente*, with all her
Vice, will bear away as much of our Good-will as the most
innocent Virgin or discreet Matron; and there cannot be
a more abject Slavery in this World, than to dote upon
what we think we ought to condemn : Yet this must be
our Condition in all the Parts of Life, if we suffer ourselves to approve any Thing but what tends to the Promo-
tion of what is good and honourable. If we would take
true Pains with ourselves to consider all Things by the
Light of Reason and Justice, tho' a Man were in the
Height

Height of Youth and amorous Inclinations, he would look upon a Coquette with the same Contempt or Indifference as he would upon a Coxcomb. The wanton Carriage in a Woman would disappoint her of the Admiration which she aims at; and the vain Dress or Discourse of a Man would destroy the Comeliness of his Shape, or Goodness of his Understanding. I say the Goodness of his Understanding, for it is too less common to see Men of Sense outrageous Coxcombs, than beautiful Women become immodest. When this happens in either, the Former we are strongly inclined to give to the good Qualities they have from Nature should shine in Proportion. But however just it is to measure the Value of Men by the Application of their Talents, and not by the Eminence of those Qualities unimproved from their Use, I say, however just such a Way of judging is, in all Ages as well as this, the Contrary has prevailed upon the Generality of Mankind. How many lewd Devices have been preserved from one Age to another, which had perished as soon as they were made, if Painters and Sculptors had been esteemed as much for the Purpose, as the Sweetness of their Designs? Modest and well-governed Imagination, have by this Means lost the Representations of Ten Thousand charming Portraitures, filled with Images of innate Truth, generous Zeal, couragious Faith, and tender Humanity; instead of which, Envy, Fury, Fancy, and Malice are transmitted by their Care to a Shameless Posterity.

THE unjust Application of laudable Talents, is the only Thing in the general Opinion of Men, not only in such Cases as we have mentioned, but also in Matters which concern ordinary Life. If a Lawyer were to be esteemed only as he uses his Parts in contending for Justice, and were immediately despicable when he appeared in a Cause which he could not but know was an unjust one, how honourable would his Character be? And how honourable is it in such among us, who follow the Profession no otherwise, than as labouring to protect the Injured, to subdue the Oppressor, to imprison the wealthy Debtor, and do right to the painted Artificer? But many of this excellent Character are overlooked by the greater Number; who affect covering a weak Place in a Client's Title, directing the Course of an Inquiry, or finding a skilful Refuge

Nº 172   *Monday, September* 17.

Non solùm Scientia, quæ est remota à Justitia, Calliditas
potiùs quàm Sapientia est appellanda; verùm etiam Ani-
mus paratus ad periculum, si sua cupiditate, non utilita-
te communi, impellitur, Audaciæ potiùs nomen habeat,
quàm Fortitudinis ————   Plato apud Tull.

As Knowledge, without Justice, ought to be called Cunning,
rather than Wisdom ; so a Mind prepared to meet Danger,
if excited by its own Eagerness, and not the Publick Good,
deserves the Name of Audacity, rather than of Courage.

THERE can be no greater Injury to human Society
than that good Talents among Men should be held
honourable to those who are endowed with them
without any Regard how they are applied. The Gifts of
Nature and Accomplishments of Art are valuable, but as
they are exerted in the Interests of Virtue, or governed
by the Rules of Honour. We ought to abstract our Minds
from the Observation of an Excellence in those we converse with, till we have taken some Notice, or received
some good Information of the Disposition of their Minds;
otherwise the Beauty of their Persons, or the Charms of
their Wit, may make us fond of those whom our Reason
and Judgment will tell us we ought to abhor.

WHEN we suffer ourselves to be thus carried away
by mere Beauty, or mere Wit, *Omniamante*, with all her
Vice, will bear away as much of our Good-will as the most
innocent Virgin or discreet Matron ; and there cannot be
a more abject Slavery in this World, than to dote upon
what we think we ought to condemn : Yet this must be
our Condition in all the Parts of Life, if we suffer ourselves to approve any Thing but what tends to the Promo-
tion of what is good and honourable. If we would take
true Pains with ourselves to consider all Things by the
Light of Reason and Justice, tho' a Man were in the
Height

Height of Youth and amorous Inclinations, he would look
upon a Coquette with the same Contempt or Indifference
as he would upon a Coxcomb: The wanton Carriage in
a Woman would disappoint her of the Admiration which
she aims at; and the vain Dress or Discourse of a Man
would destroy the Comeliness of his Shape, or Goodness
of his Underftanding. I say the Goodness of his Understanding, for it is no less common to see Men of Sense
commence Coxcombs, than beautiful Women become im-
modeft. When this happens in either, the Favour we
are naturally inclined to give to the good Qualities they
have from Nature should abate in Proportion. But however juft it is to measure the Value of Men by the Application of their Talents, and not by the Eminence of those
Qualities abstracted from their Use; I say, however juft
such a Way of judging is, in all Ages as well as this, the
Contrary has prevailed upon the Generality of Mankind.
How many lewd Devices have been preserved from one
Age to another, which had perished as soon as they were
made, if Painters and Sculptors had been esteemed as
much for the Purpose as the Execution of their Designs?
Modeft and well-governed Imaginations have by this
Means loft the Reprefentations of Ten Thousand charming Portraitures, filled with Images of innate Truth, generous Zeal, courageous Faith, and tender Humanity;
inftead of which, Satyrs, Furies, and Monfters are recommended by those Arts to a shameful Eternity.

THE unjuft Application of laudable Talents, is tolerated, in the general Opinion of Men, not only in such
Cafes as are here mentioned; but alfo in Matters which
concern ordinary Life. If a Lawyer were to be esteemed
only as he uses his Parts in contending for Justice, and
were immediately despicable when he appeared in a Caufe
which he could not but know was an unjuft one, how
honourable would his Character be? And how honourable is it in such among us, who follow the Profeffion no
otherwife, than as labouring to protect the Injured, to
fubdue the Oppreffor, to imprifon the carelefs Debtor,
and do right to the painful Artificer? But many of this
excellent Character are overlooked by the greater Number; who affect covering a weak Place in a Client's Title,
diverting the Courfe of an Inquiry, or finding a skilful
Refuge

Refuge to palliate a Falſhood: Yet it is ſtill called Eloquence in the latter, though thus unjuſtly employed: But Reſolution in an Aſſaſſin is according to Reaſon quite as laudable, as Knowledge and Wiſdom exerciſed in the Defence of an ill Cauſe.

WERE the Intention ſtedfaſtly conſidered, as the Meaſure of Approbation, all Falſhood would ſoon be out of Countenance: and an Addreſs in impoſing upon Mankind, would be as contemptible in one State of Life as another. A Couple of Courtiers, making Profeſſions of Eſteem, would make the ſame Figure after Breach of Promiſe, as two Knights of the Poſt convicted of Perjury. But Converſation is fallen ſo low in point of Morality, that as they ſay in a Bargain, *Let the Buyer look to it;* ſo in Friendſhip, he is the Man in Danger who is moſt apt to believe: He is the more likely to ſuffer in the Commerce, who begins with the Obligation of being the more ready to enter into it.

BUT thoſe Men only are truly great, who place their Ambition rather in acquiring to themſelves the Conſcience of worthy Enterpriſes, than in the Proſpect of Glory which attends them. Theſe exalted Spirits would rather be ſecretly the Authors of Events which are ſerviceable to Mankind, than, without being ſuch, to have the publick Fame of it. Where therefore an eminent Merit is robbed by Artifice or Detraction, it does but increaſe by ſuch Endeavours of its Enemies: The impotent Pains which are taken to ſully it, or diffuſe it among a Crowd to the Injury of a ſingle Perſon, will naturally produce the contrary Effect; the Fire will blaze out, and burn up all that attempt to ſmother what they cannot extinguiſh.

THERE is but one thing neceſſary to keep the Poſſeſſion of true Glory, which is, to hear the Oppoſers of it with Patience, and preſerve the Virtue by which it was acquired. When a Man is thoroughly perſuaded that he ought neither to admire, wiſh for, or purſue any thing but what is exactly his Duty, it is not in the Power of Seaſons, Perſons or Accidents, to diminiſh his Value. He only is a great Man who can neglect the Applauſe of the Multitude, and enjoy himſelf independent of its Favour. This is indeed an arduous Taſk; but it ſhould comfort a glorious Spirit that it is the higheſt Step to which

human

human Nature can arrive. Triumph, Applaufe, Acclamation, are dear to the Mind of Man; but it is ftill a more exquifite Delight to fay to yourfelf, you have done well, than to hear the whole human Race pronounce you glorious, except you yourfelf can join with them in your own Reflexions. A Mind thus equal and uniform may be deferted by little fafhionable Admirers and Followers, but will ever be had in Reverence by Souls like itfelf. The Branches of the Oak endure all the Seafons of the Year, though its Leaves fall off in Autumn; and thefe too will be reftor'd with the returning Spring. T

Nº 173. *Tuefday, September* 18.

—— *Remove fera monftra, tuæque*
Saxificos vultus, quæcunque ea, tolle Medufæ.
Ovid. Met. l. 5. v. 216.

Remove that horrid Monfter, and take hence
Medufa's *petrifying Countenance.*

IN a late Paper I mention'd the Projeƈt of an ingenious Author for the ereƈting of feveral Handicraft Prizes to be contended for by our *Britiſh* Artifans, and the Influence they might have towards the Improvement of our feveral Manufaƈtures. I have fince that been very much furprifed by the following Advertifement which I find in the *Poft-Boy* of the 11th Inftant, and again repeated in the *Poft-Boy* of the 15th.

ON the 9th of Oƈtober next will be run for upon Colefhill-Heath in Warwickfhire, a Plate of 6 Guineas Value, 3 Heats, by any Horfe, Mare or Gelding that hath not won above the Value of 5 l. the winning Horfe to be Sold for 10 l. to carry 10 Stone Weight, if 14 Hands high; if above or under to carry or be allowed Weight for Inches, and to be entered Friday the 5th at the Swan in Colefhill, before Six in the Evening. Alfo a Plate of lefs Value to be run for by Affes. The fame Day a Gold Ring to be Grinn'd for by Men.

THE

THE firft of thefe Divifions that is to be exhibited by the 10*l.* Race-Horfes, may probably have its Ufe.; but the two laft, in which the Affes and Men are concerned, feem to me altogether extraordinary and unaccountable. Why they fhould keep Running Affes at *Colefhill,* or how making Mouths turns to account in *Warwickfhire,* more than in any other Parts of *England,* I cannot comprehend. I have looked over all the Olympic Games, and do not find any thing in them like an Afs-Race, or a Match at Grinning. However it be, I am informed that feveral Affes are now kept in Body-Clothes, and fweated every Morning upon the Heath, and that all the Country-Fellows within ten Miles of the *Swan,* grin an Hour or two in their Glaffes every Morning, in order to qualify themfelves for the 9th of *October.* The Prize, which is propofed to be Grinn'd for, has raifed fuch an Ambition among the Common People of out-grinning one another, that many very difcerning Perfons are afraid it fhould fpoil moft of the Faces in the County ; and that a *Warwickfhire* Man will be known by his Grin, as Roman-Catholicks imagine a *Kentifh* Man is by his Tail. The Gold Ring which is made the Prize of Deformity, is juft the Reverfe of the Golden Apple that was formerly made the Prize of Beauty, and fhould carry for its Pofy the old Motto inverted.

Detur tetriori.

Or to accommodate it to the Capacity of the Combatants,

The frightfull'ft Grinner
Be the Winner.

IN the mean while I would advife a *Dutch* Painter to be prefent at this great Controverfy of Faces, in order to make a Collection of the moft remarkable Grins that fhall be there exhibited.

I muft not here omit an Account which I lately received of one of thefe Grinning-Matches from a Gentleman, who, upon reading the abovementioned Advertifement, entertained a Coffee-houfe with the following Narrative. Upon the taking of *Namure,* amidft other publick Rejoicings made on that Occafion, there was a Gold Ring given by a Whig Juftice of Peace to be grinn'd for. The firft

Competitor

Competitor that entered the Lifts, was a black fwarthy *Frenchman*, who accidentally paffed that way, and being a Man naturally of a wither'd Look, and hard Features, promifed himfelf good Succefs: He was placed upon a Table in the great Point of View, and looking upon the Company like *Milton*'s Death,

> *Grinn'd horribly a Ghaftly Smile* ——

HIS Mufcles were fo drawn together on each Side of his Face; that he fhew'd twenty Teeth at a Grin, and put the Country in fome Pain, left a Foreigner fhould carry away the Honour of the Day; but upon a farther Trial they found he was Mafter only of the merry Grin.

THE next that mounted the Table was a Malecontent in thofe Days, and a great Mafter in the whole Art of Grinning, but particularly excelled in the angry Grin. He did his Part fo well, that he is faid to have made half a dozen Women mifcarry; but the Juftice being apprifed by one who ftood near him, that the Fellow who grinn'd in his Face was a *Jacobite*, and being unwilling that a Difaffected Perfon fhould win the Gold Ring, and be look-ed upon as the beft Grinner in the Country, he ordered the Oaths to be tendered unto him upon his quitting the Ta-ble, which the Grinner refufing, he was fet afide as an un-qualified Perfon. There were feveral other Grotesk Fi-gures that prefented themfelves, which it would be too te-dious to defcribe, I muft not however omit a Ploughman, who lived in the farther Part of the Country, and being very lucky in a Pair of long Lanthorn-Jaws, wrung his Face into fuch an hideous Grimace, that every Feature of it appeared under a different Diftortion. The whole Com-pany ftood aftonifh'd at fuch a complicated Grin, and were ready to affign the Prize to him, had it not been proved by one of his Antagonifts, that he had practifed with Ver-juice for fome Days before, and had a Crab found upon him at the very time of Grinning; upon which the beft Judges of Grinning declared it as their Opinion, that he was not to be looked upon as a fair Grinner, and there-fore ordered him to be fet afide as a Cheat.

THE Prize, it feems, fell at length upon a Cobler, *Giles Gorgon* by Name, who produced feveral new Grins of his own Invention, having been ufed to cut Faces for many Years together over his Laſt. At the very firſt Grin he caſt every human Feature out of his Countenance, at the ſecond he became the Face of a Spout, at the third a Baboon, at the fourth the Head of a Baſs-Viol, and at the fifth a Pair of Nut-crackers. The whole Aſſembly wondered at his Accompliſhments, and beſtowed the Ring on him unanimouſly; but, what he eſteemed more than all the reſt, a Country Wench, whom he had wooed in vain for above five Years before, was ſo charmed with his Grins, and the Applauſes which he received on all Sides, that ſhe married him the Week following, and to this Day wears the Prize upon her Finger, the Cobler having made uſe of it as his Wedding-Ring.

THIS Paper might perhaps ſeem very impertinent, if it grew ſerious in the Concluſion. I would nevertheleſs leave it to the Conſideration of thoſe who are the Patrons of this monſtrous Trial of Skill, whether or no they are not guilty, in ſome meaſure, of an Affront to their Species, in treating after this manner the *Human Face Divine,* and turning that Part of us, which has ſo great an Image impreſſed upon it, into the Image of a Monkey; whether the raiſing ſuch ſilly Competitions among the Ignorant, propoſing Prizes for ſuch uſeleſs Accompliſhments, filling the common People's Heads with ſuch ſenſeleſs Ambitions, and inſpiring them with ſuch abſurd Ideas of Superiority and Preeminence, has not in it ſomething immoral as well as ridiculous.   L.

N° 174   *Wedneſday, September* 19.

Hæc memini & victum fruſtra contendere Thyrſin.
                                   Virg. Ecl. 7. v. 69.

Theſe Rhymes I did to Memory commend,
When vanquiſh'd Thyrſis *did in vain contend.* DRYDEN.

THERE is ſcarce any thing more common than Animoſities between Parties that cannot ſubſiſt but by their Agreement: this was well repreſented in the Sedition of the Members of the Human Body in the old
                                   Roman

Roman Fable. It is often the Cafe of leffer confederate States againft a fuperior Power, which are hardly held together, though their Unanimity is neceffary for their common Safety: And this is always the Cafe of the landed and trading Intereft of *Great Britain:* the Trader is fed by the Product of the Land, and the landed Man cannot be clothed but by the Skill of the Trader; and yet thofe Interefts are ever jarring.

WE had laft Winter an Inftance of this at our Club, in Sir ROGER DE COVERLEY and Sir ANDREW FREEPORT, between whom there is generally a conftant, though friendly, Oppofition of Opinions. It happened that one of the Company, in an hiftorical Difcourfe, was obferving, that *Carthaginian* Faith was a proverbial Phrafe to intimate Breach of Leagues. Sir ROGER faid it could hardly be otherwife: That the *Carthaginians* were the greateft Traders in the World; and as Gain is the chief End of fuch a People, they never purfue any other: The Means to it are never regarded; they will, if it comes eafily, get Money honeftly; but if not, they will not fcruple to attain it by Fraud or Cozenage: And indeed, what is the whole Bufinefs of the Trader's Account, but to over-reach him who trufts to his Memory? But were that not fo, what can there great and noble be expected from him whofe Attention is for ever fixed upon balancing his Books, and watching over his Expences? And at beft, let Frugality and Parfimony be the Virtues of the Merchant, how much is his punctual Dealing below a Gentleman's Charity to the Poor, or Hofpitality among his Neighbours?

CAPTAIN SENTRY obferved Sir ANDREW very diligent in hearing Sir ROGER, and had a mind to turn the Difcourfe, by taking notice in general, from the higheft to the loweft Parts of human Society, there was a fecret, tho' unjuft, Way among Men, of indulging the Seeds of Ill-nature and Envy, by comparing their own State of Life to that of another, and grudging the Approach of their Neighbour to their own Happinefs; and on the other Side, he, who is the lefs at his Eafe, repines at the other, who he thinks, has unjuftly the Advantage over him. Thus the Civil and Military Lifts look upon each other with much Ill-nature; the Soldier repines at

the Courtier's Power, and the Courtier rallies the Soldier's
Honour; or, to come to lower Instances, the private Men
in the Horse and Foot of an Army, the Carmen and
Coachmen in the City Streets, mutually look upon each
other with Ill-will, when they are in Competition for Quarters or the Way, in their respective Motions.

IT is very well, good Captain, interrupted Sir AN-
DREW: You may attempt to turn the Discourse if you
think fit; but I must however have a Word or two with
Sir ROGER, who, I see, thinks he has paid me off, and
been very severe upon the Merchant. I shall not, continued he, at this Time remind Sir ROGER of the great
and noble Monuments of Charity and Publick Spirit,
which have been erected by Merchants since the Refor-
mation, but at present content myself with what he allows us, Parsimony and Frugality. If it were consistent
with the Quality of so ancient a Baronet as Sir ROGER,
to keep an Account, or measure Things by the most infallible Way, that of Numbers, he would prefer our Parsimony to his Hospitality. If to drink so many Hogsheads
is to be Hospitable, we do not contend for the Fame of
that Virtue; but it would be worth while to consider,
whether so many Artificers at work ten Days together by
my Appointment, or so many Peasants made merry on Sir
ROGER's Charge, are the Men more obliged? I believe
the Families of the Artificers will thank me, more than
the Houshold of the Peasants shall Sir ROGER. Sir
ROGER gives to his Men, but I place mine above the
Necessity or Obligation of my Bounty. I am in very little Pain for the *Roman* Proverb upon the *Carthaginian*
Traders; the *Romans* were their professed Enemies: I
am only sorry no *Carthaginian* Histories have come to
our Hands; we might have been taught perhaps by them
some Proverbs against the *Roman* Generosity, in fighting
for and bestowing other People's Goods. But since Sir
ROGER has taken Occasion from an old Proverb to be
out of Humour with Merchants, it should be no Offence
to offer one not quite so old in their Defence. When a
Man happens to break in *Holland*, they say of him that
he has not kept true Accounts. This Phrase, perhaps
among us, would appear a soft or humorous way of
speaking, but with that exact Nation it bears the highest
Reproach;

Reproach; for a Man to be miftaken in the Calculation of
his Expence, in his Ability to anfwer future Demands,
or to be impertinently fanguine in putting his Credit to
too great Adventure, are all Inftances of as much Infamy
as with gayer Nations to be failing in Courage or common
Honefty.

NUMBERS are fo much the Meafure of every
thing that is valuable, that it is not poffible to demonftrate
the Succefs of any Action, or the Prudence of any Under-
taking without them. I fay this in Anfwer to what Sir
ROGER is pleafed to fay, That little that is truly noble can be expected from one who is ever poring on his
Cafh-book, or balancing his Accounts. When I have my
Returns from abroad, I can tell to a Shilling, by the
Help of Numbers, the Profit or Lofs by my Adventure;
but I ought alfo to be able to fhew that I had Reafon for
making it, either from my own Experience, or that of
other People, or from a reafonable Prefumption that my
Returns will be fufficient to anfwer my Expence and
Hazard; and this is never to be done without the Skill
of Numbers. For Inftance, if I am to trade to *Turkey*, I
ought beforehand to know the Demand of our Manufactures there, as well as of their Silks in *England*, and
the cuftomary Prices that are given for both in each
Country. I ought to have a clear Knowledge of thefe
Matters beforehand, that I may prefume upon fufficient
Returns to anfwer the Charge of the Cargo I have fitted out, the Freight and Affurance out and home, the Cuftoms to the Queen, and the Intereft of my own Money,
and befides all thefe Expences a reafonable Profit to myfelf. Now what is there of Scandal in this Skill?
What has the Merchant done, that he fhould be fo little
in the good Graces of Sir ROGER? He throws down
no Man's Inclofures, and tramples upon no Man's Corn;
he takes nothing from the induftrious Labourer; he pays
the poor Man for his Work; he communicates his Profit with Mankind; by the Preparation of his Cargo, and
the Manufacture of his Returns, he furnifhes Employment and Subfiftence to greater Numbers than the rich-
eft Nobleman; and even the Nobleman is obliged to
him for finding out foreign Markets for the Produce of
his Eftate, and for making a great Addition to his Rents;

and

and yet 'tis certain, that none of all thefe Things could be done by him without the Exercife of his Skill in Numbers.

THIS is the Oeconomy of the Merchant; and the Conduct of the Gentleman muft be the fame, unlefs by fcorning to be the Steward, he refolves the Steward fhall be the Gentleman. The Gentleman, no more than the Merchant, is able, without the Help of Numbers, to account for the Succefs of any Action, or the Prudence of any Adventure. If, for Inftance, the Chace is his whole Adventure, his only Returns muft be the Stag's Horns in the great Hall, and the Fox's Nofe upon the Stable Door. Without Doubt Sir ROGER knows the full Value of thefe Returns; and if beforehand he had computed the Charges of the Chace, a Gentleman of his Difcretion would certainly have hanged up all his Dogs, he would never have brought back fo many fine Horfes to the Kennel, he would never have gone fo often, like a Blaft, over Fields of Corn. If fuch too had been the Conduct of all his Anceftors, he might truly have boafted at this Day, that the Antiquity of his Family had never been fullied by a Trade; a Merchant had never been permitted with his whole Eftate to purchafe a Room for his Picture in the Gallery of the COVERLEYS, or to claim his Defcent from the Maid of Honour. But 'tis very happy for Sir ROGER that the Merchant paid fo dear for his Ambition. 'Tis the Misfortune of many other Gentlemen to turn out of the Seats of their Anceftors, to make way for fuch new Mafters as have been more exact in their Accounts than themfelves; and certainly he deferves the Eftate a great deal better, who has got it by his Induftry, than he who has loft it by his Negligence.   T.

N° 175 *Thursday, September* 20.

Proximus à tectis ignis defenditur ægrè. ——
Ovid. Rem. Am. v. 625.

To save your House from neighb'ring Fire is hard. TATE.

I SHALL this Day entertain my Readers with two or three Letters I have received from my Correspondents : The first discovers to me a Species of Females which have hitherto escaped my Notice, and is as follows.

Mr. SPECTATOR,

'I Am a young Gentleman of a competent Fortune,
' and a sufficient Taste of Learning, to spend five or
' six Hours every Day very agreeably among my Books.
' That I might have nothing to divert me from my Stu-
' dies, and to avoid the Noises of Coaches and Chairmen,
' I have taken Lodgings in a very narrow Street not far
' from *Whitehall;* but it is my Misfortune to be so post-
' ed, that my Lodgings are directly opposite to those of a
' *Jezebel.* You are to know, Sir, that a *Jezebel* (so
' call'd by the Neighbourhood from displaying her perni-
' cious Charms at her Window) appears constantly dress'd
' at her Sash, and has a thousand little Tricks and Foole-
' ries to attract the Eyes of all the idle young Fellows in
' the Neighbourhood. ' I have seen more than six Persons
' at once from their several Windows observing the *Je-*
' *zebel* I am now complaining of. I at first looked on her
' myself with the highest Contempt, could divert myself
' with her Airs for half an hour, and afterwards take up
' my *Plutarch* with great Tranquillity of Mind ; but was
' a little vexed to find that in less than a Month she had
' considerably stolen upon my Time; so that I resolved to
' look at her no more. But the *Jezebel,* who, as I sup-
' pose, might think it a Diminution to her Honour, to

B 3   ' have

' have the Number of her Gazers leſſen'd, reſolved not
' to part with me ſo, and began to play ſo many new
' Tricks at her Window, that it was impoſſible for me to
' forbear obſerving her. I verily believe ſhe put herſelf to
' the Expence of a new Wax-Baby on purpoſe to plague
' me; ſhe us'd to dandle and play with this Figure as im-
' pertinently as if it had been a real Child: ſometimes
' ſhe would let fall a Glove or a Pin-Cuſhion in the Street,
' and ſhut or open her Caſement three or four times in a
' Minute. When I had almoſt wean'd myſelf from this,
' ſhe came in her Shift-Sleeves, and dreſs'd at the Win-
' dow. I had no Way left but to let down my Curtains,
' which I ſubmitted to though it conſiderably darkened
' my Room, and was pleaſed to think that I had at laſt
' got the better of her; but was ſurpriſed the next Morn-
' ing to hear her talking out of her Window quite croſs
' the Street, with another Woman that lodges over me:
' I am ſince informed, that ſhe made her a Viſit, and got
' acquainted with her within three Hours after the Fall of
' my Window-Curtains.
'   ' SIR, I am plagued every Moment in the Day, one
' way or other, in my own Chambers; and the *Jezebel*
' has the Satisfaction to know, that tho' I am not look-
' ing at her, I am liſt'ning to her impertinent Dialogues
' that paſs over my Head. I would immediately change
' my Lodgings, but that I think it might look like a
' plain Confeſſion, that I am conquer'd; and beſides this,
' I am told that moſt Quarters of the Town are infeſted
' with theſe Creatures. If they are ſo, I am ſure 'tis ſuch
' an Abuſe, as a Lover of Learning and Silence ought to
' take notice of.

I am, SIR,

Yours, &c.

 I am afraid, by ſome Lines in this Letter, that my
young Student is touched with a Diſtemper which he hardly ſeems to dream of, and is too far gone in it to receive
Advice. However, I ſhall animadvert in due time on the
Abuſe which he mentions, having myſelf obſerved a Neſt
of *Jezebels* near the *Temple*, who make it their Diverſion
to draw up the Eyes of young Templars, that at the ſame
time

time they may see them stumble in an unlucky Gutter
which runs under the Window.

Mr. SPECTATOR,

'I HAVE lately read the Conclusion of your forty-
' seventh Speculation upon *Butts* with great Pleasure,
' and have ever since been thoroughly persuaded that one
' of those Gentlemen is extremely necessary to enliven
' Conversation. I had an Entertainment last Week upon
' the Water for a Lady to whom I make my Addresses,
' with several of our Friends of both Sexes. To divert
' the Company in general, and to shew my Mistress in
' particular my Genius for Rallery, I took one of the
' most celebrated *Butts* in Town along with me. It is
' with the utmost Shame and Confusion that I must
' acquaint you with the Sequel of my Adventure : As
' soon as we were got into the Boat, I played a Sentence
' or two at my *Butt* which I thought very smart, when
' my ill Genius, who I verily believe inspir'd him purely
' for my Destruction, suggested to him such a Reply, as
' got all the Laughter on his Side. I was dashed at so
' unexpected a Turn ; which the *Butt* perceiving, resol-
' ved not to let me recover myself, and pursuing his
' Victory, rallied and tossed me in a most unmerciful
' and barbarous manner till we came to *Chelsea*. I had
' some small Success while we were eating Cheese-Cakes ;
' but coming home, he renewed his Attacks with his for-
' mer Good-fortune, and equal Diversion to the whole
' Company. In short, Sir, I must ingenuously own that
' I was never so handled in all my Life ; and to complete
' my Misfortune, I am since told that the *Butt*, flushed
' with his late Victory, has made a Visit or two to the
' dear Object of my Wishes, so that I am at once in dan-
' ger of losing all my Pretensions to Wit, and my Mistress
' into the Bargain. This, Sir, is a true Account of my
' present Troubles, which you are the more obliged to
' assist me in, as you were yourself in a great measure the
' Cause of them, by recommending to us an Instrument,
' and not instructing us at the same time how to play
' upon it.
' I have been thinking whether it might not be highly
' convenient, that all *Butts* should wear an Inscription

' affixed

'affixed to fome Part of their Bodies, fhewing on which
'Side they are to be come at, and that if any of them
'are Perfons of unequal Tempers, there fhould be fome
'Method taken to inform the World at what Time it is.
'fafe to attack them, and when you had beft to let them
'alone. But, fubmitting thefe Matters to your more fe-
'rious Confideration,

I am, SIR, yours, &c.

I have, indeed, feen and heard of feveral young Gentlemen under the fame Misfortune with my prefent Correfpondent. The beft Rule I can lay down for them to
avoid the like Calamities for the future, is thoroughly to
confider not only *Whether their Companions are weak*, but
Whether themfelves are Wits.

THE following Letter comes to me from *Exeter*, and
being credibly informed that what it contains is Matter of
Fact, I fhall give it my Reader as it was fent me.

Mr. SPECTATOR, 　　　　　　　*Exeter, Sept.* 7.

'YOU were pleafed in a late Speculation to take no-
'tice of the Inconvenience we lie under in the
'Country, in not being able to keep Pace with the Fa-
'fhion: But there is another Misfortune which we are
'fubject to, and is no lefs grievous than the former, which
'has hitherto efcaped your Obfervation. I mean, the
'having Things palmed upon us for *London* Fafhions,
'which were never once heard of there.

'A Lady of this Place had fome time fince a Box of
'the neweft Ribbons fent down by the Coach: Whether
'it was her own malicious Invention, or the Wantonnefs
'of a *London* Milliner, I am not able to inform you; but,
'among the reft, there was one Cherry-coloured Ribbon,
'confifting of about half a dozen Yards, made up in the
'Figure of a fmall Head-Drefs. The aforefaid Lady had
'the Affurance to affirm, amidft a Circle of Female In-
'quifitors, who were prefent at the opening of the Box,
'that this was the neweft Fafhion worn at Court. Ac-
'cordingly the next *Sunday* we had feveral Females, who
'came to Church with their Heads drefs'd wholly in
'Ribbons, and looked like fo many Victims ready to be
'facrificed. This is ftill a reigning Mode among us. At
'the

' the fame time we have a Set of Gentlemen who take
' the Liberty to appear in all publick Places without any
' Buttons to their Coats, which they fupply with feveral
' little Silver Hafps, tho' our frefheft Advices from *London*
' make no mention of any fuch Fafhion ; and we are
' fomething fhy of affording Matter to the Button-makers
' for a fecond Petition.

 ' WHAT I would humbly propofe to the Publick is,
' that there may be a Society erected in *London*, to con-
' fift of the moft fkilful Perfons of both Sexes, for the *In-*
' *fpection of Modes and Fafhions* ; and that hereafter no
' Perfon or Perfons fhall prefume to appear fingularly ha-
' bited in any Part of the Country, without a Teftimonial
' from the aforefaid Society, that their Drefs is anfwera-
' ble to the Mode at *London.* By this means, Sir, we
' fhall know a little whereabout we are.

 ' IF you could bring this Matter to bear, you would
' very much oblige great Numbers of your Country
' Friends, and among the reft,

Your very humble Servant,

X   Jack Modifh.

Nº 176. *Friday, September* 21.

Parvula, pumilio, χαείτων μία, tota merum fal.

Lucr. l. 4. v. 1155.

A little, pretty, witty, charming She!

THERE are in the following Letter Matters,
which I, a Bachelor, cannot be fuppofed to be
acquainted with ; therefore fhall not pretend to
explain upon it till farther Confideration, but leave
the Author of the Epiftle to exprefs his Condition his
own Way.

Mr. SPECTATOR,

' I DO not deny but you appear in many of your Papers
' to underſtand Human Life pretty well; but there are
' very many Things which you cannot poſſibly have a true
' Notion of, in a ſingle Life; theſe are ſuch as reſpect
' the married State; otherwiſe I cannot account for your
' having overlooked a very good Sort of People, which are
' commonly called in Scorn the *Hen-peckt.* You are to un-
' derſtand that I am one of thoſe innocent Mortals who
' ſuffer Deriſion under that Word, for being governed by
' the beſt of Wives. It would be worth your Conſidera-
' tion to enter into the Nature of Affection itſelf, and tell
' us, according to your Philoſophy, why it is that our
' Dears ſhould do what they will with us, ſhall be froward,
' ill-natured, aſſuming, ſometimes whine, at others rail,
' then ſwoon away, then come to Life, have the Uſe of
' Speech to the greateſt Fluency imaginable, and then ſink
' away again, and all becauſe they fear we do not love
' them enough; that is, the poor Things love us ſo hear-
' tily, that they cannot think it poſſible we ſhould be able
' to love them in ſo great a Degree, which makes them
' take on ſo. I ſay, Sir, a true good-natured Man,
' whom Rakes and Libertines call *Hen-peckt,* ſhall fall in-
' to all theſe different Moods with his dear Life, and at
' the ſame time ſee they are wholly put on; and yet not
' be hard-hearted enough to tell the dear good Creature
' that ſhe is an Hypocrite.

' THIS ſort of good Men is very frequent in the popu-
' lous and wealthy City of *London,* and is the true *Hen-*
' *peckt* Man; the kind Creature cannot break through his
' Kindneſſes ſo far as to come to an Explanation with the
' tender Soul, and therefore goes on to comfort her when
' nothing ails her, to appeaſe her when ſhe is not angry,
' and to give her his Caſh when he knows ſhe does not
' want it; rather than be uneaſy for a whole Month,
' which is computed by hard-hearted Men the Space of
' Time which a froward Woman takes to come to herſelf,
' if you have Courage to ſtand out.

' THERE are indeed ſeveral other Species of the
' *Hen-peckt,* and in my Opinion they are certainly the beſt
' Subjects the Queen has; and for that Reaſon I take it to
' be your Duty to keep us above Contempt.

I do

'I do not know whether I make myself underſtood in
'the Repreſentation of an Hen-peckt Life, but I ſhall take
'leave to give you an Account of myſelf, and my own
'Spouſe. You are to know that I am reckoned no Fool,
'have on ſeveral Occaſions been tried whether I will take
'Ill-uſage, and the Event has been to my Advantage ;
'and yet there is not ſuch a Slave in *Turkey* as I am to my
'Dear. She has a good Share of Wit, and is what you
'call a very pretty agreeable Woman. I perfectly dote
'on her, and my Affection to her gives me all the Anxie-
'ties imaginable but, that of Jealouſy. My being thus
'confident of her, I take, as much as I can judge of my
'Heart, to be the Reaſon, that whatever ſhe does, tho' it
'be never ſo much againſt my Inclination, there is ſtill
'left ſomething in her Manner that is amiable. She will
'ſometimes look at me with an aſſumed Grandeur, and
'pretend to reſent that I have not had Reſpect enough for
'her Opinion in ſuch an Inſtance in Company. I cannot
'but ſmile at the pretty Anger ſhe is in, and then ſhe pre-
'tends ſhe is uſed like a Child. In a word, our great De-
'bate is, which has the Superiority in point of Under-
'ſtanding. She is eternally forming an Argument of De-
'bate ; to which I very indolently anſwer, Thou art mighty
'pretty. To this ſhe anſwers, All the World but you think
'I have as much Senſe as yourſelf. I repeat to her, In-
'deed you are pretty. Upon this there is no Patience ;
'ſhe will throw down any thing about her, ſtamp and pull
'off her Head-Clothes. Fy, my Dear, ſay I ; how can
'a Woman of your Senſe fall into ſuch an intemperate
'Rage ? This is an Argument which never fails. Indeed,
'my Dear, ſays ſhe, you make me mad ſometimes, ſo
'you do, with the ſilly Way you have of treating me
'like a pretty Idiot. Well, what have I got by putting
'her into Good-humour ? Nothing, but that I muſt con-
'vince her of my good Opinion by my Practice; and
'then I am to give her Poſſeſſion of my little Ready-
'Money, and, for a Day and a half following, diſlike all
'ſhe diſlikes, and extol every thing ſhe approves. I am
'ſo exquiſitely fond of this Darling, that I ſeldom ſee any
'of my Friends, am uneaſy in all Companies till I ſee
'her again ; and when I come home ſhe is in the Dumps,
'becauſe ſhe ſays ſhe is ſure I came ſo ſoon only becauſe I
　　　　　　　　　　　　　　　　　　　　　'think

' think her handfom. I dare not upon this Occafion
' laugh; but tho' I am one of the warmeft Churchmen in
' the Kingdom, I am forced to rail at the Times, becaufe
' fhe is a violent Whig. Upon this we talk Politicks fo
' long, that fhe is convinc'd I kifs her for her Wifdom.
' It is a common Practice with me to afk her fome Que-
' ftion concerning the Conftitution, which fhe anfwers me
' in general out of *Harrington*'s *Oceana :* Then I com-
' mend her ftrange Memory, and her Arm is immediately
' lock'd in mine. While I keep her in this Temper fhe
' plays before me, fometimes dancing in the midft of the
' Room, fometimes ftriking an Air at her Spinnet, vary-
' ing her Pofture and her Charms in fuch a manner that
' I am in continual Pleafure : She will play the Fool, if I
' allow her to be wife; but if fhe fufpects I like her for
' her Trifling, fhe immediately grows grave.

' T H E S E are the Toils in which I am taken, and I
' carry off my Servitude as well as moft Men; but my
' Application to you is in behalf of the *Hen-peckt* in ge-
' neral, and I defire a Differtation from you in Defence
' of us. You have, as I am informed, very good Au-
' thorities in our Favour, and hope you will not omit the
' mention of the Renowned *Socrates,* and his Philofophick
' Refignation to his Wife *Xantippe.* This would be a very
' good Office to the World in general, for the *Hen-peckt*
' are powerful in their Quality and Numbers, not only in
' Cities but in Courts; in the latter they are ever the moft
' obfequious, in the former the moft wealthy of all Men.
' When you have confidered Wedlock thoroughly, you
' ought to enter into the Suburbs of Matrimony, and give
' us an Account of the Thraldom of kind Keepers, and
' irrefolute Lovers; the Keepers who cannot quit their
' Fair Ones, tho' they fee their approaching Ruin; the
' Lovers who dare not marry, tho' they know they never
' fhall be happy without the Miftreffes whom they cannot
' purchafe on other Terms.

' W H A T will be a great Embellifhment to your Dif-
' courfe, will be, that you may find Inftances of the
' Haughty, the Proud, the Frolick, the Stubborn, who
' are each of them in fecret downright Slaves to their
' Wives or Miftreffes. I muft beg of you in the laft Place
' to dwell upon this, That the Wife and Valiant in all
' Ages

' Ages have been *Hen-peckt* : and that the sturdy Tempers
' who are not Slaves to Affection, owe that Exemption
' to their being inthralled by Ambition, Avarice, or some
' meaner Passion. I have ten thousand thousand Things
' more to say, but my Wife sees me Writing, and will,
' according to Custom, be consulted, if I do not seal this
' immediately.

Yours,

T   Nathaniel Henroost.

Nº 177   *Saturday, September 22.*

——*Quis enim bonus, aut face dignus*
Arcanâ, qualem Cereris vult esse sacerdos,
Ulla aliena sibi credat mala?—— Juv. Sat. 15. v. 140.

Who can all Sense of others Ills escape,
Is but a Brute, at best, in human Shape.   TATE.

IN one of my last Week's Papers I treated of Good-
nature, as it is the Effect of Constitution ; I shall now
speak of it as it is a Moral Virtue. The first may
make a Man easy in himself and agreeable to others, but
implies no Merit in him that is possessed of it. A Man is
no more to be praised upon this Account, than because he
has a regular Pulse or a good Digestion. This Good-
nature however in the Constitution, which Mr. *Dryden*
somewhere calls a *Milkiness of Blood,* is an admirable
Groundwork for the other. In order therefore to try our
Good-nature, whether it arises from the Body or the
Mind, whether it be founded in the Animal or Rational
Part of our Nature ; in a word, whether it be such as is
intitled to any other Reward, besides that secret Satisfaction and Contentment of Mind which is essential to it,
and the kind Reception it procures us in the World, we
must examine it by the following Rules.

FIRST, whether it acts with Steadiness and Unifor-
mity in Sickness and in Health, in Prosperity and in Adversity ;

verfity; if otherwife, it is to be looked upon as nothing elfe but an Irradiation of the Mind from fome new Supply of Spirits, or a more kindly Circulation of the Blood. Sir *Francis Bacon* mentions a cunning Solicitor, who would never ask a Favour of a great Man before Dinner; but took care to prefer his Petition at a Time when the Party petitioned had his Mind free from Care, and his Appetites in good Humour. Such a tranfient temporary Good-nature as this, is not that *Philanthropy*, that Love of Mankind, which deferves the Title of a Moral Virtue.

THE next way of a Man's bringing his Good-nature to the Teft, is, to confider whether it operates according to the Rules of Reafon and Duty: For if, notwithftanding its general Benevolence to Mankind, it makes no diftinction between its Objects, if it exerts itfelf promifcuoufly towards the Deferving and Undeferving, if it relieves alike the Idle and the Indigent, if it gives itfelf up to the firft Petitioner, and lights upon any one rather by Accident than Choice, it may pafs for an amiable Inftinct, but muft not affume the Name of a Moral Virtue.

THE third Trial of Good-nature will be, the examining ourfelves, whether or no we are able to exert it to our own Difadvantage, and employ it on proper Objects, notwithftanding any little Pain, Want, or Inconvenience which may arife to ourfelves from it: In a word, whether we are willing to risk any Part of our Fortune, our Reputation, or Health or Eafe, for the Benefit of Mankind. Among all thefe Expreffions of Good-nature, I fhall fingle out that which goes under the general Name of Charity, as it confifts in relieving the Indigent; that being a Trial of this Kind which offers itfelf to us almoft at all Times and in every Place.

I fhould propofe it as a Rule to every one who is provided with any Competency of Fortune more than fufficient for the Neceffaries of Life, to lay afide a certain Proportion of his Income for the Ufe of the Poor. This I would look upon as an Offering to him who has a Right to the whole, for the Ufe of thofe whom, in the Paffage hereafter mentioned, he has defcribed as his own Reprefentatives upon Earth. At the fame time we fhould manage our Charity with fuch Prudence and Caution, that we may not hurt our own Friends or Relations,

whilft

whilst we are doing Good to those who are Strangers to us.

. THIS may possibly be explained better by an Example than by a Rule.

EUGENIUS is a Man of an universal Good-nature, and generous beyond the Extent of his Fortune; but withal so prudent, in the Oeconomy of his Affairs, that what goes out in Charity is made up by good Management. *Eugenius* has what the World calls Two hundred Pounds a Year; but never values himself above Ninescore, as not thinking he has a Right to the tenth Part, which he always appropriates to charitable Uses. To this Sum he frequently makes other voluntary Additions, insomuch that in a good Year, for such he accounts those in which he has been able to make greater Bounties than ordinary, he has given above twice that Sum to the Sickly and Indigent. *Engenius* prescribes to himself many particular Days of Fasting and Abstinence, in order to increase his private Bank of Charity, and sets aside what would be the current Expences of those Times for the Use of the Poor. He often goes afoot where his Business calls him, and at the End of his Walk has given a Shilling, which in his ordinary Methods of Expence would have gone for Coach-hire, to the first Necessitous Person that has fallen in his way. I have known him, when he has been going to a Play or an Opera, divert the Money which was designed for that Purpose, upon an Object of Charity whom he has met with in the Street; and afterwards pass his Evening in a Coffee-house, or at a Friend's Fire-side, with much greater Satisfaction to himself than he could have received from the most exquisite Entertainments of the Theatre. By these means he is generous, without impoverishing himself, and enjoys his Estate by making it the Property of others.

. THERE are few Men so cramped in their private Affairs, who may not be charitable after this manner, without any Disadvantage to themselves, or Prejudice to their Families. It is but sometimes sacrificing a Diversion or Convenience to the Poor, and turning the usual Course of our Expences into a better Channel. This is, I think, not only the most prudent and convenient, but the most meritorious Piece of Charity, which we can put

in

in practice. By this Method we in some measure share the Neceffities of the Poor at the same time that we relieve them, and make ourselves not only their Patrons, but their Fellow-sufferers.

SIR *Thomas Brown*, in the last Part of his *Religio Medici*, in which he describes his Charity in several Heroick Instances, and with a noble Heat of Sentiments, mentions that Verse in the Proverbs of *Solomon, He that giveth to the Poor, lendeth to the Lord:* ' There is more Rhetorick ' in that one Sentence, says he, than in a Library of Ser- ' mons ; and indeed if those Sentences were understood ' by the Reader, with the same Emphasis as they are ' delivered by the Author, we needed not those Vo- ' lumes of Instructions, but might be honest by an ' Epitome.

THIS Passage in Scripture is indeed wonderfully persuasive ; but I think the same Thought is carried much farther in the New Testament, where our Saviour tells us in a most pathetick manner, that he shall hereafter regard the Clothing of the Naked, the Feeding of the Hungry, and the Visiting of the Imprisoned, as Offices done to himself, and reward them accordingly. Pursuant to those Passages in Holy Scripture, I have somewhere met with the Epitaph of a charitable Man, which has very much pleased me. I cannot recollect the Words, but the Sense of it is to this Purpose ; What I spent I lost ; what I possessed is left to others ; what I gave away remains with me.

SINCE I am thus insensibly engaged in Sacred Writ, I cannot forbear making an Extract of several Passages which I have always read with great Delight in the Book of *Job*. It is the Account which that Holy Man gives of his Behaviour in the Days of his Prosperity, and, if considered only as a human Composition, is a finer Picture of a charitable and good-natured Man than is to be met with in any other Author.

O H that I were as in Months past, as in the Days when God preserved me : When his Candle shined upon my head, and when by his light I walked through darkness: When the Almighty was yet with me: when my Children were about me : When I washed my steps with butter, and the rock poured out rivers of oil.

W H E N

WHEN the Ear heard me, then it bleſſed me; and when the Eye ſaw me, it gave witneſs to me. Becauſe I deliver-ed the poor that cried, and the fatherleſs, and him that had none to help him. The bleſſing of him that was ready to pe-riſh came upon me, and I cauſed the Widow's Heart to ſing for joy. I was eyes to the blind, and feet was I to the lame; I was a father to the poor, and the cauſe which I knew not I ſearched out. Did not I weep for him that was in trouble? was not my Soul grieved for the poor? Let me be weighed in an even balance, that God may know mine Integrity. If I did deſpiſe the cauſe of my man-ſervant or of my maid-ſervant when they contended with me; What then ſhall I do when God riſeth up? and when he viſiteth, what ſhall I anſwer him? Did not he that made me in the womb, make him? and did not one faſhion us in the womb? If I have withheld the poor from their deſire, or have cauſed the eyes of the Widow to fail: Or have eaten my morſel myſelf alone, and the fatherleſs hath not eaten thereof: If I have ſeen any periſh for want of clothing, or any poor without covering: If his loins have not bleſſed me, and if he were not warmed with the fleece of my ſheep: If I have lift up my hand againſt the fatherleſs, when I ſaw my help in the gate; then let mine arm fall from my ſhoulder-blade, and mine arm be broken from the bone. If I have rejoiced at the deſtruc-tion of him that hated me, or lift up myſelf when evil found him: (Neither have I ſuffered my mouth to ſin, by wiſhing a curſe to his ſoul.) The ſtranger did not lodge in the ſtreet; but I opened my doors to the traveller. If my land cry againſt me, or that the furrows likewiſe there-of complain: If I have eaten the fruits thereof without money, or have cauſed the owners thereof to loſe their life; Let thiſtles grow inſtead of wheat, and cockle inſtead of barley.   L.

Nº 178 *Monday, September* 24.

Comis in uxorem —— Hor. Ep. 2. I. 2. v. 133.
Civil to his Wife,   P o p e.

I Cannot defer taking notice of this Letter.

Mr. S p e c t a t o r,

'I Am but too good a Judge of your Paper of the 15th
' Inſtant, which is a Maſter-piece; I mean that of
' Jealouſy: But I think it unworthy of you to ſpeak of
' that Torture in the Breaſt of a Man, and not to men-
' tion alſo the Pangs of it in the Heart of a Woman. You
' have very judiciouſly, and with the greateſt Penetration
' imaginable, conſidered it as Woman is the Creature of
' whom the Diffidence is raiſed: but not a Word of a
' Man, who is ſo unmerciful as to move Jealouſy in his
' Wife, and not care whether ſhe is ſo or not. It is poſ-
' ſible you may not believe there are ſuch Tyrants in the
' World; but alas, I can tell you of a Man who is ever
' out of Humour in his Wife's Company, and the plea-
' ſanteſt Man in the World every where elſe; the greateſt
' Sloven at home when he appears to none but his Fa-
' mily, and moſt exactly well-dreſſed in all other Places.
' Alas, Sir, is it of courſe, that to deliver one's ſelf
' wholly into a Man's Power without Poſſibility of Ap-
' peal to any other Juriſdiction but his own Reflexions, is
' ſo little an Obligation to a Gentleman, that he can be
' offended and fall into a Rage, becauſe my Heart ſwells
' Tears into my Eyes when I ſee him in a cloudy Mood?
' I pretend to no Succour, and hope for no Relief but
' from himſelf; and yet he that has Senſe and Juſtice in
' every thing elſe, never reflects, that to come home only
' to ſleep off an Intemperance, and ſpend all the Time
' he is there as if it were a Puniſhment, cannot but give
                                                   ' the

' the Anguiſh of a jealous Mind. He always leaves his
' Home as if he were going to Court, and returns as if he
' were entring a Goal. I could add to this, that from his
' Company and his uſual Diſcourſe, he does not ſcruple
' being thought an abandoned Man, as to his Morals.
' Your own Imagination will ſay enough to you concern-
' ing the Condition of me his Wife; and I wiſh you
' would be ſo good as to repreſent to him, for he is not
' ill-natured, and reads you much, that the Moment I
' hear the Door ſhut after him, I throw myſelf upon my
' Bed, and drown the Child he is ſo fond of with my
' Tears, and often frighten it with my Cries; that I curſe
' my Being; that I run to my Glaſs all over bathed in
' Sorrows, and help the Utterance of my inward Anguiſh
' by beholding the Guſh of my own Calamities as my
' Tears fall from my Eyes. This looks like an imagined
' Picture to tell you, but indeed this is one of my Paſtimes.
' Hitherto I have only told you the general Temper of
' my Mind, but how ſhall I give you an Account of the
' Diſtraction of it? Could you but conceive how cruel I
' am one Moment in my Reſentment, and at the enſuing
' Minute; when I place him in the Condition my Anger
' would bring him to, how compaſſionate, it would give
' you ſome Notion how miſerable I am, and how little I
' deſerve it. When I remonſtrate with the greateſt Gen-
' tleneſs that is poſſible againſt unhandſom Appearances,
' and that married Perſons are under particular Rules;
' when he is in the beſt Humour to receive this, I am an-
' ſwered only, That I expoſe my own Reputation and
' Senſe if I appear jealous. I wiſh, good Sir, you would
' take this into ſerious Conſideration, and admoniſh Huſ-
' bands and Wives what Terms they ought to keep to-
' wards each other. Your Thoughts on this important
' Subject will have the greateſt Reward, that which de-
' ſcends on ſuch as feel the Sorrows of the Afflicted. Give
' me leave to ſubſcribe myſelf,

Your unfortunate

humble Servant,

CELINDA.

I had it in my Thoughts, before I received the Letter
of this Lady, to conſider this dreadful Paſſion in the Mind

of

of a Woman; and the Smart she seems to feel does not abate the Inclination I had to recommend to Husbands a more regular Behaviour, than to give the most exquisite of Torments to those who love them, nay whose Torment would be abated if they did not love them.

IT is wonderful to observe how little is made of this inexpressible Injury, and how easily Men get into a Habit of being least agreeable where they are most obliged to be so. But this Subject deserves a distinct Speculation, and I shall observe for a Day or two the Behaviour of two or three happy Pair I am acquainted with, before I pretend to make a System of conjugal Morality. I design in the first place to go a few Miles out of Town, and there I know where to meet one who practises all the Parts of a fine Gentleman in the Duty of an Husband. When he was a Bachelor much Business made him particularly negligent in his Habit; but now there is no young Lover living so exact in the Care of his Person. One who asked why he was so long washing his Mouth, and so delicate in the Choice and Wearing of his Linen, was answered, Because there is a Woman of Merit obliged to receive me kindly, and I think it incumbent upon me to make her Inclination go along with her Duty.

IF a Man would give himself leave to think, he would not be so unreasonable as to expect Debauchery and Innocence could live in Commerce together; or hope that Flesh and Blood is capable of so strict an Alliance, as that a fine Woman must go on to improve herself 'till she is as good and impassive as an Angel, only to preserve a Fidelity to a Brute and a Satyr. The Lady who desires me for her Sake to end one of my Papers with the following Letter, I am persuaded, thinks such a Perseverance very impracticable.

Husband,

'STAY more at home. I know where you visited
'at Seven of the Clock on *Thursday* Evening. The
'Colonel, whom you charged me to see no more, is in
'Town.

T   *Martha Housewife.*

Tuesday,

Nº 179 *Tuesday, September* 25.

Centuriæ seniorum agitant expertia frugis :
Celsi prætereunt austera Poemata Rhamnes.
Omne tulit punctum qui miscuit utile dulci,
Lectorem delectando, pariterque monendo.

                   Hor. Ars Poet. v. 341.

Old Age explodes all but Morality ;
Austerity offends aspiring Youth :
But he that joins Instruction with Delight,
Profit with Pleasure, carries all the Votes.

                       ROSCOMMON.

I MAY cast my Readers under two general Divisions, the *Mercurial* and the *Saturnine.* The first are the gay Part of my Disciples, who require Speculations of Wit and Humour ; the others are those of a more solemn and sober Turn, who find no Pleasure but in Papers of Morality and sound Sense. The former call every thing that is Serious, Stupid ; the latter look upon every thing as Impertinent that is Ludicrous. Were I always Grave, one half of my Readers would fall off from me : Were I always Merry, I should lose the other. I make it therefore my Endeavour to find out Entertainments of both Kinds, and by that means perhaps consult the Good of both, more than I should do, did I always write to the particular Taste of either. As they neither of them know what I proceed upon, the sprightly Reader, who takes up my Paper in order to be diverted, very often finds himself engaged unawares in a serious and profitable Course of Thinking ; as on the contrary, the thoughtful Man, who perhaps may hope to find something Solid, and full of deep Reflexion, is very often insensibly betrayed into a Fit of Mirth. In a word, the Reader sits down to my Entertainment without knowing his Bill of Fare, and has therefore at least the Pleasure of hoping there may be a Dish to his Palate.

                               I must

I muſt confeſs, were I left to myſelf, I ſhould rather aim at Inſtructing than Diverting; but if we will be uſeful to the World, we muſt take it as we find it. Authors of profeſſed Severity diſcourage the looſer Part of Mankind from having any thing to do with their Writings. A Man muſt have Virtue in him, before he will enter upon the reading of a *Seneca* or an *Epictetus*. The very Title of a Moral Treatiſe has ſomething in it auſtere and ſhocking to the Careleſs and Inconſiderate.

FOR this Reaſon ſeveral unthinking Perſons fall in my way, who would give no Attention to Lectures delivered with a Religious Seriouſneſs or a Philoſophick Gravity. They are inſnared into Sentiments of Wiſdom and Virtue when they do not think of it; and if by that means they arrive only at ſuch a Degree of Conſideration as may diſpoſe them to liſten to more ſtudied and elaborate Diſcourſes, I ſhall not think my Speculations uſeleſs. I might likewiſe obſerve, that the Gloomineſs in which ſometimes the Minds of the beſt Men are involved, very often ſtands in need of ſuch little Incitements to Mirth and Laughter, as are apt to diſperſe Melancholy, and put our Faculties in good Humour. To which ſome will add, that the *British* Climate, more than any other, makes Entertainments of this Nature in a manner neceſſary.

IF what I have here ſaid does not recommend, it will at leaſt excuſe the Variety of my Speculations. I would not willingly Laugh but in order to inſtruct, or if I ſometimes fail in this Point, when my Mirth ceaſes to be Inſtructive, it ſhall never ceaſe to be Innocent. A ſcrupulous Conduct in this Particular, has, perhaps, more Merit in it than the Generality of Readers imagine; did they know how many Thoughts occur in a Point of Humour, which a diſcreet Author in Modeſty ſuppreſſes; how many Strokes of Rallery preſent themſelves, which could not fail to pleaſe the ordinary Taſte of Mankind, but are ſtifled in their Birth by reaſon of ſome remote Tendency which they carry in them to corrupt the Minds of thoſe who read them; did they know how many Glances of Ill-nature are induſtriouſly avoided for fear of doing Injury to the Reputation of another, they would be apt to think kindly of thoſe Writers who endeavour to make themſelves Diverting, without being

Im-

Immoral.   One may apply to thefe Authors that Paffage in *Waller*.

> *Poets lofe half the Praife they would have got,*
> *Were it but known what they difcreetly blot.*

As nothing is more eafy than to be a Wit, with all the above-mentioned Liberties, it requires fome Genius and Invention to appear fuch without them.

WHAT I have here faid is not only in regard to the Publick, but with an Eye to my particular Correfpondent, who has fent me the following Letter, which I have caftrated in fome Places upon thefe Confiderations.

SIR,

'HAVING lately feen your Difcourfe upon a Match
' of Grinning, I cannot forbear giving you an Ac-
' count of a Whiftling Match, which, with many others,
' I was entertained with about three Years fince, at the
' *Bath*. The Prize was a Guinea, to be conferred upon
' the ableft Whiftler, that is, on him who could whiftle
' cleareft, and go through his Tune without Laughing,
' to which at the fame time he was provoked by the
' antick Poftures of a *Merry-Andrew*, who was to ftand
' upon the Stage and play his Tricks in the Eye of the
' Performer. There were three Competitors for the Ring.
' The firft was a Plough-man of a very promifing Afpect;
' his Features were fteady, and his Mufcles compofed in
' fo inflexible a Stupidity, that upon his firft Appearance
' every one gave the Guinea for loft. The Pickled Her-
' ring however found the way to fhake him ; for upon his
' Whiftling a Country Jig, this unlucky Wag danced to
' it with fuch Variety of Diftortions and Grimaces, that
' the Countryman could not forbear fmiling upon him,
' and by that means fpoiled his Whiftle, and loft the
' Prize.

' THE next that mounted the Stage, was an Under-
' Citizen of the *Bath*, a Perfon remarkable among the
' inferior People of that Place for his great Wifdom and
' his Broad Band. He contracted his Mouth with much
' Gravity, and, that he might difpofe his Mind to be
' more ferious than ordinary, begun the Tune of *The*
' *Children in the Wood*, and went through part of it with
                                                    ' good

'good Succefs; when on a fudden the Wit at his Elbow,
' who had appeared wonderfully grave and attentive for
' fome time, gave him a Touch upon the left Shoulder,
' and ftared him in the Face with fo bewitching a Grin,
' that the Whiftler relaxed his Fibres into a kind of Sim-
' per, and at length burft out into an open Laugh. The
' third who entered the Lifts was a Footman, who in
' Defiance of the *Merry-Andrew*, and all his Arts, whift-
' led a *Scotch* Tune and an *Italian* Sonata, with fo fettled
' a Countenance, that he bore away the Prize, to the great
' Admiration of fome Hundreds of Perfons, who, as well
' as myfelf, were prefent at this Trial of Skill. Now,
' Sir, I humbly conceive, whatever you have determined
' of the Grinners, the Whiftlers ought to be encouraged,
' not only as their Art is practifed without Diftortion, but
' as it improves Country Mufick, promotes Gravity, and
' teaches ordinary People to keep their Countenances, if
' they fee any thing ridiculous in their Betters; befides
' that it feems an Entertainment very particularly adapt-
' ed to the *Bath*, as it is ufual for a Rider to whiftle to his
' Horfe when he would make his Waters pafs.

I am, Sir, &c.

POSTSCRIPT.

' AFTER having difpatched thefe two important
' Points of Grinning and Whiftling, I hope you will ob-
' lige the World with fome Reflexions upon Yawning,
' as I have feen it practifed on a Twelfth-Night among
' other *Chriftmas* Gambols at the Houfe of a very wor-
' thy Gentleman, who always entertains his Tenants at
' that time of the Year. They Yawn for a *Chefhire*
' Cheefe, and begin about Midnight, when the whole
' Company is difpofed to be droufy. He that Yawns
' wideft, and at the fame time fo naturally as to produce
' the moft Yawns among the Spectators, carries home
' the Cheefe. If you handle this Subject as you ought,
' I queftion not but your Paper will fet half the King-
' dom a Yawning, tho' I dare promife you it will never
' make any body fall afleep. L

Wednefday,

N°. 180. *Wednesday, September* 26.

——Delirant Reges, plectuntur Achivi.

Hor. Ep. 2. l. 1. v. 14.

The People suffer when the Prince offends. CREECH.

THE following Letter has so much Weight and good Sense, that I cannot forbear inserting it, tho' it relates to an hardened Sinner, whom I have very little Hopes of reforming, *viz.* Lewis XIV. of *France.*

Mr. SPECTATOR,

'AMIDST the Variety of Subjects of which you
' have treated, I could wish it had fallen in your
' way, to expose the Vanity of Conquests. This Thought
' would naturally lead one to the *French* King, who has
' been generally esteemed the greatest Conqueror of our
' Age, 'till her Majesty's Armies had torn from him so
' many of his Countries, and deprived him of the Fruit
' of all his former Victories. For my own part, if I
' were to draw his Picture, I should be for taking him
' no lower than to the Peace of *Reswick,* just at the End
' of his Triumphs, and before his Reverse of Fortune:
' and even then I should not forbear thinking his Am-
' bition had been vain and unprofitable to himself and
' his People.

' AS for himself, it is certain he can have gained no-
' thing by his Conquests, if they have not rendered him
' Master of more Subjects, more Riches, or greater Power.
' What I shall be able to offer upon these Heads, I resolve
' to submit to your Consideration.

' TO begin then with his Increase of Subjects. From
' the time he came of Age, and has been a Manager for
' himself, all the People he had acquired were such only
' as he had reduced by his Wars, and were left in his
' Possession by the Peace; he had conquered not above one

' third

' third Part of *Flanders*, and confequently no more than
' one third Part of the Inhabitants of that Province.

' ABOUT 100 Years ago the Houfes in that Country
' were all numbered, and by a juft Computation the In-
' habitants of all Sorts could not then exceed 750000
' Souls. And if any Man will confider the Defolation by
' almoft perpetual Wars, the numerous Armies that have
' lived almoft ever fince at Difcretion upon the People,
' and how much of their Commerce has removed for
' more Security to other Places, he will have little Reafon
' to imagine that their Numbers have fince increafed;
' and therefore with one third Part of that Province that
' Prince can have gained no more than one third Part of
' the Inhabitants, or 250000 new Subjects, even tho' it
' fhould be fuppofed they were all contented to live ftill
' in their native Country, and transfer their Allegiance to
' a new Mafter.

' THE Fertility of this Province, its convenient Si-
' tuation for Trade and Commerce, its Capacity for fur-
' nifhing Employment and Subfiftence to great Num-
' bers, and the vaft Armies that have been maintained
' here, make it credible that the remaining two Thirds
' of *Flanders* are equal to all his other Conquefts; and
' confequently by all he cannot have gained more than
' 750000 new Subjects, Men, Women and Children,
' efpecially if a Deduction fhall be made of fuch as
' have retired from the Conqueror to live under their
' old Mafters.

' IT is time now to fet his Lofs againft his Profit,
' and to fhew for the new Subjects he had acquired,
' how many old ones he had loft in the Acquifition: I
' think that in his Wars he has feldom brought lefs into
' the Field in all Places than 200000 fighting Men, be-
' fides what have been left in Garrifons; and I think the
' common Computation is, that of an Army, at the
' End of a Campaign, without Sieges or Battles, fcarce
' four Fifths can be muftered of thofe that came into
' the Field at the Beginning of the Year. His Wars
' at feveral Times till the laft Peace have held about 20
' Years; and if 40000 yearly loft, or a fifth Part of his
' Armies, are to be multiplied by 20, he cannot have
' loft lefs than 800000 of his old Subjects, and all able-
                                    ' body'd

‘ body’d Men; a greater Number than the new Subjects
‘ he had acquired.

‘ BUT this Lofs is not all: Providence feems to have
‘ equally divided the whole Mafs of Mankind into dif-
‘ ferent Sexes, that every Woman may have her Husband,
‘ and that both may equally contribute to the Continuance
‘ of the Species. It follows then, that for all the Men
‘ that have been loft, as many Women muft have lived
‘ fingle, and it were but Charity to believe they have not
‘ done all the Service they were capable of doing in their
‘ Generation. In fo long a Courfe of Years great part
‘ of them muft have died, and all the reft muft go off
‘ at laft without leaving any Reprefentatives behind. By
‘ this Account he muft have loft not only 800000 Subjects,
‘ but double that Number, and all the Increafe that was
‘ reafonably to be expected from it.

‘ IT is faid in the laft War there was a Famine in his
‘ Kingdom, which fwept away two Millions of his Peo-
‘ ple. This is hardly credible: If the lofs was only of
‘ one fifth Part of that Sum, it was very great. But ’tis
‘ no wonder there fhould be Famine, where fo much
‘ of the People’s Subftance is taken away for the King’s
‘ Ufe, that they have not fufficient left to provide againft
‘ Accidents; where fo many of the Men are taken from
‘ the Plough to ferve the King in his Wars, and a great
‘ part of the Tillage is left to the weaker Hands of fo
‘ many Women and Children. Whatever was the Lofs,
‘ it muft undoubtedly be placed to the Account of his
‘ Ambition.

‘ AND fo muft alfo the Deftruction or Banifhment of
‘ 3 or 400000 of his reformed Subjects; he could have
‘ no other Reafons for valuing thofe Lives fo very cheap,
‘ but only to recommend himfelf to the Bigotry of the
‘ *Spanifh* Nation.

‘ HOW fhould there be Induftry in a Country where
‘ all Property is precarious? What Subject will fow his
‘ Land that his Prince may reap the whole Harveft?
‘ Parfimony and Frugality muft be Strangers to fuch
‘ a People; for will any Man fave to-day what he has
‘ Reafon to fear will be taken from him to-morrow?
‘ And where is the Encouragement for marrying? Will
‘ any Man think of raifing Children, without any Affu-

' rance of Clothing for their Backs, or fo much as Food
' for their Bellies? And thus by his fatal Ambition he
' muft have leffened the Number of his Subjects not only
' by Slaughter and Deftruction, but by preventing their
' very Births, he has done as much as was poffible to-
' wards deftroying Pofterity itfelf.

' IS this then the great, the invincible *Lewis* ? This
' the immortal Man, the *tout-puiffant*, or the Almighty,
' as his Flatterers have called him ? Is this the Man that
' is fo celebrated for his Conquefts ? For every Subject
' he has acquired, has he not loft three that were his In-
' heritance ? Are not his Troops fewer, and thofe nei-
' ther fo well fed, or clothed, or paid, as they were for-
' merly, tho' he has now fo much greater Caufe to exert
' himfelf ? And what can be the Reafon of all this, but
' that his Revenue is a great deal lefs, his Subjects are
' either poorer, or not fo many to be plundered by con-
' ftant Taxes for his Ufe ?

' IT is well for him he had found out a Way to fteal
' a Kingdom; if he had gone on conquering as he did
' before, his Ruin had been long fince finifhed. This
' brings to my Mind a Saying of King *Pyrrhus*, after he
' had a fecond time beat the *Romans* in a pitched Battle,
' and was complimented by his Generals; *Yes*, fays he,
' *fuch another Victory and I am quite undone*. And fince
' I have mentioned *Pyrrhus*, I will end with a very
' good, though known Story of this ambitious mad Man.
' When he had fhewn the utmoft Fondnefs of his Ex-
' pedition againft the *Romans*, *Cyneas* his chief Minifter
' asked him what he propofed to himfelf by this War ?
' Why, fays *Pyrrhus*, to conquer the *Romans*, and reduce
' all *Italy* to my Obedience. What then ? fays *Cyneas*.
' To pafs over into *Sicily*, fays *Pyrrhus*, and then all the
' *Sicilians* muft be our Subjects. And what does your
' Majefty intend next ? Why truly, fays the King, to
' conquer *Carthage*, and make myfelf mafter of all
' *Africa*. And what, Sir, fays the Minifter is to be the
' End of all your Expeditions ? Why then, fays the King,
' for the reft of our Lives we'll fit down to good Wine.
' How, Sir, replied *Cyneas*, to better than we have now
' before us ? Have we not already as much as we can
' drink ?

'   ' RIOT

' RIOT and Excefs are not the becoming Characters
' of Princes; but if *Pyrrhus* and *Lewis* had debauched like
' *Vitellius*, they had been lefs hurtful to their People.

Your humble Servant,

T　　　　　　　　　　　　　PHILARITHMUS.

Nº 181　*Thurfday, September* 27.

His lacrymis vitam damus, & miferefcimus ultrò.
　　　　　　　　　　　Virg. Æn. 2. v. 145.

Mov'd by thefe Tears, we pity and protect.

I AM more pleafed with a Letter that is filled with
Touches of Nature than of Wit. The following one
is of this Kind.

S I R,

AMONG all the Diftreffes which happen in Families, I do not remember that you have touched
' upon the Marriage of Children without the Confent
' of their Parents. I am one of thefe unfortunate Per-
' fons. I was about fifteen when I took the Liberty to
' choofe for myfelf; and have ever fince languifhed
' under the Difpleafure of an inexorable Father, who,
' though he fees me happy in the beft of Husbands, and
' bleffed with very fine Children, can never be prevailed
' upon to forgive me. He was fo kind to me before
' this unhappy Accident, that indeed it makes my Breach
' of Duty, in fome meafure, inexcufable; and at the
' fame times creates in me fuch a Tendernefs towards
' him, that I love him above all things, and would die
' to be reconciled to him. I have thrown myfelf at his
' Feet, and befought him with Tears to pardon me; but
' he always pufhes me away, and fpurns me from him;
' I have written feveral Letters to him, but he will nei-
' ther open nor receive them. About two Years ago I
' fent my little Boy to him, dreffed in a new Apparel;
　　　　　　　　　C 3　　　　　　　　　' but

' but the Child returned to me crying, becaufe he faid
' his Grandfather would not fee him, and had ordered
' him to be put out of his Houfe.   My Mother is won
' over to my Side, but dares not mention me to my Fa-
' ther for fear of provoking him. About a Month ago he
' lay fick upon his Bed, and in great Danger of his Life: I
' was pierced to the Heart at the News, and could not
' forbear going to inquire after his Health. My Mother
' took this Opportunity of fpeaking in my Behalf: fhe
' told him with abundance of Tears, that I was come to
' fee him, that I could not fpeak to her for weeping, and
' that I fhould certainly break my Heart if he refus'd at
' that Time to give me his Bleffing, and be reconciled to
' me. He was fo far from relenting towards me, that he
' bid her fpeak no more of me, unlefs fhe had a mind to
' difturb him in his laft Moments; for, Sir, you muft
' know that he has the Reputation of an honeft and reli-
' gious Man, which makes my Misfortune fo much the
' greater. God be thanked he is fince recovered: But
' his fevere Ufage has given me fuch a Blow, that I
' fhall foon fink under it, unlefs I may be relieved by
' any Impreffions which the reading of this in your Paper
' may make upon him.

I am, &c.

O F all Hardneffes of Heart there is none fo inexcufable as that of Parents towards their Children. An obftinate, inflexible, unforgiving Temper is odious upon all
Occafions; but here it is unnatural. The Love, Tendernefs, and Compaffion, which are apt to arife in us towards
thofe who depend upon us, is that by which the whole
World of Life is upheld. The Supreme Being, by the
tranfcendent Excellency and Goodnefs of his Nature,
extends his Mercy towards all his Works; and becaufe
his Creatures have not fuch a fpontaneous Benevolence
and Compaffion towards thofe who are under their Care
and Protection, he has implanted in them an Inftinct,
that fupplies the Place of this inherent Goodnefs. I
have illuftrated this kind of Inftinct in former Papers,
and have fhewn how it runs thro' all the Species of brute
Creatures, as indeed the whole Animal Creation fubfifts
by it.

THIS

THIS Inſtinct in Man is more general and uncircum-ſcribed than in Brutes, as being enlarged by the Dictates of Reaſon and Duty. For if we conſider ourſelves attentively, we ſhall find that we are not only inclined to love thoſe who deſcend from us, but that we bear a kind of ςopyή, or natural Affection, to every thing which relies upon us for its Good and Preſervation. Dependence is a perpetual Call upon Humanity, and a greater Incitement to Tenderneſs and Pity than any other Motive whatſoever.

THE Man therefore who, notwithſtanding any Paſſion or Reſentment, can overcome this powerful Inſtinct, and extinguiſh natural Affection, debaſes his Mind even below Brutality, fruſtrates, as much as in him lies, the great Deſign of Providence, and ſtrikes out of his Nature one of the moſt Divine Principles that is planted in it.

AMONG innumerable Arguments which might be brought againſt ſuch an unreaſonable Proceeding, I ſhall only inſiſt on one. We make it the Condition of our Forgiveneſs that we forgive others. In our very Prayers we deſire no more than to be treated by this kind of Retaliation. The Caſe therefore before us ſeems to be what they call a *Caſe in Point;* the Relation between the Child and Father being what comes neareſt to that between a Creature and its Creator. If the Father is inexorable to the Child who has offended, let the Offence be of never ſo high a Nature, how will he addreſs himſelf to the Supreme Being under the tender Appellation of a Father, and deſire of him ſuch a Forgiveneſs as he himſelf refuſes to grant?

TO this I might add many other religious, as well as many prudential Conſiderations; but if the laſt mentioned Motive does not prevail, I deſpair of ſucceeding by any other, and ſhall therefore conclude my Paper with a very remarkable Story, which is recorded in an old Chronicle publiſhed by *Freher,* among the Writers of the *German* Hiſtory.

EGINHART, who was Secretary to *Charles the Great,* became exceeding popular by his Behaviour in that Poſt. His great Abilities gain'd him the Favour of his Maſter, and the Eſteem of the whole Court. *Imma,* the Daughter of the Emperor, was ſo pleaſed with his Perſon and

Con-

Conversation, that she fell in Love with him. As she was one of the greatest Beauties of the Age, *Eginhart* answer'd her with a more than equal Return of Passion. They stifled their Flames for some time, under Apprehension of the fatal Consequences that might ensue. *Eginhart* at length resolving to hazard all, rather than be deprived of one whom his Heart was so much set upon, conveyed himself one Night into the Princess's Apartment, and knocking gently at the Door, was admitted as a Person who had something to communicate to her from the Emperor. He was with her in private most part of the Night; but upon his preparing to go away about Break of Day, he observed that there had fallen a great Snow during his Stay with the Princess. This very much perplexed him, lest the Prints of his Feet in the Snow might make Disco-veries to the King, who often used to visit his Daughter in the Morning. He acquainted the Princess *Imma* with his Fears; who, after some Consultations upon the Mat-ter, prevailed upon him to let her carry him through the Snow upon her own Shoulders. It happened, that the Emperor not being able to sleep, was at that time up and walking in his Chamber, when upon looking through the Window he perceived his Daughter tottering under her Burden, and carrying his first Minister across the Snow; which she had no sooner done, but she returned again with the utmost Speed to her own Apartment. The Emperor was extremely troubled and astonished at this Accident; but resolved to speak nothing of it till a proper Opportu-nity. In the mean time, *Eginhart* knowing that what he had done could not be long a Secret, determined to retire from Court; and in order to it begged the Emperor that he would be pleased to dismiss him, pretending a kind of Discontent at his not having been rewarded for his long Services. The Emperor would not give a direct Answer to his Petition, but told him he would think of it, and appointed a certain Day when he would let him know his Pleasure. He then called together the most faithful of his Counsellors, and acquainting them with his Secretary's Crime, asked them their Advice in so delicate an Affair. They most of them gave their Opinion, that the Person could not be too severely punished who had thus disho-noured his Master. Upon the whole Debate, the Empe-ror

ror declared it was his Opinion, that *Eginhart*'s Punishment would rather increase than diminish the Shame of
his Family, and that therefore he thought it the most ad-
viseable to wear out the Memory of the Fact, by marrying him to his Daughter. Accordingly *Eginhart* was
called in, and acquainted by the Emperor, that he
should no longer have any Pretence of complaining his
Services were not rewarded, for that the Princess *Imma*
should be given him in Marriage, with a Dower suitable
to her Quality; which was soon after performed accordingly.   L.

Nº 182 *Friday, September* 28.

Plus aloës quàm mellis habet—— Juv. Sat. 6. v.180.

The Bitter overbalances the Sweet.

AS all Parts of human Life come under my Observation, my Reader must not make uncharitable In-
ferences from my speaking knowingly of that Sort
of Crime which is at present treated of. He will, I hope,
suppose I know it only from the Letters of Correspondents, two of which you shall have as follow.

Mr. SPECTATOR,

'IT is wonderful to me that among the many Enor-
' mities which you have treated of, you have not men-
' tioned that of Wenching, and particularly the Insnar-
' ing Part; I mean, that it is a Thing very fit for your
' Pen, to expose the Villany of the Practice of deluding
' Women. You are to know, Sir, that I myself am a
' Woman who have been one of the Unhappy that have
' fallen into this Misfortune, and that by the Insinuations
' of a very worthless Fellow, who served others in the
' same manner both before my Ruin and since that Time.
' I had, as soon as the Rascal left me, so much Indigna-
' tion and Resolution, as not to go upon the Town, as
' the

' the Phrafe is, but took to Work for my Living in an
' obfcure Place, out of the Knowledge of all with whom
' I was before acquainted.

   ' IT is the ordinary Practice and Bufinefs of Life with
' a Set of idle Fellows about this Town, to write Letters,
' fend Meffages, and form Appointments with little raw
' unthinking Girls, and leave them after Poffeffion of
' them, without any Mercy, to Shame, Infamy, Poverty,
' and Difeafe. Were you to read the naufeous Imperti-
' nences which are written on thefe Occafions, and to fee
' the filly Creatures fighing over them, it could not but be
' Matter of Mirth as well as Pity. A little Prentice Girl
' of mine has been for fome time applied to by an *Irifh*
' Fellow, who dreffes very fine, and ftruts in a laced Coat,
' and is the Admiration of Seamftreffes who are under
' Age in Town, ever fince I have had fome Knowledge
' of the Matter, I have debarred my Prentice from Pen,
' Ink and Paper. But the other Day he befpoke fome Cra-
' vats of me: I went out of the Shop, and left his Miftrefs
' to put them up into a Bandbox in order to be fent to him
' when his Man called. When I came into the Shop
' again, I took occafion to fend her away, and found in
' the Bottom of the Box written thefe Words, *Why would*
' *you ruin a harmlefs Creature that loves you ?* then in the
' Lid, *There is no refifting* Strephon : I fearched a little
' farther, and found in the Rim of the Box, *At Eleven*
' *o' clock at Night come in an Hackney-Coach at the End of*
' *our Street.* This was enough to alarm me; I fent away
' the things, and took my Meafures accordingly. An
' Hour or two before the appointed Time I examined my
' young Lady, and found her Trunk ftuffed with imper-
' tinent Letters, and an old Scroll of Parchment in *Latin,*
' which her Lover had fent her as a Settlement of Fifty
' Pounds a Year: Among other things, there was alfo the
' beft Lace I had in my Shop to make him a Prefent for
' Cravats. I was very glad of this laft Circumftance, be-
' caufe I could very confcientioufly fwear againft him that
' he had enticed my Servant away, and was her Accom-
' plice in robbing me: I procured a Warrant againft him
' accordingly. Every thing was now prepared, and the
' tender Hour of Love approaching, I, who had acted for
' myfelf in my Youth the fame fenfelefs Part, knew how
                            ' to

' to manage accordingly: Therefore, after having locked
' up my Maid, and not being so much unlike her in
' Height and Shape, as in a huddled way not to pass for
' her, I delivered the Bundle designed to be carried off to
' her Lover's Man, who came with the Signal to receive
' them. Thus I followed after to the Coach, where when
' I saw his Master take them in, I cried out, Thieves!
' Thieves! and the Constable with his Attendants seized
' my expecting Lover. I kept myself unobserved till I
' saw the Crowd sufficiently increased, and then appeared
' to declare the Goods to be mine; and had the Satis-
' faction to see my Man of Mode put into the *Round-*
' *House,* with the stolen Wares by him, to be produced
' in Evidence against him the next Morning. This Mat-
' ter is notoriously known to be Fact; and I have been
' contented to save my Prentice, and take a Year's Rent
' of this mortified Lover, not to appear farther in the
' Matter. This was some Penance; but, Sir, is this enough
' for a Villany of much more pernicious Consequence than
' the Trifles for which he was to have been indicted?
' Should not you, and all Men of any Parts or Honour,
' put things upon so right a Foot, as that such a Rascal
' should not laugh at the Imputation of what he was
' really guilty, and dread being accused of that for
' which he was arrested?

' IN a word, Sir, it is in the Power of you, and
' such as I hope you are, to make it as infamous to rob
' a poor Creature of her Honour as her Clothes. I leave
' this to your Consideration, only take leave (which I
' cannot do without sighing) to remark to you, that if
' this had been the Sense of Mankind thirty Years ago,
' I should have avoided a Life spent in Poverty and
' Shame.

I am, S I R,
Your most humble Servant,
Alice Threadneedle.

Mr. SPECTATOR,   *Round-House, Sept.* 9.

I Am a Man of Pleasure about Town, but by the
' Stupidity of a dull Rogue of a Justice of Peace, and
' an insolent Constable, upon the Oath of an old Harri-
' dan

'dan, am imprifoned here for Theft, when I defigned
'only Fornication. The Midnight Magiftrate, as he con-
'veyed me along, had you in his Mouth, and faid, this
'would make a pure Story for the SPECTATOR. I
'hope, Sir, you won't pretend to Wit, and take the Part
'of dull Rogues of Bufinefs. The World is fo altered of
'late Years, that there was not a Man who would knock
'down a Watchman in my Behalf, but I was carried off
'with as much Triumph as if I had been a Pick-pocket.
'At this rate, there is an end of all the Wit and Humour
'in the World. The Time was when all the honeft
'Whore-mafters in the Neighbourhood would have rofe
'againft the Cuckolds in my Refcue. If Fornication is
'to be fcandalous, half the fine things that have been
'writ by moft of the Wits of the laft Age may be burnt
'by the common Hangman. Harkee, Mr. SPEC, do not
'be queer ; after having done fome things pretty well,
'don't begin to write at that rate that no Gentleman
'can read thee. Be true to Love, and burn your *Seneca*.
'You do not expect me to write my Name from hence,
'but I am

Your unknown humble, &c.

Nº 183   *Saturday*, *September* 29.

Ἴδμεν ψεύδεα πολλὰ λέγειν ἐτύμοισιν ὁμοῖα,
Ἴδμεν δ' εὖτ' ἐθέλωμεν, ἀληθέα μυθήσασθαι.

Hefiod.

Sometimes fair Truth in Fiction we difguife,
Sometimes prefent her naked to Mens Eyes.

FABLES were the firft Pieces of Wit that made their
Appearance in the World, and have been ftill highly
valued not only in Times of the greateft Simplicity,
but among the moft polite Ages of Mankind. *Jotham*'s
Fable of the Trees is the oldeft that is extant, and as
beautiful

beautiful as any which have been made since that Time. *Nathan*'s Fable of the poor Man and his Lamb is likewise more ancient than any that is extant, besides the above-mentioned, and had so good an Effect, as to convey Instruction to the Ear of a King without offending it, and to bring the Man after God's own Heart to a right Sense of his Guilt and his Duty. We find *Æsop* in the most distant Ages of *Greece*; and if we look into the very Beginnings of the Commonwealth of *Rome*, we see a Mutiny among the common People appeased by a Fable of the Belly and the Limbs, which was indeed very proper to gain the Attention of an incensed Rabble, at a time when perhaps they would have torn to pieces any Man who had preached the same Doctrine to them in an open and direct manner. As Fables took their Birth in the very Infancy of Learning, they never flourished more than when Learning was at its greatest Height. To justify this Assertion, I shall put my Reader in mind of *Horace*, the greatest Wit and Critick in the *Augustan* Age; and of *Boileau*, the most correct Poet among the Moderns: Not to mention *La Fontaine*, who by this Way of Writing is come more into vogue than any other Author of our Times.

THE Fables I have here mentioned are raised altogether upon Brutes and Vegetables, with some of our own Species mixt among them, when the Moral hath so required. But besides this kind of Fable, there is another in which the Actors are Passions, Virtues, Vices, and other imaginary Persons of the like Nature. Some of the ancient Criticks will have it, that the Iliad and Odyssey of *Homer* are Fables of this Nature; and that the several Names of Gods and Heroes are nothing else but the Affections of the Mind in a visible Shape and Character. Thus they tell us, that *Achilles*, in the first Iliad, represents Anger, or the Irascible Part of Human Nature; That upon drawing his Sword against his Superior in a full Assembly, *Pallas* is only another Name for Reason, which checks and advises him upon that Occasion; and at her first Appearance touches him upon the Head, that Part of the Man being looked upon as the Seat of Reason. And thus of the rest of the Poem. As for the Odyssey, I think it is plain that *Horace* considered it as one of these Allegorical Fables, by the Moral which he has given us of several Parts of it. The greatest

Italian

Italian Wits have applied themselves to the Writing of this latter kind of Fables: As *Spenser's Fairy-Queen* is one continued Series of them from the Beginning to the End of that admirable Work. If we look into the fineft Profe-Authors of Antiquity, fuch as *Cicero, Plato, Xenophon*, and many others, we fhall find that this was likewife their Favourite Kind of Fable. I fhall only farther obferve upon it, that the firft of this Sort that made any confiderable Figure in the World, was that of *Hercules* meeting with Pleafure and Virtue ; which was invented by *Prodicus*, who lived before *Socrates*, and in the firft Dawnings of Philofophy. He ufed to travel through *Greece* by virtue of this Fable, which procured him a kind of Reception in all the Market-towns, where he never failed telling it as foon as he had gathered an Audience about him.

AFTER this fhort Preface, which I have made up of fuch Materials as my Memory does at prefent fuggeft to me, before I prefent my Reader with a Fable of this Kind, which I defign as the Entertainment of the prefent Paper, I muft in a few Words open the Occafion of it.

IN the Account which *Plato* gives us of the Converfation and Behaviour of *Socrates*, the Morning he was to die, he tells the following Circumftance.

WHEN *Socrates* his Fetters were knocked off (as was ufual to be done on the Day that the condemned Perfon was to be executed) being feated in the midft of his Difciples, and laying one of his Legs over the other, in a very unconcerned Pofture, he began to rub it where it had been galled by the Iron ; and whether it was to fhew the Indifference with which he entertained the Thoughts of his approaching Death, or (after his ufual manner) to take every Occafion of Philofophifing upon fome ufeful Subject, he obferved the Pleafure of that Senfation which now arofe in thofe very Parts of his Leg, that juft before had been fo much pained by the Fetter. Upon this he reflected on the Nature of Pleafure and Pain in general, and how conftantly they fucceeed one another. To this he added, That if a Man of a good Genius for a Fable were to reprefent the Nature of Pleafure and Pain in that Way of Writing, he would probably join them together after fuch a manner, that it would be impoffible for the one to come into any Place without being followed by the other.

IT

IT is possible, that if *Plato* had thought it proper at such a Time to describe *Socrates* lanching out into a Discourse which was not of a piece with the Business of the Day, he would have enlarged upon this Hint, and have drawn it out into some beautiful Allegory or Fable. But since he has not done it, I shall attempt to write one myself in the Spirit of that Divine Author.

THERE were two Families which from the Beginning of the World were, as opposite to each other as Light and Darkness. The one of them lived in Heaven, and the other in Hell. The youngest Descendent of the first Family was Pleasure, who was the Daughter of Happiness, who was the Child of Virtue, who was the Offspring of the Gods. These, as I said before, had their Habitation in Heaven. The youngest of the opposite Family was Pain, who was the Son of Misery, who was the Child of Vice, who was the Offspring of the Furies. The Habitation of this Race of Beings was in Hell.

THE middle Station of Nature between these two opposite Extremes was the Earth, which was inhabited by Creatures of a middle Kind, neither so Virtuous as the one, nor so Vicious as the other, but partaking of the good and bad Qualities of these two opposite Families. Jupiter *considering that this Species commonly called Man, was too virtuous to be miserable, and too vicious to be happy; that he might make a Distinction between the Good and the Bad, ordered the two youngest of the above-mentioned Families, Pleasure who was the Daughter of Happiness, and Pain who was the Son of Misery, to meet one another upon this Part of Nature which lay in the Half-way between them, having promised to settle it upon them both, provided they could agree upon the Division of it, so as to share Mankind between them.*

PLEASURE and Pain were no sooner met in their new Habitation, but they immediately agreed upon this Point, that Pleasure should take possession of the Virtuous, and Pain of the Vicious Part of that Species which was given up to them. But upon examining to which of them any Individual they met with belonged, they found each of them had a right to him; for that, contrary to what they had seen, in their old Places of Residence, there was no Person so Vicious who had not some Good in him, nor any Person so Virtuous who had not in him some

some Evil. The Truth of it is, they generally found upon Search, that in the most vicious Man Pleasure might lay a Claim to an hundredth Part, and that in the most virtuous Man Pain might come in for at least two Thirds. This they saw would occasion endless Disputes between them, unless they could come to some Accommodation. To this end there was a Marriage proposed between them, and at length concluded: By this means it is that we find Pleasure and Pain are such constant Yoke-fellows, and that they either make their Visits together, or are never far asunder. If Pain comes into an Heart, he is quickly followed by Pleasure; and if Pleasure enters, you may be sure Pain is not far off.

BUT notwithstanding this Marriage was very convenient for the two Parties, it did not seem to answer the Intention of Jupiter in sending them among Mankind. To remedy therefore this Inconvenience, it was stipulated between them by Article, and confirmed by the Consent of each Family, that notwithstanding they here possessed the Species indifferently; upon the Death of every single Person, if he was found to have in him a certain Proportion of Evil, he should be dispatched into the infernal Regions by a Passport from Pain, there to dwell with Misery, Vice, and the Furies. Or on the contrary, if he had in him a certain Proportion of Good, he should be dispatched into Heaven by a Passport from Pleasure, there to dwell with Happiness, Virtue and the Gods. L

Nº 184 *Monday, October* 1.

—— *Opera in longo fas est obrepere somnum.*
Hor. Ars Poet. v. 360.

—— *In long Works Sleep will sometimes surprise.*
ROSCOMMON.

WHEN a Man has discovered a new Vein of Humour, it often carries him much farther than he expected from it. My Correspondents take the Hint I give them, and pursue it into Speculations which
I never

I never thought of at my firſt ſtarting it. This has been the Fate of my Paper on the Match of Grinning, which has already produced a ſecond Paper on parallel Subjects, and brought me the following Letter by the'laſt Poſt. I ſhall not premiſe any thing to it farther, than that it is built on Matter of Fact, and is as follows.

SIR,

'YOU have already obliged the World with a Diſ-
' courſe upon Grinning, and have ſince proceeded
' to Whiſtling, from whence you at length came to Yawn-
' ing; from this, I think, you may make a very natural
' Tranſition to Sleeping. I therefore recommend to you
' for the Subject of a Paper the following Advertiſement,
' which about two Months ago was given into every bo-
' -dy's Hands, and may be ſeen with ſome Additions in the
' *Daily Courant* of *Auguſt* the Ninth.

' NICHOLAS HART, *who ſlept laſt Year in*
' *St.* Bartholomew's *Hoſpital, intends to ſleep this Year at*
' *the* Cock and Bottle *in* Little-Britain.

' HAVING ſince inquired into the Matter of Fact, I
' find that the above-mentioned *Nicholas Hart* is every
' Year ſeized with a periodical Fit of Sleeping, which
' begins upon the Fifth of *Auguſt*, and ends on the Eleventh
' of the ſame Month : That

' On the Firſt of that Month he grew dull;
' On the Second, appeared drouſy;
' On the Third, fell a yawning;
' On the Fourth, began to nod;
' On the Fifth, dropped aſleep;
' On the Sixth, was heard to ſnore;
' On the Seventh, turned himſelf in his Bed;
' On the Eighth, recovered his former Poſture;
' On the Ninth fell a ſtretching;
' On the Tenth about Midnight, awaked;
' On the Eleventh in the Morning, call'd for a little
' Small-Beer.

' THIS Account I have extracted out of the Journal
' of this ſleeping Worthy, as it has been faithfully kept
' by a Gentleman of *Lincoln's-Inn*, who has undertaken

' to

' to be his Hiftriographer. I have fent it to you, not only
' as it reprefents the Actions of *Nicholas Hart*, but as it
' feems a very natural Picture of the Life of many an ho-
' neft *Englifh* Gentleman, whofe whole Hiftory very often
' confifts of Yawning, Nodding, Stretching, Turning,
' Sleeping, Drinking, and the like extraordinary Particu-
' lars. I do not queftion, Sir, that, if you pleafed, you could
' put out an Advertifement not unlike the above-mention-
' ed, of feveral Men of Figure; that Mr. *John* fuch-a-one,
' Gentleman, or *Thomas* fuch-a-one, Efquire, who flept in
' the Country laft Summer, intends to fleep in Town this
' Winter. The worft of it is, that the droufy Part of our
' Species is chiefly made up of very honeft Gentlemen,
' who live quietly among their Neighbours, without ever
' difturbing the publick Peace : They are Drones without
' Stings. I could heartily wifh, that feveral turbulent, reft-
' lefs, ambitious Spirits, would for a-while change Places
' with thefe good Men, and enter themfelves into *Nicho-*
' *las Hart*'s Fraternity. Could one but lay afleep a few
' bufy Heads which I could name, from the Firft of *No-*
' *vember* next to the Firft of *May* enfuing, I queftion not
' but it would very much redound to the Quiet of parti-
' cular Perfons, as well as to the Benefit of the Publick.

   ' BUT to return to *Nicholas Hart* : I believe, Sir, you
' will think it a very extraordinary Circumftance for a Man
' to gain his Livelihood by Sleeping, and that Reft fhould
' procure a Man Suftenance as well as Induftry ; yet fo it
' is that *Nicholas* got laft Year enough to fupport himfelf
' for a Twelvemonth. I am likewife informed that he has
' this Year had a very comfortable Nap. The Poets value
' themfelves very much for fleeping on *Parnaſſus*, but I
' never heard they got a Groat by it : On the contrary,
' our Friend *Nicholas* gets more by Sleeping than he could
' by Working, and may be more properly faid, than ever
' *Homer* was, to have had Golden Dreams. *Juvenal* in-
' deed mentions a droufy Husband who raifed an Eftate
' by Snoring, but then he is reprefented to have flept
' what the common People call a *Dog's Sleep* ; or if his
' Sleep was real, his Wife was awake, and about her Bu-
' finefs. Your Pen, which loves to moralize upon all Sub-
' jects, may raife fomething, methinks, on this Circum-
' ftance alfo, and point out to us thofe Sets of Men, who
                       ' inftead

' inſtead of growing rich by an honeſt Induſtry, recom-
' mend themſelves to the Favours of the Great, by mak-
' ing themſelves agreeable Companions in the Participa-
' tions of Luxury and Pleaſure.

' I muſt further acquaint you, Sir, that one of the moſt
' eminent Pens in *Grubſtreet* is now employed in Writ-
' ing the Dream of this miraculous Sleeper, which I hear
' will be of a more than ordinary Length, as it muſt con-
' tain all the Particulars that are ſuppoſed to have paſſed in
' his Imagination during ſo long a Sleep. He is ſaid to have
' gone already through three Days and three Nights of it,
' and to have compriſed in them the moſt remarkable Paſ-
' ſages of the four firſt Empires of the World. If he can
' keep free from Party-ſtrokes, his Work may be of Uſe;
' but this I much doubt, having been informed by one of
' his Friends and Confidents, that he has ſpoken ſome
' things of *Nimrod* with too great Freedom.

L   *I am ever, Sir, &c.*

Nº 185   *Tueſday, October* 2.

—— *Tantæne Animis cœleſtibus Iræ?* Virg. Æn. 1, v. 15.

And dwells ſuch Fury in celeſtial Breaſts?

THERE is nothing in which Men more deceive themſelves than in what the World call Zeal. There are
ſo many Paſſions which hide themſelves under it,
and ſo many Miſchiefs ariſing from it, that ſome have gone
ſo far as to ſay it would have been for the Benefit of Mankind if it had never been reckoned in the Catalogue of Virtues. It is certain, where it is once Laudable and Prudential,
it is an hundred times Criminal and Erroneous; nor can it be
otherwiſe, if we conſider that it operates with equal Violence
in all Religions, however oppoſite they may be to one
another, and in all the Subdiviſions of each Religion in
particular.

WE are told by ſome of the *Jewiſh Rabbins*, that the
firſt Murder was occaſioned by a religious Controverſy;
and

and if we had the whole History of Zeal from the Days of *Cain* to our own Times, we should see it filled with so many Scenes of Slaughter and Bloodshed, as would make a wise Man very careful how he suffers himself to be actuated by such a Principle, when it only regards Matters of Opinion and Speculation.

I would have every Zealous Man examine his Heart thoroughly, and, I believe, he will often find, that what he calls a Zeal for his Religion, is either Pride, Interest, or Ill-nature. A Man, who differs from another in Opinion, sets himself above him in his own Judgment, and in several Particulars pretends to be the wiser Person. This is a great Provocation to the proud Man, and gives a very keen Edge to what he calls his Zeal. And that this is the Case very often, we may observe from the Behaviour of some of the most zealous for Orthodoxy, who have often great Friendships and Intimacies with vicious immoral Men, provided they do but agree with them in the same Scheme of Belief. The Reason is, Because the vicious Believer gives the Precedency to the virtuous Man, and allows the good Christian to be the worthier Person, at the same time that he cannot come up to his Perfections. This we find exemplified in that trite Passage which we see quoted in almost every System of Ethicks, tho' upon another Occasion.

———— *Video meliora proboque,*
Deteriora sequor ————   Ovid. Met. l. 7. v. 20.

I see the Right, and I approve it too;
Condemn the Wrong, and yet the Wrong pursue. TATE.

On the conttary, it is certain, if our Zeal were true and genuine, we should be much more angry with a Sinner than a Heretick; since there are several Cases which may excuse the latter before his great Judge, but none which can excuse the former.

INTEREST is likewise a great Inflamer, and sets a Man on Persecution under the colour of Zeal. For this Reason we find none are so forward to promote the true Worship by Fire and Sword, as those who find their present Account in it. But I shall extend the Word *Interest* to a larger Meaning than what is generally given it, as it relates to our Spiritual Safety and Welfare, as well as to our Temporal. A Man is glad to gain Numbers on his Side,

as

as they serve to strengthen him in his private Opinions. Every Proselyte is like a new Argument for the Establishment of his Faith. It makes him believe that his Principles carry Conviction with them, and are the more likely to be true, when he finds they are conformable to the Reason of others, as well as to his own. And that this Temper of Mind deludes a Man very often into an Opinion of his Zeal, may appear from the common Behaviour of the Atheist, who maintains and spreads his Opinions with as much Heat as those who believe they do it only out of a Passion for God's Glory.

ILL-NATURE is another dreadful Imitator of Zeal. Many a good Man may have a natural Rancour and Malice in his Heart, which has been in some measure quelled and subdued by Religion; but if it finds any Pretence of breaking out, which does not seem to him inconsistent with the Duties of a Christian, it throws off all Restraint, and rages in full Fury. Zeal is therefore a great Ease to a malicious Man, by making him believe he does God Service, whilst he is gratifying the Bent of a perverse revengeful Temper. For this Reason we find, that most of the Massacres and Devastations, which have been in the World, have taken their Rise from a furious pretended Zeal.

I love to see a Man zealous in a good Matter, and especially when his Zeal shews itself for advancing Morality, and promoting the Happiness of Mankind: But when I find the Instruments he works with are Racks and Gibbets, Gallies, and Dungeons; when he imprisons Mens Persons, confiscates their Estates, ruins their Families, and burns the Body to save the Soul, I cannot stick to pronounce of such a one, that (whatever he may think of his Faith and Religion) his Faith is vain, and his Religion unprofitable.

AFTER having treated of these false Zealots in Religion, I cannot forbear mentioning a monstrous Species of Men, who one would not think had any Existence in Nature, were they not to be met with in ordinary Conversation, I mean the Zealots in Atheism. One would fancy that these Men, tho' they fall short, in every other respect, of those who make a Profession of Religion, would at least outshine them in this Particular, and be exempt from
that

that fingle Fault which feems to grow out of the impru-
dent Fervours of Religion : But fo it is, that Infidelity is
propagated with as much Fiercenefs and Contention,
Wrath and Indignation, as if the Safety of Mankind depended upon it. There is fomething fo ridiculous and per-
verfe in this kind of Zealots, that one does not know
how to fet them out in their proper Colours. They are a
Sort of Gamefters who are eternally upon the Fret, though
they play for nothing. They are perpetually teizing their
Friends to come over to them, though at the fame time
they allow that neither of them fhall get any thing by the
Bargain. In fhort, the Zeal of fpreading Atheifm is, if
poffible, more abfurd than Atheifm itfelf.

SINCE I have mentioned this unaccountable Zeal
which appears in Atheifts and Infidels, I muft farther obferve that they are likewife in a moft particular manner poffeffed with the Spirit of Bigotry. They are wedded to Opinions full of Contradiction and Impoffibility, and at the
fame time look upon the fmalleft Difficulty in an Article of
Faith as a fufficient Reafon for rejecting it. Notions that
fall in with the common Reafon of Mankind, that are conformable to the Senfe of all Ages and all Nations, not to
mention their Tendency for promoting the Happinefs of
Societies, or of particular Perfons, are exploded as Errors
and Prejudices; and Schemes erected in their ftead that
are altogether monftrous and irrational, and require the
moft extravagant Credulity to embrace them. I would fain
ask one of thefe bigotted Infidels, fuppofing all the great
Points of Atheifm, as the cafual or eternal Formation of the
World, the Materiality of a thinking Subftance, the Mortality of the Soul, the fortuitous Organization of the Body,
the Motions and Gravitation of Matter, with the like Particulars, were laid together and formed into a kind of Creed,
according to the Opinions of the moft celebrated Atheifts;
I fay, fuppofing fuch a Creed as this were formed, and impofed upon any one People in the World, whether it would
not require an infinitely greater meafure of Faith, than
any Set of Articles which they fo violently oppofe. Let
me therefore advife this Generation of Wranglers, for their
own and for the publick Good, to act at leaft fo confiftent-
ly with themfelves, as not to burn with Zeal for Irreli-
gion, and with Bigotry for Nonfenfe.　　　　　　C

Wednefday,

Nᵒ 186 *Wednefday, October* 3.

Cælum ipfum petimus ſtultitiâ.——Hor. Od. 3. l. 1. v. 38.

——*Scarce the Gods and heav'nly Climes,
Are ſafe from our audacious Crimes.*   DRYDEN.

UPON my return to my Lodgings laſt Night I found a Letter from my worthy Friend the Clergy-man, whom I have given ſome Account of in my former Papers. He tells me in it that he was particu-larly pleaſed with the latter Part of my Yeſterday's Specu-lation; and at the ſame time incloſed the following Eſ-ſay, which he defires me to publiſh as the Sequel of that Difcourfe. It confiſts partly of uncommon Reflexions, and partly of ſuch as have been already uſed, but now ſet in a ſtronger Light.

'A Believer may be excuſed by the moſt hardened Atheiſt
'for endeavouring to make him a Convert, becauſe he
'does it with an Eye to both their Intereſts. The Atheiſt
'is inexcuſable who tries to gain over a Believer, becauſe
'he does not propoſe the doing himſelf or the Believer
'any Good by ſuch a Converſion.
'THE Proſpect of a future State is the ſecret Com-
'fort and Refreſhment of my Soul; it is that which makes
'Nature look gay about me; it doubles all my Pleaſures,
'and ſupports me under all my Afflictions. I can look
'at Diſappointments and Misfortunes, Pain and Sickneſs,
'Death itſelf, and, what is worſe than Death, the Loſs
'of thoſe who are deareſt to me, with Indifference, ſo
'long as I keep in view the Pleaſures of Eternity, and
'the State of Being in which there will be no Fears nor
'Apprehenſions, Pains nor Sorrows, Sickneſs nor Separa-
'tion. Why will any Man be ſo impertinently Officious
'as to tell me all this is only Fancy and Delufion? Is
'there any Merit in being the Meſſenger of ill News? If

'it

'it is a Dream, let me enjoy it, since it makes me both
'the happier and better Man.

   'I must confess I do not know how to trust a Man
'who believes neither Heaven nor Hell, or, in other
'Words, a future State of Rewards and Punishments.
'Not only natural Self-love, but Reason directs us to
'promote our own Interest above all Things. It can never
'be for the Interest of a Believer to do me a Mischief,
'because he is sure upon the Balance of Accounts to
'find himself a Loser by it. On the contrary, if he con-
'siders his own Welfare in his Behaviour towards me,
'it will lead him to do me all the Good he can, and at
'the same time restrain him from doing me any Injury.
'An Unbeliever does not act like a reasonable Creature,
'if he favours me contrary to his present Interest, or does
'not distress me when it turns to his present Advantage.
'Honour and Good-nature may indeed tie up his Hands ;
'but as these would be very much strengthened by Rea-
'son and Principle, so without them they are only In-
'stincts, or wavering unsettled Notions, which rest on
'no Foundation.

   'INFIDELITY has been attack'd with so good
'Success of late Years, that it is driven out of all its
'Out-works. The Atheist has not found his Post tenable,
'and is therefore retired into Deism, and a Disbelief of
'revealed Religion only. But the Truth of it is, the
'greatest Number of this Set of Men, are those who, for
'want of a virtuous Education, or examining the Grounds
'of Religion, know so very little of the Matter in Que-
'stion, that their Infidelity is but another Term for their
'Ignorance.

   'AS Folly and Inconsiderateness are the Foundations
'of Infidelity, the great Pillars and Supports of it are
'either a Vanity of appearing wiser than the rest of Man-
'kind, or an Ostentation of Courage in despising the
'Terrors of another World, which have so great an In-
'fluence on what they call weaker Minds ; or an Aversion
'to a Belief that must cut them off from many of those
'Pleasures they propose to themselves, and fill them with
'Remorse for many of those they have already tasted.

   'THE great received Articles of the Christian Reli-
'gion have been so clearly proved, from the Authority

' of that Divine Revelation in which they are delivered,
' that it is impossible for those who have Ears to hear, and
' Eyes to see, not to be convinced of them. But were it
' possible for any thing in the Christian Faith to be erro-
' neous, I can find no ill Consequences in adhering to it.
' The great Points of the Incarnation and Sufferings of
' our Saviour produce naturally such Habits of Virtue
' in the Mind of Man, that I say, supposing it were
' possible for us to be mistaken in them, the Infidel him-
' self must at least allow that no other System of Religion
' could so effectually contribute to the heightning of Mo-
' rality. They give us great Ideas of the Dignity of
' human Nature, and of the Love which the supreme
' Being bears to his Creatures, and consequently engage
' us in the highest Acts of Duty towards our Creator, our
' Neighbour, and ourselves. How many noble Argu-
' ments has Saint *Paul* raised from the chief Articles of our
' Religion, for the advancing of Morality in its three great
' Branches? To give a single Example in each Kind: What
' can be a stronger Motive to a firm Trust, and Reliance
' on the Mercies of our Maker, than the giving us his
' Son to suffer for us? What can make us love and esteem
' even the most inconsiderable of Mankind more than
' the Thought that Christ died for him? Or what dispose
' us to set a stricter Guard upon the Purity of our own
' Hearts, than our being Members of Christ, and a Part
' of the Society of which that immaculate Person is the
' Head? But these are only a Specimen of those admira-
' ble Inforcements of Morality, which the Apostle has
' drawn from the History of our blessed Saviour.
' IF our modern Infidels considered these Matters
' with that Candour and Seriousness which they deserve,
' we should not see them act with such a Spirit of Bitter-
' ness, Arrogance, and Malice: They would not be
' raising such insignificant Cavils, Doubts, and Scruples,
' as may be started against every thing that is not capa-
' ble of mathematical Demonstration; in order to un-
' settle the Minds of the Ignorant, disturb the publick
' Peace, subvert Morality, and throw all things into
' Confusion and Disorder. If none of these Reflexions
' can have any Influence on them, there is one that per-
' haps may, because it is adapted to their Vanity, by

'which they seem to be guided much more than their
'Reason. I would therefore have them consider, that
'the wisest and best of Men, in all Ages of the World,
'have been those who lived up to the Religion of their
'Country, when they saw nothing in it opposite to Mo-
'rality, and to the best Lights they had of the Divine
'Nature. *Pythagoras's* first Rule directs us to worship
'the Gods *as it is ordained by Law*, for that is the most
'natural Interpretation of the Precept. *Socrates*, who
'was the most renowned among the Heathens both for
'Wisdom and Virtue, in his last Moments desires his
'Friends to offer a Cock to *Æsculapius*; doubtless out
'of a submissive Deference to the established Worship of
'his Country. *Xenophon* tells us, that his Prince (whom
'he sets forth as a Pattern of Perfection) when he found
'his Death approaching, offered Sacrifices on the Moun-
'tains to the *Persian Jupiter*, and the Sun, *according to*
'*the Custom of the Persians*; for those are the Words
'of the Historian. Nay, the *Epicureans* and Atomical
'Philosophers shewed a very remarkable Modesty in
'this Particular; for though the Being of a God was in-
'tirely repugnant to their Schemes of natural Philosophy,
'they contented themselves with the Denial of a Pro-
'vidence, asserting at the same Time the Existence of
'Gods in general; because they would not shock the
'common Belief of Mankind, and the Religion of their
'Country.—   L

N° 187.   *Thursday, October* 4.

————*Miseri quibus*
    Intentata nites————   Hor. Od. 5. l. 1. v. 12.

Ah; wretched those who love, yet ne'er did try
The smiling Treachery of thy Eye!   CREECH.

THE Intelligence given by this Correspondent is so
important and useful, in order to avoid the Persons he speaks of, that I shall insert his Letter at
length.

                              Mr.

Mr. SPECTATOR,

'I Do not know that you have ever touched upon a
' certain fpecies of Women, whom we ordinarily call
' Jilts. You cannot poffibly go upon a more ufeful Work;
' than the Confideration of thefe dangerous Animals.
' The Coquette is indeed one Degree towards the Jilt; but
' the Heart of the former is bent upon admiring herfelf,
' and giving falfe Hopes to her Lovers; but the latter is
' not contented to be extremely amiable, but fhe muft add
' to that Advantage a certain Delight in being a Tor-
' ment to others. Thus when her Lover is in the full Ex-
' pectation of Succefs, the Jilt fhall meet him with a fud-
' den Indifference, and Admiration in her Face at his be-
' ing furprifed that he is received like a Stranger, and a
' Caft of her Head another Way with a pleafant Scorn of
' the Fellow's Infolence. It is very probable the Lover
' goes home utterly aftonifhed and dejected, fits down to
' his Scrutoir, fends her word in the moft abject Terms,
' That he knows not what he has done; that all which
' was defirable in this Life is fo fuddenly vanifhed from
' him, that the Charmer of his Soul fhould withdraw the
' vital Heat from the Heart which pants for her. He
' continues a mournful Abfence for fome time, pining in
' Secret, and out of Humour with all things which he
' meets with. At length he takes a Refolution to try his
' Fate, and explain with her refolutely upon her unac-
' countable Carriage. He walks up to her Apartment,
' with a thoufand Inquietudes and Doubts in what Man-
' ner he fhall meet the firft Caft of her Eye; when upon
' his firft Appearance fhe flies towards him, wonders where
' he has been, accufes him of his Abfence, and treats him
' with a Familiarity as furprifing as her former Coldnefs.
' This good Correfpondence continues till the Lady ob-
' ferves the Lover grows happy in it, and then fhe inter-
' rupts it with fome new Inconfiftency of Behaviour. For
' (as I juft now faid) the Happinefs of a Jilt confifts only
' in the Power of making others uneafy. But fuch is the
' Folly of this Sect of Women, that they carry on this
' pretty fkittifh Behaviour, till they have no Charms left
' to render it fupportable. *Corinna*, that ufed to torment
' all who converfed with her with falfe Glances, and little

D 2   ' heedlefs

' heedlefs unguarded Motions, that were to betray fome
' Inclination towards the Man fhe would infnare, finds at
' prefent all fhe attempts that way unregarded; and is
' obliged to indulge the Jilt in her Conftitution, by lay-
' ing Artificial Plots, writing perplexing Letters from un-
' known Hands, and making all the young Fellows in
' Love with her, till they find out who fhe is. Thus, as-
' before fhe gave Torment by difguifing her Inclination,
' fhe now is obliged to do it by hiding her Perfon.

'AS for my own Part, Mr. SPECTATOR, it has
' been my unhappy Fate to be jilted from my Youth up-
' ward; and as my Tafte has been very much towards
' Intrigue, and having Intelligence with Women of Wit,
' my whole Life has paffed away in a Series of Impofi-
' tions. I fhall, for the Benefit of the prefent Race of
' young Men, give fome Account of my Loves. I know
' not whether you have ever heard of the famous Girl
' about Town called *Kitty:* This Creature (for I muft take
' Shame upon myfelf) was my Miftrefs in the Days when
' Keeping was in Fafhion. *Kitty,* under the Appearance
' of being Wild, Thoughtlefs, and Irregular in all her
' Words and Actions, concealed the moft accomplifhed
' Jilt of her Time. Her Negligence had to me a Charm
' in it like that of Chaftity, and Want of Defires feemed
' as great a Merit as the Conqueft of them. The Air fhe
' gave herfelf was that of a Romping Girl, and when-
' ever I talked to her with any Turn of Fondnefs, fhe
' would immediately fnatch off my Periwig, try it upon
' herfelf in the Glafs, clap her Arms a-kimbow, draw
' my Sword, and make Paffes on the Wall, take off my
' Cravat, and feize it to make fome other Ufe of the
' Lace, or run into fome other unaccountable Rompifh-
' nefs, till the Time I had appointed to pafs away with
' her was over. I went from her full of Pleafure at the
' Reflexion that I had the keeping of fo much Beauty in a
' Woman, who, as fhe was too heedlefs to pleafe me, was
' alfo too unattentive to form a Defign to wrong me. Long
' did I divert every Hour that hung heavy upon me in the
' Company of this Creature, whom I looked upon as nei-
' ther Guilty nor Innocent, but could laugh at myfelf
' for my unaccountable Pleafure in an Expence upon her,
' till in the end it appeared my pretty Infenfible was with
' Child by my Footman. 'THIS

'THIS Accident rouſed me into a Diſdain againſt
' all Libertine Women, under what Appearance ſoever
' they hid their Inſincerity, and I reſolved after that Time
' to converſe with none but thoſe who lived within the
' Rules of Decency and Honour. To this End I formed
' myſelf into a more regular Turn of Behaviour, and
' began to make Viſits, frequent Aſſemblies, and lead out
' Ladies from the Theatres, with all the other inſigni-
' ficant Duties which the profeſſed Servants of the Fair
' place themſelves in conſtant Readineſs to perform.
' In a very little time, (having a plentiful Fortune) Fa-
' thers and Mothers began to regard me as a good Match,
' and I found eaſy Admittance into the beſt Families in
' Town to obſerve their Daughters; but I, who was born
' to follow the Fair to no Purpoſe, have by the Force of my
' ill Stars made my Application to three Jilts ſucceſſively.

' *HYÆNA* is one of thoſe who form themſelves into
' a melancholy and indolent Air, and endeavour to gain
' Admirers from their Inattention to all around them.
' *Hyæna* can loll in her Coach, with ſomething ſo fixed in
' her Countenance, that it is impoſſible to conceive her
' Meditation is employed only on her Dreſs and her Charms
' in that Poſture. If it were not too coarſe a Simile, I
' ſhould ſay, *Hyæna*, in the Figure ſhe affects to appear
' in, is a Spider in the midſt of a Cobweb, that is ſure to
' deſtroy every Fly that approaches it. The Net *Hyæna*
' throws is ſo fine, that you are taken in it before you can
' obſerve any Part of her Work. I attempted her for a
' long and weary Seaſon, but I found her Paſſion went no
' farther than to be admired; and ſhe is of that unreaſonable
' Temper, as not to value the Inconſtancy of her Lovers,
' provided ſhe can boaſt ſhe once had their Addreſſes.

' *BIBLIS* was the ſecond I aimed at, and her Vanity
' lay in purchaſing the Adorers of others, and not in rejoic-
' ing in their Love itſelf. *Biblis* is no Man's Miſtreſs, but
' every Woman's Rival. As ſoon as I found this, I fell
' in Love with *Chloe*, who is my preſent Pleaſure and Tor-
' ment. I have writ to her, danced with her, and fought
' for her, and have been her Man in the Sight and Ex-
' pectation of the whole Town theſe three Years, and
' thought myſelf near the End of my Wiſhes; when the
' other Day ſhe called me into her Cloſet, and told me,

‘ with a very grave Face that she was a Woman of Ho-
‘ nour, and scorned to deceive a Man who loved her with
‘ so much Sincerity as she saw I did, and therefore she
‘ must inform me that she was by Nature the most in-
‘ constant Creature breathing, and begg'd of me not to
‘ marry her ; If I insisted upon it, I should ; but that she
‘ was lately fallen in Love with another. What to do or
‘ say I know not, but desire you to inform me, and you
‘ will infinitely oblige,

S I R, Your most humble Servant,

Charles Yellow.

ADVERTISEMENT.

Mr. Sly, *Haberdasher of Hats, at the Corner of* Deve-
reux-Court *in the* Strand, *gives notice, That he has prepared
very neat Hats, Rubbers, and Brushes for the Use of young
Tradesmen in their last Year of Apprenticeship, at reasonable
Rates.*   T

N° 188   *Friday,* October 5.

Lætus sum Laudari à te Laudato viro.   Tull.

*It gives me Pleasure, to be prais'd by you, whom all Men
praise.*

H E is a very unhappy Man who sets his Heart upon
being admired by the Multitude, or affects a general and undistinguishing Applause among Men.
What pious Men call the Testimony of a good Consci-
ence, should be the Measure of our Ambition in this Kind ;
that is to say, a Man of Spirit should contemn the Praise
of the Ignorant, and like being applauded for nothing but
what he knows in his own Heart he deserves. Besides
which the Character of the Person who commends you is
to be considered, before you set a Value upon his Esteem.
The Praise of an ignorant Man is only Good-will, and
you should receive his Kindness as he is a good Neighbour in Society, and not as a good Judge of your Actions
in

in Point of Fame and Reputation. The Satyrift faid very well of popular Praife and Acclamations, *Give the Tinkers and Coblers their Prefents again, and learn to live of yourfelf.* It is an Argument of a loofe and ungoverned Mind to be affected with the promifcuous Approbation of the Generality of Mankind ; and a Man of Virtue fhould be too delicate for fo coarfe an Appetite of Fame. Men of Honour fhould endeavour only to pleafe the Worthy, and the Man of Merit fhould defire to be tried only by his Peers. I thought it a noble Sentiment which I heard Yefterday uttered in Converfation; *I know,* faid a Gentleman, *a Way to be greater than any Man : If he has Worth in him, I can rejoice in his Superiority to me ; and that Satisfaction is a greater Act of the Soul in me, than any in him which can poffibly appear to me.* This Thought could not proceed but from a candid and generous Spirit ; and the Approbation of fuch Minds is what may be efteemed true Praife : For with the common Rate of Men there is nothing commendable but what they themfelves may hope to be Partakers of, and arrive at : But the Motive truly glorious is, when the Mind is fet rather to do Things laudable, than to purchafe Reputation. Where there is that Sincerity as the Foundation of a good Name, the kind Opinion of virtuous Men will be an unfought, but a neceffary Confequence. The *Lacedemonians,* tho' a plain People, and no Pretenders to Politenefs had a certain Delicacy in their Senfe of Glory, and facrificed to the Mufes when they entred upon any great Enterprife. They would have the Commemoration of their Actions be tranfmitted by the pureft and moft untainted Memorialifts. The Din which attends Victories and publick Triumphs is by far lefs eligible, than the Recital of the Actions of great Men by honeft and wife Hiftorians. It is a frivolous Pleafure to be the Admiration of gaping Crouds ; but to have the Approbation of a good Man in the cool Reflexions of his Clofet, is a Gratification worthy an heroick Spirit. The Applaufe of the Croud makes the Head giddy, but the Attestation of a reafonable Man makes the Heart glad.

WHAT makes the Love of popular or general Praife ftill more ridiculous, is, that it is ufually given for Circumftances which are foreign to the Perfons admired. Thus they are the ordinary Attendants on Power and Riches,

which

which may be taken out of one Man's Hands, and put
into another's. The Application only, and not the Pof-
feſſion, makes thoſe outward Things honourable. The
Vulgar and Men of Senſe agree in admiring Men for
having what they themſelves would rather be poſ-
feſſed of ; the wiſe Man applauds him whom he thinks
moſt virtuous, the reſt of the World him who is moſt
wealthy.

WHEN a Man is in this way of Thinking, I do not
know what can occur to one more monſtrous, than to ſee
Perſons of Ingenuity addreſs their Services and Performances to Men no way addicted to Liberal Arts : In theſe
Caſes, the Praiſe on one hand, and the Patronage on the
other, are equally the Objects of Ridicule. Dedications to
ignorant Men are as abſurd as any of the Speeches of
Bulfinch in the Droll. : Such an Addreſs one is apt to
tranſlate into other Words ; and when the Different
Parties are thoroughly conſidered, the Panegyrick generally implies no more than if the Author ſhould ſay to
the Patron; my very good Lord, You and I can never
underſtand one another, therefore I humbly deſire we
may be intimate Friends for the future.

THE Rich may as well ask to borrow of the Poor, as
the Man of Virtue or Merit hope for Addition to his Character from any but ſuch as himſelf. He that commends
another engages ſo much of his own Reputation as he
gives to that Perſon commended ; and he that has nothing
laudable in himſelf is not of Ability to be ſuch a Surety.
The wiſe *Phocion* was ſo ſenſible how dangerous it was
to be touched with what the Multitude approved, that
upon a general Acclamation made when he was making
an Oration, he turned to an intelligent Friend who ſtood
near him, and asked in a ſurpriſed Manner, What Slip
have I made ?

I ſhall conclude this Paper with a Billet which has fallen into my Hands, and was written to a Lady from a
Gentleman whom ſhe had highly-commended. The Author of it had formerly been her Lover. When all Poſſibility of Commerce between them on the Subject of Love
was cut off, ſhe ſpoke ſo handſomly of him, as to give
occaſion for this Letter.

Madam,

Madam,

'I Should be infenfible to a Stupidity, if I could forbear
'making you my Acknowledgments for your late
'mention of me with fo much Applaufe. It is, I think,
'your Fate to give me new Sentiments; as you formerly
'infpired me with the true Senfe of Love, fo do you now
'with the true Senfe of Glory. As Defire had the leaft Part
'in the Paffion I heretofore profeffed towards you, fo has
'Vanity no Share in the Glory to which you have now
'raifed me. Innocence, Knowledge, Beauty, Virtue, Sin-
'cerity, and Difcretion, are the conftant Ornaments of
'her who has faid this of me. Fame is a Babbler, but I
'have arrived at the higheft Glory in this World, the
'Commendation of the moft deferving Perfon in it.   T

Nº 189. *Saturday, October 6.*

———*Patriæ pietatis imago.*   Virg. Æn. 10. v. 824.

An Image of Paternal Tendernefs!

THE following Letter being written to my Book-
feller, upon a Subjeft of which I treated fome
time fince, I fhall publifh it in this Paper, together
with the Letter that was inclofed in it.

Mr. Buckley,

'MR. SPECTATOR having of late defcanted upon
'the Cruelty of Parents to their Children, I have
'been induced (at the Requeft of feveral of Mr. SPEC-
'TATOR's Admirers) to inclofe this Letter, which I af-
'fure you is the Original from a Father to his own Son,
'notwithftanding the latter gave but little or no Provoca-
'tion. It would be wonderfully obliging to the World, if
'Mr. SPECTATOR would give his Opinion of it in
'fome of his Speculations, and particularly to
                        (Mr. *Buckley*)
                                Your humble Servant.

SIRRAH,

YOU are a faucy audacious Rascal, and both Bold
and Mad, and I care not a Farthing whether you
comply or no; that does not raise out my Impression of
your Infolence, going about railing at me, and the next
Day to folicit my Favour: Thefe are Inconfiftencies,
fuch as difcover thy Reafon depraved. To be brief, I
never defire twice your Face; and, Sirrah, if you go to
the Work-houfe, it is no Difgrace to me for you the
fuppofed there; and if you ftarve in the Street I'll
never give any thing underhand in your Behalf. If I
have any more of your fcribbling Nonfenfe I'll break
your Head the firft Time I fet Sight on you. Yours
a ftubborn Beaft; is this your Gratitude for my giving
you Money? You Rogue, I'll better your Judgment,
and give you a greater Senfe of your Duty to (I won't
fay) your Father, &c.

P. S. It's Prudence for you to keep out of my Sight;
for to reproach me, that Might overcomes Right, on
the Outfide of your Letter, I fhall give you a good
Knock on the Scull for it.

WAS there ever fuch an Image of Paternal Tendernefs! It was ufual among fome of the *Greeks* to make their
Slaves drink to Excefs, and then expofe them to their Children, who by that means conceived an early Averfio to
a Vice which makes Men appear fo monftrous and irrational. I have expofed this Picture of an unnatural Father
with the fame Intention, that its Deformity may deter
others from its Refemblance. If the Reader has a mind to
fee a Father of the fame Stamp reprefented in the moft exquifite Strokes of Humour, he may meet with it in one of
the fineft Comedies that ever appeared upon the *Englifh*
Stage: I mean the Part of Sir *Sampfon* in *Love for Love*.
I muft not however engage myfelf blindly on the fide
of the Son, to whom the fond Letter above-written was
directed. His Father calls him a *faucy and audacious Raf-
cal* in the firft Line, and I am afraid upon Examination
he will prove but an ungracious Youth. *To go about railing at his Father, and to find no other Place but the Co-
*

fide of his Letter to tell him *that Might overcomes Right,* if it does not difcover *his Reafon to be depraved,* and *that he is either Fool or Mad,* as the cholerick old Gentleman tells him, we may at leaft allow that the Father will do very well in endeavouring to *better his Judgment, and give him a greater Senfe of his Duty.* But whether this may be brought about *by breaking his Head,* or *giving him a great Knock on the Scull,* ought, I think, to be well confidered. Upon the whole, I wifh the Father has not met with his Match, and that he may not be as equally paired with a Son, as the Mother in *Virgil.*

————*Crudelis tu quoque mater ;*
Crudelis mater magis, an puer Improbus ille?
Improbus ille puer, crudelis tu quoque mater. Ecl. 8. v. 48.

Cruel alike the Mother and the Son.

Or like the Crow and her Egg, in the Greek Proverb,

Κακῖ κόρακ☉ κακὸν ᾠὸν.

Bad the Crow, bad the Egg.

I muft here take notice of a Letter which I have received from an unknown Correfpondent, upon the Subject of my Paper, upon which the foregoing Letter is likewife founded. The Writer of it feems very much concerned left that Paper fhould feem to give Encouragement to the Difobedience of Children towards their Parents ; but if the Writer of it will take the pains to read it over again attentively, I dare fay his Apprehenfions will vanifh. Pardon and Reconciliation are all the penitent Daughter requefts, and all that I contend for in her Behalf ; and in this Cafe I may ufe the Saying of an eminent Wit, who, upon fome great Mens preffing him to forgive his Daughter who had married againft his Confent, told them he could refufe nothing to their Inftances, but that he would have them remember there was Difference between *Giving* and *Forgiving.*

I muft confefs, in all Controverfies between Parents and their Children, I am naturally prejudiced in favour of the former. The Obligations on that Side can never be acquitted,

SIRRAH,

'YOU are a saucy audacious Rascal, and both Fool
'and Mad, and I care not a Farthing whether you ·
'comply or no; that does not raze out my Impressions of
'your Insolence, going about railing at me, and the next
'Day to solicit my Favour: These are Inconsistencies,
'such as discover thy Reason depraved. To be brief, I
'never desire to see your Face; and, Sirrah, if you go to
'the Work-house, it is no Disgrace to me for you to be,
'supported there; and if you starve in the Streets, I'll
'never give any thing underhand in your Behalf. If I
'have any more of your scribbling Nonsense I'll break
'your Head the first Time I set Sight on you. You are
'a stubborn Beast; is this your Gratitude for my giving
'you Money? You Rogue, I'll better your Judgment,
'and give you a greater Sense of your Duty to (I regret
'to say) your Father, &c.

'*P. S.* It's Prudence for you to keep out of my Sight;
'for to reproach me, that Might overcomes Right, on
'the Outside of your Letter, I shall give you a great
'Knock on the Scull for it.

WAS there ever such an Image of Paternal Tenderness! It was usual among some of the *Greeks* to make their
Slaves drink to Excess, and then expose them to their Children, who by that means conceived an early Aversion to
a Vice which makes Men appear so monstrous and irrational. I have exposed this Picture of an unnatural Father
with the same Intention, that its Deformity may deter
others from its Resemblance. If the Reader has a mind to
see a Father of the same Stamp represented in the most exquisite Strokes of Humour, he may meet with it in one of
the finest Comedies that ever appeared upon the *English*
Stage: I mean the Part of Sir *Sampson* in *Love for Love.*

I must not however engage myself blindly on the Side
of the Son, to whom the fond Letter above-written was
directed. His Father calls him a *saucy and audacious Rascal* in the first Line, and I am afraid upon Examination
he will prove but an ungracious Youth. *To go about railing* at his Father, and to find no other Place but *the Out-
　　　　　　　　　　　　　　　　　side*

fide of his Letter to tell him *that Might overcomes Right,*
if it does not difcover *his Reafon to be depraved,* and *that
he is either Fool or Mad,* as the cholerick old Gentleman
tells him, we may at leaft allow that the Father will do
very well in endeavouring to *better his Judgment, and
give him a greater Senfe of his Duty.* But whether this
may be brought about *by breaking his Head,* or *giving
him a great Knock on the Scull,* ought, I think, to be well
confidered. Upon the whole, I wifh the Father has not
met with his Match, and that he may not be as equally
paired with a Son, as the Mother in *Virgil.*

*———Crudelis tu quoque mater :
Crudelis mater magis, an puer Improbus ille?
Improbus ille puer, crudelis tu quoque mater.* Ecl. 8. v. 48.

Cruel alike the Mother and the Son.

Or like the Crow and her Egg, in the *Greek* Proverb,

Κακῦ κόρακΘ κακὸν ὠὸν.

Bad the Crow, bad the Egg.

I muft here take notice of a Letter which I have received from an unknown Correfpondent, upon the Subject of my Paper, upon which the foregoing Letter is
likewife founded. The Writer of it feems very much concerned left that Paper fhould feem to give Encouragement
to the Difobedience of Children towards their Parents;
but if the Writer of it will take the pains to read it over
again attentively, I dare fay his Apprehenfions will vanifh. Pardon and Reconciliation are all the penitent
Daughter requefts, and all that I contend for in her Behalf; and in this Cafe I may ufe the Saying of an eminent Wit, who, upon fome great Mens prefling him to
forgive his Daughter who had married againft his Confent, told them he could refufe nothing to their Inftances,
but that he would have them remember there was Difference between *Giving* and *Forgiving.*

I muft confefs, in all Controverfies between Parents and
their Children, I am naturally prejudiced in favour of the
former. The Obligations on that Side can never be acquitted,

quitted, and I think it is one of the greateft Reflexions
upon Human Nature that Paternal Inftinct fhould be a
ftronger Motive to Love than Filial Gratitude; that the
receiving of Favours fhould be a lefs Inducement to
Good-will, Tendernefs and Commiferation; than the conferring of them; and that the taking care of any Perfon
fhould endear the Child or Dependent more to the Parent or Benefactor, than the Parent or Benefactor to the
Child or Dependent; yet fo it happens, that for one
cruel Parent we meet with a thoufand undutiful Children. This is indeed wonderfully contrived (as I have
formerly obferved) for the Support of every living Species;
but at the fame time that it fhews the Wifdom of the
Creator, it difcovers the Imperfection and Degeneracy
of the Creature.

THE Obedience of Children to their Parents is the
Bafis of all Government, and fet forth as the Meafure of
that Obedience which we owe to thofe whom Providence
hath placed over us.

IT is Father *Le Compte*, if I am not miftaken, who tells
us how Want of Duty in this Particular is punifhed among
the *Chinefe*, infomuch that if a Son, fhould be known to
kill, or fo much as to ftrike his Father, not only the Criminal but his whole Family would be rooted out, nay the
Inhabitants of the Place where he lived would be put to
the Sword, nay the Place itfelf would be razed to the
Ground, and its Foundations fown with Salt : For, fay
they, there muft have been an utter Depravation of Manners in that Clan or Society of People who could have
bred up among them fo horrid an Offender. To this I
fhall add a Paffage out of the firft Book of *Herodotus*. That
Hiftorian in his Account of the *Perfian* Cuftoms and Religion tells us, It is their Opinion that no Man ever killed
his Father, or that it is poffible fuch a Crime fhould be in
Nature; but that if any thing like it fhould ever happen,
they conclude that the reputed Son muft have been Illegitimate, Suppofititious, or begotten in Adultery. Their Opinion in this Particular fhews fufficiently what a Notion
they muft have had of Undutifulnefs in general.   L

Nº 190. *Monday, October* 8.

Servitus crescit nova—— Hor. Od. 8. l. 2. v. 18.
A Servitude to former Times unknown.

SINCE I made some Reflexions upon the general
Negligence used in the Case of Regard towards Women, or, in other Words, since I talked of Wenching. I have had Epistles upon that Subject, which I
shall, for the present Entertainment, insert as they lie
before me.

Mr. SPECTATOR,

'AS your Speculations are not confined to any Part of
'Human Life, but concern the Wicked as well as
'the Good, I must desire your favourable Acceptance of
'what I, a poor strolling Girl about Town, have to say
'to you. I was told by a Roman Catholick Gentleman
'who picked me up last Week, and who, I hope, is ab-
'solved for what passed between us; I say I was told by
'such a Person, who endeavoured to convert me to his
'own Religion, that in Countries where Popery prevails,
'besides the Advantage of licensed Stews, there are large
'Endowments given for the *Incurabili*, I think he called
'them, such as are past all Remedy, and are allowed such
'Maintenance and Support as to keep them without far-
'ther Care till they expire. This manner of treating poor
'Sinners has, methinks, great Humanity in it; and as
'you are a Person who pretend to carry your Reflexions
'upon all Subjects whatever occur to you, with Can-
'dour, and act above the Sense of what Misinterpretation
'you may meet with, I beg the Favour of you to lay
'before all the World the unhappy Condition of us poor
'Vagrants, who are really in a Way of Labour instead of
'Idleness. There are Crouds of us whose manner of
'Livelihood has long ceased to be pleasing to us; and
'who would willingly lead a new Life, if the Rigour of
'the

‘ the Virtuous did not for ever expel us from coming in-
‘ to the World again. As it now happens, to the eternal
‘ Infamy of the Male Sex, Falſhood among you is not
‘ reproachful, but Credulity in Women is infamous.

‘GIVE me leave, Sir, to give you my Hiſtory. You
‘ are to know that I am a Daughter of a Man of a good
‘ Reputation, Tenant to a Man of Quality. The Heir of
‘ this great Houſe took it in his Head to caſt a favourable
‘ Eye upon me, and ſucceeded. I do not pretend to ſay
‘ he promiſed me Marriage: I was not a Creature ſilly
‘ enough to be taken by ſo fooliſh a Story: But he ran
‘ away with me up to this Town, and introduced me to
‘ a grave Matron, with whom I boarded for a Day or
‘ two with great Gravity, and was not a little pleaſed
‘ with the Change of my Condition, from that of a Coun-
‘ try Life to the fineſt Company, as I believed, in the
‘ whole World. My humble Servant made me underſtand
‘ that I ſhould be always kept in the plentiful Condition
‘ I then enjoyed; when after a very great Fondneſs towards
‘ me, he one Day took his leave of me for four or five Days.
‘ In the Evening of the ſame Day my good Landlady
‘ came to me, and obſerving me very penſive, began to
‘ comfort me, and with a Smile told me I muſt ſee the
‘ World. When I was deaf to all ſhe could ſay to divert
‘ me, ſhe began to tell me with a very frank Air that I
‘ muſt be treated as I ought, and not take theſe ſqueamiſh
‘ Humours upon me, for my Friend had left me to the
‘ Town; and, as their Phraſe is, ſhe expected I would ſee
‘ Company, or I muſt be treated like what I had brought
‘ myſelf to. This put me into a Fit of Crying: And I
‘ immediately, in a true Senſe of my Condition, threw
‘ myſelf on the Floor, deploring my Fate, calling upon
‘ all that was good and ſacred to ſuccour me. While I was
‘ in all this Agony, I obſerved a decrepid old Fellow come
‘ into the Room, and looking with a Senſe of Pleaſure in
‘ his Face at all my Vehemence and Tranſport. In a Pauſe
‘ of my Diſtreſs I heard him ſay to the ſhameleſs old Wo-
‘ man who ſtood by me, She is certainly a new Face, or
‘ elſe ſhe acts it rarely. With that the Gentlewoman, who
‘ was making her Market of me, in all the Turn of my
‘ Perſon, the Heaves of my Paſſion, and the ſuitable
‘ Changes of my Poſture, took occaſion to commend my

‘ Neck,

' Neck, my Shape, my Eyes, my Limbs. All this was
' accompanied with such Speeches as you may have heard,
' Horse-coursers make in the Sale of Nags, when they are
' warranted for their Soundness. You understand by this
' time that I was left in a Brothel, and exposed to the next
' Bidder that could purchase me of my Patroness. This
' is so much the Work of Hell; the Pleasure in the Pos-
' session of us Wenches, abates in proportion to the De-
' grees we go beyond the Bounds of Innocence; and no
' Man is gratified, if there is nothing left for him to de-
' bauch. Well, Sir, my first Man, when I came upon
' the Town, was Sir *Jeoffry Foible*, who was extremely
' lavish to me of his Money, and took such a fancy to
' me that he would have carried me off, if my Patroness
' would have taken any reasonable Terms for me: But
' as he was old, his Covetousness was his strongest Passion,
' and poor I was soon left exposed to be the common Re-
' fuse of all the Rakes and Debauchees in Town. I cannot
' tell whether you will do me Justice or no, till I see whe-
' ther you print this or not; otherwise, as I now live with
' *Sal*, I could give you a very just Account of who and
' who is together in this Town. You perhaps won't believe
' it; but I know of one who pretends to be a very good
' Protestant who lies with a Roman-Catholick: But more
' of this hereafter, as you please me. There do come to
' our House the greatest Politicians of the Age; and *Sal*
' is more shrewd than any body thinks: No body can
' believe that such wise Men could go to Baudy-houses out
' of idle Purposes; I have heard them often talk of *Au-*
' *gustus Cæsar*, who had Intrigues with the Wives of Se-
' nators, not out of Wantonness but Stratagem.
    ' IT is a thousand pities you should be so severely vir-
' tuous as I fear you are; otherwise, after one Visit or two,
' you would soon understand that we Women of the Town
' are not such useless Correspondents as you may imagine:
' You have undoubtedly heard that it was a Courtesan
' who discovered *Catiline*'s Conspiracy. If you print this,
' I'll tell you more; and am in the mean time,

S I R,

Your most humble Servant,

REBECCA NETTLETOP.

Mr.

Mr. S P E C T A T O R,

' I AM an idle young Woman that would work for my
' Livelihood, but that I am kept in such a manner as
' I cannot ftir out. My Tyrant is an old jealous Fellow,
' who allows me nothing to appear in. I have but one
' Shoe and one Slipper; no Head-drefs, and no upper
' Petticoat. As you fet up for a Reformer, I defire you
' would take me out of this wicked way, and keep me
' yourfelf.

E v e   A f t e r d a y.

Mr. S P E C T A T O R,

' I AM to complain to you of a Set of impertinent Cox-
' combs, who vifit the Apartments of us Women of
' the Town, only, as they call it, to fee the World. I
' muft confefs to you, this to Men of Delicacy might
' have an Effect to cure them; but as they are ftupid, noify,
' and drunken Fellows, it tends only to make Vice in
' themfelves, as they think, pleafant and humourous, and
' at the fame time naufeous in us. I fhall, Sir, hereafter
' from time to time give you the Names of thefe Wretches
' who pretend to enter our Houfes merely as Spectators.
' Thefe Men think it Wit to ufe us ill: Pray tell them,
' however worthy we are of fuch Treatment, it is un-
' worthy them to be guilty of it towards us. Pray, Sir,
' take notice of this, and pity the Oppreffed: I wifh we
' could add to it, the Innocent.　　　　　　　　　T

N.º 191　　*Tuefday,* *October* 9.

——— ἔλον ὄνειρον.　　　　Hom. Il. 2. v. 6.
——— *Deluding Vifion of the Night.*　　P o p e.

S O M E ludicrous Schoolmen have put the Cafe, that
if an Afs were placed betwen two Bundles of Hay,
which affected his Senfes equally on each Side, and
tempted him in the very fame Degree, whether it would
be poffible for him to eat of either. They generally determine

termine this Question to the Disadvantage of the Ass, who they say would starve in the Midst of Plenty, as not having a single Grain of Free-will to determine him more to the one than to the other. The Bundle of Hay on either Side striking his Sight and Smell in the same Proportion, would keep him in a perpetual Suspence, like the two Magnets which, Travellers have told us, are placed one of them in the Roof, and the other in the Floor of *Mahomet*'s Burying-place at *Mecca*, and by that means, say they, pull the Impostor's Iron Coffin with such an equal Attraction, that it hangs in the Air between both of them. As for the Ass's Behaviour in such nice Circumstances, whether he would starve sooner than violate his Neutrality to the two Bundles of Hay, I shall not presume to determine; but only take notice of the Conduct of our own Species in the same Perplexity. When a Man has a mind to venture his Money in a Lottery, every Figure of it appears equally alluring, and as likely to succeed as any of its Fellows. They all of them have the same Pretensions to Good-luck; stand upon the same Foot of Competition, and no manner of Reason can be given why a Man should prefer one to the other before the Lottery is drawn. In this Case therefore Caprice very often acts in the Place of Reason, and forms to itself some groundless imaginary Motive, where real and substantial ones are wanting: I know a well-meaning Man that is very well pleased to risk his Good-fortune upon the Number 1711, because it is the Year of our Lord. I am acquainted with a Tacker that would give a good deal for the Number 134. On the contrary, I have been told of a certain zealous Dissenter, who being a great Enemy to Popery, and believing that bad Men are the most fortunate in this World, will lay two to one on the Number 666 against any other Number, because, says he, it is the Number of the Beast. Several would prefer the Number 12000 before any other, as it is the Number of the Pounds in the great Prize. In short, some are pleased to find their own Age in their Number; some that they have got a number which makes a pretty Appearance in the Cyphers; and others, because it is the same Number that succeeded in the last Lottery. Each of these, upon no other Grounds, thinks he stands fairest for the great Lot, and that he is possessed of what may not be improperly called *The Golden Number*.   THESE

THESE Principles of Election are the Paftimes and Extravagances of Human Reafon, which is of fo bufy a Nature, that it will be exerting itfelf in the meaneft Trifles and working even when it wants Materials. The wifeft of Men are fometimes acted by fuch unaccountable Motives, as the Life of the Fool and the Superftitious is guided by nothing elfe.

I am furprifed that none of the Fortune-tellers, or, as the *French* call them, the *Difeurs de bonne Avanture*, who publifh their Bills in every Quarter of the Town, have not turned our Lotteries to their Advantage: Did any of them fet up for a Cafter of fortunate Figures, what might he not get by his pretended Difcoveries and Predictions ?

I remember among the Advertifements in the *Poft-Boy* of *September* the 27th, I was furprifed to fee the following one :

This is to give notice, That Ten Shillings over and above the Market-Price, will be given for the Ticket in 1500000 l. *Lottery,* N° 132, *by* Nath. Cliff *at the Bible and Three Crowns in Cheapfide.*

THIS Advertifement has given great Matter of Speculation to Coffee-houfe Theorifts. Mr. *Cliff*'s Principles and Converfation have been canvaffed upon this Occafion, and various Conjectures made why he fhould thus fet his Heart upon N° 132. I have examined all the Powers in thofe Numbers, broken them into Fractions, extracted the Square and Cube Root, divided and multiplied them all Ways, but could not arrive at the Secret till about three Days ago, when I received the following Letter from an unknown Hand, by which I find that Mr. *Nathaniel Cliff* is only the Agent, and not the Principal in this Advertifement.

Mr. SPECTATOR,

' I Am the Perfon that lately advertifed I would give
' ten Shillings more than the current Price for the
' Ticket N° 132 in the Lottery now drawing; which is
' a Secret I have communicated to fome Friends, who
' rally me inceffantly upon that Account. You muft
' know I have but one Ticket, for which Reafon, and a
' certain Dream I have lately had more than once, I was
                                                    ' refolved

' refolved it fhould be the Number I moft approved.   I
' am fo pofitive I have pitched upon the great Lot, that
' I could almoft lay all I am worth of it. My Vifions are
' fo frequent and ftrong upon this Occafion, that I have
' not only poffeffed the Lot, but difpofed of the Money
' which in all probability it will fell for. This Morning,
' in particular, I fet up an Equipage which I look upon
' to be the gaieft in the Town; the Liveries are very
' rich, but not gaudy. I fhould be very glad to fee a Spe-
' culation or two upon Lottery Subjects, in which you
' would oblige all People concerned, and in particular

Your moft humble Servant,

George Gofling.

P. S. 'Dear SPEC, if I get the 12000 Pound, I'll
' make thee a handfom Prefent.

AFTER having wifhed my Correfpondent good Luck,
and thanked him for his intended Kindnefs, I fhall for this
time difmifs the Subject of the Lottery, and only obferve
that the greateft Part of Mankind are in fome degree guilty of my Friend *Gofling's* Extravagance. We are apt to re-
ly upon future Profpects, and become really expenfive
while we are only rich in Poffibility. We live up to our Expectations, not to our Poffeffions, and make a Figure pro-
portionable to what we may be, not what we are. We
out-run our prefent Income, as not doubting to difburfe
ourfelves out of the Profits of fome future Place, Project,
or Reverfion that we have in view. It is through this Temper of Mind, which is fo common among us, that we fee
Tradefmen break, who have met with no Misfortunes in
their Bufinefs; and Men of Eftates reduced to Poverty,
who have never fuffered from Loffes or Repairs, Tenants,
Taxes, or Law-fuits. In fhort, it is this foolifh fanguine
Temper, this depending upon contingent Futurities, that
occafions Romantick Generofity, Chimerical Grandeur,
fenfelefs Oftentation, and generally ends in Beggary and
Ruin. The Man, who will live above his prefent Circumftances, is in great danger of living in a little time
much beneath them, or, as the *Italian* Proverb runs, The
Man who lives by Hope will die by Hunger.

IT fhould be an indifpenfable Rule in Life, to contract our Defires to our prefent Condition, and whatever

ever may be our Expectations, to live within the Compass
of what we actually possess. It will be Time enough to
enjoy an Estate when it comes into our Hands; but if we
anticipate our good Fortune, we shall lose the Pleasure of
it when it arrives, and may possibly never possess what we
have so foolishly counted upon.   L

***

N° 192 *Wednesday,* October 10.

—— Uno ore omnes omnia
Bona dicere, & laudare fortunas meas,
Qui Gnatum haberem tali ingenio præditum.

                    Ter. Andr. Act 1. Sc. 1.

All Men agreed in complimenting me, and applauded
my good Fortune in being the Father of so towardly
a Son.

I STOOD the other Day, and beheld a Father sitting
in the middle of a Room with a large Family of Children about him; and methought I could observe in
his Countenance different Motions of Delight, as he
turned his Eye towards the one and the other of them.
The Man is a Person moderate in his Designs for their
Preferment and Welfare; and as he has an easy Fortune,
he is not solicitous to make a great one. His eldest Son
is a Child of a very towardly Disposition, and as much
as the Father loves him, I dare say he will never be a
Knave to improve his Fortune. I do not know any
Man who has a juster Relish of Life than the Person I
am speaking of, or keeps a better Guard against the Terrors of Want or the Hopes of Gain. It is usual in a
Croud of Children, for the Parent to name out of his
own Flock all the great Officers of the Kingdom. There
is something so very surprising in the Parts of a Child of
a Man's own, that there is nothing too great to be expected from his Endowments. I know a good Woman
who has but three Sons, and there is, she says, nothing
she expects with more Certainty, than that she shall see
                                        one

one of them a Bishop, the other a Judge, and the third a Court-Physician. The Humour is, that any thing which can happen to any Man's Child, is expected by every Man for his own. But my Friend, whom I was going to speak of, does not flatter himself with such vain Expectations, but has his Eye more upon the Virtue and Disposition of his Children, than their Advancement or Wealth. Good Habits are what will certainly improve a Man's Fortune and Reputation; but on the other side, Affluence of Fortune will not as probably produce good Affections of the Mind.

IT is very natural for a Man of a kind Disposition, to amuse himself with the Promises his Imagination makes to him of the future Condition of his Children, and to represent to himself the Figure they shall bear in the World after he has left it. When his Prospects of this kind are agreeable, his Fondness gives as it were a longer Date to his own Life; and the Survivorship of a worthy Man in his Son is a Pleasure scarce inferior to the Hopes of the Continuance of his own Life. That Man is happy who can believe of his Son, that he will escape the Follies and Indiscretions of which he himself was guilty, and pursue and improve every thing that was valuable in him. The Continuance of his Virtue is much more to be regarded than that of his Life; but it is the most lamentable of all Reflexions, to think that the Heir of a Man's Fortune is such a one as will be a Stranger to his Friends, alienated from the same Interests, and a Promoter of every thing which he himself disapproved. An Estate in Possession of such a Successor to a good Man, is worse than laid waste; and the Family, of which he is the Head, is in a more deplorable Condition than that of being extinct.

WHEN I visit the agreeable Seat of my honoured Friend *Ruricola*, and walk from Room to Room revolving many pleasing Occurrences, and the Expressions of many just Sentiments I have heard him utter, and see the Booby his Heir in Pain while he is doing the Honours of his House to the Friend of his Father, the Heaviness it gives one is not to be expressed. Want of Genius is not to be imputed to any Man, but Want of Humanity is a Man's own Fault. The Son of *Ruricola*, (whose Life was one continued Series of worthy Actions and Gentle-

man-

man-like Inclinations) is the Companion of drunken Clowns, and knows no Senfe of Praife but in the Flattery he receives from his own Servants; his Pleafures are mean and inordinate, his Language bafe and filthy, his Behaviour rough and abfurd. Is this Creature to be accounted the Succeffor of a Man of Virtue, Wit and Breeding? At the fame time that I have this melancholy Profpeft at the Houfe where I mifs my old Friend, I can go to a Gentleman's not far off it, where he has a Daughter who is the Piâure both of his Body and Mind, but both improved with the Beauty and Modefty peculiar to her Sex. It is fhe who fupplies the Lofs of her Father to the World ; fhe, without his Name or Fortune, is a truer Memorial of him, than her Brother who fucceeds him in both. Such an Offspring as the eldeft Son of my Friend perpetuates his Father in the fame manner as the Appearance of his Ghoft would : It is indeed *Ruricola*, but it is *Ruricola* grown frightful.

I know not what to attribute the brutal Turn which this young Man has taken, except it may be to a certain Severity and Diftance which his Father ufed towards him, and might, perhaps, have occafioned a Diflike to thofe Modes of Life which were not made amiable to him by Freedom and Affability.

WE may promife ourfelves that no fuch Excrefcence will appear in the Family of the *Cornelii*, where the Father lives with his Sons like their eldeft Brother, and the Sons converfe with him as if they did it for no other Reafon but that he is the wifeft Man of their Acquaintance. As the *Cornelii* are eminent Traders, their good Correfpondence with each other is ufeful to all that know them, as well as to themfelves: And their Friendfhip, Good-will and kind Offices, are difpofed of jointly as well as their Fortune, fo that no one ever obliged one of them, who had not the Obligation multiplied in Returns from them all.

IT is the moft beautiful Objeft the Eyes of Man can behold, to fee a Man of Worth and his Son live in an intire unreferved Correfpondence. The mutual Kindnefs and Affeâion between them give an inexpreffible Satiffaâion to all who know them. It is a fublime Pleafure which increafes by the Participation. It is as facred as Friendfhip, as pleafurable as Love, and as joyful as Religion.

ligion. This State of Mind does not only diffipate Sorrow, which would be extreme without it, but enlarges Pleafures which would otherwife be contemptible. The moft indifferent thing has its Force and Beauty when it is fpoke by a kind Father, and an infignificant Trifle has its Weight when offered by a dutiful Child. I know not how to exprefs it, but I think I may call it a tranfplanted Self-love. All the Enjoyments and Sufferings which a Man meets with are regarded only as they concern him in the Relation he has to another. A Man's very Honour receives a new Value to him, when he thinks that, when he is in his Grave, it will be had in Remembrance that fuch an Action was done by fuch a one's Father. Such Confiderations fweeten the old Man's Evening, and his Soliloquy delights him when he can fay to himfelf, No Man can tell my Child his Father was either unmerciful or unjuft: My Son fhall meet many a Man who fhall fay to him, I was obliged to thy Father, and be my Child a Friend to his Child for ever.

I T is not in the Power of all Men to leave illuftrious Names or great Fortunes to their Pofterity, but they can very much conduce to their having Induftry, Probity, Valour and Juftice : It is in every Man's Power to leave his Son the Honour of defcending from a virtuous Man, and add the Bleffings of Heaven to whatever he leaves him. I fhall end this Rhapfody with a Letter to an excellent young Man of my Acquaintance, who has lately loft a worthy Father.

Dear Sir,

I Know no Part of Life more impertinent than the Office of adminiftring Confolation : I will not enter into it, for I cannot but applaud your Grief. The virtuous Principles you had from that excellent Man, whom you have loft, have wrought in you as they ought, to make a Youth of Three and Twenty incapable of Comfort upon coming into Poffeffion of a great Fortune. I doubt not but you will honour his Memory by a modeft Enjoyment of his Eftate ; and fcorn to triumph over his Grave, by employing in Riot, Excefs, and Debauchery, what he purchafed with fo much Induftry, Prudence, and Wifdom. This is the true Way

‘ to fhew the Senfe you have of your Lofs, and to take
‘ away the Diftrefs of others upon the Occafion. You
‘ cannot recal your Father by your Grief, but you may
‘ revive him to his Friends by your Conduct.　　　T

Nº 193　　*Thurfday, October* 11.

——*Ingentem foribus domus alta fuperbis*
Manè falutantum totis vomit ædibus undam.
　　　　　　　　　　　Virg. Georg. 2. v. 461.

His Lordfhip's Palace, from its ftately Doors,
A Flood of Levée-hunting Mortals pours.

WHEN we look round us, and behold the ftrange
Variety of Faces and Perfons which fill the Streets
with Bufinefs and Hurry, it is no unpleafant
Amufement to make Gueffes at their different Purfuits, and
judge by their Countenances what it is that fo anxioufly
engages their prefent Attention. Of all this bufy Croud,
there are none who would give a Man inclined to fuch
Inquiries better Diverfion for his Thoughts, than thofe
whom we call good Courtiers, and fuch as are affiduous
at the Levées of great Men. Thefe Worthies are got into an Habit of being fervile with an Air, and enjoy a
certain Vanity in being known for underftanding how
the World paffes. In the Pleafure of this they can rife
early, go abroad fleek and well-dreffed, with no other
Hope or Purpofe, but to make a Bow to a Man in Court-
Favour, and be thought, by fome infignificant Smile of
his, not a little engaged in his Interefts and Fortunes.
It is wondrous, that a Man can get over the natural Exiftence and Poffeffion of his own Mind fo far, as to take
Delight either in paying or receiving fuch cold and repeated Civilities. But what maintains the Humour is,
that outward Show is what moft Men purfue, rather than
real Happinefs. Thus both the Idol and Idolater equally
impofe upon themfelves in pleafing their Imaginations
this way. But as there are very many of her Majefty's
　　　　　　　　　　　　　　　　　(good

good Subjects, who are extremely uneafy at their own Seats in the Country, where all from the Skies to the Centre of the Earth is their own, and have a mighty longing to fhine in Courts, or to be Partners in the Power of the World; I fay, for the Benefit of thefe, and others who hanker after being in the Whifper with great Men, and vexing their Neighbours with the Changes they would be capable of making in the Appearance at a Country Seffions, it would not methinks be amifs to give an Account of that Market for Preferment, a great Man's Levée.

FOR ought I know, this Commerce between the Mighty and their Slaves, very juftly reprefented, might do fo much good, as to incline the Great to regard Bufinefs rather than Oftentation; and make the Little know the Ufe of their Time too well, to fpend it in vain Applications and Addreffes.

THE famous Doctor in *Moorfields*, who gained fo much Reputation for his Horary Predictions, is faid to have had in his Parlour different Ropes to little Bells which hung in the Room above Stairs, where the Doctor thought fit to be oraculous. If a Girl had been deceived by her Lover, one Bell was pulled; and if a Peafant had loft a Cow, the Servant rung another. This Method was kept in refpect to all other Paffions and Concerns, and the skilful Waiter below fifted the Inquirer, and gave the Doctor Notice accordingly. The Levée of a great Man is laid after the fame manner; and twenty Whifpers, falfe Alarms, and private Intimations, pafs backward and forward from the Porter, the Valet, and the Patron himfelf, before the gaping Crew, who are to pay their Court, are gathered together: When the Scene is ready, the Doors fly open and difcover his Lordfhip.

THERE are feveral Ways of making this firft Appearance: you may be either half dreffed, and wafhing yourfelf, which is indeed the moft ftately; but this Way of Opening is peculiar to Military Men, in whom there is fomething graceful in expofing themfelves naked; but the Politicians, or Civil Officers, have ufually affected to be more referved, and preferve a certain Chaftity of Deportment. Whether it be Hieroglyphical or not, this Difference in the Military and Civil Lift, I will not fay;

but have ever underftood the Fact to be, that the clofe Minifter is buttoned up, and the brave Officer open-breafted on thefe Occafions.

HOWEVER that is, I humbly conceive the Bufi-nefs of a Levée is to receive the Acknowledgments of a Multitude, that a Man is Wife, Bounteous, Valiant and Powerful. When the firft Shot of Eyes is made, it is won-derful to obferve how much Submiffion the Patron's Mo-defty can bear, and how much Servitude the Client's Spirit can defcend to. In the vaft Multiplicity of Bufinefs, and the Croud about him, my Lord's Parts are ufually fo great, that, to the Aftonifhment of the whole Affembly, he has fomething to fay to every Man there, and that fo fuitable to his Capacity as any Man may judge that it is not without Talents that Men can arrive at great Employments. I have known a great Man ask a Flag-Officer, which way was the Wind, a Commander of Horfe the prefent Price of Oats, and a Stock-Jobber at what Difcount fuch a Fund was, with as much Eafe as if he had been bred to each of thofe feveral Ways of Life. Now this is extremely obliging; for at the fame time that the Patron informs himfelf of Matters, he gives the Perfon of whom he in-quires an Opportunity to exert himfelf. What adds to the Pomp of thofe Interviews is, that it is perform'd with the greateft Silence and Order imaginable. The Patron is ufually in the Midft of the Room, and fome humble Perfon gives him a Whifper, which his Lordfhip an-fwers aloud, *It is well. Yes, I am of your Opinion. Pray inform yourfelf further, you may be fure of my Part in it.* This happy Man is difmiffed, and my Lord can turn himfelf to a Bufinefs of a quite different Nature, and off-hand give as good an Anfwer as any great Man is obliged to. For the chief Point is to keep in Generals, and if there be any thing offered that's Particular, to be in hafte.

BUT we are now in the Height of the Affair, and my Lord's Creatures have all had their Whifpers round to keep up the Farce of the Thing, and the Dumb Show is become more general. He cafts his Eye to that Cor-ner, and there to Mr. Such-a-one; to the other, *and when did you come to Town?* And perhaps juft before he nods to another; and enters with him, *but, Sir, I am glad to fee you, now I think of it.* Each of thofe are happy for the

next

next four and twenty Hours; and those who bow in Ranks undistinguished, and by Dozens at a Time, think they have very good Prospects if they may hope to arrive at such Notices half a Year hence.

THE Satyrist says, there is seldom common Sense in high Fortune; and one would think, to behold a Levée, that the Great were not only infatuated with their Station, but also that they believed all below were seized too; else how is it possible they could think of imposing upon themselves and others in such a degree, as to set up a Levée for any thing but a direct Farce? But such is the Weakness of our Nature, that when Men are a little exalted in their Condition, they immediately conceive they have additional Senses, and their Capacities enlarged not only above other Men, but above human Comprehension itself. Thus it is ordinary to see a great Man attend one listning, bow to one at a distance, and call to a third at the same instant. A Girl in new Ribbands is not more taken with herself, nor does she betray more apparent Coquetries, than even a wise Man in such a Circumstance of Courtship. I do not know any thing that I ever thought so very distasteful as the Affectation which is recorded of *Cæsar*, to wit, that he would dictate to three several Writers at the same time. This was an Ambition below the Greatness and Candour of his Mind. He indeed (if any Man had Pretensions to greater Faculties than any other Mortal) was the Person; but such a Way of acting is childish, and inconsistent with the Manner of our Being. And it appears from the very Nature of Things, that there cannot be any thing effectually dispatched in the Distraction of a publick Levée; but the whole seems to be a Conspiracy of a Set of Servile Slaves, to give up their own Liberty to take away their Patron's Understanding.   T

N° 194   *Friday, October 12.*

―――― *Difficili bile tumet jecur.* Hor. Od. 13. l. 1. v. 4.

Anger boils up in my hot lab'ring Breast.   Glanvil.

THE prefent Paper fhall confift of two Letters which
obferve upon Faults that are eafily cured, both in
Love and Friendfhip. In the latter, as far as it
merely regards Converfation, the Perfon who neglects vi-
fiting an agreeable Friend is punifhed in the very Tranf-
greflion; for a good Companion is not found in every
Room we go into. But the Cafe of Love is of a more delicate Nature, and the Anxiety is inexpreffible if every little
Inftance of Kindnefs is not reciprocal. There are Things
in this fort of Commerce which there are not Words to
exprefs, and a Man may not poffibly know how to reprefent, what yet may tear his Heart into ten thoufand Tortures. To be grave to a Man's Mirth, unattentive to his
Difcourfe, or to interrupt either with fomething that
argues a Difinclination to be entertained by him, has
in it fomething fo difagreeable, that the utmoft Steps
which may be made in farther Enmity cannot give greater Torment. The gay *Corinna*, who fets up for an Indifference and becoming Heedlefnefs, gives her Husband
all the Torment imaginable out of mere Indolence, with
this peculiar Vanity, that fhe is to look as gay as a Maid
in the Character of a Wife. It is no matter what is the
Reafon of a Man's Grief, if it be heavy as it is. Her
unhappy Man is convinced that fhe means him no Difhonour, but pines to Death becaufe fhe will not have fo
much Deference to him as to avoid the Appearances of
it. The Author of the following Letter is perplexed with
an Injury that is in a Degree yet lefs criminal, and yet
the Source of the utmoft Unhappinefs.

Mr. SPECTATOR,

' I Have read your Papers which relate to Jealoufy,
' and defire your Advice in my Cafe, which you will
' fay is not common. I have a Wife, of whofe Virtue I

                                                    ' am

' am not in the least doubtful ; yet I cannot be satisfied she
' loves me, which gives me as great Uneasiness as being
' faulty the other Way would do. I know not whether I
' am not yet more miserable than in that Case, for she
' keeps Possession of my Heart, without the Return of
' hers. I would desire your Observations upon that Tem-
' per in some Women, who will not condescend to con-
' vince their Husbands of their Innocence or their Love,
' but are wholly negligent of what Reflexions the poor
' Men make upon their Conduct (so they cannot call it
' Criminal,) when at the same time a little Tenderness
' of Behaviour, or Regard to shew an Inclination to
' please them, would make them intirely at Ease. Do
' not such Women deserve all the Misinterpretation which
' they neglect to avoid ?   Or are they not in the actual
' Practice of Guilt, who care not whether they are
' thought guilty or not ? If my Wife does the most or-
' dinary Thing, as visiting her Sister, or taking the Air
' with her Mother, it is always carried with the Air of a
' Secret: Then she will sometimes tell a Thing of no
' Consequence, as if it was only Want of Memory made
' her conceal it before ; and this only to dally with my
' Anxiety.   I have complained to her of this Behaviour
' in the gentlest Terms imaginable, and beseeched her
' not to use him, who desired only to live with her like
' an indulgent Friend, as the most morose and unsociable
' Husband in the World. It is no easy Matter to describe
' our Circumstance, but it is miserable with this Aggra-
' vation, That it might be easily mended, and yet no
' Remedy endeavoured.   She reads you, and there is a
' Phrase or two in this Letter which she will know came
' from me. If we enter into an Explanation which may
' tend to our future Quiet by your Means, you shall have
' our joint Thanks; in the mean time I am (as much as
' I can in this ambiguous Condition be any Thing)

S I R,

Your humble Servant.

E 3

Mr.

Mr. SPECTATOR,

'GIVE me leave to make you a Present of a Cha-
'racter not yet defcribed in your Papers, which is
'that of a Man who treats his Friend with the fame odd
'Variety which a fantaftical Female Tyrant practifes to-
'wards her Lover. I have for fome time had a Friend-
'fhip with one of thefe Mercurial Perfons: The Rogue I
'know loves me, yet takes Advantage of my Fondnefs
'for him to ufe me as he pleafes. We are by Turns the
'beft Friends and the greateft Strangers imaginable ;
'Sometimes you would think us infeparable; at other
'times he avoids me for a long time, yet neither he
'nor I know why. When we meet next by Chance,
'he is amazed he has not feen me, is impatient for an
'Appointment the fame Evening: and when I expect
'he fhould have kept it, I have known him flip away to
'another Place; where he has fat reading the News,
'when there is no Poft; fmoking his Pipe, which he
'feldom cares for; and ftaring about him in Company
'with whom he has had nothing to do, as if he won-
'dered how he came there.
' THAT I may ftate my Cafe to you the more
'fully, I fhall tranfcribe fome fhort Minutes I have taken
'of him in my Almanack fince laft Spring; for you muft
'know there are certain Seafons of the Year, according
'to which, I will not fay our Friendfhip, but the Enjoy-
'ment of it rifes or falls. In *March* and *April* he was as
'various as the Weather; In *May* and part of *June* I
'found him the fprightlieft beft-humoured Fellow in the
'World; In the Dog-Days he was much upon the In-
'dolent; In *September* very agreeable but very bufy; and
'fince the Glafs fell laft to changeable, he has made three
'Appointments with me, and broke them every one.
'However I have good Hopes of him this Winter, efpe-
'cially if you will lend me your Affiftance to reform him,
'which will be a great Eafe and Pleafure to,

October 9,   S I R,
1711.

                         Your moft humble Servant.

T

                               Saturday,

Νήπιοι, ἐδ᾽ ἴσασιν ὅσῳ πλέον ἥμισυ παντός,
Οὐδ᾽ ὅσον ἐν μαλάχῃ τε ἢ ἀσφοδέλῳ μέγ᾽ ὄνειαρ.

Hef. Oper. & Dier. l. 1. v. 40.

*Fools, not to know that Half exceeds the Whole,
Nor the great Bleffings of a frugal Board!*

THERE is a Story in the *Arabian Nights Tales*
of a King who had long languifhed under an ill
Habit of Body, and had taken abundance of Remedies to no purpofe. At length, fays the Fable, a Phyfician cured him by the following Method: He took an
hollow Ball of Wood, and filled it with feveral Drugs;
after which he clos'd it up fo artificially that nothing appeared. He likewife took a Mall, and after having hollow-
ed the Handle, and that Part which ftrikes the Ball, he
inclofed in them feveral Drugs after the fame Manner as
in the Ball itfelf. He then ordered the Sultan, who was
his Patient, to exercife himfelf early in the Morning with
thefe *rightly prepared* Inftruments, till fuch time as he
fhould fweat: When, as the Story goes, the Virtue of
the Medicaments perfpiring through the Wood, had fo
good an Influence on the Sultan's Conftitution, that they
cured him of an Indifpofition which all the Compofitions
he had taken inwardly had not been able to remove.
This eaftern Allegory is finely contrived to fhew us how
beneficial bodily Labour is to Health, and that Exercife
is the moft effectual Phyfick. I have defcribed in my
Hundred and Fifteenth Paper, from the general Structure and Mechanifm of an human Body, how abfolutely
neceffary Exercife is for its Prefervation: I fhall in this
Place recommend another great Prefervative of Health,
which in many Cafes produces the fame Effects as Exercife, and may, in fome meafure, fupply its Place, where
Opportunities of Exercife are wanting. The Prefervative
I am fpeaking of is Temperance, which has thofe particular Advantages above all other Means of Health, that

it may be practifed by all Ranks and Conditions, at any
Seafon or in any Place. It is a kind of Regimen into
which every Man may put himfelf, without Interruption
to Bufinefs, Expence of Money, or Lofs of Time. If Exercife throws off all Superfluities, Temperance prevents
them; if Exercife clears the Veffels, Temperance neither
fatiates nor overftrains them; if Exercife raifes proper
Ferments in the Humours, and promotes the Circulation
of the Blood, Temperance gives Nature her full Play, and
enables her to exert herfelf in all her Force and Vigour;
if Exercife diffipates a growing Diftemper, Temperance
ftarves it.

  PHYSICK; for the moft part, is nothing elfe but
the Subftitute of Exercife or Temperance. Medicines
are indeed abfolutely neceffary in acute Diftempers, that
cannot wait the flow Operations of thefe two great Inftruments of Health; but did Men live in an habitual
Courfe of Exercife and Temperance, there would be but
little Occafion for them. Accordingly we find that thofe
Parts of the World are the moft healthy, where they fub-
fift by the Chace; and that Men lived longeft when their
Lives were employed in hunting, and when they had little
Food befides what they caught. Bliftering, Cupping,
Bleeding, are feldom of ufe but to the Idle and Intemperate; as all thofe inward Applications which are
fo much in Practice among us, are for the moft part
nothing elfe but Expedients to make Luxury confiftent
with Health. The Apothecary is perpetually employed in
countermining the Cook and the Vintner. It is faid of *Dib-
genes*, that meeting a young Man who was going to a
Feaft, he took him up in the Street and carried him home
to his Friends, as one who was running into imminent
Danger, had not he prevented him. What would that
Philofopher have faid, had he been prefent at the Gluttony
of a modern Meal? Would not he have thought the
Mafter of a Family mad, and have begged his Servants
to tie down his Hands, had he feen him devour Fowl,
Fifh, and Flefh; fwallow Oil and Vinegar, Wines and
Spices; throw down Salads of twenty different Herbs,
Sauces of an hundred Ingredients, Confections and Fruits
of numberlefs Sweets and Flavours? What unnatural Mo-
tions and Counterferments muft fuch a Medley of Intem-
                                                    perance

perance produce in the Body? For my part, when I
behold a fashionable Table set out in all its Magnificence,
I fancy that I see Gouts and Dropsies, Fevers and Le-
thargies, with other innumerable Distempers lying in
Ambuscade among the Dishes.

NATURE delights in the most plain and simple
Diet. Every Animal, but Man, keeps to one Dish. Herbs
are the Food of this Species, Fish of that, and Flesh of a
Third. Man falls upon every Thing that comes in his
Way, not the smallest Fruit or Excrescence of the Earth,
scarce a Berry or a Mushroom, can escape him.

IT is impossible to lay down any determinate Rule for
Temperance, because what is Luxury in one may be
Temperance in another; but there are few that have lived
any Time in the World, who are not Judges of their own
Constitutions, so far as to know what Kinds and what
Proportions of Food do best agree with them. Were I to
consider my Readers as my Patients, and to prescribe such
a Kind of Temperance as is accommodated to all Persons,
and such as is particularly suitable to our Climate and
Way of Living, I would copy the following Rules of a
very eminent Physician. Make your whole Repast out of
one Dish. If you indulge in a second, avoid drinking any
thing strong, till you have finished your Meal; at the same
time abstain from all Sauces, or at least such as are not the
most plain and simple. A Man could not be well guilty of
Gluttony, if he stuck to these few obvious and easy Rules.
In the first Case there would be no Variety of Tastes to
solicit his Palate, and occasion Excess; nor in the second
any artificial Provocatives to relieve Satiety, and create a
false Appetite. Were I to prescribe a Rule for drinking, it
should be form'd upon a Saying quoted by Sir *William*
Temple; *The first Glass for myself, the second for my Friends,*
the third for Good-humour, and the fourth for mine Enemies.
But because it is impossible for one who lives in the World
to diet himself always in so philosophical a manner, I
think every Man should have his Days of Abstinence, according as his Constitution will permit. These are great
Reliefs to Nature, as they qualify her for struggling with
Hunger and Thirst, whenever any Distemper or Duty of
Life may put her upon such Difficulties; and at the same
time give her an Opportunity of extricating herself from
her

her Oppreſſions, and recovering the ſeveral Tones and Springs of her diſtended Veſſels; Beſides that Abſtinence well timed often kills a Sickneſs in Embryo, and deſtroys the firſt Seeds of an Indiſpoſition. It is obſerved by two or three ancient Authors, that *Socrates*, notwithſtanding he lived in *Athens* during that great Plague, which has made ſo much Noiſe through all Ages, and has been celebrated at different Times by ſuch eminent Hands; I ſay, notwithſtanding that he lived in the time of this devouring Peſtilence, he never caught the leaſt Infection, which thoſe Writers unanimouſly aſcribe to that uninterrupted Temperance which he always obſerved.

A N D here I cannot but mention an Obſervation which I have often made, upon reading the Lives of the Philoſophers, and comparing them with any Series of Kings, or great Men of the ſame Number. If we conſider theſe ancient Sages, a great Part of whoſe Philoſophy conſiſted in a temperate and abſtemious Courſe of Life, one would think the Life of a Philoſopher and the Life of a Man were of two different Dates. For we find that the Generality of theſe wiſe Men were nearer an hundred than ſixty Years of Age at the Time of their reſpective Deaths. But the moſt remarkable Inſtance of the Efficacy of Temperance towards the procuring of long Life, is what we meet with in a little Book publiſhed by *Lewis Cornaro* the *Venetian*; which I the rather mention, becauſe it is of undoubted Credit, as the late *Venetian* Ambaſſador, who was of the ſame Family, atteſted more than once in Converſation, when he reſided in *England*. *Cornaro*, who was the Author of the little Treatiſe I am mentioning, was of an infirm Conſtitution, till about forty, when by obſtinately perſiſting in an exact Courſe of Temperance, he recovered a perfect State of Health; inſomuch that at fourſcore he publiſhed his Book, which has been tranſlated into *Engliſh* under the Title of *Sure and certain Methods of attaining a long and healthy Life.* He lived to give a 3d or 4th Edition of it, and after having paſſed his hundredth Year, died without Pain or Agony, and like one who falls aſleep. The Treatiſe I mention has been taken notice of by ſeveral eminent Authors, and is written with ſuch a Spirit of Chearfulneſs, Religion, and good Senſe, as are the natural Concomitants of Temperance

rance and Sobriety: The Mixture of the old Man in it
is rather a Recommendation than a Difcredit to it.

HAVING defigned this Paper as the Sequel to that
upon Exercife, I have not here confidered Temperance as
it is a moral Virtue, which I fhall make the Subject of a
future Speculation, but only as it is the Means of Health.

L.

***

Nº 196. *Monday, October* 15.

Eft Ulubris, animus fi te non deficit æquus.

Hor. Ep. II. l. I. v. 30.

True Happinefs is to no Place confin'd,
But ftill is found in a contented Mind.

Mr. SPECTATOR,

'THERE is a particular Fault which I have ob-
'ferved in moft of the Moralifts in all Ages, and
'that is, that they are always profeffing themfelves,
'and teaching others to be happy. This State is not to
'be arrived at in this Life, therefore I would recommend
'to you to talk in an humbler Strain than your Prede-
'ceffors have done, and inftead of prefuming to be hap-
'py, inftruct us only to be eafy. The Thoughts of him
'who would be difcreet, and aim at practicable things,
'fhould turn upon allaying our Pain rather than pro-
'moting our Joy. Great Inquietude is to be avoided, but
'great Felicity is not to be attained. The great Leffon is
'Æquanimity, a Regularity of Spirit, which is a little
'above Chearfulnefs and below Mirth. Chearfulnefs is
'always to be fupported if a Man is out of Pain, but
'Mirth to a prudent Man fhould always be accidental:
'It fhould naturally arife out of the Occafion, and the
'Occafion feldom be laid for it; for thofe Tempers who
'want Mirth to be pleafed, are like the Conftitutions
'which flag without the ufe of Brandy. Therefore, I fay,
'let your Precept be, *Be eafy*. That Mind is diffolute
'and ungoverned, which muft be hurried out of itfelf

by

'by loud Laughter or senfual Pleafure, or elfe be wholly
'unactive.

'THERE are a Couple of old Fellows of my Ac-
'quaintance who meet every Day and fmoke a Pipe,
'and by their natural Love to each other, tho' they have
'been Men of Bufinefs and Buftle in the World, enjoy a
'greater Tranquillity than either could have worked him-
'felf into by any Chapter of *Seneca.* Indolence of Body
'and Mind, when we aim at no more, is very frequently
'enjoyed; but the very Inquiry after Happinefs has fome-
'thing reftlefs in it, which a Man who lives in a Series of
'temperate Meals, friendly Converfations, and eafy Slum-
'bers, gives himfelf no Trouble about. While Men of
'Refinement are talking of Tranquillity, he poffeffes it.

'WHAT I would by thefe broken Expreffions re-
'commend to you, *Mr.* SPECTATOR, is, that you
'would fpeak of the Way of Life, which plain Men may
'purfue, to fill up the Spaces of Time with Satisfaction.
'It is a lamentable Circumftance, that Wifdom, or, as you
'call it, Philofophy, fhould furnifh Ideas only for the
'Learned; and that a Man muft be a Philofopher to know
'how to pafs away his Time agreeably. It would there-
'fore be worth your Pains to place in an handfom Light
'the Relations and Affinities among Men, which render
'their Converfation with each other fo grateful, that the
'higheft Talents give but an impotent Pleafure in Com-
'parifon with them. You may find Defcriptions and Dif-
'courfes which will render the Fire-fide of an honeft
'Artificer as entertaining as your own Club is to you.
'Good-nature has an endlefs Source of Pleafures in it;
'and the Reprefentation of domeftick Life filled with its
'natural Gratifications, (inftead of the neceffary Vexa-
'tions which are generally infifted upon in the Writings
'of the Witty) will be a very good Office to Society.

'THE Viciffitudes of Labour and Reft in the lower
'Part of Mankind, make their Being pafs away with that
'Sort of Relifh which we exprefs by the Word Com-
'fort; and fhould be treated of by you, who are a SPEC-
'TATOR, as well as fuch Subjects which appear indeed
'more fpeculative, but are lefs inftructive. In a word,
'Sir, I would have you turn your Thoughts to the Ad-
'vantage of fuch as want you moft; and fhew that Sim-
'plicity,

' plicity, Innocence, Industry and Temperance, are Arts '
' which lead to Tranquillity, as much as Learning, Wif- '
' dom, Knowledge, and Contemplation. '

I am, SIR,

Your most Humble Servant,

T. B.

Mr. SPECTATOR, *Hackney, October* 12.

' I Am the young Woman whom you did fo much
' Juftice to fome time ago, in acknowledging that I
' am perfect Miftrefs of the Fan, and ufe it with the
' utmoft Knowledge and Dexterity. Indeed the World, as
' malicious as it is, will allow, that from an Hurry of
' Laughter I recollect myfelf the moft fuddenly, make a
' Curtfy, and let fall my Hands before me, clofing my
' Fan at the fame inftant, the beft of any Woman in
' *England.* I am not a little delighted that I have had
' your Notice and Approbation; and however other
' young Women may rally me out of Envy, I triumph
' in it, and demand a Place in your Friendfhip. You
' muft therefore permit me to lay before you the pre-
' fent State of my Mind. I was reading your *Spectator*
' of the 9th Inftant, and thought the Circumftance of
' the Afs divided between two Bundels of Hay which
' equally affected his Senfes, was a lively Reprefentation
' of my prefent Condition. For you are to know that I
' am extremely enamoured with two young Gentlemen
' who at this Time pretend to me. One muft hide no-
' thing when one is afking Advice, therefore I will own
' to you, that I am very amorous and very covetous.
' My Lover *Will* is very rich, and my Lover *Tom* very
' handfom. I can have either of them when I pleafe:
' But when I debate the Queftion in my own Mind, I
' cannot take *Tom* for fear of lofing *Will's* Eftate, nor
' enter upon *Will's* Eftate, and bid adieu to *Tom's* Per-
' fon. I am very young, and yet no one in the World,
' dear Sir, has the main Chance more in her Head than
' myfelf. *Tam* is the gayeft, the blitheft Creature! He
' dances well, is very civil, and diverting at all Hours
' and Seafons: Oh he is the Joy of my Eyes? But then
' again *Will* is fo very rich and careful of the Main. How
' many

'many pretty Dreſſes does *Tom* appear in to charm me!
'But then it immediately occurs to me, that a Man of his
'Circumſtances is ſo much the poorer. Upon the whole,
'I have at laſt examined both theſe Deſires of Love and
'Avarice, and upon ſtrictly weighing the Matter I be-
'gin to think I ſhall be covetous longer than fond;
'therefore if you have nothing to ſay to the contrary,
'I ſhall take *Will.* Alas, poor *Tom!*

Your Humble Servant,

BIDDY LOVELESS.

T

Nº 197   *Tueſday, October* 16.

Alter rixatur de lanâ ſæpe caprinâ, et
Propugnat nugis armatus: ſcilicet, ut non
Sit mihi prima fides? &, verè quod placet, ut non
Acriter elatrem? pretium ætas altera ſordet.
Ambigitur quid enim! Caſtor ſciat, an Docilis plus,
Brunduſium Numici meliùs via ducat, an Appî.

Hor. Ep. 18. l. 1. v. 15.

One ſtrives for Trifles, and for Toys contends:
He is in earneſt; what he ſays, defends:
'That I ſhould not be truſted, right or wrong,
'Or be debarr'd the Freedom of my Tongue,
'And not bawl what I pleaſe! To part with this,
'I think another Life too mean a Price.'
The Queſtion is—Pray, what?—Why, which can boaſt
Or Docilis, or Caſtor, knowing moſt;
Or whether thro' Numicum ben't as good
To fair Brunduſium, as the Appian Road.   Creech.

E VERY Age a Man paſſes through, and Way of
Life he engages in, has ſome particular Vice or Imperfection naturally cleaving to it, which it will require his niceſt Care to avoid. The ſeveral Weakneſſes,
to which Youth, Old Age, and Manhood are expoſed,
have long ſince been ſet down by many both of the Poets

and

and Philofophers; but I do not remember to have met
with any Author who has treated of thofe ill Habits Men
are fubject to, not fo much by reafon of their different
Ages and Tempers, as the particular Profeffions or Bufinefs in which they were educated and brought up.

I am the more furprifed to find this Subject fo little
touched on, fince what I am here fpeaking of is fo apparent, as not to efcape the moft vulgar Obfervation.
The Bufinefs Men are chiefly converfant in, does not only
give a certain Caft or Turn to their Minds, but is very
often apparent in their outward Behaviour, and fome of
the moft indifferent Actions of their Lives. It is this Air
diffufing itfelf over the whole Man, which helps us to
find out a Perfon at his firft Appearance; fo that the
moft carelefs Obferver fancies he can fcarce be miftaken
in the Carriage of a Seaman or the Gate of a Tailor.

THE liberal Arts, though they may poffibly have
lefs Effect on our external Mien and Behaviour, make fo
deep an Impreffion on the Mind, as is very apt to bend
it wholly one Way.

THE Mathematician will take little lefs than De-
monftration in the moft common Difcourfe, and the
Schoolman is as great a Friend to Definitions and Syllo-
gifms. The Phyfician and Divine are often heard to
dictate in private Companies with the fame Authority
which they exercife over their Patients and Difciples;
while the Lawyer is putting Cafes and raifing Matter for
Difputation out of every thing that occurs.

I may poffibly fome time or other animadvert more
at large on the particular Fault each Profeffion is moft
infected with; but fhall at prefent wholly apply myfelf
to the Cure of what I laft mentioned, namely that Spirit
of Strife and Contention in the Converfations of Gentlemen of the long Robe.

THIS is the more ordinary, becaufe thefe Gentlemen regarding Argument as their own proper Province,
and very often making Ready-money of it, think it un-
fafe to yield before Company. They are fhewing in
common Talk how zealoufly they could defend a Caufe
in Court, and therefore frequently forget to keep that
Temper which is abfolutely requifite to render Converfation pleafant and inftructive.

CAP-

CAPTAIN SENTRY pushes this Matter so far, that I have heard him say, *He has known but few Pleaders that were tolerable Company.*

THE Captain, who is a Man of good Sense, but dry Conversation, was last Night giving me an Account of a Discourse, in which he had lately been engaged with a young Wrangler in the Law. I was giving my Opinion, says the Captain, without apprehending any Debate that might arise from it, of a General's Behaviour in a Battle that was fought some Years before either the Templar or myself were born. The young Lawyer immediately took me up, and by reasoning above a Quarter of an Hour upon a Subject which I saw he understood nothing of, endeavoured to shew me that my Opinions were ill-grounded. Upon which, says the Captain, to avoid any farther Contests, I told him, That truly I had not consider'd those several Arguments which he had brought against me, and that there might be a great deal in them. Ay, but says my Antagonist, who would not let me escape so, there are several Things to be urged in favour of your Opinion which you have omitted; and thereupon begun to shine on the other Side of the Question. Upon this, says the Captain, I came over to my first Sentiments, and intirely acquiesced in his Reasons for my so doing. Upon which the Templar again recovered his former Posture, and confuted both himself and me a third Time. In short, says my Friend, I found he was resolved to keep me at Sword's Length, and never let me close with him, so that I had nothing left but to hold my tongue, and give my Antagonist free leave to smile at his Victory, who I found, like *Hudibras, could still change Sides, and still confute.*

FOR my own part, I have ever regarded our Inns of Court as Nurseries of Statesmen and Lawgivers, which makes me often frequent that Part of the Town with great Pleasure.

UPON my calling in lately at one of the most noted *Temple* Coffee-houses, I found the whole Room, which was full of young Students, divided into several Parties, each of which was deeply engaged in some Controversy. The Management of the late Ministry was attacked and defended with great Vigour; and several Preliminaries to the Peace were propofed by fome, and rejected by others ; the demolifhing of *Dunkirk* was fo eagerly infifted on, and fo warmly controverted, as had like to have produced a Challenge. In fhort, I obferved that the Defire of Victory, whetted with the little Prejudices of Party and Intereft, generally carried the Argument to fuch a Height, as made the Difputants infenfibly conceive an Averfion towards each other, and part with the higheft Diffatisfaction on both Sides.

THE managing an Argument handfomly being fo nice a Point, and what I have feen fo very few excel in, I fhall here fet down a few Rules on that Head, which, among other things, I gave in writing to a young Kinfman of mine, who had made fo great a Proficiency in the Law, that he began to plead in Company, upon every Subject that was ftarted.

HAVING the intire Manufcript by me, I may, perhaps, from time to time, publifh fuch Parts of it as I fhall think requifite for the Inftruction of the *Britifh* Youth. What regards my prefent Purpofe is as follows:

AVOID Difputes as much as poffible. In order to appear eafy and well-bred in Converfation, you may affure yourfelf that it requires more Wit, as well as more Good-humour, to improve than to contradict the Notions of another : but if you are at any time obliged to enter on an Argument, give your Reafons with the utmoft Coolnefs and Modefty, two Things which fcarce ever fail of making an Impreffion on the Hearers. Befides, if you are neither dogmatical, nor fhew either by your Actions or Words, that you are full of yourfelf, all will the more heartily rejoice at your Victory. Nay, fhould you be pinched in your Argument, you may make your Retreat with a very good Grace : You were never pofitive, and are now glad to be better informed. This has made fome approve the Socratical Way of Reafoning, where while you fcarce affirm any thing, you can hardly be caught in an Abfurdity, and tho' poffibly you are endeavouring to bring over another to your Opinion, which is firmly fix'd, you feem only to defire Information from him.

IN order to keep that Temper which is fo difficult, and yet fo neceffary to preferve, you may pleafe to confider, that nothing can be more unjuft or ridiculous, than to be angry with another becaufe he is not of your Opinion. The Interefts, Education, and Means by which Men attain their Knowledge, are fo very different, that it is impoffible they fhould all think alike; and he has at leaft as much Reafon to be angry with you, as you with him. Sometimes to keep yourfelf cool, it may be of Service to ask yourfelf fairly, What might have been your Opinion, had you all the Biafes of Education and Intereft your Adverfary may poffibly have? but if you contend for the Honour of Victory alone, you may lay down this as an infallible Maxim, That you cannot make a more falfe Step, or give your Antagonifts a greater Advantage over you, than by falling into a Paffion.

WHEN an Argument is over, how many weighty Reafons does a Man recollect, which his Heat and Violence made him utterly forget?

IT is yet more abfurd to be angry with a Man becaufe he does not apprehend the Force of your Reafons, or give weak ones of his own. If you argue for Reputation, this makes your Victory the eafier; he is certainly in all refpects an Object of your Pity, rather than Anger; and if he cannot comprehend what you do, you ought to thank Nature for her Favours, who has given you fo much the clearer Underftanding.

YOU may pleafe to add this Confideration, That among your Equals no one values your Anger, which only preys upon its Mafter; and perhaps you may find it not very confiftent either with Prudence or your Eafe, to punifh yourfelf whenever you meet with a Fool or a Knave.

LASTLY, If you propofe to yourfelf the true End of Argument, which is Information, it may be a feafonable Check to your Paffion; for if you fearch purely after Truth, 'twill be almoft indifferent to you where you find it. I cannot in this Place omit an Obfervation which I have often made, namely, That nothing procures a Man more Efteem and lefs Envy from the whole Company, than if he choofes the Part of Moderator, without engaging directly on either Side in a Difpute. This gives him the Character of Impartial, furnifhes him with an Opportunity of fifting Things to the Bottom, fhewing his Judgment, and of fometimes making handfom Compliments to each of the contending Parties.

I fhall

I shall close this Subject with giving you one Caution: When you have gained a Victory, do not push it too far; 'tis sufficient to let the Company and your Adversary see 'tis in your Power, but that you are too generous to make use of it.   X

N° 198 *Wednesday, October* 17.

Cervæ luporum præda rapacium
Sectamur ultrò, quos optimus
Fallere & effugere est triumphus. Hor. Od. 4. l. 4. v. 50.

We, like the Stag, the brinded Wolf provoke,
  And, when Retreat is Victory,
  Rush on, tho' sure to die.   Anon.

THERE is a Species of Women, whom I shall distinguish by the Name of Salamanders. Now a Salamander is a kind of Heroine in Chastity, that treads upon Fire, and lives in the midst of Flames without being hurt. A Salamander knows no Distinction of Sex in those she converses with, grows familiar with a Stranger at first Sight, and is not so narrow-spirited as to observe whether the Person she talks to be in Breeches or Petticoats. She admits a Male Visitant to her Bed-side, plays with him a whole Afternoon at Piquet, walks with him two or three Hours by Moon-light, and is extremely scandalized at the Unreasonableness of an Husband, or the Severity of a Parent, that would debar the Sex from such innocent Liberties. Your Salamander is therefore a perpetual Declaimer against Jealousy, and Admirer of the *French* Good-breeding, and a great Stickler for Freedom in Conversation. In short, the Salamander lives in an invincible State of Simplicity and Innocence. Her Constitution is *preserv'd* in a kind of natural Frost; she wonders what People mean by Temptations, and defies Mankind to do their worst. Her Chastity is engaged in a constant *Ordeal*, or fiery
                                                    Trial;

Trial: Like good Queen *Emma*, the pretty innocent walks blindfold among burning Plough-fhares, without being fcorched or finged by them.

IT is not therefore for the Ufe of the Salamander, whether in a married or fingle State of Life, that I defign the following Paper; but for fuch Females only as are made of Flefh and Blood, and find themfelves fubject to human Frailties.

AS for this Part of the fair Sex who are not of the Salamander Kind, I would moft earneftly advife them to obferve a quite different Conduct in their Behaviour; and to avoid as much as poffible what Religion calls *Temptations*, and the World *Opportunities*. Did they but know how many Thoufands of their Sex have been gradually betrayed from innocent Freedoms to Ruin and Infamy; and how many Millions of ours have begun with Flatteries, Proteftations and Endearments, but ended with Reproaches, Perjury, and Perfidioufnefs; they would fhun like Death the very firft Approaches of one that might lead them into inextricable Labyrinths of Guilt and Mifery: I muft fo far give up the Caufe of the Male World, as to exhort the Female Sex in the Language of *Chamont* in the *Orphan*;

> *Truft not a Man, we are by Nature Falfe,*
> *Diffembling, Subtle, Cruel, and Unconftant:*
> *When a Man talks of Love, with Caution truft him:*
> *But if he fwears, he'll certainly deceive thee.*

I might very much enlarge upon this Subject, but fhall conclude it with a Story which I lately heard from one of our *Spanifh* Officers, and which may fhew the Danger a Woman incurs by too great Familiarities with a Male Companion.

AN Inhabitant of the Kingdom of *Caftile*, being a Man of more than ordinary Prudence, and of a grave compofed Behaviour, determined about the fiftieth Year of his Age to enter upon Wedlock: In order to make himfelf eafy in it, he caft his Eye upon a young Woman who had nothing to recommend her but her Beauty and her Education, her Parents having been reduced to great Poverty by the Wars, which for fome Years have

laid

laid, that whole Country waste. The *Castilian* having made his Addresses to her, and married her, they lived together in perfect Happiness for some time; when at length the Husband's Affairs made it necessary for him to take a Voyage to the Kingdom of *Naples*, where a great Part of his Estate lay. The Wife loved him too tenderly to be left behind him. They had not been a Shipboard above a Day, when they unluckily fell into the Hands of an *Algerine* Pirate, who carried the whole Company on Shore, and made them Slaves. The *Castilian* and his Wife had the Comfort to be under the same Master; who seeing how dearly they loved one another, and gasped after their Liberty, demanded a most exorbitant Price for their Ransom. The *Castilian*, though he would rather have died in Slavery himself, than have paid such a Sum as he found would go near to ruin him, was so moved with Compassion towards his Wife, that he sent repeated Orders to his Friend in *Spain*, (who happened to be his next Relation) to sell his Estate, and transmit the Money to him. His Friend hoping that the Terms of his Ransom might be made more reasonable, and unwilling to sell an Estate which he himself had some Prospect of inheriting, formed so many Delays, that three whole Years passed away without any thing being done for the setting them at Liberty.

THERE happened to live a *French* Renegado in the same Place where the *Castilian* and his Wife were kept Prisoners. As this Fellow had in him all the Vivacity of his Nation, he often entertained the Captives with Accounts of his own Adventures; to which he sometimes added a Song or a Dance, or some other Piece of Mirth, to divert them during their Confinement. His Acquaintance with the Manners of the *Algerines*, enabled him likewise to do them several good Offices. The *Castilian*, as he was one Day in Conversation with this Renegado, discovered to him the Negligence and Treachery of his Correspondent in *Castile*; and at the same time asked his Advice how he should behave himself in that Exigency: He further told the Renegado, that he found it would be impossible for him to raise the Money, unless he himself might go over to dispose of his Estate. The Renegado, after having represented to him that his *Algerine* Master would

never

never consent to his Releafe upon such a Pretence, at
length contrived a Method for the *Caftilian* to make his
Efcape in the Habit of a Seaman. The *Caftilian* fucceeded
in his Attempt; and having fold his Eftate, being afraid
left the Money fhould mifcarry by the Way, and deter-
mining to perifh with it rather than lofe one who was
much dearer to him than his Life, he returned himfelf in
a little Veffel that was going to *Algiers*. It is impoffible to
defcribe the Joy he felt on this Occafion, when he confidered that he fhould foon fee the Wife whom he fo much
loved, and endear himfelf more to her by this uncommon
Piece of Generofity.

THE Renegado, during the Hufband's Abfence, fo
infinuated himfelf into the good Graces of his young
Wife, and fo turned her Head with Stories of Galantry,
that fhe quickly thought him the fineft Gentleman fhe
had ever converfed with. To be brief, her Mind was
quite alienated from the honeft *Caftilian*, whom fhe was
taught to look upon as a formal old Fellow unworthy the
Poffeffion of fo charming a Creature. She had been inftructed by the Renegado how to manage herfelf upon
his Arrival; fo that fhe received him with an Appearance
of the utmoft Love and Gratitude, and at length perfuaded him to truft their common Friend the Renegado
with the Money he had brought over for their Ranfom;
as not queftioning but he would beat down the Terms of
it, and negotiate the Affair more to their Advantage than
they themfelves could do. The good Man admired her
Prudence, and followed her Advice. I wifh I could
conceal the Sequel of this Story; but fince I cannot I
fhall difpatch it in as few Words as poffible. The *Caftilian* having flept longer than ordinary the next Morning,
upon his awaking found his Wife had left him: He
immediately arofe and inquired after her, but was told
that fhe was feen with the Renegado about Break of
Day. In a word, her Lover having got all things ready
for their Departure, they foon made their Efcape out of
the Territories of *Algiers*, carried away the Money, and
left the *Caftilian* in Captivity; who partly through the
cruel Treatment of the incenfed *Algerine* his Mafter, and
partly through the unkind Ufage of his unfaithful Wife,
died fome few Months after.   L

                                        Thurfday,

N° 199. *Thurſday, October* 18.

——— *Scribere juſſit amor.* ——— Ovid. Ep. 4. v. 10.

Love bid me write.

THE following Letters are written with ſuch an Air of Sincerity, that I cannot deny the inſerting of them.

Mr. SPECTATOR,

'THO' you are every where in your Writings a
' Friend to Women, I do not remember that you
' have directly conſidered the mercenary Practice of
' Men in the Choice of Wives. If you would pleaſe to
' employ your Thoughts upon that Subject, you would
' eaſily conceive the miſerable Condition many of us are
' in, who not only from the Laws of Cuſtom and Mo-
' deſty are reſtrained from making any Advances towards
' our Wiſhes, but are alſo, from the Circumſtance of
' Fortune, out of all Hope of being addreſſed to by
' thoſe whom we love. Under all theſe Diſadvantages I
' am obliged to apply myſelf to you, and hope I ſhall
' prevail with you to Print in your very next Paper the
' following Letter, which is a Declaration of Paſſion to
' one who has made ſome faint Addreſſes to me for ſome
' time. I believe he ardently loves me, but the Inequality
' of my Fortune makes him think he cannot anſwer it to
' the World, if he purſues his Deſigns by way of Mar-
' riage ; and I believe, as he does not want Diſcerning,
' he diſcovered me looking at him the other Day una-
' wares in ſuch a Manner as has raiſed his Hopes of
' gaining me on Terms the Men call eaſier. But my
' Heart was very full on this Occaſion, and if you know
' what Love and Honour are, you will pardon me that I
' uſe no farther Arguments with you, but haſten to my
' Letter to him, whom I call *Oroondates*, becauſe if I do
' not ſucceed, it ſhall look like Romance ; and if I am
' regarded,

' regarded, you shall receive a Pair of Gloves at my
' Wedding, sent you under the Name of *Statira*.'

.: *To* OROONDATES.

SIR,

' AFTER very much Perplexity in myself, and re-
' volving how to acquaint you with my own Sen-
' timents, and expostulate with you concerning yours, I
' have chosen this Way, by which means I can be at once
' revealed to you, or, if you please, lie concealed.
' If I do not within few Days find the Effect which I
' hope from this, the whole Affair shall be buried in Ob-
' livion. But, alas! what am I going to do, when I am
' about to tell you that I love you?' But after I have done
' so, I am to assure you, that with all the Passion which
' ever entered a tender Heart, I know I can banish you
' from my Sight for ever, when I am convinced that you
' have no Inclinations towards me but to my Dishonour.
' But, alas! Sir, why should you sacrifice the real and
' essential Happiness of Life, to the Opinion of a
' World, that moves upon no other Foundation but
' profess'd Error and Prejudice? You all can observe
' that Riches alone do not make you happy, and yet
' give up every Thing else when it stands in Com-
' petition with Riches. Since the World is so bad,
' that Religion is left to us silly Women, and you Men
' act generally upon Principles of Profit and Pleasure,
' I will talk to you without arguing from any Thing
' but what may be most to your Advantage, as a Man
' of the World. And I will lay before you the State
' of the Case, supposing that you had it in your Power
' to make me your Mistress, or your Wife, and
' hope to convince you that the latter is more for your
' Interest, and will contribute more to your Plea-
' sure.

' WE will suppose then the Scene was laid, and you
' were now in Expectation of the approaching Even-
' ing wherein I was to meet you, and be carried to what
' convenient Corner of the Town you thought fit, to
' confummate all which your wanton Imagination has
' promised you in the Possession of one who is in the
' Bloom

' Bloom of Youth, and in the Reputation of Innocence :
' you would soon have enough of me, as I am sprightly,
' Young, Gay, and Airy. When Fancy is sated, and finds
' all the Promises it made itself false, where is now the
' Innocence which charmed you ? The first Hour you
' are alone you will find that the Pleasure of a Debauchée
' is only that of a Destroyer ; He blasts all the Fruit he
' tastes, and where the Brute has been devouring, there
' is nothing left worthy the Relish of the Man.   Reason
' resumes her Place after Imagination is cloyed ; and I
' am, with the utmost Distress and Confusion, to behold
' myself the Cause of uneasy Reflexions to you, to be
' visited by Stealth, and dwell for the future with the
' two Companions (the most unfit for each other in the
' World) Solitude and Guilt.   I will not insist upon the
' shameful Obscurity we should pass our Time in, nor run
' over the little short Snatches of fresh Air, and free
' Commerce which all People must be satisfied with,
' whose Actions will not bear Examination, but leave
' them to your Reflexions, who have seen of that Life,
' of which I have but a mere Idea.
' ON the other hand, if you can be so good and ge-
' nerous as to make me your Wife, you may promise
' yourself all the Obedience and Tenderness with which
' Gratitude can inspire a virtuous Woman. Whatever
' Gratifications you may promise yourself from an
' agreeable Person, whatever Compliances from an easy
' Temper, whatever Consolations from a sincere Friend-
' ship, you may expect as the Due of your Generosity.
' What at present in your ill View you promise your-
' self from me, will be followed by Distaste and Satiety ;
' but the Transports of a virtuous Love are the least
' Part of its Happiness. The Raptures of innocent
' Passion are but like Lightning to the Day, they rather
' interrupt than advance the Pleasure of it. How happy
' then is that Life to be, where the highest Pleasures of
' Sense are but the lowest Parts of its Felicity ?
' NOW am I to repeat to you the unnatural Request
' of taking me in direct Terms. I know there stands
' between me and that Happiness, the haughty Daughter
' of a Man who can give you suitably to your Fortune.
' But if you weigh the Attendance and Behaviour of her

' who comes to you in Partnerſhip of your Fortune, and
' expects an Equivalent, with that of her who enters
' your Houſe as honoured and obliged by that Permiſ-
' ſion, whom of the two will you chooſe? You, perhaps,
' will think fit to ſpend a Day abroad in the common
' Entertainments of Men of Senſe and Fortune ; ſhe will
' think herſelf ill-uſed in that Abſence, and contrive at
' Home an Expence proportioned to the Appearance
' which you make in the World; She is in all things
' to have a Regard to the Fortune which ſhe brought
' you, I to the Fortune to which you introduced me.
' The Commerce between you two will eternally have
' the Air of a Bargain, between us of a Friendſhip:
' Joy will ever enter into the Room with you, and kind
' Wiſhes attend my Benefactor when he leaves it. Ask
' yourſelf, how would you be pleaſed to enjoy for ever
' the Pleaſure of having laid an immediate Obligation
' on a grateful Mind ? ſuch will be your Caſe with me.
' In the other Marriage you will live in a conſtant Com-
' pariſon of Benefits, and never know the Happineſs
' of conferring or receiving any.

' IT may be you will, after all, act rather in the
' prudential Way, according to the Senſe of the ordi-
' nary World. I know not what I think or ſay, when
' that melancholy Reflexion comes upon me ; but ſhall
' only add more, that it is in your Power to make me
' your grateful Wife, but never your abandoned
' Miſtreſs.   T

N° 200   *Friday, October* 19.

Vincit Amor Patriæ————   Virg. Æn. 6. v. 823.

The nobleſt Motive is the Publick Good.

THE Ambition of Princes is many times as hurtful to themſelves as to their People. This cannot
be doubted of ſuch as prove unfortunate in their
Wars, but it is often true too of thoſe who are celebrated for
their

their Succeſſes. If a ſevere View were to be taken of their Conduct, if the Profit and Loſs by their Wars could be juſtly balanced, it would be rarely found that the Conqueſt is ſufficient to repay the Coſt.

AS I was the other Day looking over the Letters of my Correſpondents, I took this Hint from that of *Philarithmus*; which has turned my preſent Thoughts upon Political Arithmetick, an Art of greater Uſe than Entertainment. My Friend has offered an Eſſay towards proving that *Lewis* XIV. with all his Acquiſitions is not Maſter of more People than at the Beginning of his Wars, nay that for every Subject he had acquired, he had loſt Three that were his Inheritance: If *Philarithmus* is not miſtaken in his Calculations, *Lewis* muſt have been impoveriſhed by his Ambition.

THE Prince for the Publick Good has a Sovereign Property in every Private Perſon's Eſtate, and conſequently his Riches muſt increaſe or decreaſe in proportion to the Number and Riches of his Subjects. For example: If Sword or Peſtilence ſhould deſtroy all the People of this Metropolis, (God forbid there ſhould be Room for ſuch a Suppoſition! but if this ſhould be the Caſe) the Queen muſt needs loſe a great Part of her Revenue, or, at leaſt, what is charged upon the City muſt increaſe the Burden upon the reſt of her Subjects. Perhaps the Inhabitants here are not above a Tenth Part of the Whole; yet as they are better fed, and cloth'd, and lodg'd, than her other Subjects, the Cuſtoms and Exciſes upon their Conſumption, the Impoſts upon their Houſes, and other Taxes, do very probably make a fifth Part of the whole Revenue of the Crown. But this is not all; the Conſumption of the City takes off a great Part of the Fruits of the whole Iſland; and as it pays ſuch a Proportion of the Rent or Yearly-Value of the Lands in the Country, ſo it is the Cauſe of paying ſuch a Proportion of Taxes upon thoſe Lands. The Loſs then of ſuch a People muſt needs be ſenſible to the Prince, and viſible to the whole Kingdom.

ON the other hand, if it ſhould pleaſe God to drop from Heaven a new People equal in Number and Riches to the City, I ſhould be ready to think their Exciſes, Cuſtoms, and Houſe-Rent would raiſe as great a Revenue to the

Crown as would be loft in the former Cafe. And as the Confumption of this New Body would be a new Market for the Fruits of the Country, all the Lands, efpecially thofe moft adjacent, would rife in their yearly Value, and pay greater yearly Taxes to the Publick. The Gain in this Cafe would be as fenfible as the former Lofs.

WHATSOEVER is affefs'd upon the General, is levied upon Individuals. It were worth the while then to confider what is paid by, or by means of, the meaneft Subjects, in order to compute the Value of every Subject to the Prince.

FOR my own part, I fhould believe that Seven Eighths of the People are without Property in themfelves or the Heads of their Families, and forced to work for their daily Bread; and that of this Sort there are Seven Millions in the whole Ifland of *Great Britain:* And yet one would imagine that Seven Eighths of the whole People fhould confume at leaft three Fourths of the whole Fruits of the Country. If this is the Cafe, the Subjects without Property pay three Fourths of the Rents, and confequently enable the Landed Men to pay Three Fourths of their Taxes. Now if fo great a Part of the Land-Tax were to be divided by Seven Millions, it would amount to more than three Shillings to every Head. And thus as the Poor are the Caufe, without which the Rich could not pay this Tax, even the pooreft Subject is upon this Account worth three Shillings yearly to the Prince.

AGAIN; One would imagine the Confumption of feven Eighths of the whole People, fhould pay two Thirds of all the Cuftoms and Excifes. And if this Sum too fhould be divided by feven Millions, *viz.* the Number of poor People, it would amount to more than feven Shillings to every Head: And therefore with this and the former Sum every poor Subject, without Property, except of his Limbs or Labour, is worth at leaft ten Shillings yearly to the Sovereign. So much then the Queen lofes with every one of her old, and gains with every one of her new Subjects.

WHEN I was got into this Way of thinking, I prefently grew conceited of the Argument, and was juft preparing to write a Letter of Advice to a Member of Parliament,

liament, for opening the Freedom of our Towns and
Trades, for taking away all manner of Diſtinctions between the Natives and Foreigners, for repealing our
Laws of Pariſh Settlements, and removing every other
Obſtacle to the Increaſe of the People. But as ſoon as I
had recollected with what inimitable Eloquence my Fel-
low-Labourers had exaggerated the Miſchiefs of ſelling
the Birth right of *Britons* for a Shilling, of ſpoiling the
pure *Britiſh* Blood with Foreign Mixtures, of introduc-
ing a Confuſion of Languages and Religions, and of letting in Strangers to eat the Bread out of the Mouths of
our own People, I became ſo humble as to let my Project
fall to the Ground, and leave my Country to increaſe
by the ordinary Way of Generation.

AS I have always at Heart the Publick Good, ſo I
am ever contriving Schemes to promote it; and I think I
may without Vanity pretend to have contrived ſome as
wiſe as any of the Caſtle-builders. I had no ſooner given
up my former Project, but my Head was preſently full of
draining Fens and Marſhes, banking out the Sea, and join-
ing new Lands to my Country; for ſince it is thought
impracticable to increaſe the People to the Land, I fell
immediately to conſider how much would be gained to
the Prince by increaſing the Land to the People.

IF the ſame omnipotent Power, which made the World,
ſhould at this time raiſe out of the Ocean and join to
Great Britain an equal Extent of Land, with equal Buildings, Corn, Cattle and other Conveniences and Neceſ-
ſaries of Life, but no Men, Women, nor Children, I
ſhould hardly believe this would add either to the Riches
of the People, or Revenue of the Prince; for ſince the
preſent Buildings are ſufficient for all the Inhabitants, if
any of them ſhould forſake the old to inhabit the new Part
of the Iſland, the Increaſe of Houſe-Rent in this would
be attended with at leaſt an equal Decreaſe of it in the
other: Beſides, we have ſuch a Sufficiency of Corn and
Cattle, that we give Bounties to our Neighbours to take
what exceeds of the former off our Hands, and we will
not ſuffer any of the latter to be imported upon us by our
Fellow-Subjects; and for the remaining Product of the
Country 'tis already equal to all our Markets. But if all
theſe Things ſhould be doubled to the ſame Buyers, the

Owners muſt be glad with half their preſent Prices, the
Landlords with half their preſent Rents; and thus by ſo
great an Enlargement of the Country, the Rents in the
whole would not increaſe, nor the Taxes to the Publick.

ON the contrary, I ſhould believe they would be very
much diminiſhed; for as the Land is only valuable for its
Fruits, and theſe are all periſhable, and for the moſt part
muſt either be uſed within the Year, or periſh without
Uſe, the Owners will get rid of them at any rate, rather
than they ſhould waſte in their Poſſeſſion: So that it is
probable the annual Production of thoſe periſhable things,
even of the tenth Part of them, beyond all Poſſibility of
Uſe, will reduce one Half of their Value. It ſeems to be
for this Reaſon that our Neighbour Merchants who ingroſs
all the Species, and know how great a Quantity is equal
to the Demand, deſtroy all that exceeds it. It were natural then to think that the Annual Production of twice
as much as can be uſed, muſt reduce all to an Eighth
Part of their preſent Prices; and thus this extended Iſland
would not exceed one fourth Part of its preſent Value,
or pay more than one fourth Part of the preſent Tax.

IT is generally obſerved, That in Countries of the
greateſt Plenty there is the pooreſt Living; like the
Schoolmens Aſs in one of my Speculations, the People
almoſt ſtarve between two Meals. The Truth is, the
Poor, which are the Bulk of a Nation, work only that
they may live; and if with two Days Labour they can
get a wretched Subſiſtence, they will hardly be brought
to work the other four: But then with the Wages of
two Days they can neither pay ſuch Prices for their Pro-
viſions, nor ſuch Exciſes to the Government.

THAT Paradox therefore in old *Heſiod* πλέον ἥμισυ
παντός, or Half is more than the Whole, is very appli-
cable to the preſent Caſe; ſince nothing is more true in
political Arithmetick, than that the ſame People with half
a Country is more valuable than with the Whole. I begin
to think there was nothing abſurd in Sir *W. Petty*, when
he fancied if all the Highlands of *Scotland* and the whole
Kingdom of *Ireland* were ſunk in the Ocean, ſo that the
People were all ſaved and brought into the Lowlands of
Great Britain; nay, though they were to be reimburſt the
Value of their Eſtates by the Body of the People, yet
both

both the Sovereign and the Subjects in general would be enriched by the very Lofs.

IF the People only make the Riches, the Father of ten Children is a greater Benefactor to his Country, than he who has added to it 10000 Acres of Land and no People. It is certain *Lewis* has join'd vaft Tracts of Land to his Dominions: But if *Philarithmus* fays true, that he is not now Mafter of fo many Subjects as before; we may then account for his not being able to bring fuch mighty Armies into the Field, and for their being neither fo well fed, nor clothed, nor paid, as formerly. The Reafon is plain, *Lewis* muft needs have been impoverifhed not only by his Lofs of Subjects, but by his Acquifition of Lands.   T

Nº 201   *Saturday, October* 20.

Religentem effe oportet, Religiofum nefas.
            Incerti Autoris apud Aul. Gell.

A Man fhou'd be Religious, not Superftitious.

IT is of the laft Importance to feafon the Paffions of a Child with Devotion, which feldom dies in a Mind that has received an early Tincture of it. Though it may feem extinguifhed for a while by the Cares of the World, the Heats of Youth, or the Allurements of Vice, it generally breaks out and difcovers itfelf again as foon as Difcretion, Confideration, Age, or Misfortunes have brought the Man to himfelf. The Fire may be covered and overlaid, but cannot be intirely quenched and fmothered. A State of Temperance, Sobriety, and Juftice, without Devotion, is a cold, lifelefs, infipid Condition of Virtue; and is rather to be ftiled Philofophy than Religion. Devotion opens the Mind to great Conceptions, and fills it with more fublime Ideas than any that are to be met with in the moft exalted Science; and at the fame time warms and agitates the Soul more than fenfual Pleafure.

IT has been obferved by fome Writers, that Man is more diftinguifhed from the Animal World by Devotion than by Reafon, as feveral Brute Creatures difcover in their Actions fomething like a faint Glimmering of Reafon, though they betray in no fingle Circumftance of their Behaviour any Thing that bears the leaft Affinity to Devotion. It is certain, the Propenfity of the Mind to Religious Worfhip, the natural Tendency of the Soul to fly to fome fuperior Being for Succour in Dangers and Diftreffes, the Gratitude to an invifible Superintendent which arifes in us upon receiving any extraordinary and unexpected good Fortune, the Acts of Love and Admiration with which the Thoughts of Men are fo wonderfully tranfported in meditating upon the Divine Perfections, and the univerfal Concurrence of all the Nations under Heaven in the great Article of Adoration, plainly fhew that Devotion or Religious Worfhip muft be the Effect of Tradition from fome firft Founder of Mankind, or that it is conformable to the natural Light of Reafon, or that it proceeds from an Inftinct implanted in the Soul itfelf. For my part, I look upon all thefe to be the concurrent Caufes: but which ever of them fhall be affigned as the Principle of Divine Worfhip, it manifeftly points to a Supreme Being as the firft Author of it.

I may take fome other Opportunity of confidering thofe particular Forms and Methods of Devotion which are taught us by Chriftianity ; but fhall here obferve into what Errors even this Divine Principle may fometimes lead us, when it is not moderated by that right Reafon which was given us as the Guide of all our Actions.

THE two great Errors into which a miftaken Devotion may betray us, are Enthufiafm and Superftition.

THERE is not a more melancholy Object than a Man who has his Head turned with religious Enthufiafm. A Perfon that is crazed, tho' with Pride or Malice, is a Sight very mortifying to Human Nature; but when the Diftemper arifes from any indifcreet Fervours of Devotion, or too intenfe an Application of the Mind to its miftaken Duties, it deferves our Compaffion in a more particular Manner. We may however learn this Leffon from it, that fince Devotion itfelf (which one would be apt

apt to think could not be too warm) may diforder the Mind, unlefs its Heats are tempered with Caution and Prudence, we fhould be particularly careful to keep our Reafon as cool as poffible, and to guard ourfelves in all Parts of Life againft the Influence of Paffion, Imagination, and Conftitution.

DEVOTION, when it does not lie under the Check of Reafon, is very apt to degenerate into Enthufiafm. When the Mind finds herfelf very much inflamed with her Devotions, fhe is too much inclined to think they are not of her own kindling, but blown up by fomething Divine within her. If fhe indulges this Thought too far, and humours the growing Paffion, fhe at laft flings herfelf into imaginary Raptures and Ecftafies; and when once fhe fancies herfelf under the Influence of a Divine Impulfe, it is no Wonder if fhe flights human Ordinances, and refufes to comply with any eftablifhed Form of Religion, as thinking herfelf directed by a much fuperior Guide.

AS Enthufiafm is a kind of Excefs in Devotion, Superftition is the Excefs not only of Devotion, but of Religion in general, according to an old Heathen Saying, quoted by *Aulus Gellius, Religentem effe oportet, Religiofum nefas*; A Man fhould be Religious, not Superftitious: For as the Author tells us, *Nigidius* obferved upon this Paffage, that the *Latin* Words which terminate in *ofus* generally imply vicious Characters, and the having of any Quality to an Excefs.

AN Enthufiaft in Religion is like an obftinate Clown, a Superftitious Man like an infipid Courtier. Enthufiafm has fomething in it of Madnefs, Superftition of Folly. Moft of the Sects that fall fhort of the Church of *England* have in them ftrong Tinctures of Enthufiafm, as the *Roman* Catholick Religion is one huge over-grown Body of childifh and idle Superftitions.

THE *Roman* Catholick Church feems indeed irrecoverably loft in this Particular. If an abfurd Drefs or Behaviour be introduced in the World, it will foon be found out and difcarded: On the contrary, a Habit or Ceremony, tho' never fo ridiculous, which has taken Sanctuary in the Church, fticks in it for ever. A *Gothic* Bifhop perhaps, thought it proper to repeat fuch a Form in

fuch a

such particular Shoes or Slippers; another fancied it would be very decent if such a Part of publick Devotions were performed with a Mitre on his Head, and a Crosier in his Hand: To this a Brother *Vandal*, as wise as the others, adds an antick Dress, which he conceived would allude very aptly to such and such Mysteries, till by Degrees the whole Office has degenerated into an empty Show.

THEIR Successors see the Vanity and Inconvenience of the Ceremonies; but instead of reforming, perhaps add others, which they think more significant, and which take possession in the same manner, and are never to be driven out after they have been once admitted. I have seen the Pope officiate at St. *Peter*'s, where, for two Hours together, he was busied in putting on or off his different Accoutrements, according to the different Parts he was to act in them.

NOTHING is so glorious in the Eyes of Mankind, and ornamental to human Nature, setting aside the infinite Advantages which arise from it, as a strong, steady, masculine Piety; but Enthusiasm and Superstition are the Weaknesses of human Reason, that expose us to the Scorn and Derision of Infidels, and sink us even below the Beasts that perish.

IDOLATRY may be looked upon as another Error arising from mistaken Devotion; but because Reflexions on that Subject would be of no use to an *English* Reader, I shall not enlarge upon it. L

Sæpe decem vitiis instructior odit & horret.
                              Hor. Ep. 18. l. 1. v. 25.

Many, tho' faultier much Themselves, pretend
Their less offending Neighbours Faults to mend.

THE other Day as I passed along the Street, I saw
a sturdy Prentice-Boy disputing with an Hackney-
Coachman; and in an Instant, upon some Word
of Provocation, throw off his Hat and Periwig, clench
his Fist, and strike the Fellow a Slap on the Face; at
the same time calling him Rascal, and telling him he was
a Gentleman's Son. The young Gentleman was, it seems,
bound to a Blacksmith; and the Debate arose about Pay-
ment for some Work done about a Coach, near which
they fought. His Master, during the Combat, was full of
his Boy's Praises; and as he called to him to play with
his Hand and Foot, and throw in his Head, he made all
us who stood round him of his Party, by declaring the
Boy had very good Friends, and he could trust him with
untold Gold. As I am generally in the Theory of Mankind, I could not but make my Reflexions upon the sudden Popularity which was raised about the Lad; and perhaps with my Friend *Tacitus*, fell into Observations upon
it, which were too great for the Occasion; or ascribed
this general Favour to Causes which had nothing to do
towards it. But the young Blacksmith's being a Gentleman was, methought, what created him Good-will from
his present Equality with the Mob about him: Add to
this, that he was not so much a Gentleman, as not, at
the same time that he called himself such, to use as rough
Methods for his Defence as his Antagonist. The Advantage of his having good Friends, as his Master expressed it, was not lazily urged; but he shewed himself
superior to the Coachman in the personal Qualities of
Courage and Activity, to confirm that of his being well
allied, before his Birth was of any Service to him.

                                                    IF

IF one might moralize from this filly Story, a Man would fay, that whatever Advantages of Fortune, Birth, or any other Good, People poffefs above the reft of the World, they fhould fhew collateral Eminences befides thofe Diftinctions; or thofe Diftinctions will avail only to keep up common Decencies and Ceremonies, and not to preferve a real Place of Favour or Efteem in the Opinion and common Senfe of their Fellow-Creatures.

THE Folly of People's Procedure, in imagining that nothing more is neceffary than Property and fuperior Circumftances to fupport them in Diftinction, appears in no way fo much as in the Domeftick Part of Life. It is ordinary to feed their Humours into unnatural Excrefcences, if I may fo fpeak, and make their whole Being a wayward and uneafy Condition, for want of the obvious Reflexion that all Parts of human Life is a Commerce. It is not only paying Wages, and giving Commands, that conftitutes a Mafter of a Family; but Prudence, equal Behaviour, with Readinefs to protect and cherifh them, is what intitles a Man to that Character in their very Hearts and Sentiments. It is pleafant enough to obferve, that Men expect from their Dependents, from their fole Motive of Fear, all the good Effects which a liberal Education, and affluent Fortune, and every other Advantage, cannot produce in themfelves. A Man will have his Servant juft, diligent, fober and chafte, for no other Reafons but the Terror of lofing his Mafter's Favour; when all the Laws Divine and Human cannot keep him whom he ferves within Bounds, with relation to any one of thofe Virtues. But both in great and ordinary Affairs, all Superiority, which is not founded on Merit and Virtue, is fupported only by Artifice and Stratagem. Thus you fee Flatterers are the Agents in Families of Humourifts, and thofe who govern themfelves by any Thing but Reafon. Make-Bates, diftant Relations, poor Kinfmen, and indigent Followers, are the Fry which fupport the Oeconomy of an humourfom rich Man. He is eternally whifpered with Intelligence of who are true or falfe to him in Matters of no Confequence, and he maintains twenty Friends to defend him againft the Infinuations of one who would perhaps cheat him of an old Coat.

I

I shall not enter into farther Speculation upon this Subject at present, but think the following Letters and Petition are made up of proper Sentiments on this Occasion.

Mr. SPECTATOR,

'I Am a Servant to an old Lady who is governed by
' one she calls her Friend; who is so familiar an one,
' that she takes upon her to advise her without being
' called to it, and makes her uneasy with all about her.
' Pray, Sir, be pleased to give us some Remarks upon
' voluntary Counsellors; and let these People know
' that to give any Body Advice, is to say to that Person,
' I am your Betters. Pray, Sir, as near as you can,
' describe that eternal Flirt and Disturber of Families,
' Mrs. *Taperty*, who is always visiting, and putting People
' in a Way, as they call it. If you can make her stay
' at home one Evening, you will be a general Bene-
' factor to all the Ladies Women in Town, and particu-
' larly to

Your loving Friend,

Susan Civil.

Mr. SPECTATOR,

'I Am a Footman, and live with one of those Men,
' each of whom is said to be one of the best humoured
' Men in the World, but that he is passionate. Pray be
' pleased to inform them, that he who is passionate, and
' takes no care to command his Hastiness, does more
' Injury to his Friends and Servants in one half Hour,
' than whole Years can atone for. This Master of mine,
' who is the best Man alive in common Fame, dis-
' obliges some Body every Day he lives; and strikes me
' for the next thing I do, because he is out of humour at
' it. If these Gentlemen knew that they do all the Mis-
' chief that is ever done in Conversation, they would re-
' form; and I who have been a Spectator of Gentlemen
' at Dinner for many Years, have seen that Indiscretion
' does ten times more Mischief than Ill-nature. But you
' will represent this better than

Your abused humble Servant,

Thomas Smoky.

To

To the SPECTATOR,

The humble Petition of *John Steward, Robert Butler, Harry Cook,* and *Abigail Chambers,* in Behalf of themselves and their Relations, belonging to and difperfed in the feveral Services of moft of the great Families within the Cities of *London* and *Weſtminſter.*

Sheweth,.

'THAT in many of the Families in which your
' Petitioners live and are employed, the feveral
' Heads of them are wholly unacquainted with what is
' Bufinefs, and are very little Judges when they are well
' or ill ufed by us your faid Petitioners.
' THAT for want of fuch Skill in their own Affairs,
' and by Indulgence of their own Lazinefs and Pride,
' they continually keep about them certain mifchievous
' Animals called Spies.
' THAT whenever a Spy is entertained, the Peace
' of that Houfe is from that Moment banifhed.
' THAT Spies never give an Account of good Ser-
' vices, but reprefent our Mirth and Freedom by the
' Words, Wantonnefs and Diforder.
' THAT in all Families where there are Spies, there
' is a general Jealoufy and Mifunderftanding.
' THAT the Mafters and Miftreffes of fuch Houfes
' live in continual Sufpicion of their ingenuous and true
' Servants, and are given up to the Management of thofe
' who are falfe and perfidious.
' THAT fuch Mafters and Miftreffes who entertain
' Spies, are no longer more than Cyphers in their own
' Families; and that we your Petitioners are with great
' Difdain obliged to pay all our Refpect, and expect all
' our Maintenance from fuch Spies.

' YOUR Petitioners therefore moft humbly Pray,
' that you would reprefent the Premifes to all Per-
' fons of Condition; and your Petitioners, as in
' Duty bound, fhall for ever Pray, *&c.* T

Tuefday,

Phœbe pater, ſi das hujus mihi nominis uſum,
Nec falſâ Clymene culpam ſub imagine celat ;
Pignora da, Genitor————   Ovid. Met. l. 2. v. 36.

Illuſtrious Parent ! ſince you don't deſpiſe
A Parent's Name, ſome certain Token give,
That I may Clymene's proud Boaſt believe,
Nor longer under falſe Reproaches grieve. ADDISON.

THERE is a looſe Tribe of Men whom I have not
yet taken notice of, that ramble into all the Corners of this great City, in order to ſeduce ſuch unfortunate Females as fall into their Walks. Theſe abandoned Profligates raiſe up Iſſue in every Quarter of the
Town, and very often, for a valuable Conſideration, father it upon the Church-warden. By this means there are
ſeveral married Men who have a little Family in moſt of
the Pariſhes of *London* and *Weſtminſter*, and ſeveral Ba-
chelors who are undone by a Charge of Children.

WHEN a Man once gives himſelf this Liberty of
preying at large, and living upon the Common, he finds
ſo much Game in a populous City, that it is ſurpriſing to
conſider the Numbers which he ſometimes propagates.
We ſee many a young Fellow who is ſcarce of Age, that
could lay his Claim to the *Jus Trium Liberorum*, or the
Privileges, which were granted by the *Roman* Laws to all
ſuch as were Fathers of three Children : Nay, I have
heard a Rake, who was not quite five and twenty, declare himſelf the Father of a ſeventh Son, and very pru-
dently determine to breed him up a Phyſician. In ſhort,
the Town is full of theſe young Patriarchs, not to mention ſeveral batter'd Beaus, who, like heedleſs Spend-
thrifts that ſquander away their Eſtates before they are
Maſters of them, have raiſed up their whole Stock of
Children before Marriage.

I muſt not here omit the particular Whim of an Impudent Libertine, that had a little Smattering of Heraldry ;
and

and observing how the Genealogies of great Families were often drawn up in the Shape of Trees, had taken a Fancy to difpofe of his own illegitimate Iffue in a Figure of the fame kind.

> ———*Nec longum tempus & ingens*
> *Exiit ad cœlum ramis felicibus arbos,*
> *Miraturque novas frondes, & non fua poma.*
>   Virg. Georg. 2. v. 80.

And in fhort Space the laden Boughs arife,
With happy Fruit advancing to the Skies :
The Mother Plant admires the Leaves unknown
Of alien Trees, and Apples not her own.   DRYDEN.

THE Trunk of the Tree was mark'd with his own Name, *Will Maple.* Out of the Side of it grew a large barren Branch, infcribed *Mary Maple,* the Name of his unhappy Wife. The Head was adorned with five huge Boughs. On the Bottom of the firft was written in Capital Characters *Kate Cole,* who branched out into three Sprigs, *viz. William, Richard,* and *Rebecca, Sal Twiford* gave Birth to another Bough that fhot up into *Sarah, Tom, Will,* and *Frank.* The third Arm of the Tree had only a fingle Infant on it, with a Space left for a fecond, the Parent from whom it fprung being near her Time when the Author took this ingenious Device into his Head. The two other great Boughs were very plentifully loaden with Fruit of the fame kind ; befides which there were many ornamental Branches that did not bear. In fhort, a more flourifhing Tree never came out of the Herald's Office.

WHAT makes this Generation of Vermin fo very prolifick, is the indefatigable Diligence with which they apply themfelves to their Bufinefs. A Man does not undergo more Watchings and Fatigues in a Campaign, than in the Courfe of a vicious Amour. As it is faid of fome Men, that they make their Bufinefs their Pleafure, thefe Sons of Darknefs may be faid to make their Pleafure their Bufinefs. They might conquer their corrupt Inclinations with half the pains they are at in gratifying them.

NOR is the Invention of thefe Men lefs to be admired than their Induftry and Vigilance. There is a Fragment of *Apollodorus* the Comic Poet (who was Contemporary

with

with *Menander*) which is full of Humour, as follows: *Thou mayest shut up thy Doors*, says he, *with Bars and Bolts: It will be impossible for the Blacksmith to make them so fast, but a Cat and a Whoremaster will find a Way through them.* In a word, there is no Head so full of Stratagems as that of a libidinous Man.

WERE I to propose a Punishment for this infamous Race of Propagators, it should be to send them, after the second or third Offence, into our *American* Colonies, in order to people those Parts of her Majesty's Dominions where there is a want of Inhabitants, and in the Phrase of *Diogenes*, to *plant Men*. Some Countries punish this Crime with Death; but I think such a Banishment would be sufficient, and might turn this generative Faculty to the Advantage of the Publick.

IN the mean time, till these Gentlemen may be thus disposed of, I would earnestly exhort them to take care of those unfortunate Creatures whom they have brought into the World by these indirect Methods, and to give their spurious Children such an Education as may render them more virtuous than their Parents. This is the best Atonement they can make for their own Crimes, and indeed the only Method that is left them to repair their past Miscarriages.

I would likewise desire them to consider, whether they are not bound in common Humanity, as well as by all the Obligations of Religion and Nature, to make some Provision for those whom they have not only given life to, but entail'd upon them, tho' very unreasonably, a Degree of Shame and Disgrace. And here I cannot but take notice of those depraved Notions which prevail among us, and which must have taken rise from our natural Inclination to favour a Vice to which we are so very prone, namely, that *Bastardy* and *Cuckoldom* should be look'd upon as Reproaches, and that the Ignominy, which is only due to Lewdness and Falshood, should fall in so unreasonable a manner upon the Persons who are innocent.

I have been insensibly drawn into this Discourse by the following Letter, which is drawn up with such a Spirit of Sincerity, that I question not but the Writer of it has represented his Case in a true and genuine Light.

S I R,

S I R,

' I Am one of thofe People who by the General Opi-
' nion of the World are counted both infamous and
' unhappy.

' MY Father is a very eminent Man in this King-
' dom, and one who bears confiderable Offices in it.
' I am his Son, but my Misfortune is, That I dare
' not call him Father, nor he without Shame own
' me as his Iffue, I being illegitimate, and therefore
' deprived of that endearing Tendernefs and unpa-
' rallel'd Satisfaction which a good Man finds in the
' Love and Converfation of a Parent. Neither have I
' the Opportunities to render him the Duties of a Son,
' he having always carried himfelf at fo vaft a Diftance,
' and with fuch Superiority towards me, That by long
' Ufe I have contracted a Timoroufnefs when before
' him, which hinders me from declaring my own Ne-
' ceffities, and giving him to underftand the Inconve-
' niences I undergo.

' IT is my Misfortune to have been neither bred a
' Scholar, a Soldier, nor to any kind of Bufinefs, which
' renders me intirely uncapable of making Provifion for
' myfelf without his Affiftance; and this creates a con-
' tinual Uneafinefs in my Mind, fearing I fhall in time
' want Bread; my Father, if I may fo call him, giving
' me but very faint Affurances of doing any thing for me.

' I have hitherto lived fomewhat like a Gentleman,
' and it would be very hard for me to labour for my
' Living. I am in continual Anxiety for my future For-
' tune, and under a great Unhappinefs in lofing the
' fweet Converfation and friendly Advice of my Pa-
' rents; fo that I cannot look upon myfelf otherwife
' than as a Monfter, ftrangely fprung up in Nature,
' which every one is afhamed to own.

' I am thought to be a Man of fome natural Parts,
' and by the continual Reading what you have offered
' the World, become an Admirer thereof, which has
' drawn me to make this Confeffion; at the fame time
' hoping, if any thing herein fhall touch you with a
' Senfe of Pity, you would then allow me the Favour
' of your Opinion thereupon; as alfo what Part I, be-
' ing unlawfully born, may claim of the Man's Affection
                                        ' who

'who begot me; and how far in your Opinion I am to
'be thought his Son, or he acknowledged as my Fa-
'ther. Your Sentiments and Advice herein will be a
'great Consolation and Satisfaction to,

S I R,

Your Admirer and

Humble Servant,

W. B.

C

━━━━━━━━━━━━━━━━━━━━━━━━━━━━━━━

Nº 204 *Wednesday, October* 24.

Urit grata protervitas,
 Et vultus nimium lubricus aspici.

Hor. Od. 19. l. 1. v. 7.

With winning Coyness she, my Soul disarms:
 Her Face darts forth a thousand Rays;
 My Eye-balls swim, and I grow giddy while I gaze.

CONGREVE.

I Am not at all displeased that I am become the Courier of Love, and that the Distressed in that Passion convey their Complaints to each other by my Means. The following Letters have lately come to my hands, and shall have their Place with great Willingness. As to the Reader's Entertainment, he will, I hope, forgive the inserting such Particulars as to him may perhaps seem frivolous, but are to the Persons who wrote them of the highest Consequence. I shall not trouble you with the Prefaces, Compliments, and Apologies made to me before each Epistle when it was desired to be inserted; but in general they tell me, that the Persons to whom they are addressed have Intimations, by Phrases and Allusions in them, from whence they came.

To the Sothades.

THE Word, by which I address you, gives you, who understand *Portuguese,* a lively Image of the tender Regard I have for you. The SPECTATOR's

' late

' late Letter from *Statira* gave me the Hint to ufe
' the fame Method of explaining myfelf to you. I
' am not affronted at the Defign your late Behaviour
' difcovered you had in your Addreffes to me; but I
' impute it to the Degeneracy of the Age, rather than
' your particular Fault. As I aim at nothing more than
' being yours, I am willing to be a Stranger to your
' Name, your Fortune, or any Figure which your Wife
' might expect to make in the World, provided my Com-
' merce with you is not to be a guilty one. I refign gay
' Drefs, the Pleafures of Vifits, Equipage, Plays, Balls, and
' Operas, for that one Satisfaction of having you for ever
' mine. I am willing you fhall induftrioufly conceal the
' only Caufe of Triumph which I can know in this
' Life. I wifh only to have it my Duty, as well as my
' Inclination, to ftudy your Happinefs. If this has not
' the Effect this Letter feems to aim at, you are to un-
' derftand that I had a mind to be rid of you, and took
' the readieft Way to pall you with an Offer of what you
' would never defift purfuing while you received ill Ufage.
' Be a true Man; be my Slave while you doubt me, and
' neglect me when you think I love you. I defy you to
' find out what is your prefent Circumftance with me;
' but I know while I can keep this Sufpence,

I am your admired

Belinda.

Madam,

' IT is a ftrange State of Mind a Man is in, when the
' very Imperfections of a Woman he loves turn into
' Excellencies and Advantages. I do affure you, I am
' very much afraid of venturing upon you. I now like
' you in fpite of my Reafon, and think it an ill Circum-
' ftance to owe one's Happinefs to nothing but Infatua-
' tion. I can fee you ogle all the young Fellows who
' look at you, and obferve your Eye wander after new
' Conquefts every Moment you are in a publick Place;
' and yet there is fuch a Beauty in all your Looks and
' Geftures, that I cannot but admire you in the very Act of
' endeavouring to gain the Hearts of others. My Condi-
' tion is the fame with that of the Lover in the *Way of*
' *the World.* I have ftudied your Faults fo long, that
' they

‘ they are become as familiar to me, and I like them as
‘ well as I do my own.   Look to it, Madam; and con-
‘ fider whether you think this gay Behaviour will appear
‘ to me as amiable when an Hufband, as it does now to me
‘ a Lover.   Things are fo far advanced, that we muſt
‘ proceed; and I hope you will lay it to heart, that it
‘ will be becoming in me to appear ſtill your Lover, but
‘ not in you to be ſtill my Miſtreſs. Gaiety in the Matri-
‘ monial Life is graceful in one Sex, but exceptionable in
‘ the other.   As you improve theſe little Hints, you will
‘ aſcertain the Happineſs or Uneaſineſs of,

Madam,

Your moſt obedient,

Moſt humble Servant,

T. D.

S I R,

‘ WHEN I ſat at the Window, and you at the
‘   other End of the Room by my Couſin, I ſaw
‘ you catch me looking at you. Since you have the
‘ Secret at laſt, which I am ſure you ſhould never have
‘ known but by Inadvertency, what my Eyes ſaid was
‘ true. But it is too ſoon to confirm it with my Hand,
‘ therefore ſhall not ſubſcribe my Name.

S I R,

‘ THERE were other Gentlemen nearer, and I
‘   know no Neceſſity you were under to take up
‘ that flippant Creature’s Fan laſt Night; but you ſhall
‘ never touch a Stick of mine more, that’s pos.

Phillis.

To Colonel R———s *in* Spain.

‘ BEFORE this can reach the beſt of Huſbands and
‘   the fondeſt Lover, thoſe tender Names will be no
‘ more of Concern to me. The Indiſpoſition in which you,
‘ to obey the Dictates of your Honour and Duty, left me,
‘ has increaſed upon me; and I am acquainted by my
‘ Phyſicians I cannot live a Week longer. At this time
‘ my Spirits fail me; and it is the ardent Love I
‘ have for you that carries me beyond my Strength, and
‘ enables me to tell you, The moſt painful Thing in the

‘ Proſpect

'Prospect of Death, is, that I must part with you. But let
'it be a Comfort to you, that I have no Guilt hangs
'upon me, no unrepented Folly that retards me; but I
'pass away my last Hours in Reflexion upon the Happi-
'ness we have lived in together, and in Sorrow that it is
'so soon to have an End. This is a Frailty which I hope
'is so far from criminal, that methinks there is a kind of
'Piety in being so unwilling to be separated from a State
'which is the Institution of Heaven, and in which we
'have lived according to its Laws. As we know no more
'of the next Life, but that it will be an happy one to the
'Good, and miserable to the Wicked, why may we not
'please ourselves at least, to alleviate the Difficulty of
'resigning this Being, in imagining that we shall have a
'Sense of what passes below, and may possibly be em-
'ployed in guiding the Steps of those with whom we walk-
'ed with Innocence when mortal? Why may not I hope
'to go on in my usual Work, and, tho' unknown to you,
'be assistant in all the Conflicts of your Mind? Give me
'leave to say to you, O best of Men, that I cannot
'figure to myself a greater Happiness than in such an
'Employment: To be present at all the Adventures to
'which human Life is exposed, to administer Slumber
'to thy Eyelids in the Agonies of a Fever, to cover thy
'beloved Face in the Day of Battle, to go with thee a
'Guardian Angel incapable of Wound or Pain, where
'I have longed to attend thee when a weak, a fearful
'Woman: These, my Dear, are the Thoughts with
'which I warm my poor languid Heart; but indeed I
'am not capable under my present Weakness of bearing
'the strong Agonies of Mind I fall into, when I form
'to myself the Grief you will be in upon your first hear-
'ing of my Departure. I will not dwell upon this, be-
'cause your kind and generous Heart will be but the
'more afflicted, the more the Person for whom you la-
'ment offers you Consolation. My last Breath will, if
'I am myself, expire in a Prayer for you. I shall never
'see thy Face again. Farewel for ever.   T.

Thursday,

Nº 205   *Thurſday, October 25.*

Decipimur ſpecie recti ———   Hor. Ars Poet. v. 25.
Deluded by a ſeeming Excellence.   ROSCOMMON.

WHEN I meet with any vicious Character that is not generally known, in order to prevent its doing Miſchief, I draw it at length, and ſet it up as a Scarecrow; by which means I do not only make an Example of the Perſon to whom it belongs, but give Warning to all Her Majeſty's Subjects, that they may not ſuffer by it. Thus, to change the Alluſion, I have marked out ſeveral of the Shoals and Quickſands of Life, and am continually employed in diſcovering thoſe which are ſtill concealed, in order to keep the Ignorant and Unwary from running upon them. It is with this Intention that I publiſh the following Letter, which brings to light ſome Secrets of this Nature.

Mr. SPECTATOR,

'THERE are none of your Speculations which I
' read over with greater Delight, than thoſe which
' are deſigned for the Improvement of our Sex: You
' have endeavoured to correct our unreaſonable Fears
' and Superſtitions, in your Seventh and Twelfth Paper;
' our Fancy for Equipage, in your Fifteenth; our Love
' of Puppet-Shows, in your Thirty-Firſt; our Notions of
' Beauty, in your Thirty-Third; our Inclination for
' Romances, in your Thirty-Seventh; our Paſſion for
' *French* Fopperies, in your Forty-Fifth; our Manhood
' and Party-zeal, in your Fifty-Seventh; our Abuſe of
' Dancing, in your Sixty-Sixth and Sixty-Seventh; our
' Levity, in your Hundred and Twenty Eighth; our
' Love of Coxcombs in your Hundred and Fifty-Fourth,
' and Hundred and Fifty-Seventh; our Tyranny over
' the Henpeckt, in your Hundred and Seventy-Sixth.
' You have deſcribed the *Pict* in your Forty-firſt; the
' Idol,

'Idol, in your Seventy-Third; the Demurrer, in your
'Eighty-Ninth; the Salamander, in your Hundred and
'Ninety-Eighth. You have likewise taken to pieces our
'Drefs, and reprefented to us the Extravagances we are
'often guilty of in that Particular. You have fallen upon
'our Patches, in your Fiftieth and Eighty-Firft; our
'Commodes, in your Ninety-Eighth; our Fans in your
'Hundred and Second; our Riding Habits in your Hun-
'dred and Fourth; our Hoop-petticoats, in your Hun-
'dred and Twenty-Seventh; befides a great many little
'Blemifhes which you have touched upon in your feve-
'ral other Papers, and in thofe many Letters that are
'fcattered up and down your Works. At the fame
'Time we muft own, that the Compliments you pay
'our Sex are innumerable, and that thofe very Faults
'which you reprefent in us, are neither black in them-
'felves, nor as you own, univerfal among us. But,
'Sir, it is plain that thefe your Difcourfes are calculated
'for none but the fafhionable Part of Womankind, and
'for the Ufe of thofe who are rather indifcreet than
'vicious. But, Sir, there is a Sort of Proftitutes in the
'lower Part of our Sex, who are a Scandal to us, and
'very well deferve to fall under your Cenfure. I know
'it would debafe your Paper too much to enter into the
'Behaviour of thefe Female Libertines; but as your
'Remarks on fome Part of it would be a doing of Juf-
'tice to feveral Women of Virtue and Honour, whofe
'Reputations fuffer by it, I hope you will not think it
'improper to give the Publick fome Accounts of this
'Nature. You muft know, Sir, I am provoked to write
'you this Letter by the Behaviour of an infamous Wo-
'man, who having paffed her Youth in a moft fhame-
'lefs State of Proftitution, is now one of thofe who
'gain their Livelihood by feducing others, that are
'younger than themfelves, and by eftablifhing a crimi-
'nal Commerce between the two Sexes. Among feve-
'ral of her Artifices to get Money, fhe frequently per-
'fuades a vain young Fellow, that fuch a Woman of
'Quality, or fuch a celebrated Toaft, entertains a fe-
'cret Paffion for him, and wants nothing but an Oppor-
'tunity of revealing it: Nay, fhe has gone fo far as
'to write Letters in the Name of a Woman of Figure,

'to

'to borrow Money of one of thefe foolifh *Roderigo*'s,
' which fhe has afterwards appropriated to her own Ufe.
' In the mean time, the Perfon who has lent the Money,
' has thought a Lady under Obligations to him, who
' fcarce knew his Name; and wondered at her Ingrati-
' tude when he has been with her, that fhe has not owned
' the Favour, though at the fame time he was too much
' a Man of Honour to put her in mind of it.

' WHEN this abandoned Baggage meets with a Man
' who has Vanity enough to give Credit to Relations of
' this nature, fhe turns him to very good Account, by
' repeating Praifes that were never uttered, and delivering
' Meffages that were never fent. As the Houfe of this
' fhamelefs Creature is frequented by feveral Foreigners,
' I have heard of another Artifice, out of which fhe often
' raifes Money. The Foreigner fighs after fome *Britifh*
' Beauty, whom he only knows by Fame: Upon which
' fhe promifes, if he can be fecret, to procure him a
' Meeting. The Stranger, ravifhed at his good For-
' tune, gives her a Prefent, and in a little time is in-
' troduced to fome imaginary Title; for you muft know
' that this cunning Purveyor has her Reprefentatives
' upon this Occafion, of fome of the fineft Ladies in the
' Kingdom. By this Means, as I am informed, it is
' ufual enough to meet with a *German* Count in foreign
' Countries, that fhall make his Boafts of Favours he has
' received from Women of the higheft Ranks, and the
' moft unblemifhed Characters. Now, Sir, what Safety
' is there for a Woman's Reputation, when a Lady may
' be thus proftituted as it were by Proxy, and be reputed
' an unchafte Woman; as the Hero in the ninth Book
' of *Dryden*'s Virgil is looked upon as a Coward, becaufe
' the Phantom which appeared in his Likenefs ran away
' from *Turnus?* You may depend upon what I relate to
' you to be Matter of Fact, and the Practice of more
' than one of thefe female Pandars. If you print this
' Letter, I may give you fome farther Accounts of this
' vicious Race of Women.

Your humble Servant,

BELVIDERA

I fhall

I fhall add two other Letters on different Subjects to fill up my Paper.

Mr. SPECTATOR,

'I Am a Country Clergyman, and hope you will lend
' me your Affiftance in ridiculing fome little Inde-
' cencies which cannot fo properly be expofed from the
' Pulpit.

' A Widow Lady, who ftraggled this Summer from
' *London* into my Parifh for the Benefit of the Air, as fhe
' fays, appears every *Sunday* at Church with many
' fafhionable Extravagancies, to the great Aftonifhment
' of my Congregation.

'.BUT what gives us the moft Offence is her thea-
' trical Manner of Singing the Pfalms. She introduces
' above fifty *Italian* Airs into the hundredth Pfalm, and
' whilft we begin *All People* in the old folemn Tune of
' our Forefathers, fhe in a quite different Key runs Di-
' vifions on the Vowels, and adorns them with the Graces
' of *Nicolini;* if fhe meets with Eke or Aye, which are
' frequent in the Metre of *Hopkins* and *Sternhold,* we are
' certain to hear her quavering them half a Minute after
' us to fome fprightly Airs of the Opera.

' I am very far from being an Enemy to Church Mu-
' fick; but fear this Abufe of it may make my *Parifh*
' ridiculous, who already look on the Singing Pfalms as
' an Entertainment, and not Part of their Devotion:
' Befides, I am apprehenfive that the Infection may fpread,
' for Squire *Squeekum,* who by his Voice feems (if I may
' ufe the Expreffion) to be cut out for an *Italian* Singer,
' was laft *Sunday* practifing the fame Airs.

' I know the Lady's Principles, and that fhe will plead
' the Toleration, which (as fhe fancies) allows her Non-
' Conformity in this Particular; but I beg you to acquaint
' her, That Singing the Pfalms in a different Tune from
' the reft of the Congregation, is a Sort of Schifm not
' tolerated by that Act.

I am, S I R,

Your very humble Servant,

R. S.

Mr. SPEC-

Mr. SPECTATOR,

'IN your Paper upon Temperance, you prescribe to
' us a Rule of drinking, out of Sir *William Temple*, in
' the following Words; *The first Glass for myself, the
' second for my Friends, the third for Good-humour, and
' the fourth for mine Enemies.* Now, Sir, you must
' know, that I have read this your *Spectator*, in a Club
' whereof I am a member; when our President told us,
' there was certainly an Error in the Print, and that the
' Word *Glass* should be *Bottle*; and therefore has ordered
' me to inform you of this Mistake, and to desire you
' to publish the following *Errata*: In the Paper of *Sa-
' turday, Octob.* 13, Col. 3, Line 11, for *Glass* read
' *Bottle*.

L   *Yours,* Robin Good-fellow.

Nᵒ 206   *Friday, October 26.*

*Quanto quisque sibi plura negaverit,
A Diis plura feret*————   Hor. Od. 16. l. 3. v. 21.

*They that do much Themselves deny,
Receive more Blessings from the Sky.*   CREECH.

THERE is a Call upon Mankind to value and esteem
those who set a moderate Price upon their own
Merit; and Self-denial is frequently attended with
unexpected Blessings, which in the End abundantly recom-
pense such Losses as the Modest seem to suffer in the ordinary Occurrences of Life. The Curious tell us, a De-
termination in our Favour or to our Disadvantage is made
upon our first Appearance, even before they know any
thing of our Characters, but from the Intimations Men
gather from our Aspect. A Man, they say, wears the
Picture of his Mind in his Countenance; and one
Man's Eyes are Spectacles to his who looks at him to
read his Heart. But tho' that Way of raising an Opinion
of those we behold in Publick is very fallacious, certain it
is, that those, who by their Words and Actions take as
much upon themselves, as they can but barely demand in
                    G 2   the

the ſtrict Scrutiny of their Deſerts, will find their Account
leſſen every Day. A modeſt Man preſerves his Character,
as a frugal Man does his Fortune; if either of them live
to the Height of either, one will find Loſſes, the other
Errors, which he has not Stock by him to make up. It
were therefore a juſt Rule, to keep your Deſires, your
Words and Actions, within the Regard you obſerve your
Friends have for you; and never, if it were in a Man's
Power, to take as much as he poſſibly might either in
Preferment or Reputation. My Walks have lately been
among the mercantile Part of the World; and one gets
Phraſes naturally from thoſe with whom one converſes:
I ſay then, he that in his Air, his Treatment of others,
or an habitual Arrogance to himſelf, gives himſelf Credit
for the leaſt Article of more Wit, Wiſdom, Goodneſs, or
Valour than he can poſſibly produce if he is called upon,
will find the World break in upon him, and conſider him
as one who has cheated them of all the Eſteem they had
before allowed him. This brings a Commiſſion of Bank-
ruptcy upon him; and he that might have gone on to his
Life's End in a proſperous Way, by aiming at more than
he ſhould, is no longer Proprietor of what he really had
before, but his Pretenſions fare as all Things do which
are torn inſtead of being divided.

THERE is no one living would deny *Cinna* the Applauſe of an agreeable and facetious Wit; or could poſſibly
pretend that there is not ſomething inimitably unforced
and diverting in his Manner of delivering all his Sentiments in his Converſation, if he were able to conceal the
ſtrong Deſire of Applauſe which he betrays in every Syl-
lable he utters. But they who converſe with him, ſee that
all the Civilities they could do to him, or the kind Things
they could ſay to him, would fall ſhort of what he expects; and therefore inſtead of ſhewing him the Eſteem
they have for his Merit, their Reflexions turn only upon
that they obſerve he has of it himſelf.

IF you go among the Women, and behold *Gloriana*
trip into a Room with that theatrical Oſtentation of her
Charms, *Mirtilla* with that ſoft Regularity in her Motion,
Chloe with ſuch an indifferent Familiarity, *Corinna* with
ſuch a fond Approach, and *Roxana* with ſuch a Demand of
Reſpect in the great Gravity of her Entrance; you find all
the

the Sex, who underſtand themſelves and act naturally, wait only for their Abſence, to tell you that all theſe Ladies would impoſe themſelves upon you; and each of them carry in their Behaviour a Conſciouſneſs of ſo much more than they ſhould pretend to, that they loſe what would otherwiſe be given them.

I remember the laſt time I ſaw *Macbeth*, I was wonderfully taken with the Skill of the Poet, in making the Murderer form Fears to himſelf from the Moderation of the Prince whoſe Life he was going to take away. He ſays of the King, *He bore his Faculties ſo meekly*; and juſtly inferred from thence, That all divine and human Power would join to avenge his Death, who had made ſuch an abſtinent Uſe of Dominion. All that is in a Man's Power to do to advance his own Pomp and Glory, and forbears, is ſo much laid up againſt the Day of Diſtreſs; and Pity will always be his Portion in Adverſity, who acted with Gentleneſs in Proſperity.

THE great Officer who foregoes the Advantages he might take to himſelf, and renounces all prudential Regards to his own Perſon in Danger, has ſo far the Merit of a Volunteer; and all his Honours and Glories are unenvied, for ſharing the common Fate with the ſame Fran12neſs as they do who have no ſuch endearing Circumſtances to part with. But if there were no ſuch Conſiderations as the good Effect which Self-denial has upon the Senſe of other Men towards us, it is of all Qualities the moſt deſirable for the agreeable Diſpoſition in which it places our own Minds. I cannot tell what better to ſay of it, than that it is the very Contrary of Ambition; and that Modeſty allays all thoſe Paſſions and Inquietudes to which that Vice expoſes us. He that is moderate in his Wiſhes from Reaſon and Choice, and not reſigned from Sourneſs, Diſtaſte, or Diſappointment, doubles all the Pleaſures of his Life. The Air, the Seaſon, a Sun-ſhiny Day, or a fair Proſpect, are Inſtances of Happineſs, and that which he enjoys in common with all the World, (by his Exemption from the Inchantments by which all the World are betwitched) are to him uncommon Benefits and new Acquiſitions. Health is not eaten up with Care, nor Pleaſure interrupted by Envy. It is not to him of any Conſequence what this Man is famed for, or for what the other is preferred.

He

He knows there is in ſuch a Place an uninterrupted Walk; he can meet in ſuch a Company an agreeable Converſation: He has no Emulation, he is no Man's Rival, but every Man's Well-wiſher; can look at a proſperous Man, with a Pleaſure in reflecting that he hopes he is as happy as himſelf; and has his Mind and his Fortune (as far as Prudence will allow) open to the Unhappy and to the Stranger.

LUCCEIUS has Learning, Wit, Humour, Eloquence, but no ambitious Proſpects to purſue with theſe Advantages; therefore to the ordinary World he is perhaps thought to want Spirit, but known among his Friends to have a Mind of the moſt conſummate Greatneſs. He wants no Man's Admiration, is in no Need of Pomp. His Clothes pleaſe him if they are faſhionable and warm; his Companions are agreeable if they are civil and well-natured. There is with him no Occaſion for Superfluity at Meals, for Jollity in Company, in a word, for any thing extraordinary to adminiſter Delight to him. Want of Prejudice and Command of Appetite are the Companions which make his Journey of Life ſo eaſy, that he in all Places meets with more Wit, more good Cheer and more Good-humour, than is neceſſary to make him enjoy himſelf with Pleaſure and Satisfaction.   T

※※※※※※※※※※※※※

N° 207   *Saturday, October* 27.

Omnibus in terris, quæ ſunt à Gadibus uſque
Auroram & Gangem, pauci dignoſcere poſſunt
Vera bona, atque illis multùm diverſa, remotâ
Erroris nebulâ——   Juv. Sat. 10. v. 1.

Look round the habitable World, how few
Know their own Good, or, knowing it, purſue. DRYDEN.

IN my laſt *Saturday's* Paper I laid down ſome Thoughts upon Devotion in general, and ſhall here ſhew what were the Notions of the moſt refined Heathens on this Subject, as they are repreſented in *Plato's* Dialogue upon Prayer, intitled, *Alcibiades the Second*, which doubtleſs
gave

gave Occasion to *Juvenal's* tenth Satire, and to the second Satire of *Persius*; as the last of these Authors has almost transcribed the preceding Dialogue, intitled *Alcibiades the First*, in his Fourth Satire.

THE Speakers in this Dialogue upon Prayer, are *Socrates* and *Alcibiades*; and the Substance of it (when drawn together out of the Intricacies and Digressions) as follows.

SOCRATES meeting his Pupil *Alcibiades*, as he was going to his Devotions, and observing his Eyes to be fixed upon the Earth with great Seriousness and Attention, tells him, that he had reason to be thoughtful on that Occasion, since it was possible for a Man to bring down Evils upon himself by his own Prayers, and that those things, which the Gods send him in Answer to his Petitions, might turn to his Destruction: This, says he, may not only happen when a Man prays for what he knows is mischievous in its own Nature, as *Oedipus* implored the Gods to sow Dissension between his Sons; but when he prays for what he believes would be for his Good, and against what he believes would be to his Detriment. This the Philosopher shews must necessarily happen among us, since most Men are blinded with Ignorance, Prejudice, or Passion, which hinder them from seeing such Things as are really beneficial to them. For an Instance, he asks *Alcibiades*, Whether he would not be thoroughly pleased and satisfied if that God, to whom he was going to address himself, should promise to make him the Sovereign of the whole Earth? *Alcibiades* answers, That he should doubtless look upon such a Promise as the greatest Favour that could be bestowed upon him. *Socrates* then asks him, If after receiving this great Favour he would be contented to lose his Life? or if he would receive it though he was sure he should make an ill Use of it? To both which Questions *Alcibiades* answers in the Negative. *Socrates* then shews him, from the Examples of others, how these might very probably be the Effects of such a Blessing. He then adds, That other reputed Pieces of Good-fortune, as that of having a Son, or procuring the highest Post in a Government, are subject to the like fatal Consequences; which nevertheless, says he, Men ardently desire, and would not fail to pray for, if

they

they thought their Prayers might be effectual for the obtaining of them.

HAVING established this great Point, That all the most apparent Blessings in this Life are obnoxious to such dreadful Consequences, and that no Man knows what in its Events would prove to him a Blessing or a Curse, he teaches *Alcibiades* after what manner he ought to pray.

IN the first Place, he recommends to him, as the Model of his Devotions, a short Prayer, which a *Greek* Poet composed for the Use of his Friends, in the following Words; *O* Jupiter, *give us those Things which are good for us, whether they are such Things as we pray for, or such Things as we do not pray for: and remove from us those Things which are hurtful, though they are such Things as we pray for.*

IN the second Place, that his Disciple may ask such Things as are expedient for him, he shews him, that it is absolutely necessary to apply himself to the Study of true Wisdom, and to the Knowledge of that which is his chief Good, and the most suitable to the Excellency of his Nature.

IN the third and last Place he informs him, that the best Methods he could make use of to draw down Blessings upon himself, and to render his Prayers acceptable, would be to live in a constant Practice of his Duty towards the Gods, and towards Men. Under this Head he very much recommends a Form of Prayer the *Lacedemonians* make use of, in which they petition the Gods, *to give them all good Things so long as they were virtuous.* Under this Head likewise he gives a very remarkable Account of an Oracle to the following Purpose.

WHEN the *Athenians* in the War with the *Lacedemonians* received many Defeats both by Sea and Land, they sent a Message to the Oracle of *Jupiter Ammon*, to ask the Reason why they who erected so many Temples to the Gods, and adorned them with such costly Offerings; why they who had instituted so many Festivals, and accompanied them with such Pomps and Ceremonies; in short, why they who had slain so many Hecatombs at their Altars, should be less successful than the *Lacedemonians*, who fell so short of them in all these

Parti-

Particulars. To this, fays he, the Oracle made the following Reply ; *I am better pleafed with the Prayers of the* Lacedemonians, *than with all the Oblations of the Greeks.* As this Prayer implied and encouraged Virtue in thofe who made it ; the Philofopher proceeds to fhew how the moft vicious Man might be devout, fo far as Victims could make him, but that his Offerings were regarded by the Gods as Bribes, and his Petitions as Blafphemies. He likewife quotes on this Occafion two Verfes out of *Homer,* in which the Poet fays, That the Scent of the *Trojan* Sacrifices was carried up to Heaven by the Winds ; but that it was not acceptable to the Gods, who were difpleafed with *Priam* and all his People.

THE Conclufion of this Dialogue is very remarkable. *Socrates* having deterred *Alcibiades* from the Prayers and Sacrifice which he was going to offer, by fetting forth the above-mentioned Difficulties of performing that Duty as he ought, adds thefe Words, *We muft therefore wait till fuch Time as we may learn how we ought to behave ourfelves towards the Gods, and towards Men.* But when will that Time come, fays *Alcibiades,* and who is it that will inftruct us ? For I would fain fee this Man, whoever he is. It is one, fays *Socrates,* who takes care of you ; but as *Homer* tells us, that *Minerva* removed the Mift from *Diomedes* his Eyes, that he might plainly difcover both Gods and Men ; fo the Darknefs that hangs upon your Mind muft be removed before you are able to difcern what is Good and what is Evil. Let him remove from my Mind, fays *Alcibiades,* the Darknefs, and what elfe he pleafes, I am determined to refufe nothing he fhall order me, whoever he is, fo that I may become the better Man by it. The remaining Part of this Dialogue is very obfcure : There is fomething in it that would make us think *Socrates* hinted at himfelf, when he fpoke of this Divine Teacher who was to come into the World, did not he own that he himfelf was in this refpect as much at a Lofs, and in as great Diftrefs as the reft of Mankind.

SOME learned Men look upon this Conclufion as a Prediction of our Saviour, or at leaft that *Socrates,* like the High-Prieft, prophefied unknowingly, and pointed at

at that Divine Teacher who was to come into the World
fome Ages after him. However that may be, we find
that this great Philofopher faw, by the Light of Reafon,
that it was fuitable to the Goodnefs of the Divine Nature, to fend a Perfon into the World who fhould inftruct
Mankind in the Duties of Religion, and, in particular,
teach them how to Pray.

WHOEVER reads this Abftract of *Plato*'s Difcourfe
on Prayer, will, I believe, naturally make this Reflexion,
That the great Founder of our Religion, as well by
his own Example, as in the Form of Prayer which he
taught his Difciples, did not only keep up to thofe
Rules which the Light of Nature had fuggefted to this
great Philofopher, but inftructed his Difciples in the
whole Extent of this Duty, as well as of all others.
He directed them to the proper Object of Adoration,
and taught them, according to the third Rule above-
mentioned, to apply themfelves to him in their Clofets,
without Show or Oftentation, and to worfhip him in Spirit and in Truth. As the *Lacedemonians* in their Form
of Prayer implored the Gods in general to give them
all good things fo long as they were virtuous, we ask in
particular *that our Offences may be forgiven, as we forgive
thofe of others.* If we look into the fecond Rule which
Socrates has prefcribed, namely, That we fhould apply
ourfelves to the Knowledge of fuch Things as are beft for
us, this too is explain'd at large in the Doctrines of the
Gofpel, where we are taught in feveral Inftances to regard thofe things as Curfes, which appear as Bleffings
in the Eye of the World; and on the contrary, to efteem
thofe things as Bleffings, which to the Generality of
Mankind appear as Curfes. Thus in the Form which is
prefcribed to us we only pray for that Happinefs which
is our chief Good, and the great End of our Exiftence,
when we petition the fupreme Being for *the coming of his
Kingdom,* being folicitous for no other temporal Bleffings but our *daily Suftenance.* On the other fide, We
pray againft nothing but Sin, and againft *Evil* in general,
leaving it with Omnifcience to determine what is really
fuch. If we look into the firft of *Socrates* his Rules of
Prayer, in which he recommends the above-mentioned
Form of the ancient Poet, we find that Form not only
compre-

comprehended, but very much improved in the Petition, wherein we pray to the Supreme Being that *his Will may be done:* which is of the same Force with that Form which our Saviour used, when he prayed against the most painful and most ignominious of Deaths, *Nevertheless not my Will, but thine be done.* This comprehensive Petition is the most humble, as well as the most prudent, that can be offered up from the Creature to his Creator, as it supposes the Supreme Being wills nothing but what is for our Good, and that he knows better than ourselves what is so.　　　　　　　　　　　　　　　　　　L

Nº 208　*Monday, October* 29.

——*Veniunt spectentur ut ipsæ.*

Ovid. Ars Am. l. 1. v. 99.

To be Themselves a Spectacle, they come.

I Have several Letters of People of good Sense, who lament the Depravity or Poverty of Taste the Town is fallen into with relation to Plays and publick Spectacles. A Lady in particular observes, that there is such a Levity in the Minds of her own Sex, that they seldom attend any thing but Impertinences. It is indeed prodigious to observe how little Notice is taken of the most exalted Parts of the best Tragedies in *Shakespear*; nay, it is not only visible that Sensuality has devoured all Greatness of Soul, but the Under-Passion (as I may so call it) of a noble Spirit, Pity, seems to be a Stranger to the Generality of an Audience. The Minds of Men are indeed very differently disposed; and the Reliefs from Care and Attention are of one Sort in a great Spirit, and of another in an ordinary one. The Man of a great Heart and a serious Complexion, is more pleased with Instances of Generosity and Pity, than the light and ludicrous Spirit can possibly be with the highest Strains of Mirth and Laughter: It is therefore a melancholy Prospect when we see a numerous Assembly lost to all serious Entertainments,

tainments, and such Incidents, as should move one
Sort of Concern, excite in them a quite contrary one.
In the Tragedy of *Macbeth*, the other Night, when
the Lady who is conscious of the Crime of murdering the
King, seems utterly astonished at the News, and makes
an Exclamation at it, instead of the Indignation which
is natural to the Occasion, that Expression is received
with a loud Laugh: They were as merry when a Criminal was stabbed. It is certainly an occasion of re-
joicing when the wicked are seized in their Designs;
but I think it is not such a Triumph as is exerted by
Laughter.

YOU may generally observe, that the Appetites are
sooner moved than the Passions: A sly Expression which
alludes to Baudry, puts a whole Row into a pleasing
Smirk; when a good Sentence that describes an inward
Sentiment of the Soul, is received with the greatest Cold-
ness and Indifference. A Correspondent of mine, upon
this Subject, has divided the Female Part of the Audience, and accounts for their Prepossessions against this
reasonable Delight in the following manner. The Prude,
says he, as she acts always in Contradiction, so she is
gravely sullen at a Comedy, and extravagantly gay at a
Tragedy. The Coquette is so much taken up with throwing her Eyes around the Audience, and considering the
Effect of them, that she cannot be expected to observe
the Actors but as they are her Rivals, and take off the
Observation of the Men from herself. Besides these Species
of Women, there are the *Examples*, or the first of the
Mode: These are to be supposed too well acquainted with
what the Actor was going to say to be moved at it. After
these one might mention a certain flippant Set of Females
who are Mimicks, and are wonderfully diverted with the
Conduct of all the People around them, and are Spectators only of the Audience. But what is of all the most
to be lamented, is the Loss of a Party whom it would be
worth preserving in their right Senses upon all Occasions,
and these are those whom we may indifferently call the
Innocent or the Unaffected. You may sometimes see
one of these sensibly touched with a well-wrought Incident; but then she is immediately so impertinently observed by the Men, and frowned at by some insensible
Supe-

Superior of her own Sex, that she is ashamed, and loses the Enjoyment of the most laudable Concern, Pity. Thus the whole Audience is afraid of letting fall a Tear, and shun as a Weakness the best and worthiest Part of our Sense.

SIR,

'AS you are one that doth not only pretend to re-
'   form, but effects it amongst People of any Sense;
' makes me (who am one of the greatest of your Ad-
' mirers) give you this Trouble to desire you will settle
' the Method of us Females knowing when one another
' is in Town: For they have now got a Trick of never
' sending to their Acquaintance when they first come;
' and if one does not visit them within the Week which
' they stay at home, it is a mortal Quarrel. Now, Dear
' Mr. SPEC, either command them to put it in the Ad-
' vertisement of your Paper, which is generally read by
' our Sex, or else order them to breathe their saucy Foot-
' men (who are good for nothing else) by sending them
' to tell all their Acquaintance. If you think to print this,
' pray put it into a better Stile as to the spelling Part.
' The Town is now filling every Day, and it cannot be
' deferred, because People take Advantage of one ano-
' ther by this Means and break off Acquaintance, and are
' rude: Therefore pray put this in your Paper as soon
' as you can possibly, to prevent any future Miscarriages
' of this Nature. I am, as I ever shall be,

Dear SPEC,

Your most obedient humble Servant,

Mary Meanwell.

' PRAY settle what is to be a proper Notification of
'   a Person's being in Town, and how that differs
' according to People's Quality.

Mr. SPECTATOR,   October *the* 20th.

' I Have been out of Town, so did not meet with your
' Paper dated *September* the 28th, wherein you, to my
' Heart's Desire, expose that cursed Vice of insnaring poor
young

' young Girls, and drawing them from their Friends. I
' affure you without Flattery it has faved a Prentice of
' mine from Ruin; and in Token of Gratitude as well
' as for the Benefit of my Family, I have put it in a
' Frame and Glafs, and hung it behind my Counter. I
' fhall take care to make my young ones read it every
' Morning, to fortify them againft fuch pernicious Raf-
' cals. I know not whether what you writ was Matter
' of Fact, or your own Invention; but this I will take
' my Oath on, the firft Part is fo exactly like what hap-
' pened to my Prentice, that had I read your Paper
' then, I fhould have taken your Method to have fe-
' cured a Villain. Go on and profper.

Your moft obliged humble Servant.

Mr. SPECTATOR,

' WITHOUT Rallery, I defire you to infert this
' Word for Word in your next, as you value a
' Lover's Prayers. You fee it is an Hue and Cry after
' a ftray Heart (with the Marks and Blemifhes under-
' written) which whoever fhall bring to you, fhall re-
' ceive Satisfaction. Let me beg of you not to fail, as
' you remember the Paffion you had for her to whom
' you lately ended a Paper.

Noble, Generous, Great and Good,
But never to be underftood;
Fickle as the Wind, ftill changing,
After every Female ranging,
Panting, trembling, fighing, dying,
But addicted much to Lying:
When the Siren Songs repeats,
Equal Meafures ftill it beats;
Who-e'er fhall wear it, it will fmart her,
And who-e'er takes it, takes a Tartar.   T

Tuefday,

N.° 209   Tuesday, October 30.

Γυναικὸς ὐδὲ χρῆμ' ἀνὴρ ληίζεται
'Εϑλῆς ἄμεινον, ὐδὲ ρίγιον κακῆς.   Simonides.

Of earthly Goods the best, is a Good Wife;
A Bad, the bitterest Curse of human Life.

THERE are no Authors I am more pleased with,
than those who shew human Nature in a Variety
of Views, and describe the several Ages of the
World in their different Manners. A Reader cannot be
more rationally entertained, than by comparing the Virtues and Vices of his own Times with those which prevailed in the Times of his Forefathers; and drawing a
Parallel in his Mind between his own private Character,
and that of other Persons, whether of his own Age, or
of the Ages that went before him. The Contemplation
of Mankind under these changeable Colours, is apt to
shame us out of any particular Vice, or animate us to
any particular Virtue; to make us pleased or displeased
with ourselves in the most proper Points, to clear our
Minds of Prejudice and Prepossession, and rectify that
Narrowness of Temper which inclines us to think amiss
of those who differ from ourselves.

IF we look into the Manners of the most remote Ages
of the World, we discover human Nature in her Simplicity; and the more we come downward towards our
own Times, may observe her hiding herself in Artifices
and Refinements, polished insensibly out of her Original
Plainness, and at length intirely lost under Form and Ceremony, and (what we call) Good-breeding. Read the
Accounts of Men and Women as they are given us by
the most ancient Writers, both Sacred and Profane, and
you would think you were reading the History of another Species,

AMONG the Writers of Antiquity, there are none
who instruct us more openly in the Manners of their respective

spective Times in which they lived, than those who have employed themselves in Satire, under what Dress soever it may appear; as there are no other Authors whose Province it is to enter so directly into the Ways of Men, and set their Miscarriages in so strong a Light.

SIMONIDES, a Poet famous in his Generation, is, I think, Author of the oldest Satire that is now extant; and, as some say, of the first that was ever written. This Poet flourished about four hundred Years after the Siege of *Troy*; and shews, by his way of Writing, the Simplicity, or rather Coarseness, of the Age in which he lived. I have taken notice, in my hundred and sixty first Speculation, that the Rule of observing what the *French* call the *Bienséance*, in an Allusion, has been found out of later Years; and that the Ancients, provided there was a Likeness in their Similitudes, did not much trouble themselves about the Decency of the Comparison. The Satire or Iambicks of *Simonides*, with which I shall entertain my Readers in the present Paper, are a remarkable Instance of what I formerly advanced. The Subject of this Satire is Woman. He describes the Sex in their several Characters, which he derives to them from a fanciful Supposition raised upon the Doctrine of Præ-existence. He tells us, That the Gods formed the Souls of Woman out of those Seeds and Principles which compose several Kinds of Animals and Elements; and that their good or bad Dispositions arise in them according as such and such Seeds and Principles predominate in their Constitutions. I have translated the Author very faithfully, and if not Word for Word (which our Language would not bear) at least so as to comprehend every one of his Sentiments, without adding any thing of my own. I have already apologized for this Author's Want of Delicacy, and must further premise, That the following Satire affects only some of the lower Part of the Sex, and not those who have been refined by a polite Education, which was not so common in the Age of this Poet.

IN the Beginning God made the Souls of Womankind out of different Materials, and in a separate State from their Bodies.

THE

THE Souls of one Kind of Women were formed out of those Ingredients which compose a Swine. A Woman of this Make is a Slut in her House and a Glutton at her Table. She is constantly in her Person, a Slattern in her Dress, and her Family is no better than a Dunghil.

A Second Sort of Female Soul was formed out of the same Materials that enter into the Composition of a Fox. Such an one is what we call a notable discerning Woman, who has an Insight into every Thing, whether it be good or bad. In this Species of Females there are some virtuous and some vicious.

A Third Kind of Women were made up of Canine Particles. These are what we commonly call Scolds, who imitate the Animals out of which they were taken, that are always busy and barking, that snarl at every one who comes in their Way, and live in perpetual Clamour.

THE Fourth Kind of Women were made out of the Earth. These are your Sluggards, who pass away their Time in Indolence and Ignorance, hover over this Fire a whole Winter, and apply themselves with Alacrity to no kind of Business but Eating.

THE Fifth Species of Females were made out of the Sea. These are Women of variable uneven Tempers, sometimes all Storm and Tempest, sometimes all Calm and Sunshine. The Stranger who sees one of them in her Smiles and Smoothness, would cry her up for a Miracle of Good-humour; but on a sudden her Looks and her Words are changed, she is nothing but Fury and Outrage, Noise and Hurricane.

THE Sixth Species were made up of the Ingredients which compose an Ass, or a Beast of Burden. These are naturally exceeding slothful, but, upon the Husband's exerting his Authority, will live upon hard Fare, and do every Thing to please him. They are however far from being averse to Venereal Pleasures, and seldom refuse a Male Companion.

THE Cat furnished Materials for a Seventh Species of Women, who are of a melancholy, froward, unamiable Nature, and so repugnant to the Offices of Love, that they fly in the Face of their Husband when he approaches them with conjugal Endearments. This Species of Women are likewise subject to little Thefts, Cheats and Pilferings.

THE Mare with a flowing Mane, which was never broke to any servile Toil and Labour, composed an Eighth Species of Women. These are they who have little Regard

fpective Times in which they lived, than thofe who have employed themfelves in Satire, under what Drefs foever it may appear; as there are no other Authors whofe Province it is to enter fo directly into the Ways of Men, and fet their Mifcarriages in fo ftrong a Light.

SIMONIDES, a Poet famous in his Generation, is, I think, Author of the oldeft Satire that is now extant; and, as fome fay, of the firft that was ever written. This Poet flourifhed about four hundred Years after the Siege of *Troy*; and fhews, by his way of Writing, the Simplicity, or rather Coarfenefs, of the Age in which he lived. I have taken notice, in my hundred and fixty firft Speculation, that the Rule of obferving what the *French* call the *Bienfeance*, in an Allufion, has been found out of latter Years; and that the Ancients, provided there was a Likenefs in their Similitudes, did not much trouble themfelves about the Decency of the Comparifon. The Satire or Iambicks of *Simonides*, with which I fhall entertain my Readers in the prefent Paper, are a remarkable Inftance of what I formerly advanced. The Subject of this Satire is Woman. He defcribes the Sex in their feveral Characters, which he derives to them from a fanciful Suppofition raifed upon the Doctrine of Præexiftence. He tells us, That the Gods formed the Souls of Women out of thofe Seeds and Principles which compofe feveral Kinds of Animals and Elements; and that their good or bad Difpofitions arife in them according as fuch and fuch Seeds and Principles predominate in their Conftitutions. I have tranflated the Author very faithfully, and if not Word for Word (which our Language would not bear) at leaft fo as to comprehend every one of his Sentiments, without adding any thing of my own. I have already apologized for this Author's Want of Delicacy, and muft further premife, That the following Satire affects only fome of the lower Part of the Sex, and not thofe who have been refined by a polite Education, which was not fo common in the Age of this Poet.

IN the Beginning God made the Souls of Womankind out of different Materials, and in a feparate State from their Bodies.

THE

THE Souls *of one Kind of Women were formed out of those Ingredients which compose a Swine. A Woman of this Make is a* Slut *in her House and a* Glutton *at her Table. She is uncleanly in her Person, a Slattern in her Dress, and her Family is no better than a Dunghil.*

A Second Sort of Female Soul was formed out of the same Materials that enter into the Composition of a Fox. Such an one is what we call a notable discerning Woman, who has an Insight into every Thing, whether it be good or bad. In this Species of Females there are some virtuous and some vicious.

A Third Kind of Women were made up of Canine Particles. These are what we commonly call Scolds, *who imitate the Animals out of which they were taken, that are always busy and barking, that snarl at every one who comes in their Way, and live in perpetual Clamour.*

THE Fourth Kind of Women were made out of the Earth. These are your Sluggards, who pass away their Time in Indolence and Ignorance, hover over the Fire a whole Winter, and apply themselves with Alacrity to no kind of Business but Eating.

THE Fifth Species of Females were made out of the Sea. These are Women of variable uneven Tempers, sometimes all Storm and Tempest, sometimes all Calm and Sunshine. The Stranger who sees one of these in her Smiles and Smoothness, would cry her up for a Miracle of Good-humour ; but on a sudden her Looks and her Words are changed, she is nothing but Fury and Outrage, Noise and Hurricane.

THE Sixth Species were made up of the Ingredients which compose an Ass, or a Beast of Burden. These are naturally exceeding slothful, but, upon the Husband's exerting his Authority, will live upon hard Fare, and do every Thing to please him. They are however far from being averse to Venereal Pleasure, and seldom refuse a Male Companion.

THE Cat furnished Materials for a Seventh Species of Women, who are of a melancholy, froward, unamiable Nature, and so repugnant to the Offers of Love, that they fly in the Face of their Husband when he approaches them with conjugal Endearments. This Species of Women are likewise subject to little Thefts, Cheats and Pilferings.

THE Mare with a flowing Mane, which was never broke to any servile Toil and Labour, composed an Eighth Species of Women. These are they who have little Regard
for

for their Husbands, who pass away their Time in Dressing, Bathing, and Perfuming; who throw their Hair into the nicest Curls, and trick it up with the fairest Flowers and Garlands. A Woman of this Species is a very pretty Thing for a Stranger to look upon, but very detrimental to the Owner, unless it be a King or Prince who takes a Fancy to such a Toy.

THE Ninth Species of Females were taken out of the Ape. These are such as are both ugly and ill-natured, who have nothing beautiful in themselves, and endeavour to detract from or ridicule every Thing which appears so in others.

THE Tenth and last Species of Women were made out of the Bee; and happy is the Man who gets such an one for his Wife. She is altogether faultless and unblameable; her Family flourishes and improves by her good Management. She loves her Husband, and is beloved by him. She brings him a Race of beautiful and virtuous Children. She distinguishes herself among her Sex. She is surrounded with Graces. She never sits among the loose Tribe of Women, nor passes away her Time with them in wanton Discourses. She is full of Virtue and Prudence, and is the best Wife that Jupiter can bestow on Man.

I shall conclude these Iambicks with the Motto of this Paper, which is a Fragment of the same Author: *A Man cannot possess any Thing that is better than a good Woman, nor any thing that is worse than a bad one.*

AS the Poet has shewn a great Penetration in this Diversity of Female Characters, he has avoided the Fault which *Juvenal* and Monsieur *Boileau* are guilty of, the former in his sixth, and the other in his last Satire, where they have endeavoured to expose the Sex in general, without doing Justice to the valuable Part of it. Such levelling Satires are of no Use to the World, and for this Reason I have often wondered how the *French* Author abovementioned, who was a Man of exquisite Judgment, and a Lover of Virtue, could think human Nature a proper Subject for Satire in another of his celebrated Pieces, which is called *The Satire upon Man*. What Vice or Frailty can a Discourse correct, which censures the whole Species alike, and endeavours to shew by some superficial Strokes of Wit, that Brutes are the most excellent Creatures of the two? A Satire should expose nothing but what is

corrigible,

corrigible, and make a due Difcrimination between thofe who are, and thofe who are not the proper Objects of it.   L

Nefcio quomodo inhæret in mentibus quaſi feculorum quoddam augurium futurorum; idque in maximis ingeniis altiſſimiſque animis & exiſtit maximè & apparet facillimè.

Cic. Tuſc. Quæſt.

There is, I know not how, in the Minds of Men a certain Prefage, as it were, of a future Exiſtence; and this takes the deepeſt Root, and is moſt diſcoverable in the greateſt Genius's and moſt exalted Souls.

To the SPECTATOR.

S I R,

I Am fully perſuaded that one of the beſt Springs of generous and worthy Actions, is the having generous and worthy Thoughts of ourſelves. Whoever has a mean Opinion of the Dignity of his Nature, will act in no higher a Rank than he has allotted himſelf in his own Eſtimation. If he confiders his Being as circumſcribed by the uncertain Term of a few Years, his Defigns will be contracted into the fame narrow Span he imagines is to bound his Exiſtence. How can he exalt his Thoughts to any thing great and noble, who only believes that, after a ſhort Turn on the Stage of this World, he is to fink into Oblivion, and to loſe his Confcioufnefs for ever?

'FOR this Reafon I am of Opinion, that fo ufeful and elevated a Contemplation as that of the *Soul's Immortality* cannot be refumed too often. There is not a more improving Exercife to the human Mind, than to be frequently reviewing its own great Privileges and Endowments; nor a more effectual Means to awaken in us an Ambition raifed above low Objects and little Purfuits, than to value ourfelves as Heirs of Eternity.

'IT

' IT is a very great Satisfaction to confider the beſt
' and wiſeſt of Mankind in all Nations and Ages, aſſert-
' ing, as with one Voice, this their Birthright, and to
' find it ratify'd by an expreſs Revelation. At the ſame
' time if we turn our Thoughts inward upon ourſelves,
' we may meet with a kind of ſecret Senſe concurring
' with the Proofs of our own Immortality.

' YOU have, in my Opinion, raiſed a good preſump-
' tive Argument from the increaſing Appetite the Mind
' has to Knowledge, and to the extending its own Facul-
' ties, which cannot be accompliſhed, as the more re-
' ſtrained Perfection of lower Creatures may, in the Limits
' of a ſhort Life. I think another probable Conjecture
' may be raiſed from our Appetite to Duration itſelf, and
' from a Reflexion on our Progreſs through the ſeveral
' Stages of it : *We are complaining,* as you obſerve in a
' former Speculation, *of the Shortneſs of Life, and yet are*
' *perpetually hurrying over the Parts of it, to arrive at*
' *certain little Settlements, or imaginary Points of Reſt,*
' *which are diſperſed up and down in it.*

' NOW let us confider what happens to us when we
' arrive at theſe *imaginary Points of Reſt :* Do we ſtop our
' Motion, and ſit down ſatisfied in the Settlement we have
' gain'd ? or are we not removing the Boundary, and
' marking out new Points of Reſt, to which we preſs for-
' ward with the like Eagerneſs, and which ceaſe to be
' ſuch as faſt as we attain them ? Our Caſe is like that
' of a Traveller upon the *Alps,* who ſhould fancy that
' the Top of the next Hill muſt end his Journey, be-
' cauſe it terminates his Proſpect ; but he no ſooner ar-
' rives at it, than he ſees new Ground and other Hills
' beyond it, and continues to travel on as before.

' THIS is ſo plainly every Man's Condition in Life,
' that there is no one who has obſerved any thing, but
' may obſerve, that as faſt as his Time wears away, his
' Appetite to ſomething future remains. The Uſe there-
' fore I would make of it is this, That ſince Nature (as
' ſome love to expreſs it) does nothing in vain, or, to
' ſpeak properly, ſince the Author of our Being has
' planted no wandering Paſſion in it, no Deſire which has
' not its Object, Futurity is the proper Object of the
' Paſſion ſo conſtantly exercis'd about it ; and this Reſt-

' leſneſs

' lefnefs in the prefent, this affigning ourfelves over to
' farther Stages of Duration, this fucceffive grafping at
' fomewhat ftill to come, appears to me (whatever it may
' to others) as a kind of Inftinct or natural Symptom
' which the Mind of Man has of its own Immortality.

' I take it at the fame time for granted, that the Im-
' mortality of the Soul is fufficiently eftablifhed by other
' Arguments: And if fo, this Appetite, which otherwife
' would be very unaccountable and abfurd, feems very
' reafonable, and adds Strength to the Conclufion. But
' I am amazed when I confider there are Creatures capable
' of Thought, who, in fpite of every Argument, can
' form to themfelves a fullen Satisfaction in thinking other-
' wife. There is fomething fo pitifully mean in the in-
' verted Ambition of that Man who can hope for Annihi-
' lation, and pleafe himfelf to think that his whole Fabrick
' fhall one Day crumble into Duft, and mix with the Mafs
' of inanimate Beings, that it equally deferves our Admi-
' ration and Pity. The Myftery of fuch Mens Unbelief is
' not hard to be penetrated; and indeed amounts to no-
' thing more than a fordid Hope that they fhall not be
' immortal, becaufe they dare not be fo.

' THIS brings me back to my firft Obfervation, and
' gives me Occafion to fay further, That as worthy Actions
' fpring from worthy Thoughts, fo worthy Thoughts are
' likewife the Confequence of worthy Actions: But the
' Wretch who has degraded himfelf below the Character
' of Immortality, is very willing to refign his Pretenfions
' to it, and to fubftitute in its Room a dark negative
' Happinefs in the Extinction of his Being.

' THE admirable *Shakefpear* has given us a ftrong
' Image of the unfupported Condition of fuch a Perfon
' in his laft Minutes in the fecond Part of King *Henry* the
' Sixth, where Cardinal *Beaufort*, who had been con-
' cerned in the Murder of the good Duke *Humphrey*, is
' reprefented on his Death-bed. After fome fhort confufed
' Speeches which fhew an Imagination difturbed with
' Guilt, juft as he was expiring, King *Henry* ftanding by
' him full of Compaffion, fays,

' *Lord Cardinal! if thou think'ft on Heaven's Blifs,*
' *Hold up thy Hand, make Signal of that Hope!*
' *He dies, and makes no Sign!*———   ' THE

' THE Defpair which is here fhewn, without a Word
' or Action on the Part of the dying Perfon, is beyond
' what could be painted by the moft forcible Expreffions
' whatever.

' I fhall not purfue this Thought farther, but only add,
' That as Annihilation is not to be had with a Wifh, fo
' it is the moft abject Thing in the World to wifh it.
' What are Honour, Fame, Wealth, or Power when com-
' pared with the generous Expectation of a Being with-
' out End, and a Happinefs adequate to that Being?

' I fhall trouble you no farther; but with a certain
' Gravity which thefe Thoughts have given me, I reflect
' upon fome Things People fay of you, (as they will of
' Men who diftinguifh themfelves) which I hope are not
' true; and wifh you as good a Man as you are an
' Author.

I am, S I R,

Your moft obedient humble Servant,

Z.   T. D.

Nº 211   *Thurfday, November* 1.

Fictis meminerit nos jocari Fabulis.   Phædr. l. 1. Prol.

Let it be remember'd that we fport in fabled Stories.

HAVING lately tranflated the Fragment of an old
Poet which defcribes Womankind under feveral
Characters, and fuppofes them to have drawn
their different Manners and Difpofitions from thofe Animals and Elements out of which he tells us they were
compounded; I had fome Thoughts of giving the Sex
their Revenge, by laying together in another Paper the
many vicious Characters which prevail in the Male World,
and fhewing the different Ingredients that go to the
making up of fuch different Humours and Conftitutions.
Horace has a Thought which is fomething akin to this,
when, in order to excufe himfelf to his Miftrefs, for an

Invective

Inveſtive which he had written againſt her, and to account for that unreaſonable Fury with which the Heart of Man is often transported, he tells us that, when *Prometheus* made his Man of Clay, in the kneading up of the Heart, he ſeaſon'd it with ſome furious Particles of the Lion. But upon turning this Plan to and fro in my Thoughts, I obſerved ſo many unaccountable Humours in Man, that I did not know out of what Animals to fetch them. Male Souls are diverſify'd with ſo many Characters, that the World has not Variety of Materials ſufficient to furniſh out their different Tempers and Inclinations. The Creation, with all its Animals and Elements, would not be large enough to ſupply their ſeveral Extravagancies.

INSTEAD therefore of purſuing the Thought of *Simonides*, I ſhall obſerve, that as he has expoſed the vicious Part of Women from the Doctrine of Præexiſtence, ſome of the ancient Philoſophers have, in a manner, ſatirized the vicious Part of the human Species in general, from a Notion of the Soul's Poſtexiſtence, if I may ſo call it; and that as *Simonides* deſcribes Brutes entring into the Compoſition of Women, others have repreſented human Souls as entring into Brutes. This is commonly termed the Doctrine of Tranſmigration, which ſuppoſes that human Souls, upon their leaving the Body, become the Souls of ſuch Kinds of Brutes as they moſt reſemble in their Manners; or to give an Account of it as Mr. *Dryden* has deſcribed it in his Tranſlation of *Pythagoras* his Speech in the fifteenth Book of *Ovid*, where that Philoſopher diſſuades his Hearers from eating Fleſh:

Thus all things are but alter'd, nothing dies,
And here and there th' unbody'd Spirit flies:
By Time, or Force, or Sickneſs diſpoſſeſs'd,
And lodges where it lights, in Bird or Beaſt,
Or hunts without till ready Limbs it find,
And actuates thoſe according to their Kind:
From Tenement to Tenement is toſs'd:
The Soul is ſtill the ſame, the Figure only loſt.

Then

Then let not Piety be put to Flight,
To please the Taste of Glutton-Appetite;
But suffer inmate Souls secure to dwell,
Lest from their Seats your Parents you expel;
With rabid Hunger feed upon your Kind,
Or from a Beast dislodge a Brother's Mind.

PLATO in the Vision of *Erus* the *Armenian*, which I may possibly make the Subject of a future Speculation, records some beautiful Transmigrations; as that the Soul of *Orpheus*, who was musical, melancholy, and a Woman-hater, entered into a Swan; the Soul of *Ajax*, which was all Wrath and Fierceness, into a Lion; the Soul of *Agamemnon*, that was rapacious and imperial, into an Eagle; and the Soul of *Thersites*, who was a Mimick and a Buffoon, into a Monkey.

Mr. *Congreve*, in a Prologue to one of his Comedies, has touch'd upon this Doctrine with great Humour.

Thus Aristotle's Soul of old that was,
May now be damn'd to animate an Ass;
Or in this very House, for ought we know,
Is doing painful Penance in some Beau.

I shall fill up this Paper with some Letters which my last *Tuesday's* Speculation has produced. My following Correspondents will shew, what I there observed, that the Speculation of that Day affects only the lower Part of the Sex.

From my House in the Strand, October 30, 1711.

Mr. SPECTATOR,

' UPON reading your *Tuesday's* Paper, I find by se-
' veral Symptoms in my Constitution that I am a
' Bee. My Shop, or, if you please to call it so, my Cell,
' is in that great Hive of Females which goes by the
' Name of *The New-Exchange*; where I am daily em-
' ployed in gathering together a little Stock of Gain
' from the finest Flowers about the Town, I mean the La-
' dies and the Beaus. I have a numerous Swarm of Chil-
' dren, to whom I give the best Education I am able: But,
' Sir, it is my Misfortune to be married to a Drone, who
                                                    ' lives

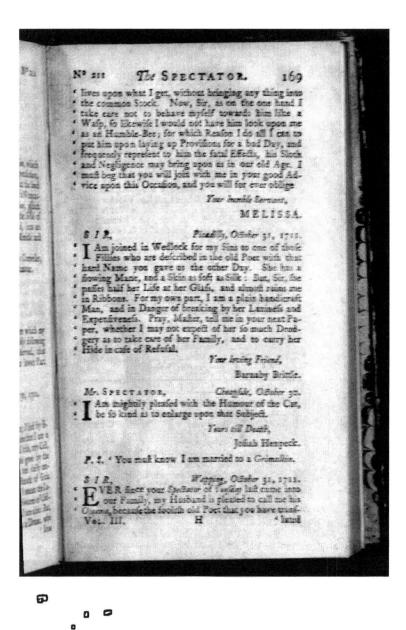

' lives upon what I get, without bringing any thing into
' the common Stock. Now, Sir, as on the one hand I
' take care not to behave myself towards him like a
' Wasp, so likewise I would not have him look upon me
' as an Humble-Bee; for which Reason I do all I can to
' put him upon laying up Provisions for a bad Day, and
' frequently represent to him the fatal Effects, his Sloth
' and Negligence may bring upon us in our old Age. I
' must beg that you will join with me in your good Ad-
' vice upon this Occasion, and you will for ever oblige

Your humble Servant,

MELISSA.

SIR,   *Picadilly, October* 31, 1711.

' I Am joined in Wedlock for my Sins to one of those
' Fillies who are described in the old Poet with that
' hard Name you gave us the other Day. She has a
' flowing Mane, and a Skin as soft as Silk : But, Sir, she
' passes half her Life at her Glass, and almost ruins me
' in Ribbons. For my own part, I am a plain hardieved
' Man, and in Danger of breaking by her Laziness and
' Expensiveness. Pray, Master, tell me in your next Pa-
' per, whether I may not expect of her so much Drud-
' gery as to take care of her Family, and to curry her
' Hide in case of Refusal.

Your loving Friend,

Barnaby Brittle.

Mr. SPECTATOR,   *Cheapside, October* 30.

' I Am mightily pleased with the Humour of the Cat,
' be so kind as to enlarge upon that Subject.

Yours till Death,

Josiah Henpeck.

P. S. ' You must know I am married to a Grimalkin.

SIR,   *Wapping, October* 31, 1711.

' E VER since your *Spectator* of *Tuesday* last came into
' our Family, my Husband is pleased to call me his
' Oenone, because the foolish old Poet that you have transf-

‘ lated fays, That the Souls of fome Women are made of
‘ Sea-Water. This, it feems, has encouraged my Sauce-
‘ Box to be witty upon me. When I am angry, he cries
‘ Pr'ythee my Dear *be calm*; when I chide one of my Ser-
‘ vants, Pr'ythee Child *do not bluſter*. He had the Impu-
‘ dence about an Hour ago to tell me, That he was a Sea-
‘ faring Man, and muſt expect to divide his Life between
‘ *Storm* and *Sunſhine*. When I beſtir myſelf with any
‘ Spirit in my Family, it is *high Sea* in his Houſe; and
‘ when I fit ſtill without doing any thing, his Affairs for-
‘ footh are *Wind-bound*. When I ask him whether it rains,
‘ he makes Anſwer, It is no Matter, ſo that it be *fair*
‘ *Weather* within Doors. In ſhort, Sir, I cannot ſpeak
‘ my Mind freely to him, but I either *ſwell* or *rage*, or
‘ do ſomething that is not fit for a civil Woman to hear.
‘ Pray, *Mr.* SPECTATOR, ſince you are ſo ſharp upon
‘ other Women, let us know what Materials your Wife
‘ is made of, if you have one. I ſuppoſe you would
‘ make us a Parcel of poor-ſpirited tame inſipid Crea-
‘ tures; but, Sir, I would have you to know, we have
‘ as good Paſſions in us as yourſelf, and that a Woman
‘ was never deſigned to be a Milk-Sop.

L *MARTHA TEMPEST.*

Nº 212 *Friday, November* 2.

———*Eripe turpi*
Colla jugo, liber, liber ſum, dic age—Hor. Sat. 7. l. 2. v. 92.
———*Looſe thy Neck from this ignoble Chain,*
And boldly ſay thou'rt free. CREECH.

Mr. SPECTATOR,

‘ I Never look upon my dear Wife, but I think of the
‘ Happineſs Sir ROGER DE COVERLEY enjoys, in
‘ having ſuch a Friend as you to expoſe in proper
‘ Colours the Cruelty and Perverſeneſs of his Miſtreſs.
‘ I have very often wiſhed you viſited in our Family, and
‘ were acquainted with my Spouſe; ſhe would afford
‘ you for ſome Months at leaſt Matter enough for one

‘ *Spectator*

'*Spectator* a Week. Since we are not so happy as to be of
'your Acquaintance, give me leave to represent to you
'our present Circumstances as well as I can in Writing.
'You are to know then that I am not of a very different
'Constitution from *Nathaniel Henroost*, whom you have
'lately recorded in your Speculations ; and have a
'Wife who makes a more tyrannical Use of the Know-
'ledge of my easy Temper than that Lady ever pre-
'tended to. We had not been a Month married, when
'she found in me a certain Pain to give Offence, and an
'Indolence that made me bear little Inconveniences ra-
'ther than dispute about them. From this Observation it
'soon came to that pass, that if I offered to go abroad,
'she would get between me and the Door, kiss me, and
'say she could not part with me ; and then down again
'I sat. In a Day or two after this first pleasant Step to-
'wards confining me, she declared to me, that I was all
'the World to her, and she thought she ought to be all
'the World to me. If, said she, my Dear loves me as
'much as I love him, he will never be tired of my Com-
'pany. This Declaration was followed by my being
'denied to all my Acquaintance; and it very soon came
'to that pass, that to give an Answer at the Door before
'my Face, the Servants would ask her whether I was
'within or not; and she would answer No with great
'Fondness, and tell me I was a good Dear. I will
'not enumerate more little Circumstances to give you a
'livelier Sense of my Condition; but tell you in general,
'that from such Steps as these at first, I now live the
'Life of a Prisoner of State ; my Letters are opened,
'and I have not the Use of Pen, Ink and Paper, but in
'her Presence. I never go abroad, except she sometimes
'takes me with her in her Coach to take the Air, if it
'may be called so, when we drive, as we generally do,
'with the Glasses up. I have overheard my Servants la-
'ment my Condition, but they dare not bring me Mes-
'sages without her Knowledge, because they doubt my
'Resolution to stand by 'em. In the midst of this insipid
'Way of Life, an old Acquaintance of mine, *Tom Meggot*,
'who is a Favourite with her, and allowed to visit me in
'her Company because he sings prettily, has roused me
'to rebel, and conveyed his Intelligence to me in the fol-

lowing

' lowing Manner. My Wife is a great Pretender to Mu-
' fick, and very ignorant of it ; but far gone in the
' *Italian* Tafte. *Tom* goes to *Armftrong*, the famous fine
' Writer of Mufick, and defires him to put this Sentence
' of *Tully* in the Scale of an *Italian* Air, and write it out
' for my Spoufe from him. *An ille mihi liber cui mulier*
' *imperat ? Cui leges imponit, præfcribit, jubet, vetat, quod*
' *videtur ? Qui nihil imperanti - negare, nihil recufare*
' *audet ? Pofcit ? dandum eft. Vocat ? veniendum. Ejicit ?*
' *abeundum. Minitatur ? extimifcendum.* Does he live like
' a Gentleman who is commanded by a Woman ? He to
' whom fhe gives Law, grants and denies what fhe pleafes ?
' who can neither deny her any thing fhe asks, or refufe to do
' any thing fhe commands ?

'TO be fhort, my Wife was extremely pleafed with
' it ; faid the *Italian* was the only Language for Mufick ;
' and admired how wonderfully tender the Sentiment
' was, and how pretty the Accent is of that Language,
' with the reft that is faid by Rote on that Occafion.
' Mr. *Meggot* is fent to fing this Air, which he per-
' forms with mighty Applaufe ; and my Wife is in Ec-
' ftafy on the Occafion, and glad to find, by my being
' fo much pleafed, that I was at laft come into the No-
' tion of the *Italian* ; for, faid fhe, it grows upon one
' when one once comes to know a little of the Language ;
' and pray, Mr. *Meggot*, fing again thofe Notes, *Nihil*
' *Imperanti negare, nihil recufare.* You may believe I was
' not a little delighted with my Friend *Tom*'s Expedient
' to alarm me, and in Obedience to his Summons I
' give all this Story thus at large ; and I am refolved,
' when this appears in the *Spectator*, to declare for my-
' felf. The manner of the Infurrection I contrive by your
' Means, which fhall be no other than that *Tom Meggot*,
' who is at our Tea-table every Morning, fhall read it to
' us ; and if my Dear can take the Hint, and fay not one
' Word, but let this be the Beginning of a new Life with-
' out farther Explanation, it is very well ; for as foon as
' the *Spectator* is read out, I fhall, without more ado, call
' for the Coach, name the Hour when I fhall be at home,
' if I come at all ; if I do not, they may go to Dinner.
' If my Spoufe only fwells and fays nothing, *Tom* and I
' go out together, and all is well, as I faid before ; but if

' fhe

' she begins to command or expostulate, you shall in my
' next to you receive a full Account of her Resistance and
' Submission, for submit the dear thing must to,

S I R,

Your most obedient humble Servant,

Anthony Freeman.

P. S. ' I hope I need not tell you that I desire this
' may be in your very next.   T

N° 213   *Saturday, November* 3.

——Mens sibi conscia recti.   Virg. Æn. 1. v. 608.

A Good Intention.

IT is the great Art and Secret of Christianity, if I may
use that Phrase, to manage our Actions to the best Advantage, and direct them in such a manner, that every
thing we do may turn to Account at that great Day,
when every thing we have done will be set before us.

IN order to give this Consideration its full Weight, we
may cast all our Actions under the Division of such as are
in themselves either Good, Evil, or Indifferent. If we
divide our Intentions after the same Manner, and consider
them with regard to our Actions, we may discover that
great Art and Secret of Religion which I have here mentioned.

A good Intention joined to a good Action, gives it its
proper Force and Efficacy; joined to an Evil Action, ex-
tenuates its Malignity, and in some Cases may take it
wholly away; and joined to an indifferent Action turns
it to a virtue, and makes it meritorious as far as human
Actions can be so.

IN the next Place, to consider in the same manner the
Influence of an Evil Intention upon our Actions. An
Evil Intention perverts the best of Actions, and makes
them in reality, what the Fathers with a witty kind of
Zeal have termed the Virtues of the Heathen World, so

H 3

many

many *shining Sins*. It destroys the Innocence of an indifferent Action, and gives an evil Action all possible Blackness and Horror, or in the emphatical Language of Sacred Writ, makes *Sin exceeding sinful*.

I F, in the last Place, we consider the Nature of an indifferent Intention, we shall find that it destroys the Merit of a good Action; abates, but never takes away, the Malignity of an evil Action; and leaves an indifferent Action in its natural State of Indifference.

I T is therefore of unspeakable Advantage to possess our Minds with an habitual good Intention, and to aim all our Thoughts, Words, and Actions at some laudable End, whether it be the Glory of our Maker, the Good of Mankind, or the Benefit of our own Souls.

THIS is a sort of Thrift or Good-Husbandry in moral Life, which does not throw away any single Action, but makes every one go as far as it can. It multiplies the Means of Salvation, increases the Number of our Virtues, and diminishes that of our Vices.

THERE is something very devout, though not solid, in *Acosta*'s Answer to *Limborch*, who objects to him the Multiplicity of Ceremonies in the *Jewish* Religion, as Washings, Dresses, Meats, Purgations, and the like. The Reply which the *Jew* makes upon this Occasion, is, to the best of my Remembrance, as follows: ' There are ' not Duties enough (says he) in the essential Parts of the ' Law for a zealous and active Obedience. Time, Place, ' and Person are requisite, before you have an Opportu- ' tunity of putting a Moral Virtue into Practice. We have ' therefore, says he, enlarged the Sphere of our Duty, ' and made many Things, which are in themselves indif- ' ferent, a Part of our Religion, that we may have more ' Occasions of shewing our Love to God, and in all the ' Circumstances of Life be doing something to please him.

MONSIEUR *St. Evremond* has endeavoured to palliate the Superstitions of the Roman-Catholick Religion with the same kind of Apology, where he pretends to consider the different Spirit of the Papists and the Calvinists, as to the great Points wherein they disagree. He tells us, that the former are actuated by Love, and the other by Fear; and that in their Expressions of Duty and Devotion towards the Supreme Being, the former

seem

seem particularly careful to do every thing which may possibly please him; and the other to abstain from every thing which may possibly displease him.

BUT notwithstanding this plausible Reason with which both the Jew and the Roman-Catholick would excuse their respective Superstitions, it is certain there is something in them very pernicious to Mankind, and destructive to Religion; because the Injunction of superfluous Ceremonies makes such Actions Duties, as were before indifferent, and by that means renders Religion more burdensom and difficult than it is in its own Nature, betrays many into Sins of Omission which they could not otherwise be guilty of, and fixes the Minds of the Vulgar to the shadowy unessential Points, instead of the more weighty and more important Matters of the Law.

THIS zealous and active Obedience however takes place in the great Point we are recommending; for, if, instead of prescribing to ourselves indifferent Actions as Duties, we apply a good Intention to all our most indifferent Actions, we make our very Existence one continued Act of Obedience, we turn our Diversions and Amusements to our eternal Advantage, and are pleasing him (whom we are made to please) in all the Circumstances and Occurrences of Life.

IT is this excellent Frame of Mind, this *holy Officiousness* (if I may be allowed to call it such) which is recommended to us by the Apostle in that uncommon Precept, wherein he directs us to propose to ourselves the Glory of our Creator in all our most indifferent Actions, *whether we eat or drink, or whatsoever we do.*

A Person therefore who is possessed with such an habitual good Intention, as that which I have been here speaking of, enters upon no single Circumstance of Life, without considering it as well-pleasing to the great Author of his Being, conformable to the Dictates of Reason, suitable to human Nature in general, or to that particular Station in which Providence has placed him. He lives in a perpetual Sense of the Divine Presence, regards himself as acting, in the whole Course of his Existence, under the Observation and Inspection of that Being, who is privy to all his Motions and all his Thoughts, who knows his *Down-fitting and his Up-rifing, who is about his Path, and about his Bed, and spieth out all his Ways.* In a word, he remembers that the Eye of his Judge is always upon him, and in every Action he reflects that he is doing what is commanded or allowed by Him who will hereafter either reward or punish it. This was the Character of those holy Men of old, who in that beautiful Phrase of Scripture are said to have *walked with God.*

WHEN I employ myself upon a Paper of Morality, I generally consider how I may recommend the particular Virtue which I treat of, by the Precepts or Examples of the ancient Heathens; by that Means, if possible, to shame those who have greater Advantages of knowing their Duty, and therefore greater Obligations to perform it, into a better Course of Life: Besides that many among us are unreasonably disposed to give a fairer hearing to a Pagan Philosopher, than to a Christian Writer.

I shall therefore produce an Instance of this excellent Frame of Mind in a Speech of *Socrates,* which is quoted by *Erasmus.* This great Philosopher on the Day of his Execution, a little before the Draught of Poison was brought to him, entertaining his Friends with a Discourse on the Immortality of the Soul, has these Words: *Whether or no God will approve of my Actions, I know not ; but this I am sure of, that I have at all Times made it my Endeavour to please him, and I have a good Hope that this my Endeavour well be accepted by him.* We find in these Words of that great Man the habitual good Intention which I would here inculcate, and with which that divine Philosopher always acted. I shall only add, that *Erasmus,* who was an unbigotted Roman-Catholick, was so much transported with this Passage of *Socrates,* that he could scarce forbear looking upon him as a Saint, and desiring him to pray for him; or as that ingenious and learned Writer has expressed himself in a much more lively manner: *When I reflect on such a Speech pronounced by such a Person, I can scarce forbear crying out,* Sancte Socrates, •ra pro nobis: O *holy* Socrates, *pray for us.* L

Nº 214. *Monday, November* 5.

———— *Perierunt tempora longi*
Servitii————
Juv. Sat. 3. v. 124.
A long Dependence in an Hour is lost. DRYDEN.

I Did some time ago lay before the World the unhappy Condition of the trading Part of Mankind, who suffer by want of Punctuality in the Dealings of Persons above them; but there is a Set of Men who are much more the Objects of Compassion than even those, and these are the Dependents on great Men, whom they are pleased to take under their Protection as such as are to share in their Friendship and Favour. These indeed, as well from the Homage that is accepted from them, as the Hopes which are given to them, are become a Sort of Creditors; and these Debts, being Debts of Honour, ought, according to the accustomed Maxim, to be first discharged.

WHEN I speak of Dependents, I would not be understood to mean those who are worthless in themselves, or who, without any Call, will press into the Company of their Betters. Nor, when I speak of Patrons, do I mean those who either have it not in their Power, or have no Obligation to assist their Friends; but I speak of such Leagues where there is Power and Obligation on the one Part, and Merit and Expectation on the other.

THE Division of Patron and Client, may, I believe, include a Third of our Nation; the Want of Merit and real Worth in the Client, will strike out about Ninety-Nine in a Hundred of these; and the Want of Ability in Patrons, as many of that Kind. But however, I must beg leave to say, that he who will take up another's Time and Fortune in his Service, though he has no Prospect of rewarding his Merit towards him, is as unjust in his Dealings as he who takes up Goods of a Tradesman without Intention or Ability to pay him. Of the few of the Class which

H 5
I think

I think fit to confider, there are not two in ten who
fucceed; infomuch that I know a Man of good Senfe
who put his Son to a Blackfmith, tho' an Offer was
made him of his being received as a Page to a Man of
Quality. There are not more Cripples come out of
the Wars than there are from thofe great Services; fome
through Difcontent lofe their Speech, fome their Me-
mories, others their Senfes or their Lives; and I feldom fee a Man thoroughly difcontented, but I conclude
he has had the Favour of fome great Man. I have
known of fuch as have been for twenty Years together
within a Month of a good Employment, but never
arrived at the Happinefs of being poffeffed of any
Thing.

THERE is nothing more ordinary, than that a Man
who is got into a confiderable Station, fhall immediately alter his Manner of treating all his Friends, and
from that Moment he is to deal with you as if he were
your Fate. You are no longer to be confulted, even
in Matters which concern yourfelf; but your Patron
is of a Species above you, and a free Communi-
cation with you is not to be expected. This perhaps
may be your Condition all the while he bears Office,
and when that is at an end, you are as intimate as
ever you were, and he will take it very ill if you
keep the Diftance he prefcribed you towards him in
his Grandeur. One would think this fhould be a Behaviour a Man could fall into, with the worft Grace
imaginable; but they who know the World have feen
it more than once. I have often, with fecret Pity,
heard the fame Man who has profeffed his Abhorrence againft all Kind of paffive Behaviour, lofe Minutes, Hours, Days, and Years in a fruitlefs Attendance
on one who had no Inclination to befriend him.
It is very much to be regarded, that the Great
have one particular Privilege above the reft of the
World, of being flow in receiving Impreffions of Kindnefs, and quick in taking Offence. The Elevation above
the reft of Mankind, except in very great Minds, makes
Men fo giddy, that they do not fee after the fame manner they did before: Thus they defpife their own Friends,
and ftrive to extend their Intereft to new Pretenders. By
this

this means it often happens, that when you come to know how you loft fuch an Employment, you will find the Man who got it never dreamed of it; but, forfooth, he was to be furprifed into it, or perhaps folicited to receive it. Upon fuch Occafions as thefe a Man may perhaps grow out of humour; if you are fo, all Mankind will fall in with the Patron, and you are an Humourift and untractable if you are capable of being four at a Difappointment: But it is the fame thing, whether you do or do not refent ill Ufage, you will be ufed after the fame manner; as fome good Mothers will be fure to whip their Children till they cry, and then whip them for crying.

THERE are but two Ways of doing any thing with great People, and thofe are by making yourfelf either confiderable or agreeable: The former is not to be attained but by finding a Way to live without them, or concealing that you want them; the latter is only by falling into their Tafte and Pleafures: This is of all the Employments in the World the moft fervile, except it happens to be of your own natural Humour. For to be agreeable to another, efpecially if he be above you, is not to be poffeffed of fuch Qualities and Accomplifhments as fhould render you agreeable in yourfelf, but fuch as make you agreeable in refpect to him. An Imitation of his Faults, or a Compliance, if not Subfervience, to his Vices, muft be the Meafures of your Conduct.

WHEN it comes to that, the unnatural State a Man lives in, when his Patron pleafes, is ended; and his Guilt and Complaifance are objected to him, tho' the Man who rejects him for his Vices was not only his Partner but Seducer. Thus the Client (like a young Woman who has given up the Innocence which made her charming) has not only loft his Time, but alfo the Virtue which could render him capable of refenting the Injury which is done him.

IT would be endlefs to recount the Tricks of turning you off from themfelves to Perfons who have lefs Power to ferve you, the Art of being forry for fuch an unaccountable Accident in your Behaviour, that fuch a one (who, perhaps, has never heard of you) oppofes your Advancement; and if you have any thing more than ordinary;

dinary in you, you are flattered with a Whisper, that 'tis no Wonder People are so slow in doing for a Man of your Talents and the like.

AFTER all this Treatment, I must still add the pleasantest Insolence of all, which I have once or twice seen; to wit, That when a silly Rogue has thrown away one Part in three of his Life in unprofitable Attendance, it is taken wonderfully ill that he withdraws, and is resolved to employ the rest for himself.

WHEN we consider these Things, and reflect upon so many honest Natures (which one, who makes Observation of what passes, may have seen) that have miscarried by such sort of Applications, it is too melancholy a Scene to dwell upon ; therefore I shall take another Opportunity to discourse of good Patrons, and distinguish such as have done their Duty to those who have depended upon them, and were not able to act without their Favour. Worthy Patrons are like *Plato*'s Guardian Angels, who are always doing good to their Wards ; but negligent Patrons are like *Epicurus*'s Gods, that lie lolling on the Clouds, and instead of Blessings pour down Storms and Tempests on the Heads of those that are offering Incense to them.   T

N° 215 *Tuesday*, November 6.

―――*Ingenuas didicisse fideliter artes*
Emollit mores, nec finit esse feros.
            Ovid. Ep. 9. l. 2. de Ponto, v. 47.

Ingenuous Arts, where they an Entrance find,
Soften the Manners, and subdue the Mind.

I Consider an human Soul without Education like Marble in the Quarry, which shews none of its inherent Beauties, 'till the Skill of the Polisher fetches out
                                                        the

the Colours, makes the Surface shine, and discovers every ornamental Cloud, Spot, and Vein that runs through the Body of it. Education, after the same manner, when it works upon a noble Mind, draws out to View every latent Virtue and Perfection, which without such Helps are never able to make their Appearance.

IF my Reader will give me leave to change the Allusion so soon upon him, I shall make use of the same Instance to illustrate the Force of Education, which *Aristotle* has brought to explain his Doctrine of Substantial Forms, when he tells us that a Statue lies hid in a Block of Marble; and that the Art of the Statuary only clears away the superfluous Matter, and removes the Rubbish. The Figure is in the Stone; the Sculptor only finds it. What Sculpture is to a Block of Marble, Education is to an human Soul. The Philosopher, the Saint, or the Hero, the Wise, the Good, or the Great Man, very often lie hid and concealed in a Plebeian, which a proper Education might have dis-interred, and have brought to light. I am therefore much delighted with reading the Accounts of savage Nations, and with contemplating those Virtues which are wild and uncultivated; to see Courage exerting itself in Fierceness, Resolution in Obstinacy, Wisdom in Cunning, Patience in Sullenness and Despair.

MENS Passions operate variously, and appear in different Kinds of Actions, according as they are more or less rectify'd and sway'd by Reason. When one hears of Negroes, who upon the Death of their Masters, or upon changing their Service, hang themselves upon the next Tree, as it frequently happens in our *American* Plantations, who can forbear admiring their Fidelity, tho' it expresses itself in so dreadful a manner? What might not that savage Greatness of Soul which appears in these poor Wretches on many Occasions, be raised to, were it rightly cultivated? And what Colour of Excuse can there be for the Contempt with which we treat this Part of our Species? That we should not put them upon the common foot of Humanity, that we should only set an insignificant Fine upon the Man who murders them; nay, that we should, as much as in us lies, cut them off from the Prospects of Happiness in another World as well as in this,

this, and deny them, that which we look upon as the proper Means for attaining it?

SINCE I am engaged on this Subject, I cannot forbear mentioning a Story which I have lately heard, and which is so well attested, that I have no manner of reason to suspect the Truth of it. I may call it a kind of wild Tragedy that passed about twelve Years ago at St. *Christophers*, one of our *British* Leeward Islands. The Negroes who were the Persons concern'd in it, were all of them the Slaves of a Gentleman who is now in *England*.

THIS Gentleman among his Negroes had a young Woman, who was look'd upon as a most extraordinary Beauty by those of her own Complexion. He had at the same time two young Fellows who were likewise Negroes and Slaves, remarkable for the Comeliness of their Persons, and for the Friendship which they bore to one another. It unfortunately happen'd that both of them fell in love with the Female Negroe above-mentioned, who would have been very glad to have taken either of them for her Husband, provided they could agree between themselves which should be the Man. But they were both so passionately in love with her, that neither of them could think of giving her up to his Rival; and at the same time were so true to one another, that neither of them would think of gaining her without his Friend's Consent. The Torments of these two Lovers were the Discourse of the Family to which they belonged, who could not forbear observing the strange Complication of Passions which perplexed the Hearts of the poor Negroes, that often dropped Expressions of the Uneasiness they underwent, and how impossible it was for either of them ever to be happy.

AFTER a long Struggle between Love and Friendship, Truth and Jealousy, they one Day took a Walk together into a Wood, carrying the Mistress along with them: Where, after abundance of Lamentations, they stabbed her to the Heart, of which she immediately died. A Slave who was at his Work not far from the Place where this astonishing Piece of Cruelty was committed, hearing the Shrieks of the dying Person, ran to see what was the Occasion of them. He there discovered the Woman

man

man lying dead upon the Ground, with the two Negroes on each fide of her, kiffing the dead Corps, weeping over it, and beating their Breafts in the utmoft Agonies of Grief and Defpair. He immediately ran to the *Englifh* Family with the News of what he had feen; who upon coming to the Place faw the Woman dead, and the two Negroes expiring by her with Wounds they had given themfelves.

WE fee in this amazing Inftance of Barbarity, what ftrange Diforders are bred in the Minds of thofe Men whofe Paffions are not regulated by Virtue, and difciplined by Reafon. Tho' the Action which I have recited is in itfelf full of Guilt and Horror, it proceeded from a Temper of Mind which might have produced very noble Fruits, had it been informed and guided by a fuitable Education.

IT is therefore an unfpeakable Bleffing to be born in thofe Parts of the World where Wifdom and Knowledge flourifh; tho' it muft be confefs'd, there are, even in thefe Parts, feveral poor uninftructed Perfons, who are but little above the Inhabitants of thofe Nations of which I have been here fpeaking; as thofe who have had the Advantages of a more liberal Education, rife above one another by feveral different Degrees of Perfection. For to return to our Statue in the Block of Marble, we fee it fometimes only begun to be chipped, fometimes roughhewn, and but juft fketched into an human Figure; fometimes we fee the Man appearing diftinctly in all his Limbs and Features, fometimes we find the Figure wrought up to a great Elegancy, but feldom meet with any to which the Hand of a *Phidias* or *Praxiteles* could not give feveral nice Touches and Finifhings.

DISCOURSES of Morality, and Reflexions upon human Nature, are the beft Means we can make ufe of to improve our Minds, and gain a true Knowledge of ourfelves, and confequently to recover our Souls out of the Vice, Ignorance, and Prejudice, which naturally cleave to them. I have all along profeft myfelf in this Paper a Promoter of thefe great Ends; and I flatter myfelf that I do from Day to Day contribute fomething to the polifhing of Mens Minds: at leaft my Defign is laudable, whatever the Execution may be. I muft confefs I am not

a little

a little encouraged in it by many Letters which I receive from unknown Hands, in Approbation of my Endeavours; and muſt take this Opportunity of returning my Thanks to thoſe who write them, and excuſing myſelf for not inſerting ſeveral of them in my Papers, which I am ſenſible would be a very great Ornament to them. Should I publiſh the Praiſes which are ſo well penned, they would do Honour to the Perſons who write them, but my publiſhing of them would I fear be a ſufficient Inſtance to the World that I did not deſerve them.   C

N° 216 *Wedneſday, November* 7.

Siquidem herclè poſſis, nil prius, neque fortius:
Verùm ſi incipies, neque perficies naviter,
Atque, ubi pati non poteris, cùm nemo expetet,
Infectâ pace, ultrò ad eam venies, indicans
Te amare, & ferre non poſſe: Actum eſt, ilicet,
Periſti: eludet, ubi te victum ſenſerit.
Ter. Eun. Act 1. Sc. 1.

If indeed you can keep to your Reſolution, you will act a noble and a manly part: but if, when you have ſet about it, your Courage fails you, and you make a voluntary Submiſſion, acknowledging the Violence of your Paſſion, and your Inability to hold out any longer; all's over with you; you are undone, and may go hang yourſelf; ſhe will inſult over you, when ſhe finds you her Slave.

To Mr. SPECTATOR.

S I R,

'THIS is to inform you, that Mr. *Freeman* had no
' ſooner taken Coach, but his Lady was taken
' with a terrible Fit of the Vapours, which 'tis
' feared will make her miſcarry, if not endanger her
' Life; therefore, dear Sir, if you know of any Receipt
' that is good againſt this faſhionable reigning Diſtem-
' per,

' per, be pleafed to communicate it for the Good of the
' Publick, and you will oblige

Yours,

A. NOEWILL.

Mr. SPECTATOR,

'THE Uproar was fo great affoon as I had read
' the *Spectator* concerning Mrs. *Freeman*, that af-
' ter many Revolutions in her Temper, of raging, fwoon-
' ing, railing, fainting, pitying herfelf, and reviling her
' Hufband, upon an accidental coming in of a neigh-
' bouring Lady (who fays fhe has writ to you alfo) fhe
' had nothing left for it but to fall in a Fit. I had the
' Honour to read the Paper to her, and have a pretty good
' Command of my Countenance and Temper on fuch
' Occafions; and foon found my hiftorical Name to be
' *Tom Meggot* in your Writings, but concealed myfelf
' till I faw how it affected Mrs. *Freeman*. She looked
' frequently at her Hufband, as often at me; and fhe
' did not tremble as fhe filled Tea, till fhe came to the
' Circumftance of *Armftrong*'s writing out a Piece of
' *Tully* for an Opera Tune: Then fhe burft out, She was
' expofed, fhe was deceiv'd, fhe was wronged and abufed:
' The Tea-cup was thrown in the Fire; and without
' taking Vengeance on her Spoufe, fhe faid of me, That
' I was a pretending Coxcomb, a Medler that knew not
' what it was to interpofe in fo nice an Affair as between
' a Man and his Wife. To which Mr. *Freeman*, Madam,
' were I lefs fond of you than I am, I fhould not have
' taken this Way of writing to the SPECTATOR, to
' inform a Woman whom God and Nature has placed
' under my Direction, with what I requeft of her; but
' fince you are fo indifcreet as not to take the Hint
' which I gave you in that Paper, I muft tell you, Ma-
' dam, in fo many Words, that you have for a long and
' tedious Space of Time acted a Part unfuitable to the
' Senfe you ought to have of the Subordination in which
' you are placed. And I muft acquaint you once for all,
' that the Fellow without, ha *Tom!* (here the Footman
' entered and anfwered Madam) Sirrah don't you know
' my Voice? look upon me when I fpeak to you: I fay,

' Madam,

' Madam, this Fellow here is to know of me myself,
' whether I am at Leisure to see Company or not. I am
' from this Hour Master of this House; and my Business
' in it, and every where else, is to behave myself in such
' a manner, as it shall be hereafter an Honour to you to
' bear my Name; and your Pride, that you are the De-
' light, the Darling and Ornament of a Man of Honour,
' useful and esteemed by his Friends; and I no longer
' one that has buried some Merit in the World, in Com-
' pliance to a froward Humour which has grown upon
' an agreeable Woman by his Indulgence. Mr. *Freeman*
' ended this with a Tenderness in his Aspect and a down-
' cast Eye, which shewed he was extremely moved at the
' Anguish he saw her in; for she sat swelling with Pas-
' sion, and her Eyes fixed on the Fire; when
' I, fearing he would lose again, took upon me to
' provoke her out of that amiable Sorrow she was in, to
' fall upon me; upon which I said very seasonably for
' my Friend, That indeed Mr. *Freeman* was become the
' common Talk of the Town; and that nothing was so
' much a Jest, as when it was said in Company he, *Free-*
' *man* has promised to come to such a Place. Upon which
' the good Lady turned her Softness into downright
' Rage, and threw the scalding Tea-kettle upon your
' humble Servant; flew into the Middle of the Room,
' and cried out she was the unfortunatest of all Women:
' Others kept Family Dissatisfactions for Hours of Pri-
' vacy and Retirement; No Apology was to be made to
' her, no Expedient to be found, no previous Manner of
' breaking what was amiss in her, but all the World was
' to be acquainted with her Errors, without the least Ad-
' monition. Mr. *Freeman* was going to make a softening
' Speech, but I interposed, Look you, Madam, I have
' nothing to say to this Matter, but you ought to con-
' sider you are now past a Chicken; this Humour, which
' was well enough in a Girl, is insufferable in one
' of your motherly Character. With that she lost all Pa-
' tience, and flew directly at her Husband's Periwig. I
' got her in my Arms, and defended my Friend: He
' making Signs at the same time that it was too much;
' I beckoning, nodding, and frowning over her Shoulder,
' that he was lost if he did not persist. In this manner she
' flew

'flew round and round the Room in a Moment, 'till the
'Lady I spoke of above and Servants entered; upon
'which she fell on a Couch as breathless. I still kept up
'my Friend; but he, with a very silly Air, bid them
'bring the Coach to the Door, and we went off, I
'forced to bid the Coachman drive on. We were no
'sooner come to my Lodgings, but all his Wife's Rela-
'tions came to enquire after him; and Mrs. *Freeman's*
'Mother writ a Note, wherein she thought never to have
'seen this Day, and so forth.

'IN a word, Sir, I am afraid we are upon a thing we
'have no Talents for; and I can observe already, my
'Friend looks upon me rather as a Man that knows a
'Weakness of him that he is ashamed of, than one who
'has rescu'd him from Slavery. Mr. SPECTATOR, I
'am but a young Fellow, and if Mr. *Freeman* submits, I
'shall be looked upon as an Incendiary, and never get a
'Wife as long as I breathe. He has indeed sent word
'home he shall lie at *Hampstead* to-night; but I believe
'Fear of the first Onset after this Rupture has too great
'a Place in this Resolution. Mrs. *Freeman* has a very
'pretty Sister; suppose I delivered him up, and articled
'with the Mother for her bringing him home. If he
'has not Courage to stand it, (you are a great Casuist)
'is it such an ill thing to bring myself off, as well as
'I can? What makes me doubt my Man,' is, that I
'find he thinks it reasonable to expostulate at least with
'her; and Capt. SENTRY will tell you, if you let
'your Orders be disputed, you are no longer a Com-
'mander. I wish you could advise me how to get clear
'of this Business handsomly.

T   *Yours,* Tom Meggot.

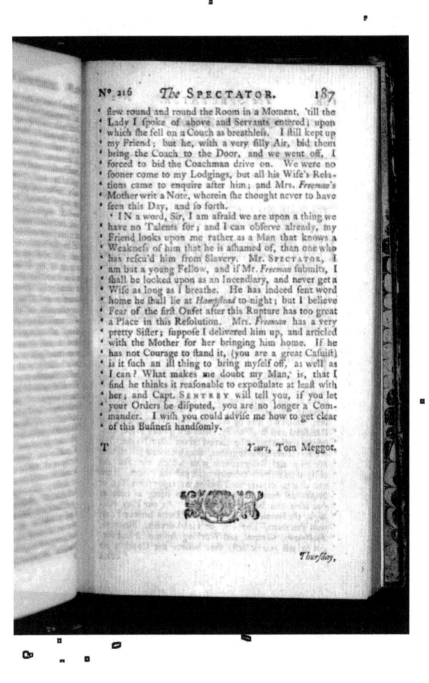

Thursday,

' Madam, this Fellow here is to know of me myself,
' whether I am at Leisure to see Company or not. I am
' from this Hour Master of this House; and my Business
' in it, and every where else, is to behave myself in such
' a manner, as it shall be hereafter an Honour to you to
' bear my Name; and your Pride, that you are the De-
' light, the Darling and Ornament of a Man of Honour,
' useful and esteemed by his Friends; and I no longer
' one that has buried some Merit in the World, in Com-
' pliance to a froward Humour which has grown upon
' an agreeable Woman by his Indulgence. Mr. *Freeman*
' ended this with a Tenderness in his Aspect and a down-
' cast Eye, which shewed he was extremely moved at the
' Anguish he saw her in; for she sat swelling with Paf-
' sion, and her Eyes firmly fixed on the Fire; when
' I, fearing he would lose again, took upon me to
' provoke her out of that amiable Sorrow she was in, to
' fall upon me; upon which I said very seasonably for
' my Friend, That indeed Mr. *Freeman* was become the
' common Talk of the Town; and that nothing was so
' much a Jest, as when it was said in Company Mr. *Free-*
' *man* has promised to come to such a Place. Upon which
' the good Lady turned her Softness into downright
' Rage, and threw the scalding Tea-kettle upon your
' humble Servant; flew into the Middle of the Room,
' and cried out she was the unfortunatest of all Women:
' Others kept Family Dissatisfactions for Hours of Pri-
' vacy and Retirement: No Apology was to be made to
' her, no Expedient to be found, no previous Manner of
' breaking what was amiss in her; but all the World was
' to be acquainted with her Errors, without the least Ad-
' monition. Mr. *Freeman* was going to make a soft'ning
' Speech, but I interposed; Look you, Madam, I have
' nothing to say to this Matter, but you ought to con-
' sider you are now past a Chicken; this Humour, which
' was well enough in a Girl, is insufferable in one
' of your motherly Character. With that she lost all Pa-
' tience, and flew directly at her Husband's Periwig. I
' got her in my Arms, and defended my Friend: He
' making Signs at the same time that it was too much;
' I beckoning, nodding, and frowning over her Shoulder,
' that he was lost if he did not persist. In this manner she
' flew

' flew round and round the Room in a Moment, 'till the
' Lady I fpoke of above and Servants entered; upon
' which fhe fell on a Couch as breathlefs. I ftill kept up
' my Friend; but he, with a very filly Air, bid them
' bring the Coach to the Door, and we went off, I
' forced to bid the Coachman drive on. We were no
' fooner come to my Lodgings, but all his Wife's Rela-
' tions came to enquire after him; and Mrs. *Freeman*'s
' Mother writ a Note, wherein fhe thought never to have
' feen this Day, and fo forth.

' IN a word, Sir, I am afraid we are upon a thing we
' have no Talents for; and I can obferve already, my
' Friend looks upon me rather as a Man that knows a
' Weaknefs of him that he is afhamed of, than one who
' has refcu'd him from Slavery. Mr. SPECTATOR, I
' am but a young Fellow, and if Mr. *Freeman* fubmits, I
' fhall be looked upon as an Incendiary, and never get a
' Wife as long as I breathe. He has indeed fent word
' home he fhall lie at *Hampftead* to-night; but I believe
' Fear of the firft Onfet after this Rupture has too great
' a Place in this Refolution. Mrs. *Freeman* has a very
' pretty Sifter; fuppofe I delivered him up, and articled
' with the Mother for her bringing him home. If he
' has not Courage to ftand it, (you are a great Cafuift)
' is it fuch an ill thing to bring myfelf off, as well as
' I can? What makes me doubt my Man, is, that I
' find he thinks it reafonable to expoftulate at leaft with
' her; and Capt. SENTREY will tell you, if you let
' your Orders be difputed, you are no longer a Com-
' mander. I wifh you could advife me how to get clear
' of this Bufinefs handfomly.

T   *Yours*, Tom Meggot.

Thurfday,

Nº 217 *Thursday, November* 8.

—— *Tunc fæmina simplex,*
Et pariter toto repetitur clamor ab antro.
Juv. Sat. 6. v. 326.

Then unreftrain'd by Rules of Decency,
Th' affembled Females raife a general Cry.

I Shall entertain my Reader to-day with fome Letters from my Correfpondents. The firft of them is the De-fcription of a Club, whether real or imaginary, I can-not determine; but am apt to fancy, that the Writer of it, whoever fhe is, has formed a kind of Nocturnal Orgie out of her own Fancy: Whether this be fo or not, her Letter may conduce to the Amendment of that Kind of Perfons who are reprefented in it, and whofe Characters are frequent enough in the World.

Mr. SPECTATOR,

' IN fome of your firft Papers you were pleafed to give ' the Publick a very diverting Account of feveral ' Clubs and nocturnal Affemblies; but I am a Member ' of a Society which has wholly efcap'd your Notice, I ' mean a Club of She-Romps. We take each a Hackney-' Coach, and meet once a Week in a large upper Cham-' ber, which we hire by the Year for that Purpofe; our ' Landlord and his Family, who are quiet People, con-' ftantly contriving to be abroad on our Club-Night. We ' are no fooner come together, than we throw off all that ' Modefty and Refervednefs with which our Sex are ' obliged to difguife themfelves in publick Places. I am ' not able to exprefs the Pleafure we enjoy from Ten at ' Night 'till four in the Morning, in being as rude as ' you Men can be for your Lives. As our Play runs ' high, the Room is immediately fill'd with broken Fans, ' torn Petticoats, Lappets, or Head-dreffes, Flounces, ' Furbelows, Garters, and Working-Aprons. I had for-' got to tell you at firft, that befides the Coaches we
' come

' come in ourselves, there is one which stands always
' empty to carry off our *dead Men*, for so we call all those
' Fragments and Tatters with which the Room is strew'd,
' and which we pack up together in Bundles and put in-
' to the aforesaid Coach: It is no small Diversion for us
' to meet the next Night at some Member's Chamber,
' where every one is to pick out what belonged to her
' from this confused Bundle of Silks, Stuffs, Laces, and
' Ribbons. I have hitherto given you an Account of our
' Diversion on ordinary Club-Nights; but must acquaint
' you further, that once a Month we *demolish a Prude*,
' that is, we get some queer formal Creature in among
' us, and unrig her in an Instant. Our last Month's Prude
' was so armed and fortified in Whalebone and Buck-
' ram, that we had much ado to come at her ; but you
' would have died with laughing to have seen how the
' sober aukward Thing looked when she was forced out
' of her Intrenchments. In short, Sir, it is impossible
' to give you a true Notion of our Sport, unless you
' would come one Night amongst us ; and tho' it be di-
' rectly against the Rules of our Society to admit a Male
' Visitant, we repose so much Confidence in your Silence
' and Taciturnity, that it was agreed by the whole Club,
' at our last Meeting, to give you Entrance for one Night
' as a Spectator.

I am your humble Servant,

Kitty Termagant.

P.S. *We shall demolish a Prude next* Thursday.

THO' I thank *Kitty* for her kind Offer, I do not at
present find in myself any Inclination to venture my Person with her and her romping Companions. I should
regard myself as a second *Clodius* intruding on the mysterious Rites of the *Bona Dea*, and should apprehend being *Demolished* as much as the *Prude*.

THE following Letter comes from a Gentleman,
whose Taste I find is much too delicate to endure the
least Advance towards Romping. I may, perhaps, hereafter improve upon the Hint he has given me, and make
it the Subject of a whole *Spectator*; in the mean time
take it as it follows in his own Words.

Mr.

Mr. SPECTATOR,

'IT is my Misfortune to be in love with a young
'Creature who is daily committing Faults, which
'though they give me the utmoſt Uneaſineſs, I know
'not how to reprove her for, or even acquaint her with.
'She is pretty, dreſſes well, is rich, and good-humour'd;
'but either wholly neglects, or has no Notion of that
'which polite People have agreed to diſtinguiſh by the
'Name of *Delicacy*. After our Return from a Walk the
'other Day ſhe threw herſelf into an Elbow-Chair, and
'profeſſed before a large Company, that *ſhe was all over
'in a Sweat*. She told me this Afternoon that her *Sto-
'mach ak'd*; and was complaining Yeſterday at Dinner
'of ſomething that *ſtuck in her Teeth*. I treated her with
'a Baſket of Fruit laſt Summer, which ſhe eat ſo very
'greedily, as almoſt made me reſolve never to ſee her
'more. In ſhort, Sir, I begin to tremble whenever I
'ſee her about to ſpeak or move. As ſhe does not want
'Senſe, if ſhe takes theſe Hints I am happy; if not, I am
'more than afraid, that theſe Things which ſhock me
'even in the Behaviour of a Miſtreſs, will appear inſup-
'portable in that of a Wife.

                              I am, SIR, *Yours,* &c.

MY next Letter comes from a Correſpondent whom
I cannot but very much value, upon the Account which
ſhe gives of herſelf.

Mr. SPECTATOR,

'I Am happily arrived at a State of Tranquillity, which
'few People envy, I mean that of an old Maid;
'therefore being wholly unconcerned in all that Medley
'of Follies which our Sex is apt to contract from their
'ſilly Fondneſs of yours, I read your Ralleries on us
'without Provocation. I can ſay with *Hamlet*,

—— *Man delights not me,*
Nor Woman neither ——

'Therefore, dear Sir, as you never ſpare your own Sex,
'do not be afraid of reproving what is ridiculous in ours,
'and you will oblige at leaſt one Woman, who is
            Your Humble Servant, Suſannah Froſt.
                                            Mr.

Mr. SPECTATOR,

"I Am Wife to a Clergyman, and cannot help think-
"ing that in your Tenth or Tithe Character, of Wo-
"mankind you meant myself, therefore I have no Quarrel
"against you for the other Nine Characters.

.X.   *Your Humble Servant,* A. B.

* * *

Nº 218 · *Friday, November* 9.

> *Quid de quoque viro, & cui dicas, fæpe caveto.*
>   Hor. Ep. 18. l. i. v. 68.

> ———————— *Have a care*
> *Of whom you talk, to whom, and what, and where.*
>   POOLY.

I Happened the other Day, as my Way is, to ftroll into a little Coffee-houfe beyond *Aldgate*; and as I fat
there, two or three very plain fenfible Men were
talking of the SPECTATOR. One faid, he had that
Morning drawn the great Benefit Ticket; another wifhed
he had; but a third fhaked his Head and faid, It was
pity that the Writer of that Paper was fuch a fort of
Man, that it was no great Matter whether he had it or
no. He is, it feems, faid the good Man, the moft extravagant Creature in the World; has run thro' vaft Sums,
and yet been in continual Want; a Man, for all he talks
fo well of Oeconomy, unfit for any of the Offices of Life
by reafon of his Profufenefs. It would be an unhappy
Thing to be his Wife, his Child, or his Friend; and
yet he talks as well of thofe Duties of Life as any one.
Much Reflexion has brought me to fo eafy a Contempt
for every thing which is falfe, that this heavy Accufation
gave me no manner of Uneafinefs; but at the fame time
it threw me into deep Thought upon the Subject of Fame
in general; and I could not but pity fuch as were fo weak,
as to value what the common People fay out of their
                                                          own

own talkative Temper to the Advantage or Diminution
of thofe whom they mention, without being moved either by Malice or Good-will. It will be too long to
expatiate upon the Senfe all Mankind have of Fame, and
the inexpreffible Pleafure which there is in the Approbation of worthy Men, to all who are capable of worthy
Actions; but methinks one may divide the general Word
Fame into three different Species, as it regards the different Orders of Mankind who have any Thing to do
with it. Fame therefore may be divided into Glory,
which refpects the Hero; Reputation, which is preferved
by every Gentleman ; and Credit, which muft be fupported by every Tradefman. Thefe Poffeffions in Fame
are dearer than Life to thefe Characters of Men, or rather
are the Life of thofe Characters. Glory, while the Hero
purfues great and noble Enterprifes, is impregnable ;
and all the Affailants of his Renown do but fhew their
Pain and Impatience of its Brightnefs, without throwing
the leaft Shade upon it. If the Foundation of an high
Name be Virtue and Service, all that is offered againft it
is but Rumour, which is too fhort-liv'd to ftand up in
Competition with Glory, which is everlafting.

REPUTATION, which is the Portion of every
Man who would live with the elegant and knowing Part
of Mankind, is as ftable as Glory, if it be as well founded ; and the common Caufe of human Society is thought
concerned when we hear a Man of good Behaviour calumniated : Befides which, according to a prevailing
Cuftom amongft us, every Man has his Defence in his
own Arm: and Reproach is foon checked, put out of
Countenance, and overtaken by Difgrace.

THE moft unhappy of all Men, and the moft expofed to the Malignity or Wantonnefs of the common
Voice, is the Trader. Credit is undone in Whifpers.
The Tradefman's Wound is received from one who is
more private and more cruel than the Ruffian with the
Lanthorn and Dagger. The Manner of repeating a
Man's Name,--As; *Mr.* Cafh, *Oh! do you leave your Money
at his Shop ? Why, do you know Mr.* Searoom ? *He is indeed a general Merchant.* I fay, I have feen, from the
Iteration of a Man's Name, hiding one Thought of him,
and explaining what you hide, by faying fomething to his

Advantage

Advantage when you fpeak, a Merchant hurt in his Credit;
and him who, every Day he lived, literally added to the
Value of his Native Country, undone by one who was
only a Burden and a Blemifh to it. Since every Body who
knows the World is fenfible of this great Evil, how careful ought a Man to be in his Language of a Merchant?
It may poffibly be in the Power of a very fhallow Creature to lay the Ruin of the beft Family in the moft opulent
City; and the more fo, the more highly he deferves of
his Country; that is to fay, the farther he places his Wealth
out of his Hands, to draw home that of another Climate.
IN this Cafe an ill-Word may change Plenty into
Want, and by a rafh Sentence a free and generous Fortune may in a few Days be reduced to Beggary. How
little does a giddy Prater imagine, that an idle Phrafe to
the Disfavour of a Merchant, may be as pernicious in the
Confequence, as the Forgery of a Deed to bar an Inheritance would be to a Gentleman? Land ftands where it
did before a Gentleman was calumniated, and the State
of a great Action is juft as it was before Calumny was offered to diminifh it; and there is Time, Place and Occafion, expected to unravel all that is contrived againft thofe
Characters; but the Trader who is ready only for probable
Demands upon him, can have no Armour againft the Inquifitive, the Malicious, and the Envious, who are prepared to fill the Cry to his Difhonour. Fire and Sword
are flow Engines of Deftruction, in Comparifon of the
Babbler in the Cafe of the Merchant.
FOR this Reafon I thought it an imitable Piece of
Humanity of a Gentleman of my Acquaintance, who had
great Variety of Affairs, and ufed to talk with Warmth
enough againft Gentlemen by whom he thought himfelf ill dealt with; but he would never let any thing be
urged againft a Merchant (with whom he had any Difference) except in a Court of Juftice. He ufed to fay, that to
fpeak ill of a Merchant, was to begin his Suit with Judgment
and Execution. One cannot, I think, fay more on this Occafion, then to repeat, That the Merit of the Merchant is
above that of all other Subjects; for while he is untouched
in his Credit, his Hand-writing is a more portable Coin
for the Service of his Fellow-Citizens, and his Word the
Gold of *Ophir* to the Country wherein he refides.   T

N°. 219 *Saturday, November* 10.

Vix ea noftra voco——— Ovid. Met. l. 13. v. 141.
Thefe I fcarce call our own.

THERE are but few Men, who are not ambitious of diftinguifhing themfelves in the Nation or Country where they live, and of growing confi-derable among thofe with whom they converfe. There is a kind of Grandeur and Refpect, which the meaneft and moft infignificant Part of Mankind endeavour to procure in the little Circle of their Friends and Acquaintance. The pooreft Mechanick, nay the Man who lives upon common Alms, gets him his Set of Admirers, and delights in that Superiority which he enjoys over thofe who are in fome refpects beneath him. This Ambition, which is natural to the Soul of Man, might methinks receive a very happy Turn ; and, if it were rightly directed, contribute as much to a Perfon's Advantage, as it generally does to his Uneafinefs and Difquiet.

I fhall therefore put together fome Thoughts on this Subject, which I have not met with in other Writers ; and fhall fet them down as they have occurred to me, without being at the pains to connect or methodife them.

ALL Superiority and Preeminence that one Man can have over another, may be reduced to the Notion of *Quality*, which, confidered at large, is either that of Fortune, Body, or Mind. The firft is that which confifts in Birth, Title, or Riches ; and is the moft foreign to our Natures, and what we can the leaft call our own of any of the three Kinds of Quality. In relation to the Body, Quality arifes from Health, Strength, or Beauty ; which are nearer to us, and more a Part of ourfelves than the former. Quality, as it regards the Mind, has its Rife from Knowledge or Virtue ; and is that which is more effential to us, and more intimately united with us than either of the other two.

THE

THE Quality of Fortune, tho' a Man has lefs Reafon to value himfelf upon it than on that of the Body or Mind, is however the kind of Quality which makes the moft fhining Figure in the Eye of the World.

AS Virtue is the moft reafonable and genuine Source of Honour, we generally find in Titles an Intimation of fome particular Merit that fhould recommend Men to the high Stations which they poffefs. Holinefs is afcribed to the Pope; Majefty to Kings; Serenity or Mildnefs of Temper to Princes; Excellence or Perfection to Ambaffadors; Grace to Archbifhops; Honour to Peers; Worfhip or Venerable Behaviour to Magiftrates; and Reverence, which is of the fame Import as the former, to the inferior Clergy.

IN the Founders of great Families, fuch Attributes of Honour are generally correfpondent with the Virtues of the Perfon to whom they are applied; but in the Defcendents they are too often the Marks rather of Grandeur than of Merit. The Stamp and Denomination ftill continues, but the intrinfick Value is frequently loft.

THE Death-bed fhews the Emptinefs of Titles in a true Light. A poor difpirited Sinner lies trembling under the Apprehenfions of the State he is entring on; and is asked by a grave Attendant how his Holinefs does? Another hears himfelf addreffed to under the Title of Highnefs or Excellency, who lies under fuch mean Circumftances of Mortality as are the Difgrace of human Nature. Titles at fuch a time look rather like Infults and Mockery than Refpect.

THE Truth of it is, Honours are in this World under no Regulation; true Quality is neglected, Virtue is oppreffed, and Vice triumphant. The laft Day will rectify this Diforder, and affign to every one a Station fuitable to the Dignity of his Character; Ranks will be then adjufted, and Precedency fet right.

METHINKS we fhould have an Ambition, if not to advance ourfelves in another World, at leaft to preferve our Poft in it, and outfhine our Inferiors in Virtue here, that they may not be put above us in a State which is to fettle the Diftinction for Eternity.

MEN in Scripture are called *Strangers* and *Sojourners upon Earth*, and Life a *Pilgrimage*. Several Heathen, as

well

well as Chriſtian Authors, under the ſame kind of Metaphor, have repreſented the World as an Inn, which
was only deſigned to furniſh us with Accommodations in
this our Paſſage. It is therefore very abſurd to think of
ſetting up our Reſt before we come to our Journey's End,
and not rather to take care of the Reception we ſhall
there meet, than to fix our Thoughts on the little Conveniences and Advantages which we enjoy one above
another in the Way to it.

E P I C T E T U S makes uſe of another Kind of
Alluſion, which is very beautiful, and wonderfully proper to incline us to be ſatisfied with the Poſt in which
Providence has placed us. We are here, ſays he, as in
a Theatre, where every one has a Part allotted to
him. The great Duty which lies upon a Man is to act
his Part in Perfection. We may indeed ſay, that our
Part does not ſuit us, and that we could act another
better. But this (ſays the Philoſopher) is not our
Buſineſs. All that we are concerned in is to excel
in the Part which is given us. If it be an improper one,
the Fault is not in us, but in him who has *caſt*
our ſeveral Parts, and is the great Diſpoſer of the
Drama.

T H E Part that was acted by this Philoſopher himſelf was but a very indifferent one, for he lived and died
a Slave. His Motive to Contentment in this Particular, receives a very great Inforcement from the above-
mentioned Conſideration, if we remember that our
Parts in the other World will be *new caſt*, and that
Mankind will be there ranged in different Stations of
Superiority and Preeminence, in Proportion as they
have here excelled one another in Virtue, and performed
in their ſeveral Poſts of Life the Duties which belong to
them.

T H E R E are many beautiful Paſſages in the little
Apocryphal Book, intitled, *The Wiſdom of* Solomon,
to ſet forth the Vanity of Honour, and the like temporal Bleſſings which are in ſo great Repute among
Men, and to comfort thoſe who have not the Poſſeſſion of them. It repreſents in very warm and noble
Terms this Advancement of a good Man in the other
World, and the great Surpriſe which it will produce
among

among thofe who are his Superiors in this. 'Then fhall
' the righteous Man ftand in great Boldnefs before the
' Face of fuch as have afflicted him, and made no Ac-
' count of his Labours. When they fee it, they fhall
' be troubled with terrible Fear, and fhall be amazed at
' the Strangenefs of his Salvation, fo far beyond all that
' they looked for. And they repenting and groaning
' for Anguifh of Spirit, fhall fay within themfelves;
' This was he whom we had fometime in Derifion, and
' a Proverb of Reproach We Fools accounted his Life
' Madnefs, and his End to be without Honour. How is
' he numbered among the Children of God, and his
' Lot is among the Saints!

IF the Reader would fee the Defcription of a Life
that is paffed away in Vanity and among the Shadows of
Pomp and Greatnefs, he may fee it very finely drawn in
the fame Place. In the mean time, fince it is neceffary
in the prefent Conftitution of Things, that Order and
Diftinction fhould be kept in the World, we fhould be
happy, if thofe who enjoy the upper Stations in it, would
endeavour to furpafs others in Virtue, as much as in
Rank, and by their Humanity and Condefcenfion make
their Superiority eafy and acceptable to thofe who are
beneath them; and if, on the contrary, thofe who are
in meaner Pofts of Life, would confider how they may
better their Condition hereafter, and by a juft Deference
and Submiffion to their Superiors, make them happy in
thofe Bleffings with which Providence has thought fit to
diftinguifh them. C

N° 220 *Monday, November* 12.

Rumoresque ferit varios—— Virg. Æn. 12. v. 228.

A thousand Rumours spreads.

SIR,

'WHY will you apply to my Father for my Love?
' I cannot help it if he will give you my Person;
'   but I assure you it is not in his Power, not
' even in my own, to give you my Heart. Dear Sir, do
' but consider the ill Consequence of such a Match; you
' are Fifty-five, I Twenty-one. You are a Man of Busi-
' ness, and mightily conversant in Arithmetick and making
' Calculations; be pleased therefore to consider what
' Proportion your Spirits bear to mine, and when you
' have made a just Estimate of the necessary Decay on
' one Side, and the Redundance on the other, you will
' act accordingly. This perhaps is such Language as you
' may not expect from a young Lady; but my Happiness
' is at Stake, and I must talk plainly. I mortally hate
' you; and so, as you and my Father agree, you may
' take me or leave me: But if you will be so good as
' never to see me more, you will for ever oblige,

SIR, Your most humble Servant,

HENRIETTA.

Mr. SPECTATOR,

'THERE are so many Artifices and Modes of false
'   Wit, and such a Variety of Humour discovers
' itself among its Votaries, that it would be impossible
' to exhaust so fertile a Subject, if you would think fit to
' resume it. The following Instances may, if you think
' fit, be added by way of Appendix to your Discourses
' on that Subject.
'   THAT Feat of Poetical Activity mentioned by
' *Horace,* of an Author who could compose two hundred
' Verses while he stood upon one Leg, has been imitated

' (as

‘ (as I have heard) by a modern Writer; who priding him-
‘ felf on the Hurry of his Invention, thought it no fmall
‘ Addition to his Fame to have each Piece minuted with
‘ the exact Number of Hours or Days it coft him in the
‘ Compofition. He could tafte no Praife till he had ac-
‘ quainted you in how fhort Space of Time he had de-
‘ ferved it ; and was not fo much led to an Oftentation
‘ of his Art, as of his Difpatch.

———————*Accipe fi vis,*
Accipiam tabulas ; *detur nobis locus, hora,*
Cuftodes : videamus uter plus fcribere poffit.

Hor. Sat. 4. l. 1. v. 14.

Here’s Pen and Ink, and Time, and Place; let’s try,
Who can write moft, and fafteft, you or I.　CREECH.

‘ THIS was the whole of his Ambition ; and there-
‘ fore I cannot but think the Flights of this rapid Author
‘ very proper to be oppofed to thofe laborious Nothings
‘ which you have obferved were the Delight of the *Ger-*
‘ *man* Wits, and in which they fo happily got rid of
‘ fuch a tedious Quantity of their Time.
‘ I have known a Gentleman of another Turn of Hu-
‘ mour, who, defpifing the Name of an Author, never
‘ printed his Works, but contracted his Talent, and by
‘ the help of a very fine Diamond which he wore on
‘ his little Finger, was a confiderable Poet upon Glafs.
‘ He had a very good Epigrammatick Wit ; and there
‘ was not a Parlour or Tavern-Window where he
‘ vifited or dined for fome Years, which did not re-
‘ ceive fome Sketches or Memorials of it. It was his
‘ Misfortune at laft to lofe his Genius and his Ring to a
‘ Sharper at Play, and he has not attempted to make a
‘ Verfe fince.
‘ BUT of all Contractions or Expedients for Wit, I
‘ admire that of an ingenious Projector whofe Book I
‘ have feen. This Virtuofo being a Mathematician, has,
‘ according to his Tafte, thrown the Art of Poetry into
‘ a fhort Problem, and contrived Tables by which any
‘ one without knowing a Word of Grammar or Senfe,
‘ may, to his great Comfort, be able to compofe, or ra-
‘ ther to erect *Latin* Verfes. His Tables are a kind of

I 4　　　　　　‘ Poetical

‘ Poetical Logarithms, which being divided into several
‘ Squares, and all inscribed with so many incoherent
‘ Words, appear to the Eye somewhat like a Fortune-
‘ telling Screen. What a Joy must it be to the unlearned
‘ Operator to find that these Words being carefully col-
‘ lected and writ down in Order according to the Pro-
‘ blem, start of themselves into Hexameter and Penta-
‘ meter Verses? A Friend of mine, who is a Student in
‘ Astrology, meeting with this Book, performed the
‘ Operation, by the Rules there set down; he shewed
‘ his Verses to the next of his Acquaintance, who happen-
‘ ed to understand *Latin*; and being informed they de-
‘ scribed a Tempest of Wind, very luckily prefixed
‘ them, together with a Translation, to an Almanack
‘ he was just then printing, and was supposed to have
‘ foretold the last great Storm.

‘ I think the only Improvement beyond this, would
‘ be that which the late Duke of *Buckingham* mentioned
‘ to a stupid Pretender to Poetry, as the Project of a
‘ *Dutch* Mechanick, *viz* a Mill to make Verses. This
‘ being the most compendious Method of all which have
‘ yet been proposed, may deserve the Thoughts of our
‘ modern Virtuosi who are employed in new Discoveries
‘ for the publick Good : and it may be worth the while
‘ to consider, whether in an Island where few are con-
‘ tent without being thought Wits, it will not be a com-
‘ mon Benefit, that Wit as well as Labour should be
‘ made cheap.

I am, S I R,

Your humble Servant, &c.

Mr. SPECTATOR,

‘ I OFTEN dine at a Gentleman's House, where
‘ there are two young Ladies in themselves very
‘ agreeable, but very cold in their Behaviour, because
‘ they understand me for a Person that is to break my
‘ Mind, as the Phrase is, very suddenly to one of them.
‘ But I take this Way to acquaint them, that I am not in
‘ Love with either of them, in Hopes they will use me
‘ with that agreeable Freedom and Indifference which

‘ they

‘ they do all the reft of the World, and not to drink to
‘ one another only, but fometimes caft a kind Look, with
‘ their Service to,

SIR, *Your humble Servant.*

Mr. SPECTATOR,

‘ I AM a young Gentleman, and take it for a Piece of
‘ Good-breeding to pull off my Hat when I fee any
‘ thing peculiarly charming in any Woman, whether I
‘ know her or not. I take care that there is nothing
‘ ludicrous or arch in my Manner, as if I were to betray
‘ a Woman into a Salutation by way of Jeft or Humour;
‘ and yet except I am acquainted with her, I find fhe
‘ ever takes it for a Rule, that fhe is to look upon this
‘ Civility and Homage I pay to her fuppofed Merit, as
‘ an Impertinence or Forwardnefs which fhe is to ob-
‘ ferve and negleft. I wifh, Sir, you would fettle the
‘ Bufinefs of Salutation; and pleafe to inform me how
‘ I fhall refift the fudden Impulfe I have to be civil to
‘ what gives an Idea of Merit; or tell thefe Creatures
‘ how to behave themfelves in Return to the Efteem I
‘ have for them. My Affairs are fuch, that your Deci-
‘ fion will be a Favour to me, if it be only to fave the
‘ unneceffary Expence of wearing out my Hat fo faft
‘ as I do at prefent.

I am,

SIR,

Yours, T. D.

P. S. ‘ THERE are fome that do know me, and
‘ won't bow to me.   T

Nº 221 *Tuesday, November* 13.

―――――*Ab Ovo*
Ufque ad Mala―――― Hor. Sat. 3. l. 1. v. **6.**

From Eggs, which first are set upon the Board,
To Apples ripe, with which it last is stor'd.

WHEN I have finished any of my Speculations, it is my Method to confider which of the ancient Authors have touched upon the Subject that I treat of. By this means I meet with fome celebrated Thought upon it, or a Thought of my own expreffed in better Words, or fome Similitude for the Illuftration of my Subject. This is what gives birth to the Motto of a Speculation, which I rather choofe to take out of the Poets than the Profe-writers, as the former generally give a finer Turn to a Thought than the latter, and by couching it in few Words, and in harmonious Numbers, make it more portable to the Memory.

MY Reader is therefore fure to meet with at leaft one good Line in every Paper, and very often finds his Imagination entertained by a Hint that awakens in his Memory fome beautiful Paffage of a Claffick Author.

IT was a Saying of an ancient Philofopher, which I find fome of our Writers have afcribed to Queen *Elizabeth*, who perhaps might have taken occafion to repeat it, That a good Face is a Letter of Recommendation. It naturally makes the Beholders inquifitive into the Perfon who is the Owner of it, and generally prepoffeffes them in his Favour. A handfom Motto has the fame Effect. Befides that it always gives a fupernumerary Beauty to a Paper, and is fometimes in a manner neceffary when the Writer is engaged in what may appear a Paradox to vulgar Minds, as it fhews that he is fupported by good Authorities, and is not fingular in his Opinion.

I muft confefs, the Motto is of little Ufe to an unlearned Reader, for which Reafon I confider it only as *a Word to the Wife*. But as for my unlearned Friends, if
they

they cannot relish the Motto, I take care to make Provision for them in the Body of my Paper. If they do not underftand the Sign that is hung out, they know very well by it, that they may meet with Entertainment in the Houfe; and I think I was never better pleafed than with a plain Man's Compliment, who, upon his Friend's telling him that he would like the *Spectator* much better if he underftood the Motto, replied, *That good Wine needs no Bufh.*

I have heard of a Couple of Preachers in a Country Town, who endeavoured which fhould outfhine one another, and draw together the greateft Congregation. One of them being well verfed in the Fathers, ufed to quote every now and then a *Latin* Sentence to his illiterate Hearers, who it feems found themfelves fo edified by it, that they flocked in greater Numbers to this learned Man than to his Rival. The other finding his Congregation mouldering every *Sunday*, and hearing at length what was the Occafion of it, refolved to give his Parifh a little *Latin* in his Turn; but being unacquainted with any of the Fathers, he digefted into his Sermons the whole Book of *Quæ Genus*, adding however fuch Explications to it as he thought might be for the Benefit of his People. He afterwards entered upon *As in præfenti,* which he converted in the fame manner to the Ufe of his Parifhioners. This in a very little time thickned his Audience, filled his Church, and routed his Antagonift.

THE natural Love to *Latin,* which is fo prevalent in our common People, makes me think that my Speculations fare never the worfe among them for that little Scrap which appears at the Head of them; and what the more encourages me in the Ufe of Quotations in an unknown Tongue, is, that I hear the Ladies, whofe Approbation I value more than that of the whole learned World, declare themfelves in a more particular manner pleafed with my *Greek* Mottos.

DESIGNING this Day's Work for a Differtation upon the two Extremities of my Paper, and having already difpatch'd my Motto, I fhall, in the next Place, difcourfe upon thofe fingle Capital Letters, which are placed at the End of it, and which have afforded great Matter of Speculation

lation to the Curious. I have heard various Conjectures upon this Subject. Some tell us that C is the Mark of those Papers that are written by the Clergyman, though others afcribe them to the Club in general: That the Papers marked with R were written by my Friend Sir ROGER: That L fignifies the Lawyer, whom I have defcribed in my fecond Speculation; and that T ftands for the Trader or Merchant: But the Letter X, which is placed at the End of fome few of my Papers, is that which has puzzled the whole Town, as they cannot think of any Name which begins with that Letter, except *Xenophon* and *Xerxes*, who can neither of them be fuppofed to have had any Hand in thefe Speculations.

I N Anfwer to thefe inquifitive Gentlemen, who have many of them made Inquiries of me by Letter, I muft tell them the Reply of an ancient Philofopher, who carried fomething hidden under his Cloke. A certain Acquaintance defiring him to let him know what it was he covered fo carefully; *I cover it,* fays he, *on purpofe that you fhould not know.* I have made ufe of thefe obfcure Marks for the fame Purpofe. They are, perhaps, little Amulets or Charms to preferve the Paper againft the Fafcination and Malice of evil Eyes; for which Reafon I would not have my Reader furprifed; if hereafter he fees any of my Papers marked with a Q, a Z, a Y, an &c. or with the Word *Abracadabra.*

I fhall, however, fo far explain myfelf to the Reader, as to let him know that the Letters, C, L, and X, are Cabaliftical, and carry more in them than it is proper for the World to be acquainted with. Thofe who are verfed in the Philofophy of *Pythagoras,* and fwear by the *Tetrachtys,* that is the Number Four, will know very well that the Number *Ten,* which is fignified by the Letter X, (and which has fo much perplexed the Town) has in it many particular Powers; that it is called by Platonick Writers the Complete Number; that One, Two, Three and Four put together make up the Number Ten; and that Ten is all. But thefe are not Myfteries for ordinary Readers to be let into. A Man muft have fpent many Years in hard Study before he can arrive at the Knowledge of them.

W R

WE had a Rabbinical Divine in *England*, who was Chaplain to the Earl of *Essex* in Queen *Elizabeth*'s Time; that had an admirable Head for Secrets of this Nature: Upon his taking the Doctor of Divinity's Degree, he preached before the University of *Cambridge*, upon the *First* Verse of the *First* Chapter of the *First* Book of *Chronicles*, in which, says he, you have the three following Words;

Adam, Sheth, Enosh.

He divided this short Text into many Parts, and by discovering several Mysteries in each Word, made a most learned and elaborate Discourse. The Name of this profound Preacher was Dr. *Alabaster*, of whom the Reader may find a more particular Account in Dr. *Fuller*'s Book of *English* Worthies. This Instance will, I hope, convince my Readers that there may be a great deal of fine Writing in the Capital Letters which bring up the Rear of my Paper, and give them some Satisfaction in that Particular. But as for the full Explication of these Matters, I must refer them to Time, which discovers all Things. C

N° 222 Wednesday, November 14.

Cur alter fratrum cessare, & ludere, & ungi,
Præferat Herodis palmetis pinguibus—
Hor. Ep. 2. l. 2. v. 183.

Why, of two Brothers, one his Pleasure loves,
Prefers his Sports to Herod's fragrant Groves. CREECH.

Mr. SPECTATOR,

THERE is one thing I have often look'd for in your Papers, and have as often wondered to find myself disappointed; the rather, because I think it a Subject every way agreeable to your Design, and by being left unattempted by others, seems reserved as a proper Employment for you; I mean a Disquisition, from whence it proceeds, that Men of the brightest Parts, and most comprehensive Genius, completely furnished with Talents for any Province in human Affairs; such as by their wise Lessons of Oeconomy to others have made it evident, that they have the justest Notions

‘ of

' of Life, and of true Senfe in the Conduct of it ——:
' from what unhappy contradictious Caufe it proceeds,
' that Perfons thus finifhed by Nature and by Art, fhould
' fo often fail in the Management of that which they fo
' well underftand, and want the Addrefs to make a right
' Application of their own Rules. This is certainly a pro-
' digious Inconfiftency in Behaviour, and makes much
' fuch a Figure in Morals as a monftrous Birth in Na-
' turals, with this Difference only, which greatly ag-
' gravates the Wonder, that it happens much more fre-
' quently; and what a Blemifh does it caft upon Wit and
' Learning in the general Account of the World? And
' in how difadvantageous a Light does it expofe them
' to the bufy Clafs of Mankind, that there fhould be
' fo many Inftances of Perfons who have fo conducted
' their Lives in fpite of thefe tranfcendent Advantages,
' as neither to be happy in themfelves, nor ufeful to their
' Friends; when every Body fees it was intirely in their
' own Power to be eminent in both thefe Characters? For
' my part, I think there is no Reflexion more aftonifhing,
' than to confider one of thefe Gentlemen fpending a fair
' Fortune, running in every Body's Debt without the
' leaft Apprehenfion of a future Reckoning, and at laft
' leaving not only his own Children, but poffibly thofe of
' other People, by his Means, in ftarving Circumftances;
' while a Fellow, whom one would fcarce fufpect to have
' a human Soul, fhall perhaps raife a vaft Eftate out of
' Nothing, and be the Founder of a Family capable of
' being very confiderable in their Country, and doing
' many illuftrious Services to it. That this Obfervation
' is juft, Experience has put beyond all Difpute. But
' though the Fact be fo evident and glaring, yet the
' Caufes of it are ftill in the Dark; which makes me
' perfuade myfelf, that it would be no unacceptable Piece
' of Entertainment to the Town, to inquire into the
' hidden Sources of fo unaccountable an Evil.

I am, S I R,

Your moft Humble Servant.

WHAT this Correfpondent wonders at, has been Matter of Admiration ever fince there was any fuch thing as
                                                    human

human Life. *Horace* reflects upon this Inconfiftency very
agreeably in the Character of *Tigellius*, whom he makes a
mighty Pretender to Oeconomy, and tells you, you might
one Day hear him fpeak the moft philofophick Things
imaginable concerning being contented with a little, and
his Contempt of every thing but mere Neceffaries, and in
half a Week after fpend a thoufand Pound. When he
fays this of him with relation to Expence, he defcribes
him as unequal to himfelf in every other Circumftance of
Life. And indeed, if we confider lavifh Men carefully,
we fhall find it always proceeds from a certain Incapacity of poffeffing themfelves, and finding Enjoyment in
their own Minds. Mr. *Dryden* has expreffed this very
excellently in the Character of *Zimri*.

A Man fo various, that he feem'd to be
Not one, but all Mankind's Epitome.
Stiff in Opinion, always in the Wrong,
Was every Thing by Starts, and Nothing long;
But in the Courfe of one revolving Moon,
Was Chymiſt, Fidler, Statefman, and Buffoon.
Then all for Women, Painting, Rhiming, Drinking,
Befides ten thoufand Freaks that died in thinking;
Bleſt Madman, who could every Hour employ
In fomething new to wifh or to enjoy!
In fquandring Wealth was his peculiar Art,
Nothing went unrewarded but Defert.

THIS loofe State of the Soul hurries the Extravagant
from one Purfuit to another; and the Reafon that his Expences are greater than another's, is, that his Wants are
alfo more numerous. But what makes fo many go on
in this Way to their Lives End, is, that they certainly do
not know how contemptible they are in the Eyes of the
reft of Mankind, or rather, that indeed they are not fo
contemptible as they deferve. *Tully* fays, it is the greateft
of Wickednefs to leffen your paternal Eftate. And if a Man
would thoroughly confider how much worfe than Banifhment it muft be to his Child, to ride by the Eftate which
fhould have been his, had it not been for his Father's In-
juftice to him, he would be fmitten with the Reflexion
more deeply than can be underftood by any but one who

Is

is a Father. Sure there can be nothing more afflicting, than to think it had been happier for his Son to have been born of any other Man living than himself.

IT is not perhaps much thought of, but it is certainly a very important Leſſon, to learn how to enjoy ordinary Life, and to be able to reliſh your Being without the Tranſport of ſome Paſſion, or Gratification of ſome Appetite. For want of this Capacity, the World is filled with Whetters, Tipplers, Cutters, Sippers, and all the numerous Train of thoſe who, for want of Thinking, are forced to be ever exerciſing their Feeling or Taſting. It would be hard on this Occaſion to mention the harmleſs Smokers of Tobacco and Takers of Snuff.

THE ſlower Part of Mankind, whom my Correſpondent wonders ſhould get Eſtates, are the more immediately formed for that Purſuit: They can expect diſtant Things without Impatience, becauſe they are not carried out of their Way either by violent Paſſion or keen Appetite to any Thing. To Men addicted to Delights, Buſineſs is an Interruption ; to ſuch as are cold to Delights, Buſineſs is an Entertainment. For which Reaſon it was ſaid to one who commended a dull Man for his Application, *No Thanks to him ; if he had no Buſineſs, he would have nothing to do.*   T

⁂⁂⁂⁂⁂⁂⁂⁂⁂

N° 223   *Saturday, November* 15.

O ſuavis Anima ! qualem te dicam bonam
Antehac fuiſſe, tales cùm ſint reliquiæ !
　　　　　　　　Phædr. Fab. 1. l. 3. v. 5.

O ſweet Soul ! how good muſt you have been heretofore, when your Remains are ſo delicious !

WHEN I reflect upon the various Fate of thoſe Multitudes of ancient Writers who flouriſhed in *Greece* and *Italy*, I conſider Time as an immenſe Ocean, in which many noble Authors are intirely ſwallowed up, many very much ſhattered and damaged, ſome quite disjointed and broken into pieces, while ſome have wholly eſcaped the common Wreck; but the Number of the laſt is very ſmall.

Appa-

Apparent rari nantes in gurgite vasto. Virg. Æn. 1. v. 122.

'One here and there floats on the vast Abyss.

AMONG the mutilated Poets of Antiquity, there is none whose Fragments are so beautiful as those of *Sappho.* They give us a Taste of her Way of Writing, which is perfectly conformable with that extraordinary Character we find of her, in the Remarks of those great Criticks who were conversant with her Works when they were intire. One may see by what is left of them, that she followed Nature in all her Thoughts, without descending to those little Points, Conceits, and Turns of Wit with which many of our modern Lyricks are so miserably infected. Her Soul seems to have been made up of Love and Poetry : She felt the Passion in all its Warmth, and described it in all its Symptoms. She is called by ancient Authors the Tenth Muse; and by *Plutarch* is compared to *Cacus* the Son of *Vulcan,* who breathed out nothing but Flame. I do not know, by the Character that is given of her Works, whether it is not for the Benefit of Mankind that they are lost. They are filled with such bewitching Tenderness and Rapture, that it might have been dangerous to have given them a Reading.

AN inconstant Lover, called *Phaon*, occasioned great Calamities to this poetical Lady. She fell desperately in Love with him, and took a Voyage into *Sicily,* in Pursuit of him, he having withdrawn himself thither on purpose to avoid her. It was in that Island, and on this Occasion, she is supposed to have made the Hymn to *Venus,* with a Translation of which I shall present my Reader. Her Hymn was ineffectual for procuring that Happiness which she prayed for in it. *Phaon* was still obdurate, and *Sappho* so transported with the Violence of her Passion, that she was resolved to get rid of it at any Price.

THERE was a Promontory in *Acarnania* called *Leucate,* on the Top of which was a little Temple dedicated to *Apollo.* In this Temple it was usual for *despairing* Lovers to make their Vows in secret, and afterwards to fling themselves from the Top of the Precipice into the Sea, where they were sometimes taken up alive. This Place was therefore called, *The Lover's Leap;* and whether or no

the

it intire in his Works, as a Pattern of Perfection in th
Structure of it.

LONGINUS has quoted another Ode of this grea
Poetcss, which is likewise admirable in its Kind, and ha
been translated by the same Hand with the foregoing one
I shall oblige my Reader with it in another Paper. I
the mean while, I cannot but wonder, that these tw
finished Pieces have never been attempted before by an
of our own Countrymen. But the Truth of it is, th
Compositions of the Ancients, which have not in the
any of those unnatural Witticisms that are the Delight
ordinary Readers, are extreme difficult to render int
another Tongue, so as the Beauties of the Original ma
not appear weak and faded in the Translation.

N° 224   *Friday, November* 16.

— *Fulgente trahit constrictos Gloria curru*
Non minus ignotos generosos —   Hor. Sat. 6. l. 1. v. 2
— *Glory's flaming Chariot fastly draws*
With equal Whirl the noble and the base.   CREECH

IF we look abroad upon the great Multitude of Mankin
and endeavour to trace out the Principles of Actio
in every Individual, it will, I think, seem highly pro
bable that Ambition runs through the whole Species, an
that every Man in Proportion to the Vigour of his Com
plexion is more or less actuated by it. It is indeed n
uncommon Thing to meet with Men, who, by the na
tural Bent of their Inclinations, and without the Disc
pline of Philosophy, aspire not to the Heights of Powe
and Grandeur; who never set their Hearts upon a nume
rous Train of Clients and Dependencies, nor other po
Appendages of Greatness; who are contented with a Com
petency, and will not molest their Tranquillity to gain a
Abundance: But it is not therefore to be concluded th
such a Man is not Ambitious; his Desires may have t
out another Channel, and determined him to other Pursuit
the Motive however may be still the same; and in the
Ca

Can likewife the Man may be equally publifh'd on with the Paine of Diftinction.

THOUGH the pure Confcioufnefs of worthy Actions abftracted from the Views of popular Applaufe, be to an generous Mind an ample Reward, yet the Defire of Diftinction was doubtlefs implanted in our Natures as an additional Incentive to exert ourfelves in virtuous Excellence.

THIS Paffion indeed, like all others, is frequently perverted to evil and ignoble Purpofes; fo that we may account for many of the Excellencies and Follies of Life upon the fame uncertain Principle, to wit, the Defire of being remarkable: For this, as it has been differently cultivated by Education, Senfe and Conceit, will bring forth fociable Effects as it falls in with an ingenuous Difpofition, or a corrupt Mind; it does exceedingly quicken it felf in Men of Magnanimity or brisk Cunning, as it meets with a good or a weak Underftanding. As it has been employed in embellifhing the Mind, or adorning the Outfide, it renders the Man extremely generous or extremely malicious. Ambition therefore is not to be confidered only to one Paffion or Purfuit, for as the fame Ground, in Conftitutions otherwife different, affords the Laft Quae different Manners, as the fame Seed yields different Products, being forced forth upon one Object...

I cannot be deubted, but that there is no great Defire of Glory in a King of Wealthm or Confpir Power, nor to any their more natural Competition for Superiority. No Matter could avoid it, would ever infer he thinks to be blam but out of a Principle of Honour. This is the fame Spring that pufhes them forward, and the fame from which they gain above the undiftinguifh't many; rather than repaire thofe Wounds they have receiv'd in a Combat. To Mr. Wake's Opinion, that Julius Cæfar had never been Mafter of the Roman Empire, would in a Probability have made an excellent Vintner:

Great Julius, on the Mountains bred,
A Flock perhaps, or Herd had led,
He that the World's jurisd, had been
But the beft Wreftler on the Green.

Thus

the Fright they had been in, or the Refolution that could puſh them to ſo dreadful a Remedy, or the Bruiſes which they often received in their Fall, baniſhed all the tender Sentiments of Love, and gave their Spirits another Turn : thoſe who had taken this Leap were obſerved never to relapſe into that Paſſion. *Sappho* tried the Cure, but pe- riſhed in the Experiment.

AFTER having given this ſhort Account of *Sappho* ſo far as it regards the following Ode, I ſhall ſub- join the Tranſlation of it as it was ſent me by a Friend, whoſe admirable Paſtorals and *Winter-Piece* have been already ſo well received. The Reader will find in it that pathetick Simplicity which is ſo peculiar to him, and ſo ſuitable to the Ode he has here tranſlated. This Ode in the Greek (beſides thoſe Beauties obſerved by Madam *Dacier*) has ſeveral harmonious Turns in the Words, which are not loſt in the *Engliſh*. I muſt farther add, that the Tranſlation has preſerved every Image and Sen- timent of *Sappho*, notwithſtanding it has all the Eaſe and Spirit of an Original. In a word, if the Ladies have a mind to know the Manner of Writing practiſed by the ſo much celebrated *Sappho*, they may here ſee it in its ge- nuine and natural Beauty, without any foreign or affected Ornaments.

An HYMN to *VENUS*.

I.

O Venus *Beauty of the Skies,*
To whom a Thouſand Temples riſe,
Gaily falſe in gentle Smiles,
Full of Love-perplexing Wiles ;
O Goddeſs ! from my Heart remove
The waſting Cares and Pains of Love.

II.

If ever thou haſt kindly heard
A Song in ſoft Diſtreſs preferr'd,
Propitious to my tuneful Vow,
O gentle Goddeſs ! hear me now.
Deſcend thou bright, immortal Gueſt,
In all thy radiant Charms confeſt.

III. *Thou*

III.

Thou once didft leave Almighty Jove,
And all the Golden Roofs above:
The Car thy wanton Sparrows drew,
Hov'ring in Air they lightly flew;
As to my Bower they wing'd their Way,
I faw their quiv'ring Pinions play.

IV.

The Birds difmifs (while you remain)
Bore back their empty Car again:
Then you with Looks divinely mild,
In ev'ry heav'nly Feature fmil'd,
And afk'd what new Complaints I made,
And why I call'd you to my Aid?

V.

What Frenzy in my Bofom rag'd,
And by what Cure to be affuag'd?
What gentle Youth I would allure,
Whom in my artful Toils fecure?
Who does thy tender Heart fubdue,
Tell me, my Sappho, *tell me who?*

VI.

Tho' now he fhuns thy longing Arms,
He foon fhall court thy flighted Charms;
Tho' now thy Off'rings he defpife,
He foon to thee fhall facrifice;
Tho' now he freeze, he foon fhall burn,
And be thy Victim in his Turn.

VII.

Celeftial Vifitant, once more
Thy needful Prefence I implore!
In Pity come and eafe my Grief,
Bring my diftemper'd Soul Relief,
Favour thy Suppliant's hidden Fires,
And give me All my Heart defires.

MADAM *Dacier* obferves, there is fomething very pretty in that Circumftance of this Ode, wherein *Venus* is defcribed as fending away her Chariot upon her Arrival at *Sappho*'s Lodgings, to denote that it was not a fhort tranfient Vifit which fhe intended to make her. This Ode was preferved by an eminent *Greek* Critick, who inferted

it

it intire in his Works, as a Pattern of Perfection in the Structure of it.

LONGINUS has quoted another Ode of this great Poetefs, which is likewife admirable in its Kind, and has been tranflated by the fame Hand with the foregoing one. I fhall oblige my Reader with it in another Paper. In the mean while, I cannot but wonder, that thefe two finifhed Pieces have never been attempted before by any of our own Countrymen. But the Truth of it is, the Compofitions of the Ancients, which have not in them any of thofe unnatural Witticifms that are the Delight of ordinary Readers, are extremely difficult to render into another Tongue, fo as the Beauties of the Original may not appear weak and faded in the Tranflation. C

N° 224 *Friday, November* 16.

— *Fulgente trahit conftrictos Gloria curru*
Non minùs ignotos generofis — Hor. Sat. 6. l. 1. v. 23.

— *Glory's fhining Chariot fwiftly draws*
With equal Whirl the noble and the bafe. CREECH.

IF we look abroad upon the great Multitude of Mankind, and endeavour to trace out the Principles of Action in every Individual, it will, I think, feem highly probable that Ambition runs through the whole Species, and that every Man in Proportion to the Vigour of his Complexion is more or lefs actuated by it. It is indeed no uncommon Thing to meet with Men, who, by the natural Bent of their Inclinations, and without the Difcipline of Philofophy, afpire not to the Heights of Power and Grandeur; who never fet their Hearts upon a numerous Train of Clients and Dependencies, nor other gay Appendages of Greatnefs; who are contented with a Competency, and will not moleft their Tranquillity to gain an Abundance: But it is not therefore to be concluded that fuch a Man is not Ambitious; his Defires may have cut out another Channel, and determined him to other Purfuits; the Motive however may be ftill the fame; and in thefe

Cafes

Cafes likewife the Man may be equally pufh'd on with the Defire of Diftinction.

THOUGH the pure Confcioufnefs of worthy Actions, abftracted from the Views of popular Applaufe, be to a generous Mind an ample Reward, yet the Defire of Diftinction was doubtlefs implanted in our Natures as an additional Incentive to exert ourfelves in virtuous Excellence.

THIS Paffion indeed, like all others, is frequently perverted to evil and ignoble Purpofes; fo that we may account for many of the Excellencies and Follies of Life upon the fame innate Principle, to wit, the Defire of being remarkable: For this, as it has been differently cultivated by Education, Study and Converfe, will bring forth fuitable Effects as it falls in with an ingenuous Difpofition, or a corrupt Mind; it does accordingly exprefs itfelf in Acts of Magnanimity or felfifh Cunning, as it meets with a good or a weak Underftanding. As it has been employed in embellifhing the Mind, or adorning the Outfide, it renders the Man eminently praife-worthy or ridiculous. Ambition therefore is not to be confined only to one Paffion or Purfuit; for as the fame Humours, in Conftitutions otherwife different, affect the Body after different Manners, fo the fame afpiring Principle within us fometimes breaks forth upon one Object, fometimes upon another.

IT cannot be doubted, but that there is as great Defire of Glory in a Ring of Wreftlers or Cudgel-Players, as in any other more refined Competition for Superiority. No Man that could avoid it, would ever fuffer his Head to be broken but out of a Principle of Honour. This is the fecret Spring that pufhes them forward; and the Superiority which they gain above the undiftinguifh'd many, does more than repair thofe Wounds they have received in the Combat. 'Tis Mr. *Waller*'s Opinion, that *Julius Cæfar*, had he not been Mafter of the *Roman* Empire, would in all Probability have made an excellent Wreftler.

> Great Julius *on the Mountains bred,*
> *A Flock perhaps or Herd had led;*
> *He that the World fubdu'd, had been*
> *But the beft Wreftler on the Green.*

That

That he subdu'd the World, was owing to the Accidents of Art and Knowledge; had he not met with those Advantages, the same Sparks of Emulation would have kindled within him, and prompted him to distinguish himself in some Enterprise of a lower Nature. Since therefore no Man's Lot is so unalterably fixed in this Life, but that a thousand Accidents may either forward or disappoint his Advancement, it is, methinks, a pleasant and inoffensive Speculation, to consider a great Man as divested of all the adventitious Circumstances of Fortune, and to bring him down in one's Imagination to that low Station of Life, the Nature of which bears some distant Resemblance to that high one he is at present possessed of. Thus one may view him exercising in Miniature those Talents of Nature, which being drawn out by Education to their full Length, enable him for the Discharge of some important Employment. On the other hand, one may raise uneducated Merit to such a Pitch of Greatness as may seem equal to the possible Extent of his improved Capacity.

THUS Nature furnishes a Man with a general Appetite of Glory, Education determines it to this or that particular Object. The Desire of Distinction is not, I think, in any Instance more observable than in the Variety of Outsides and new Appearances, which the modish Part of the World are obliged to provide, in order to make themselves remarkable; for any Thing glaring and particular, either in Behaviour or Apparel, is known to have this good Effect, that it catches the Eye, and will not suffer you to pass over the Person so adorned without due Notice and Observation. It has likewise, upon this Account, been frequently resented as a very great Slight, to leave any Gentleman out of a Lampoon or Satire, who has as much Right to be there as his Neighbour, because it supposes the Person not eminent enough to be taken notice of. To this passionate Fondness for Distinction are owing various frolicksom and irregular Practices, as sallying out into Nocturnal Exploits, breaking of Windows, singing of Catches, beating the Watch, getting drunk twice a Day, killing a great Number of Horses; with many other Enterprises of the like fiery Nature: For certainly
many

many a Man is more rakifh and extravagant than he would willingly be, were there not others to look on and give their Approbation.

ONE very common, and at the fame time the moft abfurd Ambition that ever fhewed itfelf in human Nature, is that which comes upon a Man with Experience and old Age, the Seafon when it might be expected he fhould be wifeft; and therefore it cannot receive any of thofe leffening Circumftances which do, in fome meafure, excufe the diforderly Ferments of youthful Blood: I mean the Paffion for getting Money, exclufive of the Character of the provident Father, the affectionate Husband, or the generous Friend. It may be remarked, for the Comfort of honeft Poverty, that this Defire reigns moft in thofe who have but few good Qualities to recommend them. This is a Weed that will grow in a barren Soil. Humanity, Good-nature, and the Advantages of a liberal Education, are incompatible with Avarice. 'Tis ftrange to fee how fuddenly this abject Paffion kills all the noble Sentiments and generous Ambitions that adorn human Nature; it renders the Man who is over-run with it a peevifh and cruel Mafter, a fevere Parent, an unfociable Husband, a diftant and miftruftful Friend. But it is more to the prefent Purpofe to confider it as an abfurd Paffion of the Heart, rather than as a vicious Affection of the Mind. As there are frequent Inftances to be met with of a proud Humility, fo this Paffion, contrary to moft others, affects Applaufe, by avoiding all Show and Appearance; for this Reafon it will not fometimes endure even the common Decencies of Apparel. *A covetous Man will call himfelf poor, that you may footh his Vanity by contradicting him.* Love and the Defire of Glory, as they are the moft natural, fo they are capable of being refined into the moft delicate and rational Paffions. 'Tis true, the wife Man who ftrikes out of the fecret Paths of a private Life, for Honour and Dignity, allured by the Splendor of a Court, and the unfelt Weight of publick Employment, whether he fucceeds in his Attempts or no, ufually comes near enough to this painted Greatnefs to difcern the Dawbing; he is then defirous of extricating himfelf out of the Hurry of Life, that he may pafs away the Remainder of his Days in Tranquillity and Retirement.

I T

IT may be thought then but common Prudence in a Man not to change a better State for a worfe, nor ever to quit that which he knows he fhall take up again with Pleafure; and yet if human Life be not a little moved with the gentle Gales of Hopes and Fears, there may be fome Danger of its ftagnating in an unmanly Indolence and Security. It is a known Story of *Domitian*, that after he had poffeffed himfelf of the *Roman* Empire, his Defires turn'd upon catching Flies. Active and mafculine Spirits in the Vigour of Youth neither can nor ought to remain at Reft; If they debar themfelves from aiming at a noble Object, their Defires will move downwards, and they will feel themfelves actuated by fome low and abject Paffion. Thus if you cut off the top Branches of a Tree, and will not fuffer it to grow any higher, it will not therefore ceafe to grow, but will quickly fhoot out at the Bottom. The Man indeed who goes into the World only with the narrow Views of Self-Intereft, who catches at the Applaufe of an idle Multitude, as he can find no folid Contentment at the End of his Journey, fo he deferves to meet with Difappointments in his Way; but he who is actuated by a noble Principle, whofe Mind is fo far enlarged as to take in the Profpect of his Country's Good, who is enamoured with that Praife which is one of the fair Attendants of Virtue, and values not thofe Acclamations which are not feconded by the impartial Teftimony of his own Mind; who repines not at the low Station which Providence has at prefent allotted him, but yet would willingly advance himfelf by juftifiable Means to a more-rifing and advantageous Ground; fuch a Man is warmed with a generous Emulation; it is a virtuous Movement in him to wifh and to endeavour that his Power of doing Good may be equal to his Will.

THE Man who is fitted out by Nature, and fent into the World with great Abilities, is capable of doing great Good or Mifchief in it. It ought therefore to be the Care of Education to infufe into the untainted Youth early Notices of Juftice and Honour, that fo the poffible Advantages of good Parts may not take an evil Turn, nor be perverted to bafe and unworthy Purpofes. It is the Bufinefs of Religion and Philofophy not fo much to extinguifh our Paffions, as to regulate and direct them to valuable well-chosen Objects: When these have pointed out to us which Course we may lawfully steer, 'tis no Harm to set out all our Sail; if the Storms and Tempests of Adversity should rise upon us, and not suffer us to make the Haven where we would be, it will however prove no small Consolation to us in these Circumstances, that we have neither mistaken our Course, nor fallen into Calamities of our own procuring.

RELIGION therefore (were we to consider it no farther than as it interposes in the Affairs of this Life) is highly valuable, and worthy of great Veneration; as it settles the various Pretensions, and otherwise interfering Interests of mortal Men, and thereby consults the Harmony and Order of the great Community; as it gives a Man room to play his Part, and exert his Abilities; as it animates to Actions truly laudable in themselves, in their Effects beneficial to Society; as it inspires rational Ambition, correct Love, and elegant Desire.

N° 225   *Saturday, November* 17.

Nullum numen abest si sit Prudentia——
Juv. Sat. 10. v. 365.

Prudence supplies the Want of ev'ry God.

I Have often thought if the Minds of Men were laid open, we should see but little Difference between that of the wise Man and that of the Fool. There are infinite *Reveries,* numberless Extravagancies, and a perpetual Train of Vanities which pass through both. The great Difference is that the first knows how to pick and cull his Thoughts for Conversation, by suppressing some, and communicating others; whereas the other lets them all indifferently fly out in Words. This sort of Discretion, however, has no Place in private Conversation between intimate Friends. On such Occasions the wisest Men very often talk like the weakest; for indeed the talking with a Friend is nothing else but *thinking aloud.*

TULLY has therefore very juftly expófed a Précept delivered by fome ancient Writers, That a Man fhould live with his Enemy in fuch a manner, as might leave him room to become his Friend; and with his Friend, in fuch a manner, that if he became his Enemy, it fhould not be in his Power to hurt him. The firft Part of this Rule, which regards our Behaviour towards an Enemy, is indeed very reafonable, as well as very prudential; but the latter Part of it which regards our Behaviour towards a Friend, favours more of Cunning than of Difcretion, and would cut a Man off from the greateft Pleafures of Life, which are the Freedoms of Converfation with a Bofom Friend. Befides that when a Friend is turned into an Enemy, and, (as the Son of *Sirach* calls him) a Bewrayer of Secrets, the World is juft enough to accufe the Perfidioufnefs of the Friend, rather than the Indifcretion of the Perfon who confided in him.

DISCRETION does not only fhew itfelf in Words, but in all the Circumftances of Action; and is like an Under-Agent of Providence, to guide and direct us in the ordinary Concerns of Life.

THERE are many more fhining Qualities in the Mind of Man, but there is none fo ufeful as Difcretion; it is this indeed which gives a Value to all the reft, which fets them at work in their proper Times and Places, and turns them to the Advantage of the Perfon who is poffeffed of them. Without it Learning is Pedantry, and Wit Impertinence; Virtue itfelf looks like Weaknefs; the beft Parts only qualify a Man to be more fprightly in Errors, and active to his own Prejudice.

NOR does Difcretion only make a Man the Mafter of his own Parts, but of other Mens. The difcreet Man finds out the Talents of thofe he converfes with, and knows how to apply them to proper Ufes. Accordingly if we look into particular Communities and Divifions of Men, we may obferve that it is the difcreet Man, not the Witty, nor the Learned, nor the Brave, who guides the Converfation, and gives Meafures to the Society. A Man with great Talents, but void of Difcretion, is like *Polyphemus* in the Fable, ftrong and blind, endued with an irrefiftible Force, which for want of Sight is of no Ufe to him.

THOUGH

THOUGH a Man has all other Perfections, and wants Difcretion, he will be of no great Confequence in the World ; but if he has this fingle Talent in Perfection, and but a common Share of others, he may do what he pleafes in his particular Station of Life.

AT the fame time that I think Difcretion the moft ufeful Talent a Man can be Mafter of, I look upon Cunning to be the Accomplifhment of little, mean, ungenerous Minds. Difcretion points out the nobleft Ends to us, and purfues the moft proper and laudable Methods of attaining them : Cunning has only private felfifh Aims, and fticks at nothing which may make them fucceed. Difcretion has large and extended Views, and, like a well-formed Eye, commands a whole Horizon: Cunning is a Kind of Short-fightednefs, that difcovers the minuteft Objects which are near at hand, but is not able to difcern things at a diftance. Difcretion, the more it is difcovered, gives a greater Authority to the Perfon who poffeffes it : Cunning, when it is once detected, lofes its Force, and makes a Man incapable of bringing about even thofe Events which he might have done, had he paffed only for a plain Man. Difcretion is the Perfection of Reafon, and a Guide to us in all the Duties of Life; Cunning is a kind of Inftinct, that only looks out after our immediate Intereft and Welfare. Difcretion is only found in Men of ftrong Senfe and good Underftandings : Cunning is often to be met with in Brutes themfelves, and in Perfons who are but the feweft Removes from them. In fhort Cunning is only the Mimick of Difcretion, and may pafs upon weak Men, in the fame manner as Vivacity is often miftaken for Wit, and Gravity for Wifdom.

THE Caft of Mind which is natural to a difcreet Man, makes him look forward into Futurity, and confider what will be his Condition Millions of Ages hence, as well as what it is at prefent. He knows that the Mifery or Happinefs which are referv'd for him in another World, lofe nothing of their Reality by being placed at fo great Diftance from him. The Objects do not appear little to him becaufe they are remote. He confiders that thofe Pleafures and Pains which lie hid in Eternity, approach nearer to him every Moment, and will be present with him in their full Weight and Measure, as much as those Pains and Pleasures which he feels at this very Instant. For this Reason he is careful to secure to himself that which is the proper Happiness of his Nature, and the ultimate Design of his Being. He carries his Thoughts to the End of every Action, and considers the most distant as well as the most immediate Effects of it. He supersedes every little Prospect of Gain and Advantage which offers itself here, if he does not find it consistent with his Views of an Hereafter. In a word, his Hopes are full of Immortality, his Schemes are large and glorious, and his Conduct suitable to one who knows his true Interest, and how to pursue it by proper Methods.

I have, in this Essay upon Discretion, considered it both as an Accomplishment and as a Virtue, and have therefore described it in its full Extent; not only as it is conversant about worldly Affairs, but as it regards our whole Existence; not only as it is the Guide of a mortal Creature, but as it is in general the Director of a reasonable Being. It is in this Light that Discretion is represented by the wise Man, who sometimes mentions it under the Name of Discretion, and sometimes under that of Wisdom. It is indeed (as described in the latter Part of this Paper) the greatest Wisdom, but at the same time in the Power of every one to attain. Its Advantages are infinite, but its Acquisition easy; or to speak of her in the Words of the Apocryphal Writer whom I quoted in my last *Saturday*'s Paper, *Wisdom is glorious, and never fadeth away, yet she is easily seen of them that love her, and found of such as seek her. She preventeth them that desire her, in making herself first known unto them. He that seeketh her early, shall have no great Travel: for he shall find her sitting at his Doors. To think therefore upon her is Perfection of Wisdom, and whoso watcheth for her shall quickly be without Care. For she goeth about seeking such as are worthy of her, sheweth herself favourably unto them in the Ways, and meeteth them in every Thought.*　　C

Nº 226   *Monday, November* 19.

————*Mutum eft pictura poema.*

A Picture is a Poem without Words.

I Have very often lamented and hinted my Sorrow in
several Speculations, that the Art of Painting is
made so little Use of to the Improvement of our
Manners. When we confider that it places the Action
of the Perfon represented in the moft agreeable Afpect
imaginable, that it does not only exprefs the Paffion or
Concern as it fits upon him who is drawn, but has under
thofe Features the Height of the Painter's Imagination,
What ftrong Images of Virtue and Humanity might we
not expect would be inftilled into the Mind from the
Labours of the Pencil? There is a Poetry which would
be underftood with much lefs Capacity, and lefs Expence
of Time, than what is taught by Writings; but the Ufe
of it is generally perverted, and that admirable Skill proftituted to the bafeft and moft unworthy Ends. Who is
the better Man for beholding the moft beautiful *Venus,*
the beft wrought *Bacchanal,* the Images of fleeping *Cu-*
pids, languifhing Nymphs, or any of the Reprefentations of Gods, Goddeffes, Demigods, Satyrs, *Poly-*
phemes, Sphinxes, or Fawns? But if the Virtues and
Vices, which are fometimes pretended to be reprefented
under fuch Draughts, were given us by the Painter in
the Characters of real Life, and the Perfons of Men and
Women whofe Actions have rendered them laudable
or infamous; we fhould not fee a good Hiftory-Piece
without receiving an inftructive Lecture. There needs
no other Proof of this Truth, than the Teftimony of
every reafonable Creature who has feen the Cartons in
her Majefty's Gallery at *Hampton-Court*: Thefe are Reprefentations of no lefs Actions than thofe of our bleffed Saviour and his Apoftles. As I now fit and recollect the warm Images which the admirable *Raphael* has
raifed, it is impoffible even from the faint Traces in one's

Memory of what one has not seen thefe two Years, to be unmoved at the Horror and Reverence which appear in the whole Affembly when the mercenary Man fell down dead; at the Amazement of the Man born blind, when he firft receives Sight; or at the gracelefs Indignation of the Sorcerer, when he is ftruck blind. The Lame, when they firft find Strength in their Feet, ftand doubtful of their new Vigour. The heavenly Apoftles appear acting thefe great Things, with a deep Senfe of the Infirmities which they relieve, but no Value of themfelves who adminifter to their Weaknefs. They know themfelves to be but Inftruments; and the generous Diftrefs they are painted in when divine Honours are offered to them, is a Reprefentation in the moft exquifite Degree of the Beauty of Holinefs. When St. *Paul* is preaching to the *Athenians*, with what wonderful Art are almoft all the different Tempers of Mankind reprefented in that elegant Audience? You fee one credulous of all that is faid, another wrapt up in deep Sufpence, another faying there is fome Reafon in what he fays, another angry that the Apoftle deftroys a favourite Opinion which he is unwilling to give up, another wholly convinced and holding out his Hands in Rapture, while the Generality attend, and wait for the Opinion of thofe who are of leading Characters in the Affembly. I will not pretend fo much as to mention that Chart on which is drawn the Appearance of our bleffed Lord after his Refurrection. Prefent Authority, late Sufferings, Humility and Majefty, defpotick Command, and divine Love, are at once feated in his celeftial Afpect. The Figures of the eleven Apoftles are all in the fame Paffion of Admiration, but difcover it differently according to their Characters. *Peter* receives his Mafter's Orders on his Knees with an Admiration mixed with a more particular Attention; The two next with a more open Ecftafy, though ftill conftrained by the Awe of the divine Prefence: The beloved Difciple, whom I take to be the Right of the two firft Figures, has in his Countenance Wonder drowned in Love; and the laft Perfonage, whofe Back is towards the Spectators, and his Side towards the Prefence, one would fancy to be St. *Thomas*, as abafhed by the Confcience of his former Diffidence; which perplexed

plexed Concern it is poffible *Raphael* thought too hard a
Taſk to draw but by this Acknowledgment of the Difficulty to defcribe it.

THE whole Work is an Exercife of the higheſt Piety
in the Painter; and all the Touches of a religious Mind
are expreſſed in a Manner much more forcible than can
poſſibly be performed by the moſt moving Eloquence.
Thefe invaluable Pieces are very juſtly in the Hands of
the greateſt and moſt pious Sovereign in the World; and
cannot be the frequent Objeſt of every one at their own
Leifure: But as an Engraver is to the Painter what a
Printer is to an Author, it is worthy Her Majefty's Name,
that ſhe has encouraged that noble Artiſt, Monfieur
Dorigny, to publiſh thefe Works of *Raphael*. We have of
this Gentleman a Piece of the Transfiguration, which,
I think, is held a Work fecond to none in the World.

METHINKS it would be ridiculous in our People
of Condition after their large Bounties to Foreigners
of no Name or Merit, ſhould they overlook this Occaſion of having, for a trifling Subfeription, a Work
which it is impoſſible for a Man of Senfe to behold,
without being warmed with the nobleſt Sentiments that
can be infpired by Love, Admiration, Compaſſion, Contempt of this World, and Expeſtation of a better.

IT is certainly the greateſt Honour we can do our
Country, to diſtinguiſh Strangers of Merit who apply
to us with Modefty and Diffidence, which generally accompanies Merit. No Opportunity of this Kind ought
to be negleſted; and a modeſt Behaviour ſhould alarm
us to examine whether we do not lofe fomething excellent under that Difadvantage in the Poſſeſſor of that
Quality. My Skill in Paintings, where one is not di-
reſted by the Paſſion of the Piſtures, is fo inconfidera-
ble, that I am in very great Perplexity when I offer
to ſpeak of any Performances of Painters of Landſkips,
Buildings, or fingle Figures. This makes me at a loſs
how to mention the Pieces which Mr. *Boul* expofes to
Sale by Auſtion on *Wednefday next* in *Shandois-ſtreet*:
But having heard him commended by thofe who have
bought of him heretofore for great Integrity in his Dealing, and overheard him himfelf (tho' a laudable Painter)
ſay, Nothing of his own was fit to come into the Room

with

with thofe he had to fell, I fear'd I fhould lofe an Occafion of ferving a Man of Worth, in omitting to fpeak
of his Auction.　　　　　　　　　　　　　　　T

N° 227　Tuefday, November 20.

'Ω μοι ἐγώ τι πάθω; τί ὁ δύανο͂ ; οὐχ ὑπακούεις;
Τὰν βαίταν ἀποδύς εἰς κύματα τῆνα ἀλεῦμαι
'Ωπερ τώς θύννως σκοπιάζε͂ 'Ολπις ὁ γείπευς.
Κήκα μὴ 'ποθάνω, τὸ γε μὰν τεὸν ἁδὺ τέτυκται.

Theocr.

IN my laft *Thurfday's* Paper I made mention of a Place
called *The Lover's Leap,* which I find has raifed a great
Curiofity among feveral of my Correfpondents. I
there told them that this Leap was ufed to be taken
from a Promontory of *Leucas.* This *Leucas* was formerly a Part of *Acarnania,* being joined to it by a narrow Neck of Land, which the Sea has by Length of
Time overflowed and wafhed away ; fo that at prefent
Leucas is divided from the Continent, and is a little Ifland
in the *Ionian* Sea. The Promontory of this Ifland, from
whence the Lover took his Leap, was formerly called
Leucate. If the Reader has a mind to know both the
Ifland and the Promontory by their modern Titles,
he will find in his Map the ancient Ifland of *Leucas* under
the Name of St. *Mauro,* and the ancient Promontory of
Leucate under the Name of *The Cape of St.* Mauro.

SINCE I am engaged thus far in Antiquity, I
muft obferve that *Theocritus* in the Motto prefixed to
my Paper, defcribes one of his defpairing Shepherds
addreffing himfelf to his Miftrefs after the following
manner, *Alas ! What will become of me! Wretch that
I am ! Will you not hear me ? I'll throw off my Clothes,
and take a Leap into that Part of the Sea which is
fo much frequented by* Olphis *the Fifherman. And tho'
I fhould efcape with my Life, I know you will be
pleafed with it.* I fhall leave it with the Criticks

to

to determine whether the Place, which this Shepherd so particularly points out, was not the above-mentioned *Leucate*, or at least some other Lover's Leap, which was supposed to have had the same Effect. I cannot believe, as all the Interpreters do, that the Shepherd means nothing farther here than that he would drown himself, since he represents the Issue of his Leap as doubtful, by adding, That if he should escape with Life, he knows his Mistress would be pleased with it; which is according to our Interpretation, that she would rejoice any way to get rid of a Lover who was so troublesom to her.

AFTER this short Preface, I shall present my Reader with some Letters which I have received upon this Subject. The first is sent me by a Physician.

Mr. SPECTATOR,

'THE Lover's Leap, which you mention in your
' 223d Paper, was generally, I believe, a very ef-
' fectual Cure for Love, and not only for Love, but for
' all other Evils. In short, Sir, I am afraid it was such a
' Leap as that which *Hero* took to get rid of her Pas-
' sion for *Leander*. A Man is in no Danger of breaking
' his Heart, who breaks his Neck to prevent it. I know
' very well the Wonders which ancient Authors relate
' concerning this Leap; and in particular, that very
' many Persons who tried it, escaped not only with
' their Lives but their Limbs. If by this Means they
' got rid of their Love, tho' it may in part be ascribed
' to the Reasons you give for it; why may not we
' suppose that the cold Bath into which they plunged
' themselves, had also some Share in their Cure? A
' Leap into the Sea or into any Creek of Salt Waters,
' very often gives a new Motion to the Spirits, and a new
' Turn to the Blood; for which Reason we prescribe it
' in Distempers which no other Medicine will reach. I
' could produce a Quotation out of a very venerable
' Author, in which the Frenzy produced by Love, is
' compared to that which is produced by the Biting of a
' mad Dog. But as this Comparison is a little too coarse
' for your Paper, and might look as if it were cited to
' ridicule the Author who has made use of it; I shall on-
' ly hint at it, and desire you to consider whether, if the

' Frenzy

'Frenzy produced by thefe two different Caufes be of
'the fame Nature, it may not very properly be cured by
'the fame Means.

I am, S I R,

Your moft humble Servant,

and Well-wifher,

ÆSCULAPIUS.

Mr. SPECTATOR,

'I Am a young Woman croffed in Love. My Story is
' very long and melancholy. To give you the Heads
'of it : A young Gentleman, after having made his Ap-
'plications to me for three Years together, and filled my
'Head with a thoufand Dreams of Happinefs, fome few
'Days fince married another. Pray tell me in what Part
'of the World your Promontory lies, which you call *The*
'*Lover's Leap,* and whether one may go to it by Land ?
'But, alas, I am afraid it has loft its Virtue, and that a
'Woman of our Times would find no more Relief in
'taking fuch a Leap, than in finging an Hymn to *Venus.*
'So that I muft cry out with *Dido* in *Dryden's Virgil,*

Ah! cruel Heaven, that made no Cure for Love!

Your difconfolate Servant,

ATHENAIS.

MISTER SPICTATUR,

'MY Heart is fo full of Lofes and Paffions for
' Mrs. *Gwinifrid,* and fhe is fo pettifh and over-
'run with Cholers againft me, that if I had the good
'Happinefs to have my Dwelling (which is placed by
'my Creat-Cranfather upon the Pottom of an Hill) no
'farther Diftance but twenty Mile from the Lofer's Leap,
'I would indeed indeafour to-preak my Neck upon
'it on Purpofe. Now, good Mifter SPICTATUR of
'*Crete Pritain,* you muft know it there is in *Caer-*
'*narvanfhire* a very pig Mountain, the Clory of all
'*Wales,* which is named *Penmainmaure,* and you muft
'alfo know, it is no great Journey on Foot from me;
'but the Road is ftony and bad for Shooes. Now,
'there is upon the Forehead of this Mountain a very
high

' high Rock, (like a Parish Steeple) that cometh a huge
' deal over the Sea; fo when I am in my Melancholies,.
' and I do throw myfelf from it, I do defire my fery
' good Friend to tell me in his *Spectatur*, if I fhall be
' cure of my griefous Lofes; for there is the Sea clear as
' Glafs, and as creen as the Leek: Then likewife if I be
' drown, and preak my Neck, if Mrs. *Gwinifrid* will
' not lofe me afterwards. Pray be fpeedy in your An-
' fwers, for I am in crete Hafte, and it is my Tefires to
' do my Pufinefs without Lofs of Time. I remain with
' cordial Affections, your ever lofing Friend,.

Davyth ap Shenkyn.

P. S. ' My Law-fuits have brought me to *London*, but
' I have loft my Caufes; and fo have made my Refolu-
' tions to go down and leap before the Frofts begin; for
' I am apt to take Colds.

RIDICULE, perhaps, is a better Expedient againft
Love than fober Advice, and I am of Opinion, that *Hu-
dibras* and *Don Quixote* may be as effectual to cure the
Extravagancies of this Paffion, as any of the old Philo-
fophers. I fhall therefore publifh very fpeedily the
Tranflation of a little *Greek* Manufcript, which is fent
me by a learned Friend. It appears to have been a Piece
of thofe Records which were kept in the Temple of
Apollo, that ftood upon the Promontory of *Leucate*. The
Reader will find it to be a Summary Account of feveral
Perfons who tried the Lover's Leap, and of the Succefs
they found in it. As there feem to be in it fome Ana-
chronifms and Deviations from the ancient Orthography,
I am not wholly fatisfied myfelf that it is authentick, and
not rather the Production of one of thofe *Grecian* So-
phifters, who have impofed upon the World feveral fpu-
rious Works of this Nature. I fpeak this by way of
Precaution, becaufe I know there are feveral Writers, of
uncommon Erudition, who would not fail to expofe my
Ignorance, if they caught me tripping in a Matter of
fo great Moment,   C.

Wednefday,

N°. 228 *Wednesday, November* 21.

Percunctatorem fugito, nam Garrulus idem est.
Hor. Ep. 18. l. 1. v. 69.

Shun the inquisitive and curious Man ;
For what he hears he will relate again. P O O L Y.

THERE is a Creature who has all the Organs of Speech, a tolerable good Capacity for conceiving what is said to it, together with a pretty proper Behaviour in all the Occurrences of common Life ; but naturally very vacant of Thought in itself, and therefore forced to apply itself to foreign Assistances. Of this Make is that Man who is very inquisitive. You may often observe, that tho' he speaks as good Sense as any Man upon any thing with which he is well acquainted, he cannot trust to the Range of his own Fancy to entertain himself upon that Foundation, but goes on still to new Inquiries. Thus, tho' you know he is fit for the most polite Conversation, you shall see him very well contented to sit by a Jockey, giving an Account of the many Revolutions in his Horse's Health, what Potion he made him take, how that agreed with him, how afterwards he came to his Stomach and his Exercise, or any the like Impertinence ; and be as well pleased as if you talked to him on the most important Truths. This Humour is far from making a Man unhappy, tho' it may subject him to Rallery ; for he generally falls in with a Person who seems to be born for him, which is your talkative Fellow. It is so ordered, that there is a secret Bent, as natural as the Meeting of different Sexes, in these two Characters, to supply each other's Wants. I had the Honour the other Day to sit in a publick Room, and saw an inquisitive Man look with an Air of Satisfaction upon the Approach of one of these Talkers. The Man of ready Utterance sat down by him, and rubbing his Head, leaning on his Arm, and making an uneasy Countenance, he began ; ' There is no manner of News To-
' day.

" day. I cannot tell what is the Matter with me, but
" I flept very ill laft Night; whether I caught Cold or no,
" I know not, but I fancy I do not wear Shoes thick
" enough for the Weather, and I have coughed all this
" Week: It muft be fo, for the Cuftom of wafhing my
" Head Winter and Summer with cold Water, prevents
" any Injury from the Seafon entering that Way; fo it
" muft come in at my Feet; But I take no Notice of it:
" as it comes fo it goes. Moft of our Evils proceed from
" too much Tendernefs; and our Faces are naturally as
" little able to refift the Cold as other Parts. The *Indian*
" anfwered very well to an *European*, who afked him how
" he could go naked; I am all Face.

I obferved this Difcourfe was as welcome to my general Inquirer as any other of more Confequence could
have been; but fome Body calling our Talker to
another Part of the Room, the Inquirer told the next
Man who fat by him, that Mr. fuch a one, who was
juft gone from him, ufed to wafh his Head in cold
Water every Morning; and fo repeated almoft *ver-
batim* all that had been faid to him. The Truth is,
the Inquifitive are the Funnels of Converfation; they
do not take in any thing for their own Ufe, but
merely to pafs it to another: They are the Channels
through which all the Good and Evil that is fpoken
in Town are conveyed. Such as are offended at them,
or think they fuffer by their Behaviour, may themfelves mend that Inconvenience; for they are not a malicious People, and if you will fupply them, you may
contradict any thing they have faid before by their own
Mouths. A farther Account of a thing is one of the
gratefulleft Goods that can arrive to them; and it is feldom that they are more particular than to fay, The Town
will have it, or I have it from a good Hand: So that
there is room for the Town to know the Matter more
particularly, and for a better Hand to contradict what
was faid by a good one.

I have not known this Humour more ridiculous than
in a Father, who has been earneftly folicitous to
have an Account how his Son has paffed his leifure
Hours; if it be in a Way thoroughly infignificant, there
cannot be a greater Joy than an Inquirer difcovers in
feeing

seeing him follow so hopefully his own Steps: But this Humour among Men is most pleasant when they are saying something which is not wholly proper for a third Person to hear, and yet is in itself indifferent. The other Day there came in a well-dressed young Fellow, and two Gentlemen of this Species immediately fell a whispering his Pedigree. I could overhear, by Breaks, She was his Aunt; then an Answer, Ay, she was of the Mother's Side: Then again in a little lower Voice, His Father wore generally a darker Wig: Answer, Not much. But this Gentleman wears higher Heels to his Shoes.

AS the Inquisitive, in my Opinion, are such merely from a Vacancy in their own Imaginations, there is nothing, methinks, so dangerous as to communicate Secrets to them; for the same Temper of Inquiry makes them as impertinently communicative: But no Man, though he converses with them, need put himself in their Power, for they will be contented with Matters of less Moment as well. When there is Fuel enough, no matter what it is————Thus the Ends of Sentences in the News Papers, as, *This wants Confirmation, This occasions many Speculations,* and *Time will discover the Event,* are read by them, and considered not as mere Expletives.

ONE may see now and then this Humour accompanied with an insatiable Desire of knowing what passes, without turning it to any Use in the world but merely their own Entertainment. A Mind which is gratified this Way is adapted to Humour and Pleasantry, and formed for an unconcerned Character in the World; and, like myself, to be a mere Spectator. This Curiosity, without Malice or Self-interest, lays up in the Imagination a Magazine of Circumstances which cannot but entertain when they are produced in Conversation. If one were to know, from the Man of the first Quality to the meanest Servants, the different Intrigues, Sentiments, Pleasures, and Interests of Mankind, would it not be the most pleasing Entertainment imaginable to enjoy so constant a Farce, as the observing Mankind much more different from themselves in their secret Thoughts and publick Actions, than in their Night-caps and long Periwigs?

Mr.

Mr. SPECTATOR,

'PLUTARCH tells us, that *Caius Gracchus*, the
' *Roman*, was frequently hurried by his Paffion in-
'to fo loud and tumultuous a way of Speaking, and fo
'ftrained his Voice as not to be able to proceed. To re-
'medy this Excefs, he had an ingenious Servant, by
'Name *Licinius*, always attending him with a Pitch-pipe,
'or Inftrument to regulate the Voice; who, whenever
'he heard his Mafter begin to be high, immediately
'touched a foft Note; at which, 'tis faid, *Caius* would
'prefently abate and grow calm.

' UPON recollecting this Story, I have frequently
'wondered that this ufeful Inftrument fhould have been
'fo long difcontinued; efpecially fince we find that this
'good Office of *Licinius* has preferved his Memory
'for many hundred Years, which, methinks, fhould
'have encouraged fome one to have revived it, if not
'for the publick Good, yet for his own Credit. It
'may be objected, that our loud Talkers are fo fond
'of their own Noife, that they would not take it
'well to be check'd by their Servants: But granting
'this to be true, furely any of their Hearers have a
'very good Title to play a foft Note in their own
'Defence. To be fhort, no *Licinius* appearing and
'the Noife increafing, I was refolved to give this late
'long Vacation to the Good of my Country; and I
'have at length, by the Affiftance of an ingenious
'Artift, (who works to the Royal Society) almoft
'compleated my Defign, and fhall be ready in a fhort
'Time to furnifh the Publick with what Number of
'thefe Inftruments they pleafe, either to lodge at Cof-
'fee-houfes, or carry for their own private Ufe. In the
'mean time I fhall pay that Refpect to feveral Gen-
'tlemen, who I know will be in Danger of offending
'againft this Inftrument, to give them notice of it by
'private Letters, in which I fhall only write; *Get a
'Licinius.*

' I fhould now trouble you no longer, but that I muft
'not conclude without defiring you to accept one of thefe
'Pipes; which fhall be left for you with *Buckley*; and
'which I hope will be ferviceable to you, fince as you
'   'are

' are filent yourfelf you are moft open to the Infults of
' the Noify.

                I am, SIR, &c. W. B.

' I had almoft forgot to inform you, that as an Im-
' provement in this Inftrument, there will be a particu-
' lar Note, which I call a Hufh-Note; and this is to be
' made ufe of againft a long Story, Swearing, Obfcene-
' nefs, and the like.   T

N⁰ 229   *Thurfday, November* 22.

——— *Spirat adhuc amor,*
Vivuntque commiffi calores
   Æoliæ fidibus puellæ.   Hor. Od. 9. l. 4. v. 10.

  Sappho's charming Lyre
  Preferves her foft Defire,
  And tunes our ravifh'd Souls to Love.   CREECH.

AMONG the many famous Pieces of Antiquity
which are ftill to be feen at *Rome,* there is the
Trunk of a Statue which has loft the Arms, Legs,
and Head; but difcovers fuch an exquifite Workman-
fhip in what remains of it, that *Michael Angelo* declared
he had learned his whole Art from it. Indeed he ftudied
it fo attentively, that he made moft of his Statues, and
even his Pictures in that *Gufto,* to make ufe of the *Italian*
Phrafe; for which Reafon this maimed Statue is ftill
called *Michael Angelo's* School.

A Fragment of *Sappho,* which I defign for the Subject of this Paper, is in as great Reputation among the
Poets and Criticks, as the mutilated Figure abovementioned is among the Statuaries and Painters. Several
of our Countrymen, and Mr. *Dryden* in particular, feem
very often to have copied after it in their Dramatick
Writings, and in their Poems upon Love.

WHATEVER might have been the Occafion of
this Ode, the Englifh Reader will enter into the Beau-
tiss

ties of it, if he suppofes it to have been written in the Perfon of a Lover fitting by his Miftrefs. I fhall fet to View three different Copies of this beautiful Original: The firft is a Tranflation by *Catullus,* the fecond by Monfieur *Boileau,* and the laft by a Gentleman whofe Tranflation of the *Hymn to Venus* has been fo defervedly admired.

Ad LESBIAM.

Ille mi par effe Deo videtur,
Ille, fi fas eft, fuperare Divos,
Qui fedens adverfus identidem te
    Spectat, & audit
Dulce ridentem, mifero quod omnis
Eripit fenfus mihi: nam fimul te,
Lefbia, adfpexi, nihil eft fuper mi
    Quod loquar amens.
Lingua fed torpet: tenuis fub artus
Flamma dimanat, fonitu fuopte
Tinniunt aures: gemina teguntur
    Lumina nocte.

MY learned Reader will know very well the Reafon why one of thefe Verfes is printed in *Roman* Letter; and if he compares this Tranflation with the Original, will find that the three firft Stanzas are rendred almoft Word for Word, and not only with the fame Elegance, but with the fame fhort Turn of Expreffion which is fo remarkable in the *Greek,* and fo peculiar to the *Sapphick* Ode. I cannot imagine for what Reafon Madam *Dacier* has told us, that this Ode of *Sappho* is preferved intire in *Longinus,* fince it is manifeft to any one who looks into that Author's Quotation of it, that there muft at leaft have been another Stanza, which is not tranfmitted to us.

THE fecond Tranflation of this Fragment which I fhall here cite, is that of Monfieur *Boileau.*

Heureux! qui près de toi, pour toi feul foupire:
Qui jouït du plaifir de t'entendre parler:
Qui te voit quelquefois doucement lui fourire.
Les Dieux, dans fon bonheur, peuvent-ils l'égaler?

Je sens de veine en veine une subtile flamme
Courir par tout mon corps, si-tôt que je te vois :
Et dans les doux transports, où s'egare mon âme,
Je ne sçaurois trouver de langue, ni de voix.

Un nuage confus se répand sur ma vûë,
Je n'entens plus, je tombe en de douces langueurs ;
Et pâle, sans haleine, interdite, esperdüë,
Un frisson me saisit, je tremble, je me meurs.

THE Reader will see that this is rather an Imitation than a Translation. The Circumstances do not lie so thick together, and follow one another with that Vehemence and Emotion as in the Original. In short, Monsieur *Boileau* has given us all the Poetry, but not all the Passion of this famous Fragment. I shall, in the last Place, present my Reader with the *English* Translation.

I.

Blest as th' immortal Gods is he,
The Youth who fondly sits by thee,
And hears and sees thee all the while
Softly speak and sweetly smile.

II.

'Twas this depriv'd my Soul of Rest,
And rais'd such Tumults in my Breast ;
For while I gaz'd, in Transport tost,
My Breath was gone, my Voice was lost :

III.

My Bosom glow'd ; the subtle Flame
Ran quick through all my vital Frame ;
O'er my dim Eyes a Darkness hung ;
My Ears with hollow Murmurs rung.

IV.

In dewy Damps my Limbs were chill'd ;
My Blood with gentle Horrors thrill'd ;
My feeble Pulse forgot to play ;
I fainted, sunk, and dy'd away.

INSTEAD of giving any Character of this last Translation, I shall desire my learned Reader to look into the Criticisms which *Longinus* has made upon the Original. By that means he will know to which of the Translations he ought to give the Preference. I shall only add, that this Translation is written in the very Spirit of *Sappho*, and as near the *Greek* as the Genius of our Language will possibly suffer.

LONGINUS has observed that this Description of Love in *Sappho* is an exact Copy of Nature, and that all the Circumstances which follow one another in such an hurry of Sentiments, notwithstanding they appear repugnant to each other, are really such as happen in the Phrenzies of Love.

I wonder, that not one of the Criticks or Editors, through whose Hands this Ode has passed, has taken Occasion from it to mention a Circumstance related by *Plutarch*. That Author in the famous Story of *Antiochus*, who fell in Love with *Stratonice*, his Mother-in-law, and (not daring to discover his Passion) pretended to be confined to his Bed by Sickness, tells us, that *Erasistratus*, the Physician, found out the Nature of his Distemper by those Symptoms of Love which he had learnt from *Sappho's* Writings. *Stratonice* was in the Room of the Love-sick Prince, when these Symptoms discovered themselves to his Physician; and it is probable, that they were not very different from those which *Sappho* here describes in a Lover sitting by his Mistress. The Story of *Antiochus* is so well known, that I need not add the Sequel of it, which has no Relation to my present Subject. C.

Nº 230 *Friday, November 23.*

Homines ad Deos nullâ re propiùs accedunt, quàm salutem Hominibus dando.
                                                    Tull.

Men resemble the Gods in nothing so much, as in doing good to their Fellow-creatures.

HUMAN Nature appears a very deformed, or a very beautiful Object, according to the different Lights in which it is viewed. When we see Men of inflamed Passions, or of wicked Designs, tearing one another to pieces by open Violence, or undermining each other by secret Treachery; when we observe base and narrow Ends pursued by ignominious and dishonest Means; when we behold Men mixed in Society as if it were for the Destruction of it; we are even ashamed of our Species, and out of Humour with our own Being: But in another Light, when we behold them mild, good, and benevolent, full of a generous Regard for the publick Prosperity, compassionating each other's Distresses, and relieving each other's Wants, we can hardly believe they are Creatures of the same Kind. In this View they appear Gods to each other, in the Exercise of the noblest Power, that of doing Good; and the greatest Compliment we have ever been able to make to our own Being, has been by calling this Disposition of Mind Humanity. We cannot but observe a Pleasure arising in our own Breast upon the seeing or hearing of a generous Action, even when we are wholly disinterested in it. I cannot give a more proper Instance of this, than by a Letter from *Pliny*, in which he recommends a Friend in the most handsom manner, and, methinks, it would be a great Pleasure to know the Success of this Epistle, though each Party concerned in it has been so many hundred Years in his Grave.

                                                    To

To MAXIMUS.

'WHAT I should gladly do for any Friend of
'yours, I think I may now with Confidence
'request for a Friend of mine. *Arrianus Maturius* is the
'most considerable Man of his Country; when I call him
'so, I do not speak with Relation to his Fortune, though
'that is very plentiful, but to his Integrity, Justice, Gra-
'vity, and Prudence; his Advice is useful to me in Busi-
'ness, and his Judgment in Matters of Learning: His Fi-
'delity, Truth, and good Understanding, are very great;
'besides this, he loves me as you do, than which I can-
'not say any thing that signifies a warmer Affection. He
'has nothing that's aspiring; and though he might rise
'to the highest Order of Nobility, he keeps himself in
'an inferior Rank; yet I think myself bound to use
'my Endeavours to serve and promote him; and would
'therefore find the Means of adding something to his
'Honours while he neither expects nor knows it, nay,
'though he should refuse it. Something, in short, I
'would have for him that may be honourable, but not
'troublesom; and I intreat that you will procure him
'the first thing of this kind that offers, by which you
'will not only oblige me, but him also; for though he
'does not covet it, I know he will be as grateful in ac-
'knowledging your Favour as if he had asked it.

Mr. SPECTATOR,

'THE Reflexions in some of your Papers on the
'servile manner of Education now in Use, have
'given Birth to an Ambition, which, unless you discoun-
'tenance it, will, I doubt, engage me in a very difficult,
'tho' not ungrateful Adventure. I am about to under-
'take, for the sake of the *British* Youth, to instruct
'them in such a manner, that the most dangerous Page
'in *Virgil* or *Homer* may be read by them with much
'Pleasure, and with perfect Safety to their Persons.
'COULD I prevail so far as to be honoured with the
'Protection of some few of them, (for I am not Hero
'enough to rescue many) my Design is to retire with
'them to an agreeable Solitude; though within the Neigh-
'bourhood of a City, for the Convenience of their being
'instructed

' inftructed in Mufick, Dancing, Drawing, Defigning,
' or any other fuch Accomplifhments, which it is con-
' ceived may make as proper Diverfions for them, and,
' almoft as pleafant, as the little fordid Games which
' dirty School-boys are fo much delighted with. It may
' eafily be imagined, how fuch a pretty Society, converf-
' ing with none beneath themfelves, and fometimes ad-
' mitted as perhaps not unentertaining Parties amongft
' better Company, commended and careffed for their lit-
' tle Performances, and turned by fuch Converfations to
' a certain Galantry of Soul, might be brought early
' acquainted with fome of the moft polite *Englifh* Wri-
' ters. This having given them fome tolerable Tafte of
' Books, they would make themfelves Mafters of the *La-*
' *tin* Tongue by Methods far eafier than thofe in *Lilly,*
' with as little Difficulty or Reluctance as young Ladies
' learn to fpeak *French,* or to fing *Italian* Operas. When
' they had advanced thus far, it would be time to form
' their Tafte fomething more exactly: One that had
' any true Relifh of fine Writing, might, with great
' Pleafure both to himfelf and them, run over together
' with them the beft *Roman* Hiftorians, Poets, and Ora-
' tors, and point out their more remarkable Beauties ;
' give them a fhort Scheme of Chronology, a little View
' of Geography, Medals, Aftronomy, or what elfe might
' beft feed the bufy inquifitive Humour fo natural to
' that Age. Such of them as had the leaft Spark of
' Genius, when it was once awakened by the fhining
' Thoughts and great Sentiments of thofe admired Wri-
' ters, could not, I believe be eafily withheld from
' attempting that more difficult Sifter Language, whofe
' exalted Beauties they would have heard fo often ce-
' lebrated as the Pride and Wonder of the whole
' Learned World. In the mean while, it would be
' requifite to exercife their Stile in Writing any light
' Pieces that afk more of Fancy than of Judgment: and
' that frequently in their Native Language, which every
' one methinks fhould be moft concerned to cultivate,
' efpecially Letters in which a Gentleman muft have fo
' frequent Occafions to diftinguifh himfelf. A Set of gen-
' teel good-natured Youths fallen into fuch a Manner of
' Life, would form almoft a little Academy, and doubt-
' lefs

' lefs prove no fuch contemptible Companions, as might
' not often tempt a wifer Man to mingle himfelf in their
' Diverfions, and draw them into fuch ferious Sports as
' might prove nothing lefs inftructing than the graveft
' Leffons. I doubt not but it might be made fome of
' their Favourite Plays, to contend which of them fhould
' recite a beautiful Part of a Poem or Oration moft grace-
' fully, or fometimes to join in acting a Scene of *Terence*,
' *Sophocles*, or our own *Shakefpear*. The Caufe of
' *Milo* might again be pleaded before more favourable
' Judges, *Cæfar* a fecond time be taught to tremble, and
' another Race of *Athenians* be afrefh enraged at the Am-
' bition of another *Philip*. Amidft thefe noble Amufe-
' ments, we could hope to fee the early Dawnings of
' their Imagination daily brighten into Senfe, their In-
' nocence improve into Virtue, and their unexperienced
' Good-nature directed to a generous Love of their
' Country.

T   *I am,* &c.

Nº 231   *Saturday, November* 24.

O *Pudor !* O *Pietas !* ———   Mart.
O *Modefty !* O *Piety !*

LOOKING over the Letters which I have lately
received from my Correfpondents, I met with the
following one, which is written with fuch a Spirit
of Politenefs, that I could not but be very much pleafed
with it myfelf, and queftion not but it will be as acceptable to the Reader.

Mr. SPECTATOR,

' YOU, who are no Stranger to Publick Affemblies,
'   cannot but have obferved the Awe they often
' ftrike on fuch as are obliged to exert any Talent before
' them. This is a fort of elegant Diftrefs, to which in-
' genuous Minds are the moft liable, and may therefore
' deferve fome Remarks in your Paper. Many a brave
'   Fellow,

' Fellow, who has put his Enemy to Flight in the Field,'
' has been in the utmost Disorder upon making a Speech'
' before a Body of his Friends at home: One would think'
' there was some kind of Fascination in the Eyes of a'
' large Circle of People, when darting altogether upon'
' one Person. I have seen a new Actor in a Tragedy so'
' bound up by it as to be scarce able to speak or move,'
' and have expected he would have died above three Acts'
' before the Dagger or Cup of Poison were brought in.'
' It would not be amiss, if such an one were at first in-'
' troduced as a Ghost, or a Statue, till he recovered his'
' Spirits, and grew fit for some living Part.

' AS this sudden Desertion of one's self shews a Diffi-'
' dence, which is not displeasing, it implies at the same'
' time the greatest Respect to an Audience that can be.'
' It is a sort of mute Eloquence, which pleads for their'
' Favour much better than Words could do; and we find'
' their Generosity naturally moved to support those who'
' are in so much Perplexity to entertain them. I was ex-'
' tremely pleased with a late Instance of this Kind at the'
' Opera of *Almahide*, in the Encouragement given to a'
' young Singer, whose more than ordinary Concern on'
' her first Appearance, recommended her no less than her'
' agreeable Voice, and just Performance. Meer Bash-'
' fulness without Merit is aukward; and Merit without'
' Modesty, insolent. But modest Merit has a double'
' Claim to Acceptance, and generally meets with as ma-'
' ny Patrons as Beholders.

I am, &c.

IT is impossible that a Person should exert himself
to Advantage in an Assembly, whether it be his Part
either to sing or speak, who lies under too great Oppressi-
ons of Modesty. I remember, upon talking with a Friend
of mine concerning the Force of Pronunciation, our Discourse led us into the Enumeration of the several Organs
of Speech which an Orator ought to have in Perfection,
as the Tongue, the Teeth, the Lips, the Nose, the Palate,
and the Wind-pipe. Upon which, says my Friend, you
have omitted the most material Organ of them all, and
that is the Forehead.

' BUT

BUT notwithstanding an Excess of Modesty obstructs the Tongue, and renders it unfit for its Offices, a due Porportion of it is thought so requisite to an Orator, that Rhetoricians have recommended it to their Disciples as a Particular in their Art. *Cicero* tells us that he never liked an Orator, who did not appear in some little Confusion at the Beginning of his Speech, and confesses that he himself never entered upon an Oration without Trembling and Concern. It is indeed a kind of Deference which is due to a great Assembly, and seldom fails to raise a Benevolence in the Audience towards the Person who speaks. My Correspondent has taken notice that the bravest Men often appear timorous on these Occasions, as indeed we may observe, that there is generally no Creature more impudent than a Coward.

———*Linguâ melior, sed frigida bello.*
　Dextera———　　　　　　　　Virg. Æn. 11. v. 338.

———Bold at the Council-board;
But cautious in the Field, he shunn'd the Sword.
　　　　　　　　　　　　　　　　DRYDEN.

A bold Tongue and a feeble Arm are the Qualifications of *Drances* in *Virgil*; as *Homer*, to express a Man both timorous and saucy, makes use of a kind of Point, which is very rarely to be met with in his Writings; namely, that he had the Eyes of a Dog, but the Heart of a Deer.

A just and reasonable Modesty does not only recommend Eloquence, but sets off every great Talent which a Man can be possessed of. It heightens all the Virtues which it accompanies; like the Shades in Paintings, it raises and rounds every Figure, and makes the Colours more beautiful, though not so glaring as they would be without it.

MODESTY is not only an Ornament, but also a Guard to Virtue. It is a kind of quick and delicate *Feeling* in the Soul, which makes her shrink and withdraw herself from every thing that has Danger in it. It is such an exquisite Sensibility, as warns her to shun the first Appearance of every thing which is hurtful.

I cannot at present recollect either the Place or Time of what I am going to mention; but I have read somewhere in the History of Ancient *Greece*, that the Women of the Country were seized with an unaccountable Me-

lancholy, which difpofed feveral of them to make away
with themfelves. The Senate, after having tried many
Expedients to prevent this Self-Murder, which was fo
frequent among them, publifhed an Edict, That if any
Woman whatever fhould lay violent Hands upon herfelf,
her Corps fhould be expofed naked in the Street, and
dragged about the City in the moft publick Manner.
This Edict immediately put a Stop to the Practice which
was before fo common. We may fee in this Inftance the
Strength of Female Modefty, which was able to overcome the Violence even of Madnefs and Defpair. The
Fear of Shame in the Fair Sex, was in thofe Days more
prevalent than that of Death.

IF Modefty has fo great an Influence over our Actions,
and is in many Cafes fo impregnable a Fence to Virtue;
what can more undermine Morality than that Politenefs
which reigns among the unthinking Part of Mankind,
and treats as unfafhionable the moft ingenuous Part of
our Behaviour; which recommends Impudence as Good-
breeding, and keeps a Man always in Countenance, not
becaufe he is Innocent, but becaufe he is Shamelefs?

SENECA thought Modefty fo great a Check to Vice,
that he prefcribes to us the Practice of it in Secret, and
advifes us to raife it in ourfelves upon imaginary Occafions, when fuch as are real do not offer themfelves; for
this is the Meaning of his Precept, that when we are by
ourfelves, and in our greateft Solitudes, we fhould fancy
that *Cato* ftands before us and fees every thing we do. In
fhort, if you banifh Modefty out of the World, fhe carries
away with her half the Virtue that is in it.

AFTER thefe Reflexions on Modefty, as it is a
Virtue; I muft obferve, that there is a vicious Modefty, which juftly deferves to be ridiculed, and which
thofe Perfons very often difcover, who value themfelves
moft upon a well-bred Confidence. This happens when
a Man is afhamed to act up to his Reafon, and would not
upon any Confideration be furprifed in the Practice of
thofe Duties, for the Performance of which he was fent
into the World. Many an impudent Libertine would blufh
to be caught in a ferious Difcourfe, and would fcarce be
able to fhew his Head, after having difclofed a religious
Thought. Decency of Behaviour, all outward Show of
Virtue,

Virtue, and Abhorrence of Vice, are carefully avoided by this Set of Shame-faced People, as what would disparage their Gaiety of Temper, and infallibly bring them to Dishonour. This is such a Poorness of Spirit, such a despicable Cowardise, such a degenerate abject State of Mind, as one would think human Nature incapable of, did we not meet with frequent Instances of it in ordinary Conversation.

THERE is another Kind of vicious Modesty which makes a Man ashamed of his Person, his Birth, his Profession, his Poverty, or the like Misfortunes; which it was not in his Choice to prevent, and is not in his Power to rectify. If a Man appears ridiculous by any of the aforementioned Circumstances, he becomes much more so by being out of Countenance for them. They should rather give him Occasion to exert a noble Spirit, and to palliate those Imperfections which are not in his Power, by those Perfections which are; or to use a very witty Allusion of an eminent Author, he should imitate *Cæsar,* who, because his Head was bald, cover'd that Defect with Laurels. C

Nº 232. *Monday, November* 26.

Nihil largiundo gloriam adeptus est. Salluſt.

By beſtowing nothing he acquired Glory.

MY wife and good Friend, Sir *Andrew Freeport,* divides himself almost equally between the Town and the Country: His Time in Town is given up to the Publick, and the Management of his private Fortune; and after every three or four Days spent in this manner, he retires for as many to his Seat within a few Miles of the Town, to the Enjoyment of himself, his Family, and his Friend. Thus Business and Pleasure, or rather, in Sir *Andrew,* Labour and Rest, recommend each other. They take their Turns with so quick a Vicissitude, that neither becomes a Habit, or takes possession of the whole Man; nor is it possible he should be surfeited with either. I often see him at our Club in good Humour, and yet fometimes too with an Air of Care in his Looks : But in his Country Retreat he is always unbent, and fuch a Companion as I could defire; and therefore I feldom fail to make one with him when he is pleafed to invite me.

THE other Day, as foon as we were got into his Chariot, two or three Beggars on each Side hung upon the Doors, and folicited our Charity with the ufual Rhetorick of a fick Wife or Husband at home, three or four helplefs little Children all ftarving with Cold and Hunger. We were forced to part with fome Money to get rid of their Importunity; and then we proceeded on our Journey with the Bleffings and Acclamations of thefe People.

" WELL then, fays Sir *Andrew*, we go off with the
" Prayers and good Wifhes of the Beggars, and perhaps
" too our Healths will be drunk at the next Ale-houfe:
" So all we fhall be able to value ourfelves upon, is, that
" we have promoted the Trade of the Victualler and the
" Excifes of the Government. But how few Ounces of
" Wooll do we fee upon the Backs of thofe poor Crea-
" tures ? And when they fhall next fall in our Way, they
" will hardly be better drefs'd ; they muft always live in
" Rags to look like Objects of Compaffion. If their Fa-
" milies too are fuch as they are reprefented, 'tis certain
" they cannot be better clothed, and muft be a great
" deal worfe fed : One would think Potatoes fhould be
" all their Bread, and their Drink the pure Element; and
" then what goodly Cuftomers are the Farmers like to
" have for their Wooll, Corn and Cattle ? Such Cufto-
" mers, and fuch a Confumption, cannot choofe but
" advance the landed Intereft, and hold up the Rents
" of the Gentlemen.

" BUT of all Men living, we Merchants, who live by
" Buying and Selling, ought never to encourage Beg-
" gars. The Goods which we export are indeed the Pro-
" duct of the Lands, but much the greateft Part of their
" Value is the Labour of the People: but how much of
" thefe Peoples Labour fhall we export whilft we hire
" them to fit ftill ? The very Alms they receive from
" us, are the Wages of Idlenefs. I have often thought
" that no Man fhould be permitted to take Relief from
" the Parifh, or to ask it in the Street, till he has firft pur-
" chafed

" chafed as much as poffible of his own Livelihood by
" the Labour of his own Hands; and then the Publick
" ought only to be taxed to make good the Deficiency.
" If this Rule was ftrictly obferved, we fhould fee every
" where fuch a multitude of new Labourers, as would
" in all probability reduce the Prices of all our Manufac-
" tures. It is the very Life of Merchandife to buy cheap
" and fell dear. The Merchant ought to make his Out-fet
" as cheap as poffible, that he may find the greater Profit
" upon his Returns; and nothing will enable him to do
" this like the Reduction of the Price of Labour upon all
" our Manufactures. This too would be the ready Way
" to increafe the Number of our Foreign Markets: The
" Abatement of the Price of the Manufacture would pay
" for the Carriage of it to more diftant Countries; and
" this Confequence would be equally beneficial both to
" the Landed and Trading Interefts. As fo great an
" Addition of labouring Hands would produce this
" happy Confequence both to the Merchant and the
" Gentleman; our Liberality to common Beggars, and
" every other Obftruction to the Increafe of Labourers,
" muft be equally pernicious to both.

SIR *Andrew* then went on to affirm, That the Reduction of the Prices of our Manufactures by the Addition of fo many new Hands, would be no Inconvenience to any Man: But obferving I was fomething
ftartled at the Affertion, he made a fhort Paufe, and then
refumed the Difcourfe. " It may feem, fays he, a Pa-
" radox, that the Price of Labour fhould be reduced
" without an Abatement of Wages, or that Wages can
" be abated without any Inconvenience to the Labourer,
" and yet nothing is more certain than that both thefe
" Things may happen. The Wages of the Labourers
" make the greateft Part of the Price of every Thing
" that is ufeful; and if in Proportion with the Wages
" the Prices of all other Things fhould be abated, every
" Labourer with lefs Wages would ftill be able to pur-
" chafe as many Neceffaries of Life; where then would
" be the Inconvenience? But the Price of Labour may
" be reduced by the Addition of more Hands to a Manu-
" facture, and yet the Wages of Perfons remain as high
" as ever. The admirable Sir *William Petty* has given

L 3 " Ex-

" Examples of this in fome of his Writings : One of them,
" as I remember, is that of a Watch, which I fhall en-
" deavour to explain fo as fhall fuit my prefent Purpofe.
" It is certain that a fingle Watch could not be made fo
" cheap in Proportion by one only Man, as a hundred
" Watches by a hundred ; for as there is vaft Variety in
" the Work, no one Perfon could equally fuit himfelf to
" all the Parts of it ; the Manufacture would be tedious,
" and at laft but clumfily performed : But if an hundred
" Watches were to be made by a hundred Men, the Cafes
" may be affigned to one, the Dials to another, the Wheels
" to another, the Springs to another, and every other
" Part to a proper Artift ; as there would be no need of
" perplexing any one Perfon with too much Variety,
" every one would be able to perform his fingle Part
" with greater Skill and Expedition ; and the hundred
" Watches would be finifhed in one fourth Part of the
" Time of the firft one, and every one of them at one
" fourth Part of the Coft, tho' the Wages of every Man
" were equal. The Reduction of the Price of the Manu-
" facture would increafe the Demand of it, all the fame
" Hands would be ftill employed and as well paid. The
" fame Rule will hold in the Clothing, the Shipping,
" and all other Trades whatfoever. And thus an Addi-
" tion of Hands to our Manufactures will only reduce
" the Price of them ; the Labourer will ftill have as much
" Wages, and will confequently be enabled to purchafe
" more Conveniencies of Life ; fo that every Intereft in
" the Nation would recieve a Benefit from the Increafe
" of our Working People.

" BESIDES, I fee no Occafion for this Charity to
" common Beggars, fince every Beggar is an Inhabitant
" of a Parifh, and every Parifh is taxed to the Mainte-
" nance of their own Poor. For my own part, I cannot
" be mightily pleafed with the Laws which have done
" this, which have provided better to feed than employ
" the Poor. We have a Tradition from our Forefathers,
" that after the firft of thofe Laws was made, they were
" infulted with that famous Song ;

Hang Sorrow, and caft away Care,
The Parifh is bound to find us, &c.

　　　　　　　　　　　　　　　" And

" And if we will be so good-natured as to maintain
" them without Work, they can do no less in Return
" than sing us *The Merry Beggars.*

" WHAT then? Am I against all Acts of Charity?
" God forbid! I know of no Virtue in the Gospel that
" is in more pathetick Expressions recommended to our
" Practice. *I was hungry and ye gave me no Meat; thirsty*
" *and ye gave me no Drink, naked and ye clothed me not,*
" *a Stranger and ye took me not in, sick and in prison*
" *and ye visited me not.* Our Blessed Saviour treats the
" Exercise or Neglect of Charity towards a poor Man,
" as the Performance or Breach of this Duty towards
" himself. I shall endeavour to obey the Will of my
" Lord and Master: And therefore if an industrious
" Man shall submit to the hardest Labour and coarsest
" Fare, rather than endure the Shame of taking Relief
" from the Parish, or asking it in the Street, this is the
" Hungry, the Thirsty, the Naked; and I ought to
" believe, if any Man is come hither for Shelter against
" Persecution or Oppression, this is the Stranger, and
" I ought to take him in. If any Countryman of our
" own is fallen into the Hands of Infidels, and lives in
" a State of miserable Captivity, this is the Man in
" Prison, and I should contribute to his Ransom. I
" ought to give to an Hospital of Invalids, to recover
" as many useful Subjects as I can; but I shall bestow
" none of my Bounties upon an Alms-house of idle Peo-
" ple; and for the same Reason I shall not think it a
" Reproach to me if I had withheld my Charity from
" those common Beggars. But we prescribe better Rules
" than we are able to practise; we are ashamed not to
" give into the mistaken Customs of our Country: But
" at the same time, I cannot but think it a Reproach
" worse than that of common Swearing, that the Idle
" and the Abandoned are suffered in the Name of
" Heaven and all that is sacred, to extort from christian
" and tender Minds a Supply to a profligate Way of
" Life, that is always to be supported, but never re-
" lieved. ·Z.

N° 233 *Tuesday, November* 27.

——*Tanquam hæc sint nostri medicina furoris,*
Aut Deus ille malis hominum mitescere discat.

Virg. Ecl. 10. v. 60.

As if by these my Sufferings I cou'd ease,
Or by my Pains the God of Love appease. DRYDEN.

I Shall, in this Paper, discharge myself of the Promise
I have made to the Publick, by obliging them with a
Translation of the little *Greek* Manuscript, which is
said to have been a Piece of those Records that were preserved in the Temple of *Apollo*, upon the Promontory of
Leucate: It is a short History of the Lover's Leap, and is
inscribed, *An Account of Persons Male and Female, who
offered up their Vows in the Temple of the* Pythian Apollo,
*in the Forty sixth Olympiad, and leaped from the Promontory
of* Leucate *into the* Ionian *Sea, in order to cure themselves
of the Passion of Love.*

THIS Account is very dry in many Parts, as only
mentioning the Name of the Lover who leaped, the Person he leaped for, and relating, in short, that he was either
cured, or killed, or maimed by the Fall. It indeed gives
the Names of so many who died by it, that it would have
looked like a Bill of Mortality, had I translated it at full
length; I have therefore made an Abridgment of it,
and only extracted such particular Passages as have something extraordinary, either in the Case, or in the Cure,
or in the Fate of the Person who is mentioned in it.
After this short Preface take the Account as follows.

BATTUS, the Son of *Menalcas* the *Sicilian,* leaped for
Bombyca the Musician: Got rid of his Passion with the Loss
of his Right Leg and Arm, which were broken in the Fall.

MELISSA, in Love with *Daphnis,* very much
bruised, but escaped with Life.

CYNISCA, the Wife of *Æschines,* being in Love
with *Lycus;* and *Æschines* her Husband being in Love
with *Eurilla;* (which had made this married Couple
very

very uneasy to one another for several Years) both the Husband and the Wife took the Leap by Consent; they both of them escaped, and have lived very happily together ever since.

LARISSA, a Virgin of *Thessaly*, deserted by *Plexippus*, after a Courtship of three Years; she stood upon the Brow of the Promontory for some time, and after having thrown down a Ring, a Bracelet, and a little Picture, with other Presents which she had received from *Plexippus*, she threw herself into the Sea, and was taken up alive.

N. B. Larissa, before she leaped, made an Offering of a Silver *Cupid* in the Temple of *Apollo*.

SIMÆTHA, in Love with *Daphnis* the *Myndian*, perished in the Fall.

CHARIXUS, the Brother of *Sappho*, in Love with *Rhodope* the Courtesan, having spent his whole Estate upon her, was advised by his Sister to leap in the Beginning of his Amour, but would not hearken to her till he was reduced to his last Talent; being forsaken by *Rhodope*, at length resolved to take the Leap. Perished in it.

ARIDÆUS, a beautiful Youth of *Epirus*, in Love with *Praxinoe*, the Wife of *Thespis*, escaped without Damage, saving only that two of his Foreteeth were struck out and his Nose a little flatted.

CLEORA, a Widow of *Ephesus*, being inconsolable for the Death of her Husband, was resolved to take this Leap in order to get rid of her Passion for his Memory; but being arrived at the Promontory, she there met with *Dimmachus* the *Miletian*, and after a short Conversation with him, laid aside the Thoughts of her Leap, and married him in the Temple of *Apollo*.

N. B. Her Widow's Weeds are still seen hanging up in the Western Corner of the Temple.

OLPHIS, the Fisherman, having received a Box on the Ear from *Thestylis* the Day before, and being determined to have no more to do with her, leaped, and escaped with Life.

ATALANTA, an old Maid, whose Cruelty had several Years before driven two or three despairing Lovers to this Leap; being now in the fifty fifth Year of her Age, and in Love with an Officer of *Sparta*, broke her Neck in the Fall.

HIPPARCHUS being paſſionately fond of his own Wife who was enamoured of *Bathyllus,* leaped, and died of his Fall; upon which his Wife married her Galant.

TETTYX, the Dancing-maſter, in Love with *Olympia* an *Athenian* Matron, threw himſelf from the Rock with great Agility, but was crippled in the Fall.

DIAGORAS, the Uſurer, in Love with his Cook-Maid; he peeped ſeveral times over the Precipice, but his Heart miſgiving him, he went back, and married her that Evening.

CINÆDUS, after having entred his own Name in the *Pythian* Records, being asked the Name of the Perſon whom he leaped for, and being aſhamed to diſcover it, he was ſet aſide, and not ſuffered to leap.

EUNICA, a Maid of *Paphos,* aged Nineteen, in Love with *Eurybates.* Hurt in the Fall, but recovered.

N. B. This was the ſecond Time of her Leaping.

HESPERUS, a young Man of *Tarentum,* in Love with his Maſter's Daughter. Drowned; the Boats not coming in ſoon enough to his Relief.

SAPPHO, the *Lesbian,* in Love with *Phaon,* arrived at the Temple of *Apollo,* habited like a Bride in Garments as white as Snow. She wore a Garland of Myrtle on her Head, and carried in her Hand the little Muſical Inſtrument of her own Invention. After having ſung an Hymn to *Apollo,* ſhe hung up her Garland on one Side of his Altar, and her Harp on the other. She then tuck'd up her Veſtments, like a *Spartan* Virgin, and amidſt thouſands of Spectators, who were anxious for her Safety, and offered up Vows for her Deliverance, marched directly forwards to the utmoſt Summit of the Promontory, where after having repeated a Stanza of her own Verſes, which we could not hear, ſhe threw herſelf off the Rock with ſuch an Intrepidity as was never before obſerved in any who had attempted that dangerous Leap. Many who were preſent related, that they ſaw her fall into the Sea, from whence ſhe never roſe again; tho' there were others who affirmed, that ſhe never came to the Bottom of her Leap, but that ſhe was changed into a Swan as ſhe fell, and that they ſaw her hovering in the Air under that Shape. But whether or no the whiteneſs and fluttering of her Garments might not deceive thoſe who looked upon her, or whether ſhe might not

not

not really be metamorphofed into that mufical and me-lancholy Bird, is ftill a Doubt among the *Lesbians*.

ALCÆUS, the famous *Lyrick* Poet, who had for fome time been paffionately in Love with *Sappho*, arrived at the Promontory of *Leucate* that very Evening, in order to take the Leap upon her Account; but hearing that *Sappho* had been there before him, and that her Body could be no where found, he very generoufly lamented her Fall, and is faid to have written his hundred and twenty fifth Ode upon that Occafion.

Leaped in this Olympiad 250.

Males	124
Females,	126
Cured	120
Males	51
Females	69

C.

N° 234 *Wedneſday, November* 28.

Vellem in amicitia fic erraremus. Hor. Sat. 3. l. 1. v. 41.

I wiſh this Error in our Friendſhip reign'd! CREECH.

YOU very often hear People, after a Story has been told with fome entertaining Circumftances, tell it over again with Particulars that deftroy the Jeft, but give Light into the Truth of the Narration. This fort of Veracity, though it is impertinent, has fomething amiable in it, becaufe it proceeds from the Love of Truth, even in frivolous Occafions. If fuch honeft Amendments do not promife an agreeable Companion, they do a fincere Friend; for which Reafon one fhould allow them fo much of our Time, if we fall into their Company, as to fet us right in Matters that can do us no manner of Harm, whether the Facts be one Way or the other. Lies which are told out of Arrogance and Oftentation a Man fhould detect in his own Defence, becaufe he fhould not be triumphed over; Lies which are told out of Malice he fhould expofe, both for his own fake and that of the reft of Mankind, becaufe every Man fhould rife

rife againſt a common Enemy : But the officious Liar
many have argued is to be excuſed, becauſe it does ſome
Man good, and no Man hurt. The Man who made more
than ordinary ſpeed from a Fight in which the *Athenians*
were beaten, and told them they had obtained a complete
Victory, and put the whole City into the utmoſt Joy and
Exultation, was check'd by the Magiſtrates for his Falſhood ; but excuſed himſelf by ſaying, O *Athenians* ! am I
your Enemy becauſe I gave you two happy Days ? This
Fellow did to a whole People what an Acquaintance of
mine does every Day he lives in ſome eminent Degree to
particular Perſons. He is ever lying People into good Humour, and, as *Plato* ſaid, it was allowable in Phyſicians to
lye to their Patients to keep up their Spirits, I am half
doubtful whether my Friend's Behaviour is not as excuſable.
His Manner is to expreſs himſelf ſurpriſed at the chearful
Countenance of a Man whom he obſerves diffident of himſelf ; and generally by that means makes his Lye a Truth.
He will, as if he did not know any thing of the Circumſtance, ask one whom he knows at Variance with another, what is the meaning that Mr. ſuch a one, naming his
Adverſary, does not applaud him with that Heartineſs
which formerly he has heard him ? He ſaid indeed, (continues he) I would rather have that Man for my Friend
than any Man in *England*; but for an Enemy———This
melts the Perſon he talks to, who expected nothing but
downright Rallery from that Side. According as he ſees
his Practices ſucceeded, he goes to the oppoſite Party, and
tells him, he cannot imagine how it happens that ſome
People know one another ſo little; you ſpoke with ſo
much Coldneſs of a Gentleman who ſaid more Good
of you, than, let me tell you, any Man living deſerves.
The Succeſs of one of theſe Incidents was, that the
next time that one of the Adverſaries ſpied the other,
he hems after him in the publick Street, and they
muſt crack a Bottle at the next Tavern, that uſed to
turn out of the other's Way to avoid one another's Eye-
ſhot. He will tell one Beauty ſhe was commended by
another, nay, he will ſay ſhe gave the Woman he ſpeaks
to, the Preference in a Particular for which ſhe herſelf is
admired. The pleaſanteſt Confuſion imaginable is made
through the whole Town by my Friend's indirect Offices ;

fices; you shall have a Visit returned after half a Year's
Abfence, and mutual Railing at each other every Day of
that Time. They meet with a thoufand Lamentations for
fo long a Separation, each Party naming herfelf for the
greateft Delinquent, if the other can poffibly be fo good
as to forgive her, which fhe has no reafon in the World,
but from the Knowledge of her Goodnefs, to hope for.
Very often a whole Train of Railers of each Side tire
their Horfes in fetting Matters right which they have
faid during the War between the Parties; and a whole
Circle of Acquaintance are put into a thoufand pleafing
Paffions and Sentiments, inftead of the Pangs of Anger,
Envy, Detraction, and Malice.

' THE worft Evil I ever obferved this Man's Falfhood
occafion, has been that he turned Detraction into Flattery.
He is well skilled in the Manners of the World, and by
over-looking what Men really are, he grounds his Artifices
upon what they have a mind to be. Upon this Foundation,
if two diftant Friends are brought together, and the Cement
feems to be weak, he never refts till he finds new Appearances to take off all Remains of Ill-will, and that by new
Mifunderftandings they are thoroughly reconciled.

To the SPECTATOR.

SIR,   *Devonshire, Nov.* 14, 1711.

' THERE arrived in this Neighbourhood two Days
    ' ago one of your gay Gentlemen of the Town, who
' being attended at his Entry with a Servant of his own,
' befides a Countryman he had taken up for a Guide, ex-
' cited the Curiofity of the Village to learn whence and what
' he might be. The Countryman (to whom they applied as
' moft eafy of Accefs) knew little more than that the Gentle-
' man came from *London* to travel and fee Fafhions, and was,
' as he heard fay, a Free-thinker: What Religion that might
' be, he could not tell; and for his own part, if they had
' not told him the Man was a Free-thinker, he fhould have
' gueffed, by his way of talking, he was little better than
' a Heathen; excepting only that he had been a good
' Gentleman to him, and made him drunk twice in one
' Day, over and above what they had bargained for.

' I do not look upon the Simplicity of this, and feveral
' odd Inquiries with which I fhall not trouble you to be
                                              ' won-

' wondered at, much lefs can I think that our Youths of
' fine Wit, and enlarged Underftandings, have any reafon
' to laugh. There is no Neceffity that every Squire in
' *Great Britain* fhould know what the Word Free-thinker
' ftands for; but it were much to be wifhed, that they who
' value themfelves upon that conceited Title were a little,
' better inftructed in what it ought to ftand for ; and that
' they would not perfuade themfelves a Man is really and
' truly a Free-thinker in any tolerable Senfe, meerly by
' virtue of his being an Atheift, or an Infidel of any other
' Diftinction. It may be doubted with good Reafon,
' whether there ever was in nature a more abject, flavifh,
' and bigotted Generation than the Tribe of *Beaux Efprits,*
' at prefent fo prevailing in this Ifland. Their Pretenfion
' to be Free-thinkers, is no other than Rakes have to be
' Free-livers, and Savages to be Free-men, that is, they
' can think whatever they have a mind to, and give them-
' felves up to whatever Conceit the Extravagancy of their
' Inclination, or their Fancy, fhall fuggeft; they can
' think as wildly as they talk and act, and will not endure
' that their Wit fhould be controled by fuch formal
' Things as Decency and common Senfe : Deduction,
' Coherence, Confiftency, and all the Rules of Reafon,
' they accordingly difdain, as too precife and mechani-
' cal for Men of a liberal Education.

' THIS, as far as I could ever learn from their Writings,
' or my own Obfervation, is a true Account of the *Britifh*
' Free-thinker. Our Vifitant here, who gave occafion to
' this Paper, has brought with him a new Syftem of com-
' mon Senfe, the Particulars of which I am not yet ac-
' quainted with, but will lofe no Opportunity of inform-
' ing myfelf whether it contain any thing worth Mr.
' SPECTATOR's Notice. In the mean time, Sir, I
' cannot but think it would be for the good of Mankind,
' if you would take this Subject into your Confideration,
' and convince the hopeful Youth of our Nation, that
' Licentioufnefs is not Freedom ; or, if fuch a Paradox
' will not be underftood, that a Prejudice towards
' Atheifm is not Impartiality.

I am, SIR, Your moft humble Servant,

T   PHILONOUS.

Thurfday,

N° 235. *Thurſday,* November 29.

———————*Populares*
Vincentem ſtrepitus————   Hor. Ars Poet. v. 81.
Awes the tumultuous Noiſes of the Pit. ROSCOMMON.

THERE is nothing which lies more within the Province of a Spectator than publick Shows and Diverſions; and as among theſe there are none which can pretend to vie with thoſe elegant Entertainments that are exhibited in our Theatres, I think it particularly incumbent on me to take notice of every thing that is remarkable in ſuch numerous and refined Aſſemblies.

IT is obſerved, that of late Years there has been a certain Perſon in the upper Gallery of the Play-houſe, who when he is pleaſed with any thing that is acted upon the Stage, expreſſes his Approbation by a loud Knock upon the Benches or the Wainſcot, which may be heard over the whole Theatre. The Perſon is commonly known by the Name of the *Trunk-maker in the upper Gallery.* Whether it be that the Blow he gives on theſe Occaſions reſembles that which is often heard in the Shops of ſuch Artiſans, or that he was ſuppoſed to have been a real Trunk-maker, who after the finiſhing of his Day's Work uſed to unbend his Mind at theſe publick Diverſions with his Hammer in his Hand, I cannot certainly tell. There are ſome, I know, who have been fooliſh enough to imagine it is a Spirit which haunts the upper Gallery, and from time to time makes thoſe ſtrange Noiſes; and the rather becauſe he is obſerved to be louder than ordinary every time the Ghoſt of *Hamlet* appears. Others have reported, that it is a dumb Man, who has choſen this Way of uttering himſelf when he is tranſported with any thing he ſees or hears. Others will have it to be the Play-houſe Thunderer, that exerts himſelf after this manner in the upper Gallery, when he has nothing to do upon the Roof.

BUT having made it my Buſineſs to get the beſt Information I could in a Matter of this Moment, I find that
the

the Trunk-maker, as he is commonly called, is a large black Man, whom no body knows. He generally leans forward on a huge Oaken Plant with great Attention to every thing that paffes upon the Stage. He is never feen to fmile; but upon hearing any thing that pleafes him, he takes up his Staff with both Hands, and lays it upon the next Piece of Timber that ftands in his way with exceeding Vehemence: After which, he compofes himfelf in his former Pofture, till fuch Time as fomething new fets him again at Work.

IT has been obferved, his Blow is fo well timed, that' the moft judicious Critick could never except againft it. As foon as any fhining Thought is expreffed in the Poet, or any uncommon Grace appears in the Actor, he fmites the Bench or Wainfcot. If the Audience does not concur with him, he fmites a fecond Time, and if the Audience is not yet awaked, looks round him with great Wrath, and repeats the Blow a third Time, which never fails to produce the Clap. He fometimes lets the Audience begin the Clap of themfelves, and at the Conclufion of their Applaufe ratifies it with a fingle Thwack.

He is of fo great Ufe to the Play-houfe, that it is faid a former Director of it, upon his not being able to pay his Attendance by reafon of Sicknefs kept one in pay to officiate for him till fuch time as he recovered; but the Perfon fo employed, tho' he laid about him with incredible Violence, did it in fuch wrong Places, that the Audience foon found out that it was not their old Friend the Trunk-maker.

IT has been remarked, that he has not yet exerted himfelf with Vigour this Seafon. He fometimes plies at the Opera; and upon *Nicolini*'s firft Appearance, was faid to have demolifhed three Benches in the fury of his Applaufe. He has broken half a dozen Oaken Plants upon *Dogget*, and feldom goes away from a Tragedy of *Shakefpear*, without leaving the Wainfcot extremely fhattered.

THE Players do not only connive at his obftreperous Approbation, but very chearfully repair at their own Coft whatever Damages he makes. They had once a Thought of erecting a kind of Wooden Anvil for his Ufe, that fhould be made of a very founding Plank, in order to render his Strokes more deep and mellow; but as this might not have been diftinguifhed from the Mufick of a Kettle-Drum, the Project was laid afide.

IN

IN the mean while, I cannot but take notice of the great Use it is to an Audience, that a Person should thus preside over their Heads like the Director of a Consort, in order to awaken their Attention, and beat time to their Applauses; or, to raise my Simile, I have sometimes fancied the Trunk-maker in the upper Gallery to be like *Virgil's* Ruler of the Winds, seated upon the Top of a Mountain, who, when he struck his Sceptre upon the Side of it, roused an Hurricane, and set the whole Cavern in an Uproar.

IT is certain, the Trunk-maker has saved many a good Play, and brought many a graceful Actor into Reputation, who would not otherwise have been taken notice of. It is very visible, as the Audience is not a little abashed, if they find themselves betrayed into a Clap, when their Friend in the upper Gallery does not come into it; so the Actors do not value themselves upon the Clap, but regard it as a meer *brutum fulmen*, or empty Noise, when it has not the Sound of the Oaken Plant in it. I know it has been given out by those who are Enemies to the Trunk-maker, that he has sometimes been bribed to be in the Interest of a bad Poet, or a vicious Player; but this is a Surmise which has no Foundation: his Strokes are always just, and his Admonitions seasonable; he does not deal about his Blows at Random, but always hits the right Nail upon the Head. The inexpressible Force wherewith he lays them on, sufficiently shews the Evidence and Strength of his Conviction. His Zeal for a good Author is indeed outrageous, and breaks down every Fence and Partition, every Board and Plank, that stands within the Expression of his Applause.

AS I do not care for terminating my Thoughts in barren Speculations, or in Reports of pure Matter of Fact, without drawing something from them for the Advantage of my Countrymen, I shall take the Liberty to make an humble Proposal, that whenever the Trunk-maker shall depart this Life, or whenever he shall have lost the Spring of his Arm by Sickness, old Age, Infirmity, or the like, some able-bodied Critick should be advanced to this Post, and have a competent Salary settled on him for Life, to be furnished with Bamboos for Operas, Crabtree-Cudgels for Comedies, and Oaken Plants for Tragedy, at the publick Expence. And to the End that this Place should be always disposed of according to Merit,

Merit, I would have none preferred to it, who has not
given convincing Proofs both of a sound Judgment and a
strong Arm, and who could not, upon Occasion, either
knock down an Ox, or write a Comment upon *Horace's*
Art of Poetry. In short, I would have him a due Composition of *Hercules* and *Apollo*, and so rightly qualified
for this important Office, that the *Trunk-maker* may not
be missed by our Posterity.   C

N° 236   *Friday, November* 30.

—— *Dare Jura maritis.*   - Hor. Ars Poet. v. 398.

With Laws connubial Tyrants to restrain.

Mr. SPECTATOR,

'YOU have not spoken in so direct a manner upon
'   the Subject of Marriage as that important Case
'   deserves. It would not be improper to observe
' upon the Peculiarity in the Youth of *Great Britain*, of
' railing and laughing at that Institution; and when they
' fall into it, from a profligate Habit of Mind, being in-
' sensible of the Satisfaction in that Way of Life, and
' treating their Wives with the most barbarous Disrespect.
'   PARTICULAR Circumstances and Cast of Tem-
' per, must teach a Man the Probability of mighty Uneasi-
' nesses in that State, (for unquestionably some there are
' whose very Dispositions are strangely averse to conjugal
' Friendship;) but no one, I believe, is by his own natu-
' ral Complexion prompted to teaze and torment ano-
' ther for no Reason but being nearly allied to him: And
' can there be any thing more base, or serve to sink a
' Man so much below his own distinguishing Characteri-
' stick, (I mean Reason) than returning Evil for Good in
' so open a Manner, as that of treating an helpless Creature
' with Unkindness, who has had so good an Opinion of
' him as to believe what he said relating to one of the
' greatest Concerns of Life, by delivering her Happiness
' in this World to his Care and Protection? Must not that
' Man be abandoned even to all manner of Humanity,
'   ' who

‘ who can deceive a Woman with Appearances of Affection
‘ and Kindnefs, for no other End but to torment her
‘ with more Eafe and Authority? Is any thing more un-
‘ like a Gentleman, than when his Honour is engaged for
‘ the performing his Promifes, becaufe nothing but that
‘ can oblige him to it, to become afterwards falfe to his
‘ Word, and be alone the Occafion of Mifery to one whofe
‘ Happinefs he but lately pretended was dearer to him
‘ than his own ? Ought fuch a one to be trufted in his
‘ common Affairs ? or treated but as one whofe Honefty
‘ confifted only in his Incapacity of being otherwife ?

‘ THERE is one Caufe of this Ufage no lefs abfurd
‘ than common, which takes place among the more un-
‘ thinking Men; and that is the Defire to appear to their
‘ Friends free and at Liberty, and without thofe Tram-
‘ mels they have fo much ridiculed. To avoid this they
‘ fly into the other Extreme, and grow Tyrants that they
‘ may feem Mafters. Becaufe an uncontrolable Com-
‘ mand of their own Actions is a certain Sign of intire
‘ Dominion, they won't fo much as recede from the Go-
‘ vernment even in one Mufcle of their Faces. A kind
‘ Look they believe would be fawning, and a civil An-
‘ fwer yielding the Superiority. To this muft we attri-
‘ bute an Aufterity they betray in every Action: What
‘ but this can put a Man out of Humour in his Wife's
‘ Company, tho’ he is fo diftinguifhingly pleafant every
‘ where elfe ? The Bitternefs of his Replies, and the Se-
‘ verity of his Frowns to the tendereft of Wives, clearly
‘ demonftrate, that an ill-grounded Fear of being thought
‘ too fubmiffive, is at the Bottom of this, as I am wil-
‘ ling to call it, affected Morofenefs; but if it be fuch only,
‘ put on to convince his Acquaintance of his intire Do-
‘ minion, let him take care of the Confequence, which
‘ will be certain and worfe than the prefent Evil; his
‘ feeming Indifference will by Degrees grow into real
‘ Contempt, and, if it doth not wholly alienate the Af-
‘ fections of his Wife for ever from him, make both him
‘ and her more miferable than if it really did fo.

‘ HOWEVER inconfiftent it may appear, to be
‘ thought a well-bred Perfon has no fmall Share in this
‘ clownifh Behaviour: A Difcourfe therefore relating to
‘ Good-breeding towards a loving and a tender Wife, would
‘ be

' be of great Ufe to this Sort of Gentlemen. Could you
' but once convince them, that to be civil at leaft is not
' beneath the Charaĉter of a Gentleman, nor even tender
' Affeĉtion towards one who would make it reciprocal,
' betrays any Softnefs of Effeminacy that the moft maf-
' culine Difpofition need be afhamed of; could you fatisfy
' them of the Generofity of voluntary Civility, and the
' Greatnefs of Soul that is confpicuous in Benevolence
' without immediate Obligations; could you recommend
' to People's Practice the Saying of the Gentlemen quoted
' in one of your Speculations, *That he thought it incumbent*
' *upon him to make the Inclinations of a Woman of Merit go*
' *along with her Duty:* Could you, I fay, perfuade thefe
' Men of the Beauty and Reafonablenefs of this Sort of
' Behaviour, I have fo much Charity for fome of them
' at leaft, to believe you would convince them of a
' Thing they are only afhamed to allow: Befides, you
' would recommend that State in its trueft, and confe-
' quently its moft agreeable Colours; and the Gentlemen
' who have for any Time been fuch profeffed Enemies to
' it, when Occafion fhould ferve, would return you their
' Thanks for affifting their Intereft in prevailing over
' their Prejudices. Marriage in general would by this
' Means be a more eafy and comfortable Condition; the
' Hufband would be no where fo well fatisfied as in his
' own Parlour, nor the Wife fo pleafant as in the Com-
' pany of her Hufband: A Defire of being agreeable in
' the Lover would be increafed in the Hufband, and the
' Miftrefs be more amiable by becoming the Wife. Befides
' all which, I am apt to believe we fhould find the Race
' of Men grow wifer as their Progenitors grew kinder,
' and the Affeĉtion of their Parents would be confpicuous
' in the Wifdom of their Children; in fhort, Men would
' in general be much better Humoured than they are, did
' not they fo frequently exercife the worft Turns of their
' Temper where they ought to exert the beft.

Mr. SPECTATOR,

' I AM a Woman who left the Admiration of this
' whole Town, to throw myfelf (for Love of Wealth)
' into the Arms of a Fool. When I married him, I could
' have had any one of feveral Men of Senfe who languifhed
'   ' for

'for me; but my Cafe is juft. I believed my fuperior Un-
'derftanding would form him into a tractable Creature.
'But, alas, my Spoufe has Cunning and Sufpicion, the
'infeparable Companions of little Minds; and every At-
'tempt I make to divert, by putting on an agreeable Air,
'a fudden Chearfulnefs, or kind Behaviour, he looks upon
'as the firft Act towards an Infurrection againft his un-
'deferved Dominion over me. Let every one who is ftill
'to choofe, and hopes to govern a Fool, remember

TRISTISSA.

Mr. SPECTATOR,   *St. Martins, November* 25.

'THIS is to complain of an evil Practice which I
'   think very well deferves a Redrefs, though you
'have not as yet taken any Notice of it: If you mention it
'in your Paper, it may perhaps have a very good Effect.
'What I mean is the Difturbance fome People give to
'others at Church, by their Repetition of the Prayers after
'the Minifter, and that not only in the Prayers, but alfo
'the Abfolution and the Commandments fare no better,
'which are in a particular manner the Prieft's Office:
'This I have known done in fo audible a manner, that
'fometimes their Voices have been as loud as his. As
'little as you would think it, this is frequently done by
'People feemingly devout. This irreligious Inadvertency
'is a Thing extremely offenfive: But I do not recommend
'it as a Thing I give you Liberty to ridicule, but hope it
'may be amended by the bare Mention.

T   SIR, *Your very humble Servant,* T. S.

Nº 237. *Saturday, December* 1.

Visu carentem magna pars veri latet. Seneca in OEdip.
The Blind fee Truth by halves.

IT is very reafonable to believe, that Part of the Pleafure which happy Minds fhall enjoy in a future State,
will arife from an enlarged Contemplation of the
Divine Wifdom in the Government of the World, and a
Dif-

Difcovery of the fecret and amazing Steps of Providence, from the Beginning to the End of Time. Nothing feems to be an Entertainment more adapted to the Nature of Man, if we confider that Curiofity is one of the ftrongeft and moft lafting Appetites implanted in us, and that Admiration is one of our moft pleafing Paffions; and what a perpetual Succeffion of Enjoyments will be afforded to both thefe, in a Scene fo large and various as fhall then be laid open to our View in the Society of fuperior Spirits, who perhaps will join with us in fo delightful a Profpect!

IT is not impoffible, on the contrary, that Part of the Punifhment of fuch as are excluded from Blifs, may confift not only in their being denied this Privilege, but in having their Appetites at the fame time vaftly increafed, without any Satisfaction afforded to them. In thefe, the vain Purfuit of Knowledge fhall, perhaps, add to their Infelicity, and bewilder them into Labyrinths of Error, Darknefs, Diftraction and Uncertainty of every thing but their own evil State. *Milton* has thus reprefented the fallen Angels reafoning together in a kind of Refpite from their Torments, and creating to themfelves a new Difquiet amidft their very Amufements; he could not properly have defcribed the Sports of condemned Spirits, without that Caft of Horror and Melancholy he has fo judicioufly mingled with them.

> *Others apart fat on a Hill retired,*
> *In Thoughts more elevate, and reafon'd high*
> *Of Providence, Foreknowledge, Will, and Fate,*
> *Fixt Fate, Freewill, Foreknowledge abfolute,*
> *And found no End in wandering Mazes loft.*

IN our prefent Condition, which is a middle State, our Minds are, as it were, chequered with Truth and Falfhood; and as our Faculties are narrow, and our Views imperfect, it is impoffible but our Curiofity muft meet with many Repulfes. The Bufinefs of Mankind in this Life being rather to act than to know, their Portion of Knowledge is dealt to them accordingly.

FROM hence it is, that the Reafon of the Inquifitive has fo long been exercifed with Difficulties, in accounting for the promifcuous Diftribution of Good and

Evil

Evil to the Virtuous and the Wicked in this World. From hence comes all those pathetick Complaints of so many tragical Events, which happen to the Wise and the Good; and of such surprising Prosperity, which is often the Reward of the Guilty and the Foolish; that Reason is sometimes puzzled, and at a loss what to pronounce upon so mysterious a Dispensation.

PLATO expresses his Abhorrence of some Fables of the Poets, which seem to reflect on the Gods as the Authors of Injustice; and lays it down as a Principle, That whatever is permitted to befal a just Man, whether Poverty, Sickness, or any of those Things which seem to be Evils, shall either in Life or Death conduce to his Good. My Reader will observe how agreeable this Maxim is to what we find delivered by a greater Authority. *Seneca* has written a Discourse purposely on this Subject, in which he takes pains, after the Doctrine of the *Stoicks*, to shew that Adversity is not in itself an Evil; and mentions a noble Saying of *Demetrius*, That *nothing would be more unhappy than a Man who had never known Affliction.* He compares Prosperity to the Indulgence of a fond Mother to a Child, which often proves his Ruin; but the Affection of the Divine Being to that of a wise Father who would have his Sons exercised with Labour, Disappointment, and Pain, that they may gather Strength and improve their Fortitude. On this Occasion the Philosopher rises into that celebrated Sentiment; That there is not on Earth a Spectacle more worthy the Regard of a Creator intent on his Works than a brave Man superior to his Sufferings; to which he adds, That it must be a Pleasure to *Jupiter* himself to look down from Heaven, and see *Cato* amidst the Ruins of his Country preserving his Integrity.

THIS Thought will appear yet more reasonable, if we consider human Life as a State of Probation, and Adversity as the Post of Honour in it, assigned often to the best and most select Spirits.

BUT what I would chiefly insist on here, is, that we are not at present in a proper Situation to judge of the Counsels by which Providence acts, since but little arrives at our Knowledge, and even that little we discern imperfectly; or according to the elegant Figure in Holy Writ, *We see but in part, and as in a Glass darkly.* It is to

be

be confidered, that Providence in its Oeconomy regards
the whole Syftem of Time and Things together, fo that
we cannot difcover the beautiful Connection between Incidents which lie widely feparate in Time, and by lofing
fo many Links of the Chain, our Reafonings become
broken and imperfect. Thus thofe Parts of the moral
World which have not an abfolute, may yet have a rela-
tive Beauty, in refpect of fome other Parts concealed from
us, but open to his Eye before whom *Paft, Prefent,* and
To come, are fet together in one Point of View: and thofe
Events, the Permiffion of which feems now to accufe his
Goodnefs, may in the Confummation of Things both
magnify his Goodnefs, and exalt his Wifdom. And this
is enough to check our Prefumption, fince it is in vain to
apply our Meafures of Regularity to Matters of which
we know neither the Antecedents nor the Confequents,
the Beginning nor the End.

I fhall relieve my Readers from this abftracted Thought,
by relating here a *Jewifh* Tradition concerning *Mofes,*
which feems to be a kind of Parable, illuftrating what I
have laft mentioned. That great Prophet, it is faid, was
called up by a Voice from Heaven to the top of a Mountain; where, in a Conference with the Supreme Being,
he was permitted to propofe to him fome Queftions concerning his Adminiftration of the Univerfe. In the midft
of this Divine Colloquy he was commanded to look down
on the Plain below. At the Foot of the Mountain there
iffued out a clear Spring of Water, at which a Soldier
alighted from his Horfe to drink. He was no fooner gone
than a little Boy came to the fame Place, and finding a
Purfe of Gold which the Soldier had dropped, took it up
and went away with it. Immediately after this came an infirm old Man, weary with Age and Travelling, and having quenched his Thirft, fat down to reft himfelf by the
Side of the Spring. The Soldier miffing his Purfe returns
to fearch for it, and demands it of the old Man, who affirms
he had not feen it, and appeals to Heaven in witnefs of
his Innocence. The Soldier not believing his Proteftations, kills him. *Mofes* fell on his Face with Horror and
Amazement, when the Divine Voice thus prevented his
Expoftulation: ' Be not furprifed, *Mofes,* nor afk why
' the Judge of the whole Earth has fuffer'd this Thing to
' come

' come to pass :: The Child is the Occasion that the Blood
' of the old Man is spilt; but know, that the old Man,
' whom thou saw'st, was the Murderer of that Child's
' Father. C

Nº 238 *Monday, December* 3.

Nequicquam populo bibulas, donaveris Aures;
Respue quod non es—— Persius, Sat. 4. v. 50.

Please not thyself the flatt'ring Crowd to hear ;
'Tis fulsom Stuff, to please thy itching Ear.
Survey thy Soul, not what thou dost appear,
But what thou art.—— DRYDEN.

AMONG all the Diseases of the Mind, there is not
one more epidemical or more pernicious than the
Love of Flattery. For as where the Juices of the
Body are prepared to receive a malignant Influence, there
the Disease rages with most Violence; so in this Distemper of the Mind, where there is ever a Propensity and
Inclination to suck in the Poison, it cannot be but that
the whole Order of reasonable Action must be over-
turn'd; for, like Musick, it

——*So softens and disarms the Mind,*
That not one Arrow can Resistance find.

FIRST we flatter ourselves, and then the Flattery
of others is sure of Success. It awakens our Self-love
within, a Party which is ever ready to revolt from our
better Judgment, and join the Enemy without. Hence it
is, that the Profusion of Favours we so often see poured
upon the Parasite, are represented to us, by our Self-Love,
as Justice done to the Man, who so agreeably reconciles
us to ourselves. When we are overcome by such soft
Insinuations and insnaring Compliances, we gladly re-
compense the Artifices that are made use of to blind our
Reason, and which triumph over the Weaknesses of our
Temper and Inclinations.

BUT were every Man persuaded from how mean and
low a Principle this Passion is derived, there can be no

doubt

doubt but the Perſon who ſhould attempt to gratify it, would then be as contemptible as he is now ſucceſsful. 'Tis the Deſire of ſome Quality we are not poſſeſſed of, or Inclination to be ſomething we are not, which are the Cauſes of our giving ourſelves up to that Man, who beſtows upon us the Characters and Qualities of others; which perhaps ſuit us as ill and were as little deſign'd for our wearing, as their Clothes. Inſtead of going out of our own complexional Nature into that of others, 'twere a better and more laudable Induſtry to improve our own, and inſtead of a miſerable Copy become a good Original; for there is no Temper, no Diſpoſition ſo rude and untractable, but may in its own peculiar Caſt and Turn be brought to ſome agreeable Uſe in Converſation, or in the Affairs of Life. A Perſon of a rougher Deportment, and leſs tied up to the uſual Ceremonies of Behaviour, will, like *Manly* in the Play, pleaſe by the Grace which Nature gives to every Action wherein ſhe is complied with; the Briſk and Lively will not want their Admirers, and even a more reſerved and melancholy Temper may at ſome times be agreeable.

WHEN there is not Vanity enough awake in a Man to undo him, the Flatterer ſtirs up that dormant Weakneſs, and inſpires him with Merit enough to be a Coxcomb. But if Flattery be the moſt ſordid Act that can be complied with, the Art of Praiſing juſtly is as commendable: For 'tis laudable to praiſe well; as Poets at one and the ſame time give Immortality, and receive it themſelves for a Reward: Both are pleaſed, the one whilſt he receives the Recompence of Merit, the other whilſt he ſhews he knows how to diſcern it; but above all, that Man is happy in this Art, who, like a ſkilful Painter, retains the Features and Complexion, but ſtill ſoftens the Picture into the moſt agreeable Likeneſs.

THERE can hardly, I believe, be imagin'd a more deſirable Pleaſure, than that of Praiſe unmix'd with any Poſſibility of Flattery. Such was that which *Germanicus* enjoyed, when, the Night before a Battle, deſirous of ſome ſincere Mark of the Eſteem of his Legions for him, he is deſcribed by *Tacitus* liſtening in a Diſguiſe to the Diſcourſe of a Soldier, and wrapt up in the Fruition of his Glory, whilſt with an undeſigned Sincerity they praiſed

-his

his noble and majeftick Mien, his Affability, his Valour, Conduct, and Succefs in War. How muft a Man have his Heart full-blown with Joy in fuch an Article of Glory as this ? What a Spur and Encouragement ftill to proceed in thofe Steps which had already brought him to fo pure a Tafte of the greateft of mortal Enjoyments?

IT fometimes happens, that even Enemies and envious Perfons beftow the fincereft Marks of Efteem when they leaft defign it. Such afford a greater Pleafure, as extorted by Merit, and freed from all Sufpicion of Favour or Flattery. Thus it is with *Malvolio* ; he has Wit, Learning, and Difcernment, but temper'd with an Allay of Envy, Self-Love and Detraction : *Malvolio* turns pale at the Mirth and Good-humour of the Company, if it center not in his Perfon ; he grows jealous and difpleafed when he ceafes to be the only Perfon admired, and looks upon the Commendations paid to another as a Detraction from his Merit, and an Attempt to leffen the Superiority he affects ; but by this very Method, he beftows fuch Praife as can never be fufpected of Flattery. His Uneafinefs and Diftaftes are fo many fure and certain Signs of another's Title to that Glory he defires, and has the Mortification to find himfelf not poffeffed of.

A good Name is fitly compared to a precious Ointment, and when we are praifed with Skill and Decency, 'tis indeed the moft agreeable Perfume, but if too ftrongly admitted into a Brain of a lefs vigorous and happy Texture, 'twill, like too ftrong an Odour, overcome the Senfes, and prove pernicious to thofe Nerves 'twas intended to refrefh. A generous Mind is of all others the moft fenfible of Praife and Difpraife ; and a noble Spirit is as much invigorated with its due Proportion of Honour and Applaufe, as 'tis depreffed by Neglect and Contempt : But 'tis only Perfons far above the common Level who are thus affected with either of thefe Extremes ; as in a Thermometer, 'tis only the pureft and moft fublimated Spirit that is either contracted or dilated by the Benignity or Inclemency of the Seafon.

Mr. SPECTATOR,

'THE Tranflations which you have lately given us from the *Greek*, in fome of your laft Papers, 'have been the Occafion of my looking into fome of

' thofe Authors; among whom I chanced on a Collection
' of Letters which pafs under the Name of *Ariſtænetus*:
' Of all the Remains of Antiquity, I believe there can be
' Nothing produc'd of an Air fo galant and polite; each
' Letter contains a little Novel or Adventure, which is
' told with all the Beauties of Language and heightened
' with a Luxuriance of Wit. There are feveral of them
' tranflated, but with fuch wide Deviations from the Ori-
' ginal, and in a Stile fo far differing from the Authors,
' that the Tranflator feems rather to have taken Hints for
' the expreffing his own Senfe and Thoughts, than to have
' endeavoured to render thofe of *Ariſtænetus*. In the fol-
' lowing Tranflation, I have kept as near the Meaning of
' the *Greek* as I could, and have only added a few Words
' to make the Sentences in *Engliſh* fit together a little bet-
' ter than they would otherwife have done. The Story
' feems to be taken from that of *Pygmalion* and the Statue
' in *Ovid*: Some of the Thoughts are of the fame Turn,
' and the whole is written in a kind of Poetical Profe.'

Philopinax to *Chromation*.

"NEVER was Man more overcome with fo fan-
" taftical a Paffion as mine. I have painted a beau-
" tiful Woman, and am defpairing, dying for the Picture.
" My own Skill has undone me; 'tis not the Dart of
" *Venus*, but my own Pencil has thus wounded me. Ah
" me! with what Anxiety am I neceffitated to adore
" my own Idol? How miferable am I, whilft every one
" muft as much pity the Painter as he praifes the Picture,
" and own my Torment more than equal to my Art.
" But why do I thus complain? Have there not been
" more unhappy and unnatural Paffions than mine? Yes,
" I have feen the Reprefentations of *Phædra*, *Narciſſus*,
" and *Paſiphae*. *Phædra* was unhappy in her Love; that
" of *Paſiphae* was monftrous; and whilft the other caught
" at his beloved Likenefs, he deftroyed the watery Image,
" which ever eluded his Embraces. The Fountain re-
" prefented *Narciſſus* to himfelf, and the Picture both
" that and him, thirfting after his adored Image. But I
" am yet lefs unhappy, I enjoy her Prefence continually,
" and if I touch her, I deftroy not the beauteous Form,
" but fhe looks pleafed, and a fweet Smile fits in the
　　　　　　　　　　　　　　　　　　　" charming

" charming Space which divides her Lips. One would
" fwear that Voice and Speech were iſſuing out, and that
" one's Ears felt the melodious Sound. How often have
" I, deceived by a Lover's Credulity, hearkned if ſhe
" had not ſomething to whiſper me ? and when fruſtrated
" of my Hopes, how often have I taken my Revenge in
" Kiſſes from her Cheeks and Eyes, and ſoftly wooed her
" to my Embrace, whilſt ſhe (as to me it ſeem'd) only
" withheld her Tongue the more to inflame me. But, Mad-
" man that I am, ſhall I be thus taken with the Repreſen-
" tation only of a beauteous Face, and flowing Hair, and
" thus waſte myſelf and melt to Tears for a Shadow ?
" Ah, ſure 'tis ſomething more, 'tis a Reality ! for ſee her
" Beauties ſhine out with new Luſtre, and ſhe ſeems to
" upbraid me with ſuch unkind Reproaches. Oh may I
" have a living Miſtreſs of this Form, that when I ſhall
" compare the Work of Nature with that of Art, I may
" be ſtill at a loſs which to chooſe, and be long perplex'd
" with the pleaſing Uncertainty.   T

Nº 239   *Tueſday, December* 4.

———*Bella, horrida bella!*   Virg. Æn. 6. v. 86.
Wars, horrid Wars!   DRYDEN.

I HAVE ſometimes amuſed myſelf with conſidering
the ſeveral Methods of managing a Debate which
have obtained in the World.

THE firſt Races of Mankind uſed to diſpute, as our
ordinary People do now-a-days, in a kind of wild Logick, uncultivated by Rules of Art.

SOCRATES introduced a catechetical Method of
Arguing: He would ask his Adverſary Queſtion upon
Queſtion, till he had convinced him out of his own Mouth
that his Opinions were wrong. This Way of Debating
drives an Enemy up into a Corner, ſeizes all the Paſſes
through which he can make an Eſcape, and forces him
to ſurrender at Diſcretion.

ARISTOTLE changed this Method of Attack, and invented a great Variety of little Weapons, call'd Syllogiſms. As in the *Socratick* Way of Diſpute you agree to every thing which your Opponent advances, in the *Ariſtotelick* you are ſtill denying and contradicting ſome Part or other of what he ſays. *Socrates* conquers you by Stratagem, *Ariſtotle* by Force: The one takes the Town by Sap, the other Sword in Hand.

THE Univerſities of *Europe*, for many Years, carried on their Debates by Syllogiſm, inſomuch that we ſee the Knowledge of ſeveral Centuries laid out into Objections and Anſwers, and all the good Senſe of the Age cut and minced into almoſt an Infinitude of Diſtinctions.

WHEN our Univerſities found that there was no End of Wrangling this Way, they invented a kind of Argument, which is not reducible to any Mood or Figure in *Ariſtotle*. It was called the *Argumentum Baſilinum* (others write it *Bacilinum* or *Baculinum*) which is pretty well expreſs'd in our *Engliſh* Word *Club-Law*. When they were not able to confute their Antagoniſt, they knock'd him down. It was their Method in theſe polemical Debates, firſt to diſcharge their Syllogiſms, and afterwards to betake themſelves to their Clubs, till ſuch Time as they had one Way or other confounded their Gainſayers. There is in *Oxford* a narrow Defile, (to make uſe of a military Term) where the Partiſans uſed to encounter, for which Reaſon it ſtill retains the Name of *Logick-Lane*. I have heard an old Gentleman, a Phyſician, make his Boaſts, that when he was a young Fellow he marched ſeveral Times at the Head of a Troop of *Scotiſts*, and cudgel'd a Body of *Smigleſians* half the length of *High-ſtreet*, 'till they had diſperſed themſelves for Shelter into their reſpective Garriſons.

THIS Humour, I find, went very far in *Eraſmus*'s Time. For that Author tells us, That upon the Revival of *Greek* Letters, moſt of the Univerſities in *Europe* were divided into *Greeks* and *Trojans*. The latter were thoſe who bore a mortal Enmity to the Language of the *Grecians*; inſomuch that if they met with any who underſtood it, they did not fail to treat him as a Foe. *Eraſmus* himſelf had, it ſeems, the Misfortune to fall into the Hands of a Party of *Trojans*, who laid him on with ſo

many

many Blows and Buffets that he never forgot their Hoftilities to his dying Day.

THERE is a way of managing an Argument not much unlike the former, which is made ufe of by States and Communities, when they draw up a hundred thoufand Difputants on each Side, and convince one another by Dint of Sword. A certain Grand Monarch was fo fenfible of his Strength in this way of Reafoning, that he writ upon his Great Guns----*Ratio ultima Regum*, *The Logick of Kings*; but, God be thanked, he is now pretty well baffled at his own Weapons. When one has to do with a Philofopher of this kind, one fhould remember the old Gentleman's Saying, who had been engaged in an Argument with one of the *Roman* Emperors. Upon his Friend's telling him, That he wonder'd he would give up the Queftion, when he had vifibly the Better of the Difpute; *I am never afham'd*, fays he, *to be confuted by one who is Mafter of fifty Legions*.

I fhall but juft mention another kind of Reafoning, which may be called arguing by Poll; and another which is of equal Force, in which Wagers are made ufe of as Arguments, according to the celebrated Line in *Hudibras*.

BUT the moft notable way of managing a Controverfy, is that which we may call *Arguing by Torture*. This is a Method of Reafoning which has been made ufe of with the poor Refugees, and which was fo fafhionable in our Country during the Reign of Queen *Mary*, that in a Paffage of an Author quoted by Monfieur *Bayle*, it is faid the Price of Wood was raifed in *England*, by reafon of the Executions that were made in *Smithfield*. Thefe Difputants convince their Adverfaries with a *Sorites*, commonly called a Pile of Faggots. The Rack is alfo a kind of Syllogifm which has been ufed with good Effect, and has made Multitudes of Converts. Men were formerly difputed out of their Doubts, reconciled to Truth by Force of Reafon, and won over to Opinions by the Candour, Senfe and Ingenuity of thofe who had the Right on their Side; but this Method of Conviction operated too flowly. Pain was found to be much more enlightning than Reafon. Every Scruple was looked upon as Obftinacy, and not to be removed but by feveral Engines invented for that Purpofe. In a word, the Application of

Whips,

Whips, Racks, Gibbets, Gallies, Dungeons, Fire and Faggot, in a Difpute, may be look'd upon as Popifh Refinements upon the old Heathen Logick.

THERE is another way of Reafoning which feldom fails, tho' it be of a quite different Nature to that I have laft mentioned. I mean, convincing a Man by ready Money, or as it is ordinarily called, bribing a Man to an Opinion. This Method has often proved fuccefsful, when all the others have been made ufe of to no purpofe. A Man who is furnifhed with Arguments from the Mint, will convince his Antagonift much fooner than one who draws them from Reafon and Philofophy. Gold is a wonderful Clearer of the Underftanding; it diffipates every Doubt and Scruple in an Inftant; accommodates itfelf to the meaneft Capacities; filences the Loud and Clamorous, and brings over the moft Obftinate and Inflexible. *Philip* of *Macedon* was a Man of moft invincible Reafon this Way. He refuted by it all the Wifdom of *Athens*, confounded their Statefmen, ftruck their Orators dumb, and at length argued them out of all their Liberties.

HAVING here touched upon the feveral Methods of Difputing, as they have prevailed in different Ages of the World, I fhall very fuddenly give my Reader an Account of the whole Art of Cavilling; which fhall be a full and fatisfactory Anfwer to all fuch Papers and Pamphlets as have yet appeared againft the SPECTATOR. C

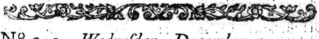

N° 240 *Wednefday, December* 5.

———*Aliter non fit, Avite, liber.* Mart. Ep. 17. l. 1.

Of fuch Materials, Sir, are Books compofed.

Mr. SPECTATOR,

'I AM of one of the moft genteel Trades in the City,
' and underftand thus much of liberal Education, as
' to have an ardent Ambition of being ufeful to Man-
' kind, and to think That the chief End of Being as to this
' Life. I had thefe good Impreffions given me from the
' handfom

' handsom Behaviour of a learned, generous, and wealthy
' Man, towards me when I first began the World. Some
' Diffatisfaction between me and my Parents made me
' enter into it with less Relish of Business than I ought;
' and to turn off this Uneasiness I gave myself to crimi-
' nal Pleasures, some Excesses, and a general loose Con-
' duct. I know not what the excellent Man above-mentioned
' saw in me, but he descended from the Superiority of his
' Wisdom and Merit, to throw himself frequently into
' my Company. This made me soon hope that I had
' something in me worth cultivating, and his Conversa-
' tion made me sensible of Satisfactions in a regular Way,
' which I had never before imagined. When he was
' grown familiar with me, he opened himself like a good
' Angel, and told me, he had long laboured to ripen me
' into a Preparation to receive his Friendship and Advice,
' both which I should daily command, and the Use of any
' Part of his Fortune, to apply the Measures he should
' propose to me, for the Improvement of my own. I
' assure you, I cannot recollect the Goodness and Confu-
' sion of the good Man when he spoke to this Purpose to
' me, without melting into Tears; but in a word, Sir, I
' must hasten to tell you, that my Heart burns with Grati-
' tude towards him, and he is so happy a Man, that it can
' never be in my Power to return him his Favours in Kind;
' but I am sure I have made him the most agreeable Satis-
' faction I could possibly, in being ready to serve others to
' my utmost Ability, as far as is consistent with the Pru-
' dence he prescribes to me. Dear Mr. SPECTATOR, I
' do not owe to him only the Good-will and Esteem of my
' own Relations, (who are People of Distinction) the pre-
' sent Ease and Plenty of my Circumstances, but also the
' Government of my Passions, and Regulation of my De-
' sires. I doubt not, Sir, but in your Imagination such Vir-
' tues as these of my worthy Friend, bear as great a Figure
' as Actions which are more glittering in the common
' Estimation. What I would ask of you, is to give us a
' whole *Spectator* upon Heroick Virtue in common Life,
' which may incite Men to the same generous Inclinati-
' ons, as have by this admirable Person been shewn to,
' and rais'd in,

S I R, Your most humble Servant.

Mr.

Mr. SPECTATOR,

'I Am a Country Gentleman, of a good plentiful Estate,
' and live as the rest of my Neighbours with great
' Hospitality. I have been ever reckoned among the La-
' dies the best Company in the World, and have Access
' as a sort of Favourite. I never came in Publick but I
' saluted them, tho' in great Assemblies, all around,
' where it was seen how genteelly I avoided hampering
' my Spurs in their Petticoats, whilst I moved amongst
' them; and on the other side how prettily they curtsied
' and received me, standing in proper Rows, and ad-
' vancing as fast as they saw their Elders, or their Betters,
' dispatch'd by me. But so it is, Mr. SPECTATOR, that
' all our Good-breeding is of late lost by the unhappy
' Arrival of a Courtier, or Town Gentleman, who came
' lately among us: This Person wherever he came into a
' Room made a profound Bow, and fell back, then reco-
' vered with a soft Air, and made a Bow to the next, and
' so to one or two more, and then took the Gross of the
' Room, by passing by them in a continued Bow till he
' arrived at the Person he thought proper particularly to
' entertain. This he did with so good a Grace and Af-
' surance, that it is taken for the present Fashion; and
' there is no young Gentlewoman within several Miles of
' this Place has been kissed ever since his first Appearance
' among us. We Country Gentlemen cannot begin again
' and learn these fine and reserved Airs; and our Conver-
' sation is at a Stand, till we have your Judgment for, or
' against Kissing, by way of Civility or Salutation;
' which is impatiently expected by your Friends of both
' Sexes, but by none so much as

> *Your humble Servant,* Rustick Sprightly.

Mr. SPECTATOR, *December* 3, 1711.

'I Was the other Night at *Philaster*, where I expected
' to hear your famous Trunk-maker, but was unhap-
' pily disappointed of his Company, and saw another
' Person who had the like Ambition to distinguish him-
' self in a noisy manner, partly by Vociferation or talk-
' ing loud, and partly by his bodily Agility. This was a
' very lusty Fellow, but withal a sort of Beau, who get-
' ting

' ting into one of the Side-boxes on the Stage before the
' Curtain drew, was difpofed to fhew the whole Audi-
' ence his Activity by leaping over the Spikes ; he pafs'd
' from thence to one of the entring Doors, where he
' took Snuff with a tolerable good Grace, difplay'd his
' fine Clothes, made two or three feint Paffes at the
' Curtain with his Cane, then faced about and appear'd
' at t'other Door : Here he affected to furvey the whole
' Houfe, bow'd and fmil'd at random, and then fhew'd
' his Teeth, which were fome of them indeed very white :
' After this he retired behind the Curtain, and obliged us
' with feveral Views of his Perfon from every Opening.'
  ' DURING the Time of Acting, he appear'd fre-
' quently in the Prince's Apartment, made one at the Hunt-
' ing-match, and was very forward in the Rebellion. If
' there were no Injunctions to the contrary, yet this Prac-
' tice muft be confefs'd to diminifh the Pleafure of the
' Audience, and for that Reafon prefumptuous and unwar-
' rantable : But fince her Majefty's late Command has
' made it criminal, you have Authority to take notice of it.

S I R, Your humble Servant,

T Charles Eafy.

Nᵒ 241 *Thurfday, December 6.*

———*Semperque relinqui*
Sola fibi, femper longam incomitata videtur
Ire viam—— Virg. Æn. 4. v. 466.

————— *She feems alone*
To wander in her Sleep thro' Ways unknown,
Guidelefs and dark. DRYDEN.

Mr. SPECTATOR,

THOUGH you have confidered virtuous Love
in moft of its Diftreffes, do not remember that
you have given us any ﬦertation upon the Ab-
' fence of Lovers, or laid down any Methods how they
' fhould fupport themfelves under thofe long Separations
' which

' which they are sometimes forced to undergo. I am at
' present in this unhappy Circumstance, having parted
' with the best of Husbands, who is abroad in the Ser-
' vice of his Country, and may not possibly return for
' some Years. His warm and generous Affection while
' we were together, with the Tenderness which he ex-
' pressed to me at parting, make his Absence almost in-
' supportable. I think of him every moment of the Day,
' and meet him every Night in my Dreams. Every thing
' I see puts me in mind of him. I apply myself with
' more than ordinary Diligence to the Care of his Fa-
' mily and his Estate; but this, instead of relieving me,
' gives me but so many Occasions of wishing for his Re-
' turn. I frequent the Rooms where I used to converse
' with him, and not meeting him there, sit down in his
' Chair, and fall a weeping. I love to read the Books he
' delighted in, and to converse with the Persons whom
' he esteemed. I visit his Picture a hundred times
' a Day, and place myself over-against it whole Hours
' together. I pass a great part of my Time in the
' Walks where I used to lean upon his Arm, and recollect
' in my Mind the Discourses which have there passed
' between us : I look over the several Prospects and Points
' of View which we used to survey together, fix my Eye
' upon the Objects which he has made me take notice
' of, and call to mind a thousand agreeable Remarks
' which he has made on those Occasions. I write to him
' by every Conveyance, and contrary to other People;
' am always in Good-humour when an East-Wind blows,
' because it seldom fails of bringing me a Letter from
' him. Let me intreat you, Sir, to give me your Ad-
' vice upon this Occasion, and to let me know how I
' may relieve myself in this my Widowhood.--

I am, S I R, Your very humble Servant,

ASTERIA.

ABSENCE is what the Poets call Death in Love;
and has given occasion to abundance of beautiful Complaints in those Authors who have treated of this Passion
in Verse. *Ovid's* Epistles are full of them. *Otway's*
Monimia talks very tenderly upon this Subject.
$\overline{\hspace{3cm}}$ *It*

> ———————*It was not kind*
> *To leave me like a Turtle, here alone,*
> *To droop and mourn the Absence of my Mate.*
> *When thou art from me, every Place is defert:*
> *And I, methinks, am favage and forlorn:*
> *Thy Prefence only 'tis can make me bleft,*
> *Heal my unquiet Mind, and tune my Soul.*

THE Confolations of Lovers on thefe Occafions are very extraordinary. Befides thofe mentioned by *Afteria*, there are many other Motives of Comfort, which are made ufe of by abfent Lovers.

I remember in one of *Scudery*'s Romances, a Couple of honourable Lovers agreed at their parting to fet afide one half Hour in the Day to think of each other during a tedious Abfence. The Romance tells us, that they both of them punctually obferved the Time thus agreed upon; and that whatever Company or Bufinefs they were engaged in, they left it abruptly as foon as the Clock warned them to retire. The Romance further adds, That the Lovers expected the Return of this ftated Hour with as much Impatience, as if it had been a real Affignation, and enjoyed an imaginary Happinefs that was almoft as pleafing to them as what they would have found from a real Meeting. It was an inexpreffible Satisfaction to thefe divided Lovers, to be affured that each was at the fame time employ'd in the fame kind of Contemplation, and making equal Returns of Tendernefs and Affection.

IF I may be allowed to mention a more ferious Expedient for the alleviating of Abfence, I fhall take notice of one which I have known two Perfons practife, who joined Religion to that Elegance of Sentiments with which the Paffion of Love generally infpires its Votaries. This was, at the Return of fuch an Hour, to offer up a certain Prayer for each other, which they had agreed upon before their Parting. The Husband, who is a Man that makes a Figure in the polite World, as well as in his own Family, has often told me, that he could not have fupported an Abfence of three Years without this Expedient.

STRADA, in one of his Prolufions, gives an Account of a chimerical Correfpondence between two Friends by

the

the Help of a certain Loadstone, which had such Virtue in it, that if it touched two several Needles, when one of the Needles so touched began to move, the other, tho' at never so great a Distance, moved at the same Time, and in the same Manner. He tells us, that the two Friends, being each of them possessed of one of these Needles, made a kind of a Dial-plate, inscribing it with the four and twenty Letters, in the same manner as the Hours of the Day are marked upon the ordinary Dial-plate. They then fixed one of the Needles on each of these Plates in such a manner, that it could move round without Impediment, so as to touch any of the four and twenty Letters. Upon their Separating from one another into distant Countries, they agreed to withdraw themselves punctually into their Closets at a certain Hour of the Day, and to converse with one another by means of this their Invention. Accordingly when they were some hundred Miles asunder, each of them shut himself up in his Closet at the Time appointed, and immediately cast his Eye upon his Dial-plate. If he had a mind to write any thing to his Friend, he directed his Needle to every Letter that formed the Words which he had occasion for, making a little Pause at the end of every Word or Sentence, to avoid Confusion. The Friend, in the mean while, saw his own sympathetick Needle moving of itself to every Letter which that of his Correspondent pointed at. By this means they talked together across a whole Continent, and conveyed their Thoughts to one another in an Instant over Cities or Mountains, Seas or Deserts.

IF Monsieur *Scudery*, or any other Writer of Romance, had introduced a Necromancer, who is generally in the Train of a Knight-Errant, making a Present to two Lovers of a Couple of those above-mentioned Needles, the Reader would not have been a little pleased to have seen them corresponding with one another when they were guarded by Spies and Watches, or separated by Castles and Adventures.

IN the mean while, if ever this Invention should be revived or put in practice, I would propose, that upon the Lover's Dial-plate there should be written not only the four and twenty Letters, but several intire Words which have always a Place in passionate Epistles, as *Flames,*

Darts,

Darts, Die, Language, Abfence, Cupid, Heart, Eyes, Hang, Drown, and the like. This would very much abridge the Lover's Pains in this way of writing a Letter, as it would enable him to expreſs the moſt uſeful and ſignificant Words with a ſingle Touch of the Needle.   C

***

N° 242   *Friday, December* 7.

Creditur, ex medio quia res arceſſit, habere
Sudoris minimum———   Hor. Ep. 1. 1. 2. v. 168.

To write on vulgar Themes, is thought an eaſy Task.

Mr. SPECTATOR,

'YOUR Speculations do not ſo generally prevail
' over Mens Manners as I could wiſh. A former
' Paper of yours concerning the Miſbehaviour of
'People, who are neceſſarily in each other's Company in
'travelling, ought to have been a laſting Admonition
'againſt Tranſgreſſions of that Kind: But I had the Fate
'of your Quaker, in meeting with a rude Fellow in a
'Stage-Coach, who entertained two or three Women of
'us (for there was no Man beſides himſelf) with Lan-
'guage as indecent as ever was heard upon the Water.
'The impertinent Obſervations which the Coxcomb
'made upon our Shame and Confuſion were ſuch, that it
'is an unſpeakable Grief to reflect upon them. As much
'as you have declaimed againſt Duelling, I hope you will
'do us the Juſtice to declare, that if the Brute has Cou-
'rage enough to ſend to the Place where he ſaw us all
'alight together to get rid of him, there is not one of
'us but has a Lover who ſhall avenge the Inſult. It
'would certainly be worth your Conſideration, to look
'into the frequent Miſfortunes of this kind, to which
'the Modeſt and Innocent are expoſed, by the licentious
'Behaviour of ſuch as are as much Strangers to Good-
'breeding as to Virtue. Could we avoid hearing what we
'do not approve, as eaſily as we can ſeeing what is diſa-
'greeable, there were ſome Conſolation; but ſince in a
'Box

' Box at a Play, in an Aſſembly of Ladies, or even in a
' Pew at Church, it is in the Power of a groſs Coxcomb
' to utter what a Woman cannot avoid hearing, how mi-
' ſerable is her Condition who comes within the Power
' of ſuch Impertinents? And how neceſſary is it to re-
' peat Invectives againſt ſuch a Behaviour? If the Li-
' centious had not utterly forgot what it is to be modeſt,
' they would know that offended Modeſty labours under
' one of the greateſt Sufferings to which human Life
' can be expoſed. If one of theſe Brutes could reflect
' thus much, tho' they want Shame, they would be
' moved, by their Pity, to abhor an impudent Behaviour
' in the Preſence of the Chaſte and Innocent. If you
' will oblige us with a *Spectator* on this Subject, and pro-
' cure it to be paſted againſt every Stage-Coach in *Great-*
' *Britain*, as the Law of the Journey, you will highly
' oblige the whole Sex, for which you have profeſſed ſo
' great an Eſteem; and in particular, the two Ladies
' my late Fellow-Sufferers, and,

S I R, *Your moſt humble Servant,*

Rebecca Ridinghood.

Mr. SPECTATOR,

'THE Matter which I am now going to ſend you,
' is an unhappy Story in low Life, and will re-
' commend itſelf, ſo that you muſt excuſe the Manner
' of expreſſing it. A poor idle drunken Weaver in *Spittle-*
' *Fields* has a faithful laborious Wife, who by her Fruga-
' lity and Induſtry had laid by her as much Money as pur-
' chaſed her a Ticket in the preſent Lottery. She had hid
' this very privately in the Bottom of a Trunk, and had
' given her Number to a Friend and Confident, who had
' promiſed to keep the Secret, and bring her News of the
' Succeſs. The poor Adventurer was one Day gone abroad,
' when her careleſs Husband, ſuſpecting ſhe had ſaved
' ſome Money, ſearches every Corner, till at length he
' finds this ſame Ticket; which he immediately carries
' abroad, ſells, and ſquanders away the Money without
' the Wife's ſuſpecting any thing of the matter. A Day or
' two after this, this Friend who was a Woman, comes
' and brings the Wife word, that ſhe had a Benefit of
' Five Hundred Pounds. The poor Creature overjoyed,

' flies

' flies up Stairs to her Husband, who was then at Work;
' and desires him to leave his Loom for that Evening;
' and come and drink with a Friend of his and hers
' below. The Man received this chearful Invitation as
' bad Husbands sometimes do, and after a cross Word or
' two, told her he wou'dn't come. His Wife with Ten-
' derness renewed her Importunity, and at length said
' to him, My Love! I have within these few Months,
' unknown to you, scraped together as much Money as
' has bought us a Ticket in the Lottery, and now here
' is Mrs. *Quick* come to tell me, that 'tis come up this
' Morning a Five hundred Pound Prize. The Husband
' replies immediately, You lye, you Slut, you have no
' Ticket, for I have sold it. The poor Woman upon
' this faints away in a Fit, recovers, and is now run dis-
' tracted. As she had no Design to defraud her Husband,
' but was willing only to participate in his good Fortune,
' every one pities her, but thinks her Husband's Punish-
' ment but just. This, Sir, is Matter of Fact, and would,
' if the Persons and Circumstances were greater, in a
' well-wrought Play be called *Beautiful Distress*. I have
' only sketched it out with Chalk, and know a good
' Hand can make a moving Picture with worse Materials.

                                             S I R, &c.

Mr. SPECTATOR,

' I AM what the World calls a warm Fellow, and by
' good Success in Trade I have raised myself to a
' Capacity of making some Figure in the World; but no
' matter for that. I have now under my Guardianship a
' couple of Neices, who will certainly make me run mad;
' which you will not wonder at, when I tell you they are
' Female Virtuosos, and during the three Years and a
' half that I have had them under my Care, they never
' in the least inclined their Thoughts towards any one
' single Part of the Character of a notable Woman. Whilst
' they should have been considering the proper Ingredi-
' ents for a Sack-posset, you should hear a dispute con-
' cerning the magnetick Virtue of the Loadstone, or per-
' haps the Pressure of the Atmosphere: Their Language
' is peculiar to themselves, and they scorn to express
' themselves on the meanest Trifle with Words that are
                                                    ' not

'not of a *Latin* Derivation. But this were supportable
'still, would they suffer me to enjoy an uninterrupted
'Ignorance; but, unless I fall in with their abstracted
'Ideas of Things (as they call them) I must not expect
'to smoke one Pipe in Quiet. In a late Fit of the Gout
'I complained of the Pain of that Distemper, when my
'Neice *Kitty* begged Leave to assure me, that whatever
'I might think, several great Philosophers, both ancient
'and modern, were of Opinion, that both Pleasure and
'Pain were imaginary Distinctions, and that there was
'no such thing as either *in rerum Natura*. I have of-
'ten heard them affirm that the Fire was not hot; and
'one Day when I, with the Authority of an old Fel-
'low, desired one of them to put my blue Cloke on
'my Knees; she answered, Sir, I will reach the Cloke;
'but take notice, I do not do it as allowing your
'Description; for it might as well be called Yellow as
'Blue; for Colour is nothing but the various In-
'fractions of the Rays of the Sun. Miss *Molly* told
'me one Day; That to say Snow was white, is allowing
'a vulgar Error; for as it contains a great Quantity of
'nitrous Particles, it might more reasonably be supposed
'to be black. In short, the young Husseys would per-
'suade me, that to believe one's Eyes is a sure way to be
'deceived; and have often advised me, by no means, to
'trust any thing so fallible as my Senses. What I have
'to beg of you now is, to turn one Speculation to the
'due Regulation of Female Literature, so far at least, as
'to make it consistent with the Quiet of such whose Fate
'it is to be liable to its Insults; and to tell us the Dif-
'ference between a Gentleman that should make Cheese-
'cakes and raise Paste, and a Lady that reads *Locke*,
'and understands the Mathematicks. In which you will
'extremely oblige

Your hearty Friend and humble Servant,

Abraham Thrifty.

T

N.º 243. *Saturday, December* 8.

*Formam quidem ipfam, Marce fili, & tanquam-facient
Honefti vides: quæ fi oculis cerneretur, mirabiles amorés
(ut ait Plato) excitaret Sapientiæ.* Tull. Offic.

You fee, my Son Marcus, *the very Shape and Countenance,
as it were, of Virtue; which if it cou'd be made the Object of Sight, would (as Plato fays) excite in us a wonderful Love of Wifdom.*

I DO not remember to have read any Difcourfe written
exprefly upon the Beauty and Lovelinefs of Virtue,
without confidering it as a Duty, and as the Means of
making us happy both now and hereafter. I defign therefore this Speculation as an Effay upon that Subject, in
which I fhall confider Virtue no farther than as it is in itfelf of an amiable Nature, after having premifed, that I
underftand by the Word Virtue fuch a general Notion as
is affixed to it by the Writers of Morality, and which by
devout Men generally goes under the Name of Religion,
and by Men of the World under the Name of Honour.

HYPOCRISY itfelf does great Honour, or rather
Juftice, to Religion, and tacitly acknowledges it to be
an Ornament to human Nature. The Hypocrite would
not be at fo much Pains to put on the Appearance of
Virtue, if he did not know it was the moft proper and
effectual Means to gain the Love and Efteem of Mankind.

WE learn from *Hierocles*, it was a common Saying
among the Heathens, that the Wife Man hates no Body,
but only loves the Virtuous.

TULLY has a very beautiful Gradation of Thoughts
to fhew how amiable Virtue is. We love a virtuous Man,
fays he, who lives in the remoteft Parts of the Earth,
though we are altogether out of the Reach of his Virtue,
and can receive from it no manner of Benefit; nay one
who died feveral Ages ago, raifes a fecret Fondnefs and
Benevolence for him in our Minds, when we read his
Story: Nay what is ftill more, one who has been the
Enemy

Enemy of our Country, provided his Wars were regulated by Juſtice and Humanity, as in the Inſtance of
Pyrrhus whom *Tully* mentions on this Occaſion in Oppo-
ſition to *Hannibal.* Such is the natural Beauty and Loveli-
neſs of Virtue.

STOICISM, which was the Pedantry of Virtue,
aſcribes all good Qualifications, of what kind ſoever, to
the virtuous Man. Accordingly *Cato,* in the Character
Tully has left of him, carried Matters ſo far, that he would
not allow any one but a virtuous Man to be handſom.
This indeed looks more like a Philoſophical Rant than the
real Opinion of a Wiſe Man; yet this was what *Cato* very
ſeriouſly maintained. In ſhort, the Stoicks thought they
could not ſufficiently repreſent the Excellence of Virtue,
if they did not comprehend in the Notion of it all poſſible
Perfections; and therefore did not only ſuppoſe, that it
was tranſcendently beautiful in itſelf, but that it made
the very Body amiable, and baniſhed every kind of Deformity from the Perſon in whom it reſided.

IT is a common Obſervation, that the moſt abandoned
to all Senſe of Goodneſs, are apt to wiſh thoſe who are
related to them of a different Character; and it is very
obſervable, that none are more ſtruck with the Charms of
Virtue in the fair Sex, than thoſe who by their very Admiration of it are carried to a Deſire of ruining it.

A virtuous Mind in a fair Body is indeed a fine Picture
in a good Light, and therefore it is no Wonder that it
makes the beautiful Sex all over Charms.

AS Virtue in general is of an amiable and lovely Nature, there are ſome particular kinds of it which are more
ſo than others, and theſe are ſuch as diſpoſe us to do Good
to Mankind. Temperance and Abſtinence, Faith and Devotion, are in themſelves perhaps as laudable as any other
Virtues; but thoſe which make a Man popular and beloved, are Juſtice, Charity, Munificence, and, in ſhort, all
the good Qualities that render us beneficial to each other.
For which Reaſon even an extravagant Man, who has nothing elſe to recommend him but a falſe Generoſity, is often more beloved and eſteemed than a Perſon of a much
more finiſhed Character, who is defective in this Particular.

THE two great Ornaments of Virtue, which ſhew her
in the moſt advantageous Views, and make her altogether
lovely,

lovely, are Chearfulnefs and Good-nature. Thefe generally go together; as a Man cannot be agreeable to others'-
who is not eafy within himfelf. They are both very requifite in a virtuous Mind, to keep out Melancholy from
the many ferious Thoughts it is engaged in, and to hinder its natural Hatred of Vice from fouring into Severity
and Cenforioufnefs.

IF Virtue is of this amiable Nature, what can we think
of thofe who can look upon it with an Eye of Hatred and
Ill-will, or can fuffer their Averfion for a Party to blot
out all the Merit of the Perfon who is engaged in it. A
Man muft be exceffively ftupid, as well as uncharitable,
who believes that there is no Virtue but on his own Side,
and that there are not Men as honeft as himfelf who may
differ from him in Political Principles. Men may oppofe
one another in fome Particulars, but ought not to carry
their Hatred to thofe Qualities which are of fo amiable a
Nature in themfelves, and have nothing to do with the
Points in Difpute. Men of Virtue, though of different
Interefts, ought to confider themfelves as more nearly
united with one another, than with the vicious Part of
Mankind, who embark with them in the fame civil
Concerns. We fhould bear the fame Love towards a Man
of Honour, who is a living Antagonift, which *Tully* tells
us in the forementioned Paffage every one naturally does
to an Enemy that is dead. In fhort, we fhould efteem
Virtue though in a Foe, and abhor Vice though in a
Friend.

I fpeak this with an Eye to thofe cruel Treatments
which Men of all fides are apt to give the Characters of
thofe who do not agree with them. How many Perfons
of undoubted Probity, and exemplary Virtue, on either
Side, are blackned and defamed? How many Men of
Honour expofed to publick Obloquy and Reproach?
Thofe therefore who are either the Inftruments or
Abettors in fuch Infernal Dealings, ought to be looked
upon as Perfons who make ufe of Religion to promote
their Caufe, not of their Caufe to promote Religion.

C.

Nº 244. *Monday, December* 10.

—— *Judex & callidus audis.* Hor. Sat. 7. l. 2. v. 101.

A Judge of Painting you, and Man of Skill. Creech.

Mr. SPECTATOR, *Covent-Garden, December* 7.

'I CANNOT, without a double Injuſtice, forbear
' expreſſing to you the Satisfaction which a whole
' Clan of Virtuoſos have received from thoſe Hints
' which you have lately given the Town on the Cartons
' of the inimitable *Raphael.* It ſhould be methinks the
' Buſineſs of a SPECTATOR to improve the Pleaſures
' of Sight, and there cannot be a more immediate Way
' to it than recommending the Study and Obſervation of
' excellent Drawings and Pictures. When I firſt went to
' view thoſe of *Raphael* which you have celebrated, I muſt
' confeſs I was but barely pleaſed ; the next time I liked
' them better, but at laſt as I grew better acquainted with
' them, I fell deeply in love with them, like wiſe Speeches
' they ſunk deep into my Heart ; for you know, *Mr.* SPEC-
' TATOR, that a Man of Wit may extremely affect one
' for the Preſent, but if he has not Diſcretion, his Merit
' ſoon vaniſhes away, while a Wiſe Man that has not ſo
' great a Stock of Wit, ſhall neverthelefs give you a far
' greater and more laſting Satisfaction : Juſt ſo it is in a
' Picture that is ſmartly touched but not well ſtudied ; one
' may call it a witty Picture, tho' the Painter in the mean
' time may be in Danger of being called a Fool. On the
' other hand, a Picture that is thoroughly underſtood in the
' Whole, and well performed in the Particulars, that is
' begun on the Foundation of Geometry, carried on by
' the Rules of Perſpective, Architecture, and Anatomy,
' and perfected by a good Harmony, a juſt and natural
' Colouring, and ſuch Paſſions, and Expreſſions of the
' Mind as are almoſt peculiar to *Raphael* ; this is what
' you may juſtly ſtile a wiſe Picture, and which ſeldom
' fails to ſtrike us Dumb, till we can aſſemble all our
' Faculties to make but a tolerable Judgment upon it.
' Other

' Other Pictures are made for the Eyes only, as Rattles
' are made for Childrens Ears; and certainly that Picture
' that only pleases the Eye, without representing some
' well-chosen Part of Nature or other, does but shew what
' fine Colours are to be sold at the Colour-shop, and mocks
' the Works of the Creator. If the best Imitator of Nature
' is not to be esteemed the best Painter, but he that makes
' the greatest Show and Glare of Colours; it will necef-
' sarily follow, that he who can array himself in the most
' gaudy Draperies is best drest, and he that can speak loudest
' the best Orator. Every Man when he looks on a Picture
' should examine it according to that share of Reason he is
' Master of, or he will be in Danger of making a wrong
' Judgment. If Men as they walk abroad would make
' more frequent Observations on those Beauties of Nature
' which every Moment present themselves to their View,
' they would be better Judges when they saw her well
' imitated at home: This would help to correct those Er-
' rors which most Pretenders fall into, who are over-hasty
' in their Judgments, and will not stay to let Reason come
' in for a share in the Decision. 'Tis for want of this that
' Men mistake in this Case, and in common Life, a wild
' extravagant Pencil for one that is truly bold and great, an
' impudent Fellow for a Man of true Courage and Bravery,
' hasty and unreasonable Actions for Enterprises of Spirit
' and Resolution, gaudy Colouring for that which is truly
' beautiful, a false and insinuating Discourse for simple
' Truth elegantly recommended. The Parallel will hold
' through all the Parts of Life and Painting too; and the
' Virtuous abovementioned will be glad to see you draw
' it with your Terms of Art. As the Shadows in Picture
' represent the serious or melancholy, so the Lights do the
' bright and lively Thoughts: As there should be but
' one forcible Light in a Picture which should catch the
' Eye and fall on the Hero, so there should be but one
' Object of our Love, even the Author of Nature. These
' and the like Reflexions well improved, might very much
' contribute to open the Beauty of that Art, and prevent
' young People from being poisoned by the ill Gusto of an
' extravagant Workman that should be imposed upon us. '

I am, S I R, *Your most humble Servant.*

Mr.

Mr. SPECTATOR,

'THOUGH I am a Woman, yet I am one of those
' who confess themselves highly pleased with a
' Speculation you obliged the World with sometime ago,
' from an old *Greek* Poet you call *Simonides,* in relation
' to the several Natures and Distinctions of our own
' Sex. I could not but admire how justly the Characters
' of Women in this Age, fall in with the times of *Simo-*
' *nides,* there being no one of those Sorts I have not at
' some time or other of my Life met with a Sample of.
' But, Sir, the Subject of this present Address, are a Set
' of Women comprehended, I think, in the Ninth Spe-
' cie of that Speculation, called the Apes; the Descrip-
' tion of whom I find to be, " That they are such as are
" both ugly and ill-natured, who have nothing beautiful
" themselves, and endeavour to detract from or ridicule
" every thing that appears so in others." Now, Sir, this
' Sect, as I have been told, is very frequent in the great
' Town where you live; but as my Circumstance of Life
' obliges me to reside altogether in the Country, though
' not many Miles from *London,* I can't have met with a
' great Number of 'em, nor indeed is it a desirable Ac-
' quaintance, as I have lately found by Experience. You
' must know, Sir, that at the Beginning of this Summer
' a Family of these Apes came and settled for the Season
' not far from the Place where I live. As they were
' Strangers in the Country, they were visited by the La-
' dies about 'em, of whom I was, with an Humanity
' usual in those that pass most of their Time in Solitude.
' The Apes lived with us very agreeably our own Way
' till towards the End of the Summer, when they began
' to bethink themselves of returning to Town; then it
' was, *Mr.* SPECTATOR, that they began to set them-
' selves about the proper and distinguishing Business of
' their Character; and, as 'tis said of evil Spirits, that they
' are apt to carry away a Piece of the House they are about
' to leave, the Apes, without Regard to common Mercy,
' Civility, or Gratitude, thought fit to mimick and fall
' foul on the Faces, Dress, and Behaviour of their inno-
' cent Neighbours, bestowing abominable Censures and
' disgraceful Appellations commonly called Nick-names,
' on all of them; and in short, like true fine Ladies made
' their

' their honeſt Plainneſs and Sincerity Matter of Ridicule.
' I could not but acquaint you with theſe Grievances, as
' well at the Deſire of all the Parties injur'd, as from
' my own Inclination. I hope, Sir, if you can't propoſe
' intirely to reform this Evil, you will take ſuch Notice
' of it in ſome of your future Speculations, as may put
' the deſerving Part of our Sex on their Guard againſt
' theſe Creatures; and at the ſame time the Apes may
' be ſenſible, that this ſort of Mirth is ſo far from an in-
' nocent Diverſion, that it is in the higheſt Degree that
' Vice which is ſaid to comprehend all others.

I am, S I R, Your humble Servant,

T   Conſtantia Field.

Nº 245.   Tueſday, December 11.

Ficta Voluptatis causâ ſint proxima veris.

Hor. Ars Poet. v. 338.

Fictions, to pleaſe, ſhou'd wear the Face of Truth.

THERE is nothing which one regards ſo much
with an Eye of Mirth and Pity as Innocence,
when it has in it a Daſh of Folly. At the ſame
time that one eſteems the Virtue, one is tempted to laugh
at the Simplicity which accompanies it. When a Man is
made up wholly of the Dove, without the leaſt Grain
of the Serpent in his Compoſition, he becomes ridiculous
in many Circumſtances of Life, and very often diſcredits
his beſt Actions. The *Cordeliers* tell a Story of their
Founder St *Francis*, that as he paſſed the Streets in the
Dusk of the Evening, he diſcovered a young Fellow with
a Maid in a Corner; upon which the good Man, ſay they,
lifted up his Hands to Heaven with a ſecret Thankſgiv-
ing, that there was ſtill ſo much Chriſtian Charity in the
World. The Innocence of the Saint made him miſtake the
Kiſs of a Lover for a Salute of Charity. I am heartily
concerned when I ſee a virtuous Man without a competent Knowledge of the World; and if there be any Uſe in

'thefe my Papers, it is this, that without reprefenting Vice
under any falfe alluring Notions, they give my Reader an
Infight into the Ways of Men, and reprefent human Nature in all its changeable Colours. The Man who has not
been engaged in any of the Follies of the World, or, as
Shakefpear expreffes it, *hackney'd in the Ways of Men,* may
here find a Picture of its Follies and Extravagancies. The
Virtuous and the Innocent may know in Speculation
what they could never arrive at by Practice, and by this
Means avoid the Snares of the Crafty, the Corruptions of
the Vicious, and the Reafonings of the Prejudiced. Their
Minds may be opened without being vitiated.

IT is with an Eye to my following Correfpondent,
Mr. *Timothy Doodle,* who feems a very well-meaning
Man, that I have written this fhort Preface, to which
I fhall fubjoin a Letter from the faid Mr. *Doodle.*

    S I R,

' I Could heartily wifh that you would let us know your
'   Opinion upon feveral innocent Diverfions which are
' in ufe among us, and which are very proper to pafs
' away a Winter Night for thofe who do not care to throw
' away their Time at an Opera, or at the Play-houfe. I
' would gladly know in particular, what Notion you have
' of Hot-Cockles; as alfo whether you think that Quefti-
' ons and Commands, Mottoes, Similes, and Crofs-Pur-
' pofes have not more Mirth and Wit in them, than thofe
' publick Diverfions which are grown fo very fafhionable
' among us. If you would recommend to our Wives and
' Daughters, who read your Papers with a great deal of
' Pleafure, fome of thofe Sports and Paftimes that may be
' practifed within Doors, and by the Fire-fide, we who are
' Mafters of Families fhould be hugely obliged to you, I
' need not tell you that I would have thefe Sports and
' Paftimes not only merry but innocent, for which Reafon
' I have not mentioned either Whisk or Lanterloo, nor
' indeed fo much as One and Thirty. After having com-
' municated to you my Requeft upon this Subject, I will
' be fo free as to tell you how my Wife and I pafs away
' thefe tedious Winter Evenings with a great deal of Plea-
' fure. Tho' fhe be young and handfom, and good-
' humoured to a Miracle, fhe does not care for gadding
                                  ' abroad

' abroad like others of her Sex. There is a very friendly
' Man, a Colonel in the Army, whom I am mightily
' obliged to for his Civilities, that comes to see me almost
' every Night; for he is not one of those giddy young
' Fellows that cannot live out of a Play-house. When we
' are together, we very often make a Party at Blind-
' Man's Buff, which is a Sport that I like the better, be-
' cause there is a good deal of Exercise in it. The Colonel
' and I are blinded by Turns, and you would laugh your
' Heart out to see what Pains my Dear takes to hoodwink
' us, so that it is impossible for us to see the least Glimpse of
' Light. The poor Colonel sometimes hits his Nose against
' a Post, and makes us die with laughing. I have generally
' the good Luck not to hurt myself, but am very often
' above half an Hour before I can catch either of them;
' for you must know we hide ourselves up and down in
' Corners, that we may have the more Sport. I only give
' you this Hint as a Sample of such innocent Diversions
' as I would have you recommend; and am,

Most esteemed S I R, your ever loving Friend,

Timothy Doodle.

THE following Letter was occasioned by my last *Thursday's* Paper upon the Absence of Lovers, and the Methods
therein mentioned of making such Absence supportable.

S I R,

'A MONG the several Ways of Consolation which
'   absent Lovers make use of while their Souls are
' in that State of Departure, which you say is Death in
' Love, there are some very material ones that have
' escaped your Notice. Among these, the first and most
' received is a crooked Shilling, which has administred
' great Comfort to our Forefathers, and is still made
' use of on this Occasion with very good Effect in most
' Parts of Her Majesty's Dominions. There are some, I
' know, who think a Crown-Piece cut into two equal
' Parts, and preserved by the distant Lovers, is of more
' sovereign Virtue than the former. But since Opinions
' are divided in this Particular, why may not the same
' Persons make use of both? The Figure of a Heart, whe-
' ther cut in Stone or cast in Metal, whether bleeding up-
' on an Altar, stuck with Darts, or held in the Hand of a
N 2   ' Cupid.

' *Cupid*, has always been looked upon as Talifmanick in
' Diftreffes of this Nature. I am acquainted with many a
' brave Fellow, who carries his Miftrefs in the Lid of his
' Snuff-box, and by that Expedient has fupported himfelf
' under the Abfence of a whole Campaign. For my own
' part, I have tried all thefe Remedies, but never found fo
' much Benefit from any as from a Ring, in which my
' Miftrefs's Hair is platted together very artificially in a
' kind of True-Lover's Knot. As I have received great Be-
' nefit from this Secret, I think myfelf obliged to com-
' municate it to the Publick, for the Good of my Fellow-
' Subjects. I defire you will add this Letter as an Appen-
' dix to your Confolations upon Abfence, and am,

Your very humble Servant, T. B.

I fhall conclude this Paper with a Letter from an
Univerfity Gentleman, occafioned by my laft *Tuefday's*
Paper, wherein I gave fome Account of the great Feuds
which happened formerly in thofe learned Bodies, between the modern *Greeks* and *Trojans*.

' S I R,

' THIS will give you to underftand, that there is at
' prefent in the Society, whereof I am a Member,
' a very confiderable Body of *Trojans*, who, upon a proper
' Occafion, would not fail to declare ourfelves. In the
' mean while we do all we can to annoy our Enemies by
' Stratagem, and are refolved by the firft Opportunity to
' attack Mr. *Jofhua Barnes*, whom we look upon as the
' *Achilles* of the oppofite Party. As for myfelf, I have had
' the Reputation ever fince I came from School, of being a
' trufty *Trojan*, and am refolved never to give Quarter to
' the fmalleft Particle of *Greek*, where-ever I chance to
' meet it. It is for this Reafon I take it very ill of you, that
' you fometimes hang out *Greek* Colours at the Head of
' your Paper, and fometimes give a Word of the Enemy
' even in the Body of it. When I meet with any thing of
' this nature, I throw down your Speculations upon the
' Table, with that Form of Words which we make ufe of
' when we declare War upon an Author.

Græcum eft, non poteft legi.

' I give you this Hint, that you may for the future abftain
' from any fuch Hoftilities at your Peril. *Troilus.*

C *Wednefday,*

━━━━━━━━━━━━━━━━━━━━━━━━━━

N° 246　*Wednefday, December* 12.

━━━━━━━━━━━━━━━━━━━━━━━━━━

——— Οὐκ ἄρα σοί γε πατὴρ ἦν ἱππότα Πηλεύς,
Οὐδὲ Θέτις μήτηρ, γλαυκὴ δέ σ᾽ ἔτικ|ε θάλασσα,
Πέτραι τ᾽ ἠλίβατοι, ὅτι τοι νόG ἐστὶν ἀπηνής.

Hom. Iliad, 16. 33.

No amorous Hero ever gave thee Birth,
Nor ever tender Goddefs brought thee forth:
Some rugged Rock's hard Entrails gave thee Form,
And raging Seas produc'd thee in a Storm:
A Soul well fuiting thy tempeftuous Kind,
So rough thy Manners, fo untam'd thy Mind. —— P O P E.

Mr. S P E C T A T O R,

‘A S your Paper is Part of the Equipage of the Tea-
‘ Table, I conjure you to print what I now write
‘　　　to you ; for I have no other Way to communi-
‘ cate what I have to fay to the fair Sex on the moft im-
‘ portant Circumftance of Life, even the Care of Children.
‘ I do not underftand that you profefs your Paper is always
‘ to confift of Matters which are only to entertain the
‘ Learned and Polite, but that it may agree with your
‘ Defign to publifh fome which may tend to the Informa-
‘ tion of Mankind in general ; and when it does fo, you do
‘ more than writing Wit and Humour. Give me leave then
‘ to tell you, that all the Abufes that ever you have as
‘ yet endeavoured to reform, certainly not one wanted fo
‘ much your Affiftance as the Abufe in nurfing Children.
‘ It is unmerciful to fee, that a Woman endowed with all
‘ the Perfections and Bleffings of Nature, can, as foon as
‘ fhe is delivered, turn off her innocent, tender, and help-
‘ lefs Infant, and give it up to a Woman that is (ten thou-
‘ fand to one) neither in Health nor good Condition,
‘ neither found in Mind nor Body, that has neither Ho-
‘ nour nor Reputation, neither Love nor Pity for the
‘ poor Babe, but more Regard for the Money than for
‘ the whole Child, and never will take farther Care of it
‘ than what by all the Encouragement of Money and Pre-

N 3　　　　　　　　fents

'ſents ſhe is forced to ; like *Æſop*'s Earth, which would
' not nurſe the Plant of another Ground, altho' never ſo
' much improved, by reaſon that Plant was not of its own
' Production. And ſince another's Child is no more natu-
' ral to a Nurſe than a Plant to a ſtrange and different
' Ground, how can it be ſuppoſed that the Child ſhould
' thrive ; and if it thrives, muſt it not imbibe the groſs
' Humours and Qualities of the Nurſe, like a Plant in a
' different Ground, or like a Graft upon a different Stock ?
' Do not we obſerve, that a Lamb ſucking a Goat changes
' very much its Nature, nay even its Skin and Wooll into
' the Goat Kind ? The Power of a Nurſe over a Child,
' by infuſing into it, with her Milk, her Qualities and
' Diſpoſition, is ſufficiently and daily obſerved : Hence
' came that old Saying concerning an ill-natured and
' malicious Fellow, that he had imbibed his Malice with
' his Nurſe's Milk, or that ſome Brute or other had been
' his Nurſe. Hence *Romulus* and *Remus* were ſaid to have
' been nurſed by a Wolf, *Telephus* the Son of *Hercules* by
' a Hind, *Pelias* the Son of *Neptune* by a Mare, and
' *Ægiſthus* by a Goat; not that they had actually ſuck'd
' ſuch Creatures, as ſome Simpletons have imagin'd,
' but that their Nurſes had been of ſuch a Nature and
' Temper, and infuſed ſuch into them.
  ' MANY Inſtances may be produced from good Au-
' thorities and daily Experience, that Children actually
' ſuck-in the ſeveral Paſſions and depraved Inclinations of
' their Nurſes, as Anger, Malice, Fear, Melancholy, Sad-
' neſs, Deſire, and Averſion. This *Diodorus, lib.* 2. witneſſes,
' when he ſpeaks, ſaying, That *Nero* the Emperor's Nurſe
' had been very much addicted to Drinking; which Ha-
' bit *Nero* received from his Nurſe, and was ſo very par-
' ticular in this, that the People took ſo much notice of it,
' as inſtead of *Tiberius Nero,* they call'd him *Biberius Mero.*
' The ſame *Diodorus* alſo relates of *Caligula,* Predeceſſor to
' *Nero,* that his Nurſe uſed to moiſten the Nipples of her
' Breaſt frequently with Blood, to make *Caligula* take
' the better hold of them ; which, ſays *Diodorus,* was
' the Cauſe that made him ſo blood-thirſty and cruel all
' his Life-time after, that he not only committed fre-
' quent Murder by his own Hand, but likewiſe wiſhed
' that all human Kind wore but one Neck, that he might
               ' have

' have the Pleasure to cut it off. Such like Degeneracies
' aftonish the Parents, who not knowing after whom the
' Child can take, see one to incline to Stealing, another to
' Drinking, Cruelty, Stupidity; yet all thefe are not mind-
' ed. Nay it is eafy to demonftrate, that a Child, altho' it
' be born from the beft of Parents, may be corrupted by
' an ill-tempered Nurfe. How many Children do we fee
' daily brought into Fits, Confumptions, Rickets, &c. mere-
' ly by fucking their Nurfes when in a Paffion or Fury?
' But indeed almoft any Diforder of the Nurfe is a Diforder
' to the Child, and few Nurfes can be found in this Town
' but what labour under fome Diftemper or other. The
' firft Queftion that is generally asked a young Woman
' that wants to be a Nurfe, Why fhe fhould be a Nurfe to
' other Peoples Children; is anfwered, by her having an ill
' Husband, and that fhe muft make fhift to live. I think
' now this very Anfwer is enough to give any Body a
' Shock, if duly confidered; for an ill Husband may, or
' ten to one if he does not, bring home to his Wife an ill
' Diftemper, or at leaft Vexation and Difturbance. Be-
' fides as fhe takes the Child out of mere Neceffity, her
' Food will be accordingly, or elfe very coarfe at beft;
' whence proceeds an ill-concocted and coarfe Food for
' the Child; for as the Blood, fo is the Milk; and hence I
' am very well affured proceeds the Scurvy, the Evil, and
' many other Diftempers. I beg of you, for the Sake of
' the many poor Infants that may and will be faved by
' weighing this Cafe ferioufly, to exhort the People with
' the utmoft Vehemence to let the Children fuck their own
' Mothers, both for the Benefit of Mother and Child. For
' the general Argument, that a Mother is weakened by
' giving fuck to her Children, is vain and fimple; I will
' maintain that the Mother grows ftronger by it, and will
' have her Health better than fhe would have otherwife:
' She will find it the greateft Cure and Prefervative
' for the Vapours and future Mifcarriages, much beyond
' any other Remedy whatfoever: Her Children will be
' like Giants, whereas otherwife they are but living Sha-
' dows and like unripe Fruit; and certainly if a Woman
' is ftrong enough to bring forth a Child, fhe is beyond
' all Doubt ftrong enough to nurfe it afterwards. It
' grieves me to obferve and confider how many poor

N 4   ' Chil-

' Children are daily ruined by careless Nurses; and yet
' how tender ought they to be of a poor Infant, since the
' least Hurt or Blow, especially upon the Head, may make
' it senseless, stupid, or otherwise miserable for ever !
' BUT I cannot well leave this Subject as yet; for it
' seems to me very unnatural, that a Woman that has fed
' a Child as part of herself for nine Months, should have
' no Desire to nurse it farther, when brought to Light and
' before her Eyes, and when by its Cry it implores her
' Assistance and the Office of a Mother. Do not the very
' cruellest of Brutes tend their young ones with all the
' Care and Delight imaginable? for how can she be call'd
' a Mother that will not nurse her young ones? The Earth
' is called the Mother of all things, not because she pro-
' duces, but because she maintains and nurses what she
' produces. The Generation of the Infant is the Effect of
' Desire, but the Care of it argues Virtue and Choice. I
' am not ignorant but that there are some Cases of Neces-
' sity where a Mother cannot give Suck, and then out of
' two Evils the least must be chosen; but there are so
' very few, that I am sure in a Thousand there is hardly
' one real Instance; for if a Woman does but know that
' her Husband can spare about three or six Shillings a
' Week extraordinary, (altho' this is but seldom consi-
' dered) she certainly, with the Assistance of her Gossips,
' will soon persuade the good Man to send the Child to
' Nurse, and easily impose upon him by pretending In-
' disposition. This Cruelty is supported by Fashion; and
' Nature gives place to Custom.

T   *S I R, Your humble Servant.*

N° 247   *Thursday, December* 13.

— Τῶν δ' ἀχδματ☉ ῥέει αὐδὴ
Ἐκ ςομάτων ἡδέα ———   Hesiod.

Their untired Lips a wordy Torrent pour.

WE are told by some ancient Authors, that *Socrates*
was instructed in Eloquence by a Woman, whose
Name, if I am not mistaken, was *Aspasia.* I have indeed
                                        very

very often looked upon that Art as the moſt proper for the Female Sex, and I think the Univerſities would do well to conſider whether they ſhould not fill the Rhetorick Chairs with She Profeſſors.

IT has been ſaid in the Praiſe of ſome Men, that they could talk whole Hours together upon any Thing; but it muſt be owned to the Honour of the other Sex, that there are many among them who can talk whole Hours together upon Nothing. I have known a Woman branch out into a long Extempore Diſſertation upon the Edging of a Petticoat, and chide her Servant for breaking a China Cup, in all the Figures of Rhetorick.

WERE Women admitted to plead in Courts of Judicature, I am perſuaded they would carry the Eloquence of the Bar to greater Heights than it has yet arrived at. If any one doubts this, let him but be preſent at thoſe Debates which frequently ariſe among the Ladies of the *Britiſh* Fiſhery.

THE firſt Kind therefore of Female Orators which I ſhall take notice of, are thoſe who are employed in ſtirring up the Paſſions, a Part of Rhetorick in which *Socrates* his Wife had perhaps made a greater Proficiency than his above-mentioned Teacher.

THE ſecond Kind of Female Orators are thoſe who deal in Invectives, and who are commonly known by the Name of the Cenſorious. The Imagination and Elocution of this Set of Rhetoricians is wonderful. With what a Fluency of Invention, and Copiouſneſs of Expreſſion, will they enlarge upon every little Slip in the Behaviour of another? With how many different Circumſtances, and with what Variety of Phraſes, will they tell over the ſame Story? I have known an old Lady make an unhappy Marriage the Subject of a Month's Converſation. She blamed the Bride in one Place; pitied her in another; laughed at her in a third; wondered at her in a fourth; was angry with her in a fifth; and in ſhort, wore out a Pair of Coach-Horſes in expreſſing her Concern for her. At length, after having quite exhauſted the Subject on this Side, ſhe made a Viſit to the new-married Pair, praiſed the Wife for the prudent Choice ſhe had made, told her the unreaſonable Reflexions which ſome malicious People had caſt upon her, and deſired that they might be better acquainted. The Cenſure and Approbation of this Kind of Women are there-

therefore only to be confider'd as Helps to Difcourfe.

A third Kind of Female Orators may be comprehended
under the Word *Goffips*. Mrs. *Fiddle Faddle* is perfectly
accomplifhed in this Sort of Eloquence; fhe lanches out
into Defcriptions of Chriftenings, runs Divifions upon an
Head-drefs, knows every Difh of Meat that is ferved up
in her Neighbourhood, and entertains her Company a
whole Afternoon together with the Wit of her little Boy,
before he is able to fpeak.

THE Coquette may be looked upon as a fourth Kind of
Female Orator. To give herfelf the larger Field for Difcourfe, fhe hates and loves in the fame Breath, talks to her
Lap-dog or Parrot, is uneafy in all kinds of Weather, and
in every Part of the Room: She has falfe Quarrels and
feigned Obligations to all the Men of her Acquaintance;
fighs when fhe is not fad, and laughs when fhe is not
merry. The Coquette is in particular a great Miftrefs of
that Part of Oratory which is called Action, and indeed
feems to fpeak for no other Purpofe, but as it gives her
an Opportunity of ftirring a Limb, or varying a Feature,
of glancing her Eyes, or playing with her Fan.

AS for News-mongers, Politicians, Mimicks, Story-
tellers, with other Characters of that Nature, which
give Birth to Loquacity, they are as commonly found
among the Men as the Women; for which Reafon I
fhall pafs them over in Silence.

I have often been puzzled to affign a Caufe why Women
fhould have this Talent of a ready Utterance in fo much
greater Perfection than Men. I have fometimes fancied that
they have not a retentive Power, or the Faculty of fuppreffing
their Thoughts, as Men have, but that they are neceffitated
to fpeak every thing they think, and if fo, it would perhaps furnifh a very ftrong Argument to the *Cartefians*, for
the fupporting of their Doctrine, that the Soul always
thinks. But as feveral are of Opinion that the Fair Sex are
not altogether Strangers to the Art of Diffembling and concealing their Thoughts, I have been forced to relinquifh
that Opinion, and have therefore endeavoured to feek after fome better Reafon. In order to it, a Friend of mine,
who is an excellent Anatomift, has promifed me by the
firft Opportunity to diffect a Woman's Tongue, and to exa-

mine

mine whether there may not be in it certain Juices which render it so wonderfully voluble or flippant, or whether the Fibres of it may not be made up of a finer or more pliant Thread, or whether there are not in it some particular Muscles which dart it up and down by such sudden Glances and Vibrations; or whether in the last place, there may not be certain undiscovered Channels running from the Head and the Heart, to this little Instrument of Loquacity, and conveying into it a perpetual Affluency of animal Spirits. Nor must I omit the Reason which *Hudibras* has given, why those who can talk on Trifles speak with the greatest Fluency; namely, that the Tongue is like a Race-Horse, which runs the faster the lesser Weight it carries.

WHICH of these Reasons soever may be looked upon as the most probable, I think the *Irishman*'s Thought was very natural, who after some Hours Conversation with a Female Orator, told her, that he believed her Tongue was very glad when she was asleep, for that it had not a Moment's Rest all the while she was awake.

THAT excellent old Ballad of *The Wanton Wife of Bath*, has the following remarkable Lines.

> *I think, quoth* Thomas, *Womens Tongues*
> *Of Aspen Leaves are made.*

AND *Ovid*, tho' in the Description of a very barbarous Circumstance, tells us, That when the Tongue of a beautiful Female was cut out, and thrown upon the Ground, it could not forbear muttering even in that Posture.

> ————*Comprensam forcipe linguam*
> *Abstulit ense fero.* *Radix micat ultima linguæ.*
> *Ipsa jacet, terræque tremens immurmurat atræ;*
> *Utque salire solet mutilatæ cauda colubræ*
> *Palpitat*———— Met. 1. 6. v. 556.

> ————————————The Blade had cut
> Her Tongue sheer of, close to the trembling root:
> The mangl'd Part still quiver'd on the Ground,
> Murmuring with a faint imperfect Sound;
> And, as a Serpent wreaths his wounded Train,
> Uneasy, panting, and possess'd with Pain. CROXAL.

IF a Tongue would be talking without a Mouth, what could it have done when it had all its Organs of Speech, and

and Accomplices of Sound about it? I might here mention the Story of the Pippin Woman, had not I some Reason to look upon it as fabulous.

I muſt confeſs I am ſo wonderfully charmed with the Muſick of this little Inſtrument, that I would by no means diſcourage it. All that I aim at by this Diſſertation is, to cure it of ſeveral diſagreeable Notes and in particular of thoſe little Jarrings and Diſſonances which ariſe from Anger, Cenſoriouſneſs, Goſſiping and Coquetry. In ſhort, I would always have it tuned by Good-nature, Truth, Diſcretion and Sincerity.   C

Nᵒ 248 *Friday, December* 14.

Hoc maximè Officii eſt, ut quiſque maximè opis indigeat,
ita ei potiſſimùm opitulari.   Tull.

It is a principal point of Duty, to aſſiſt another moſt,
when he ſtands moſt in need of Aſſiſtance.

THERE are none who deſerve Superiority over others in the Eſteem of Mankind, who do not make it their Endeavour to be beneficial to Society; and who upon all Occaſions which their Circumſtances of Life can adminiſter, do not take a certain unfeigned Pleaſure in conferring Benefits of one kind or other. Thoſe whoſe great Talents and high Birth have placed them in conſpicuous Stations of Life, are indiſpenſably obliged to exert ſome noble Inclinations for the Service of the World, or elſe ſuch Advantages become Misfortunes, and Shade and Privacy are a more eligible Portion. Where Opportunities and Inclinations are given to the ſame Perſon, we ſometimes ſee ſublime Inſtances of Virtue, which ſo dazzle our Imaginations, that we look with Scorn on all which in lower Scenes of Life we may ourſelves be able to practiſe. But this is a vicious way of thinking; and it bears ſome ſpice of romantick Madneſs, for a Man to imagine that he muſt grow ambitious, or ſeek Adventures to be able to do great Actions. It is in every Man's
Power

Power in the World who is above mere Poverty, not only
to do Things worthy but heroick. The great Foundation
of civil Virtue is Self-denial; and there is no one above
the Neceffities of Life, but has Opportunities of exercifing
that noble Quality, and doing as much as his Circumftances will bear for the Eafe and Convenience of other
Men; and he who does more than ordinary Men practife upon fuch Occafions as occur in his Life, deferves
the Value of his Friends as if he had done Enterprifes
which are ufually attended with the higheft Glory. Men
of publick Spirit differ rather in their Circumftances than
their Virtue; and the Man who does all he can, in a low
Station, is more a Hero than he who omits any worthy Action he is able to accomplifh in a great one. It is not many Years ago fince *Lapirius*, in Wrong of his elder Brother, came to a great Eftate by Gift of his Father, by reafon of the diffolute Behaviour of the Firft-born. Shame
and Contrition reformed the Life of the difinherited
Youth, and he became as remarkable for his good Qualities as formerly for his Errors. *Lapirius*, who obferved
his Brother's Amendment, fent him on a New-Year's
Day in the Morning the following Letter:

Honoured Brother,

‘ I Inclofe to you the Deeds whereby my Father gave
‘ me this Houfe and Land: Had he lived 'till now,
‘ he would not have beftowed it in that manner; he took
‘ it from the Man you were, and I reftore it to the Man
‘ you are. I am,

> *S I R, Your affectionate Brother,*
>
> *and humble Servant,* P. T.

AS great and exalted Spirits undertake the Purfuit of
hazardous Actions for the Good of others, at the fame
time gratifying their Paffion for Glory; fo do worthy
Minds, in the domeftick way of Life deny themfelves many Advantages, to fatisfy a generous Benevolence which
they bear to their Friends oppreffed with Diftreffes and
Calamities. Such Natures one may call Stores of Providence, which are actuated by a fecret Celeftial Influence
to undervalue the ordinary Gratifications of Wealth; to
give Comfort to an Heart loaded with Affliction, to fave.

a falling Family, to preserve a Branch of Trade in their Neighbourhood, and give Work to the Industrious, preserve the Portion of the helpless Infant, and raise the Head of the mourning Father. People whose Hearts are wholly bent towards Pleasure, or intent upon Gain, never hear of the noble Occurrences among Men of Industry and Humanity. It would look like a City Romance, to tell them of the generous Merchant, who the other Day sent this Billet to an eminent Trader under Difficulties to support himself, in whose Fall many hundreds besides himself had perished; but because I think there is more Spirit and true Galantry in it than in any Letter I have ever read from *Strephon* to *Phillis*, I shall insert it even in the mercantile honest Stile in which it was sent.

S I R,

‘ I Have heard of the Casualties which have involved
‘ you in extreme Distress at this time; and knowing
‘ you to be a Man of great Good-nature, Industry and
‘ Probity, have resolved to stand by you. Be of good
‘ chear, the Bearer brings with him five thousand Pounds,
‘ and has my Order to answer your drawing as much
‘ more on my Account. I did this in haste, for fear I
‘ should come too late for your Relief; but you may value
‘ yourself with me to the Sum of fifty thousand Pounds;
‘ for I can very chearfully run the Hazard of being so
‘ much less rich than I am now, to save an honest Man
‘ whom I love.

Your Friend and Servant, W. P.

I think there is somewhere in *Montaigne* mention made of a Family-book, wherein all the Occurrences that happened from one Generation of that House to another were recorded. Were there such a Method in the Families which are concerned in this Generosity, it would be an hard Task for the greatest in *Europe* to give, in their own, an Instance of a Benefit better placed, or conferred with a more graceful Air. It has been heretofore urged how barbarous and inhuman is any unjust Step made to the Disadvantage of a Trader; and by how much such an Act towards him is detestable, by so much an Act of Kindness towards him is laudable. I remember to have heard a
Bencher

Bencher of the *Temple* tell a Story of a Tradition in their House, where they had formerly a Custom of choosing Kings for such a Season, and allowing him his Expences at the Charge of the Society: One of our Kings, said my Friend, carried his Royal Inclination a little too far, and there was a Committee ordered to look into the Management of his Treasury. Among other Things it appeared, that his Majesty walking *incog.* in the Cloister, had overheard a poor Man say to another, Such a small Sum would make me the happiest Man in the World. The King out of his Royal Compassion privately inquired into his Character, and finding him a proper Object of Charity, sent him the Money. When the Committee read the Report, the House passed his Accounts with a Plaudite without farther Examination, upon the Recital of this Article in them,

	l.	s.	d.
T *For making a Man happy.*	10 :	00 :	00

N° 249   *Saturday, December* 15.

Γέλως ἄκαιρ⊕ ἐν βροτοῖς δεινὸν κακὸν. Frag. Vet. Poet.
Mirth out of season is a grievous Ill.

WHEN I make choice of a Subject that has not been treated on by others, I throw together my Reflexions on it without any Order or Method, so that they may appear rather in the Looseness and Freedom of an Essay, than in the Regularity of a set Discourse. It is after this manner that I shall consider Laughter and Ridicule in my present Paper.

MAN is the merriest Species of the Creation, all above and below him are serious. He sees things in a different Light from other Beings, and finds his Mirth arising from Objects that perhaps cause something like Pity or Displeasure in higher Natures. Laughter is indeed a very good Counterpoise to the Spleen; and it seems but reasonable that we should be capable of receiving Joy from what is no real Good to us, since we can receive Grief from what is no real Evil.

I

I have in my forty-seventh Paper raised a Speculation on the Notion of a modern Philosopher, who describes the first Motive of Laughter to be a secret Comparison which we make between ourselves, and the Persons we laugh at; or, in other Words, that Satisfaction which we receive from the Opinion of some Preeminence in ourselves, when we see the Absurdities of another, or when we reflect on any past Absurdities of our own. This seems to hold in most Cases, and we may observe that the vainest Part of Mankind are the most addicted to this Passion.

I have read a Sermon of a Conventual in the Church of *Rome*, on those Words of the Wise Man, *I said of Laughter, it is mad; and of Mirth, what does it?* Upon which he laid it down as a Point of Doctrine, that Laughter was the Effect of Original Sin, and that *Adam* could not laugh before the Fall.

LAUGHTER, while it lasts, slackens and unbraces the Mind, weakens the Faculties, and causes a kind of Remissness and Dissolution in all the Powers of the Soul: And thus far it may be looked upon as a Weakness in the Composition of human Nature. But if we consider the frequent Reliefs we receive from it, and how often it breaks the Gloom which is apt to depress the Mind and damp our Spirits, with transient unexpected Gleams of Joy, one would take care not to grow too wise for so great a Pleasure of Life.

THE Talent of turning Men into Ridicule, and exposing to Laughter those one converses with, is the Qualification of little ungenerous Tempers. A young Man with this Cast of Mind cuts himself off from all manner of Improvement. Every one has his Flaws and Weaknesses; nay, the greatest Blemishes are often found in the most shining Characters; but what an absurd Thing is it to pass over all the valuable Parts of a Man, and fix our Attention on his Infirmities? To observe his Imperfections more than his Virtues? and to make use of him for the Sport of others, rather than for our own Improvement?

WE therefore very often find, that Persons the most accomplished in Ridicule are those who are very shrewd at hitting a Blot, without exerting any thing masterly in themselves. As there are many eminent Criticks who ne-

ver

ver writ a good Line, there are many admirable Buffoons that animadvert upon every fingle Defect in another, without ever difcovering the leaft Beauty of their own. By this Means, thefe unlucky little Wits often gain Repu-tation in the Efteem of vulgar Minds, and raife themfelves above Perfons of much more laudable Characters.

IF the Talent of Ridicule were employed to laugh Men out of Vice and Folly, it might be of fome Ufe to the World; but inftead of this, we find that it is gene-rally made ufe of to laugh Men out of Virtue and good Senfe, by attacking every thing that is folemn and ferious, decent and praife-worthy in human Life.

WE may obferve, that in the firft Ages of the World, when the great Souls and Mafter-pieces of human Na-ture were produced, Men fhined by a noble Simplicity of Behaviour, and were Strangers to thofe little Em-bellifhments which are fo fafhionable in our prefent Con-verfation. And it is very remarkable, that notwith-ftanding we fall fhort at prefent of the Ancients in Poetry, Painting, Oratory, Hiftory, Architecture, and all the noble Arts and Sciences which depend more upon Genius than Experience, we exceed them as much in Doggrel, Humour, Burlefque, and all the trivial Arts of Ridicule. We meet with more Rallery among the Moderns, but more good Senfe among the Ancients.

THE two great Branches of Ridicule in Writing are Comedy and Burlefque. The firft ridicules Perfons by drawing them in their proper Characters, the other by drawing them quite unlike themfelves. Burlefque is there-fore of two Kinds; the firft reprefents mean Perfons in the Accoutrements of Heroes, the other defcribes great Perfons acting and fpeaking like the bafeft among the People. *Don Quixote* is an Inftance of the firft, and *Lu-cian*'s Gods of the fecond. It is a Difpute among the Criticks, whether Burlefque Poetry runs beft in Heroick Verfe, like that of the *Difpenfary*; or in Doggrel, like that of *Hudibras*. I think where the low Character is to be raifed, the Heroick is the proper Meafure; but when an Hero is to be pulled down and degraded, it is done beft in Doggrel.

IF *Hudibras* had been fet out with as much Wit and Humour in Heroick Verfe as he is in Doggrel, he would

have

have made a much more agreeable Figure than he does; though the generality of his Readers are so wonderfully pleased with the double Rhimes, that I do not expect many will be of my Opinion in this Particular.

I shall conclude this Essay upon Laughter with observing that the Metaphor of Laughing, applied to Fields and Meadows when they are in Flower, or to Trees when they are in Blossom, runs through all Languages; which I have not observed of any other Metaphor, excepting that of Fire and Burning when they are applied to Love. This shews that we naturally regard Laughter, as what is in itself both amiable and beautiful. For this Reason likewise *Venus* has gained the Title of Φιλομειδης, the Laughter-loving Dame, as *Waller* has translated it, and is represented by *Horace* as the Goddess who delights in Laughter. *Milton*, in a joyous Assembly of imaginary Persons, has given us a very Poetical Figure of Laughter. His whole Band of Mirth is so finely described, that I shall set down the Passage at length.

> *But come thou Goddess fair and free,*
> *In Heaven ycleped* Euphrosyne,
> *And by Men, heart-easing Mirth,*
> *Whom lovely* Venus *at a Birth,*
> *With two Sister Graces more,*
> *To Ivy-crowned* Bacchus *bore:*
> *Haste thee Nymph, and bring with thee*
> *Jest and youthful Jollity,*
> *Quips and Cranks, and wanton Wiles,*
> *Nods, and Becks, and wreathed Smiles,*
> *Such as hang on* Hebe's *Cheek,*
> *And love to live in Dimple sleek:*
> *Sport that wrinkled Care derides,*
> And Laughter holding both his Sides.
> *Come, and trip it, as you go,*
> *On the light fantastick Toe:*
> *And in thy right Hand lead with thee*
> *The Mountain Nymph, sweet Liberty;*
> *And if I give thee Honour due,*
> *Mirth, admit me of thy Crew,*
> *To live with her, and live with thee,*
> *In unreproved Pleasures free.*

Monday,

N° 250. *Monday, December* 17.

Disce docendus adhuc, quæ censet amiculus, ut si
Cæcus iter monstrare velit; tamen aspice si quid
Et nos, quod cures proprium fecisse, loquamur.

Hor. Ep. 17. l. i. v. 3.

Yet hear what thy unskilful Friend can say,
As if one blind pretends to show the way;
Yet see a while, if what is fairly shown
Be good, and such as you may make your own.

CREECH.

Mr. SPECTATOR,

'YOU see the Nature of my Request by the *Latin*
' Motto which I address to you. I am very sensible
' I ought not to use many Words to you, who are
' one of but few; but the following Piece, as it relates
' to Speculation in Propriety of Speech, being a Curiosity
' in its Kind, begs your Patience. It was found in a Poe-
' tical Virtuoso's Closet among his Rarities; and since
' the several Treatises of Thumbs, Ears, and Noses, have
' obliged the World, this of Eyes is at your Service.

' THE first Eye of Consequence (under the invi-
' sible Author of all) is the visible Luminary of the
' Universe. This glorious Spectator is said never to open
' his Eyes at his Rising in a Morning, without having
' a whole Kingdom of Adorers in *Persian* Silk waiting
' at his Levée. Millions of Creatures derive their Sight
' from this Original, who, besides his being the great
' Director of Opticks, is the surest Test whether Eyes
' be of the same Species with that of an Eagle, or that of
' an Owl: The one he emboldens with a manly Assu-
' rance to look, speak, act or plead before the Faces of a
' numerous Assembly; the other he dazzles out of Coun-
' tenance into a sheepish Dejectedness. The Sun-proof
' Eye dares lead up a Dance in a full Court; and with-
' out blinking at the Lustre of Beauty, can distribute an
' Eye of proper Complaisance to a Room crowded with
' Company, each of which deserves particular Regard:
' while

' while the other sneaks from Conversation, like a fear-
' ful Debtor, who never dares to look out, but when
' he can see no Body, and no Body him.

' THE next Instance of Opticks is the famous *Ar-*
' *gus,* who (to speak the Language of *Cambridge*) was
' one of an Hundred; and being used as a Spy in the
' Affairs of Jealousy, was obliged to have all his Eyes
' about him.   We have no Account of the particular Co-
' lours, Casts and Turns of this Body of Eyes; but as he
' was Pimp for his Mistress *Juno,* 'tis probable he used
' all the modern Leers, sly Glances, and other ocular
' Activities to serve his Purpose.   Some look upon him
' as the then King at Arms to the Heathenish Deities;
' and make no more of his Eyes than as so many Span-
' gles of his Herald's Coat.

' THE next upon the Optick List is old *Janus,* who
' stood in a double-sighted Capacity, like a Person placed
' betwixt two opposite Looking-Glasses, and so took a sort
' of retrospective Cast at one View. Copies of this double-
' faced Way are not yet out of Fashion with many Pro-
' fessions, and the ingenious Artists pretend to keep up
' this Species by double-headed Canes and Spoons; but
' there is no Mark of this Faculty, except in the emble-
' matical Way of a wise General having an Eye to both
' Front and Rear, or a pious Man taking a Review and
' Prospect of his past and future State at the same Time.

' I must own, that the Names, Colours, Qualities,
' and Turns of Eyes vary almost in every Head; for,
' not to mention the common Appellations of the Black,
' the Blue, the White, the Gray, and the like; the
' most remarkable are those that borrow their Titles from
' Animals, by Virtue of some particular Quality of Re-
' semblance they bear to the Eyes of the respective Crea-
' tures; as that of a greedy rapacious Aspect takes its
' Name from the Cat, that of a sharp piercing Nature from
' the Hawk, those of an amorous roguish Look derive
' their Title even from the Sheep, and we say such an one
' has a Sheep's Eye, not so much to denote the Innocence
' as the simple Sliness of the Cast: Nor is this metapho-
' rical Inoculation a modern Invention, for we find *Ho-*
' *mer* taking the Freedom to place the Eye of an Ox,
' Bull, or Cow in one of his principal Goddesses, by that
' frequent Expression of   Βοῶπις

Βοῶπις πότνια Ἥρη——
The Ox-eyed venerable *Juno*.

' NOW as to the peculiar Qualities of the Eye, that
' fine Part of our Conſtitution ſeems as much the Recep-
' tacle and Seat of our Paſſions, Appetites and Inclinations
' as the Mind itſelf; and at leaſt it is the outward Portal
' to introduce them to the Houſe within, or rather the
' common Thorough-fare to let our Affections paſs in and
' out. Love, Anger, Pride, and Avarice, all viſibly move
' in thoſe little Orbs. I know a young Lady that can't ſee
' a certain Gentleman paſs by without ſhewing a ſecret
' Deſire of ſeeing him again by a Dance in her Eye-balls;
' nay, ſhe can't for the Heart of her help looking Half a
' Street's Length after any Man in a gay Dreſs. You can't
' behold a covetous Spirit walk by a Goldſmith's Shop
' without caſting a wiſhful Eye at the Heaps upon the
' Counter. Does not a haughty Perſon ſhew the Temper of
' his Soul in the ſupercilious Roll of his Eye? and how
' frequently in the Height of Paſſion does that moving
' Picture in our Head ſtart and ſtare, gather a Redneſs and
' quick Flaſhes of Lightning, and make all its Humours
' ſparkle with Fire, as *Virgil* finely deſcribes it.

——— *Ardentis ab ore*
Scintillæ abſiſtunt: oculis micat acribus ignis.

Æn. 12. v. 101.

———— From his wide Noſtrils flies
A fiery Stream, and Sparkles from his Eyes. DRYDEN.

' AS for the various Turns of the Eye-ſight, ſuch as the
' voluntary or involuntary, the half or the whole Leer,
' I ſhall not enter into a very particular Account of them;
' but let me obſerve, that oblique Viſion, when natural,
' was anciently the Mark of Bewitchery and magical Fa-
' ſcination, and to this Day 'tis a malignant ill Look; but
' when 'tis forced and affected it carries a wanton Deſign,
' and in Play-houſes, and other publick Places, this ocular
' Intimation is often an Aſſignation for bad Practices: But
' this Irregularity in Viſion, together with ſuch Enormi-
' ties as Tipping the Wink, the Circumſpective Roll,
' the Side-peep through a thin Hood or Fan, muſt be put
' in the Claſs of Heteropticks, as all wrong Notions of
' Religion are ranked under the general Name of Hete-
' rodox.

' rodox. All the pernicious Applications of Sight are more
' immediately under the Direction of a SPECTATOR;
' and I hope you will arm your Readers againſt the Miſ-
' chiefs which are daily done by killing Eyes, in which you
' will highly oblige your wounded unknown Friend,

T. B.

Mr. SPECTATOR,

' YOU profeſſed in ſeveral Papers your particular
' Endeavours in the Province of SPECTATOR, to
' correct the Offences committed by Starers, who diſ-
' turb whole Aſſemblies without any Regard to Time,
' Place or Modeſty. You complained alſo, that a Starer is
' not uſually a Perſon to be convinced by the Reaſon of
' the Thing, nor ſo eaſily rebuked, as to amend by Ad-
' monitions. I thought therefore fit to acquaint you with a
' convenient Mechanical Way, which may eaſily prevent
' or correct Staring, by an Optical Contrivance of new
' Perſpective-Glaſſes, ſhort and commodious like Opera
' Glaſſes, fit for ſhort-ſighted People as well as others, theſe
' Glaſſes making the Objects appear, either as they are
' ſeen by the naked Eye, or more diſtinct, though ſome-
' what leſs than Life, or bigger and nearer. A Perſon
' may, by the Help of this Invention, take a View of ano-
' ther without the Impertinence of Staring; at the ſame
' Time it ſhall not be poſſible to know whom or what he
' is looking at. One may look towards his Right or Left
' Hand, when he is ſuppoſed to look forwards: This is
' ſet forth at large in the printed Propoſals for the Sale
' of theſe Glaſſes, to be had at Mr. *Dillon*'s in *Long-*
' *Acre*, next Door to the *White-Hart*. Now, Sir, as your
' *Spectator* has occaſioned the Publiſhing of this Inven-
' tion for the Benefit of modeſt Spectators, the Inventor
' deſires your Admonitions concerning the decent Uſe of
' it; and hopes, by your Recommendation, that for the
' future Beauty may be beheld without the Torture and
' Confuſion which it ſuffers from the Inſolence of Starers.
' By this means you will relieve the Innocent from an
' Inſult which there is no Law to puniſh, tho' it is a
' greater Offence than many which are within the
' Cogniſance of Juſtice. I am,

S I R, *Your moſt humble Servant,*

Abraham Spy.

Q

Tueſday,

N.º 251 *Tuesday,* December 18.

———*Linguæ centum funt, oraque centum,*
Ferrea Vox.———   Virg. Æn. 6. v. 625.

———*A hundred Mouths, a hundred Tongues,*
And Throats of Braſs inſpir'd with Iron Lungs. DRYDEN.

THERE is nothing which more aſtoniſhes a Foreigner, and frights a Country Squire, than the
Cries of London. My good Friend Sir ROGER often
declares, that he cannot get them out of his Head or go to
Sleep for them, the firſt Week that he is in Town. On
the contrary, WILL HONEYCOMB calls them the *Ra-*
mage de la Ville, and prefers them to the Sounds of Larks
and Nightingales, with all the Muſick of the Fields and
Woods. I have lately received a Letter from ſome very
odd Fellow upon this Subject, which I ſhall leave with
my Reader, without ſaying any thing further of it.

'*SIR,*

'I AM a Man out of all Buſineſs, and would willingly
'turn my Head to any thing for an honeſt Livelihood.
'I have invented ſeveral Projects for raiſing many Mil-
'lions of Money without burdening the Subject, but I
'cannot get the Parliament to liſten to me, who look
'upon me, forſooth, as a Crack, and a Projector; ſo that
'deſpairing to enrich either myſelf or my Country by
'this Publick-ſpiritedneſs, I would make ſome Propoſals
'to you relating to a Deſign which I have very much at
'Heart, and which may procure me a handſom Sub-
'ſiſtence, if you will be pleaſed to recommend it to the
'Cities of *London* and *Weſtminſter.*

'THE Poſt I would aim at, is to be Comptroller-
'General of the *London* Cries, which are at preſent un-
'der no manner of Rules or Diſcipline. I think I am
'pretty well qualified for this Place, as being a Man of
'very ſtrong Lungs, of great Inſight into all the Bran-
'ches of our *Britiſh* Trades and Manufactures, and of a
'competent Skill in Muſick.

'THE

' THE Cries of *London* may be divided into Vocal and
' Inftrumental. As for the latter they are at prefent under
' a very great Diforder. A Freeman of *London* has the
' Privilege of difturbing a whole Street for an Hour toge-
' ther, with the Twanking of a Brafs-Kettle or a Frying-
' Pan. The Watchman's Thump at Midnight ftartles us
' in our Beds, as much as the Breaking in of a Thief. The
' Sowgelder's Horn has indeed fomething mufical in it,
' but this is feldom heard within the Liberties. I would
' therefore propofe, that no, Inftrument of this Nature
' fhould be made ufe of, which I have not tuned and li-
' cenfed, after having carefully examined in what manner
' it may affect the Ears of her Majefty's liege Subjects.

' VOCAL Cries are of a much larger Extent, and in-
' deed fo full of Incongruities and Barbarifms, that we
' appear a diftracted City to Foreigners, who do not com-
' prehend the Meaning of fuch enormous Outcries. Milk
' is generally fold in a Note above *Ela*, and in Sounds fo
' exceeding fhrill, that it often fets our Teeth on Edge.
' The Chimney-fweeper is confined to no certain Pitch ;
' he fometimes utters himfelf in the deepeft Bafe, and
' fometimes in the fharpeft Treble ; fometimes in the
' higheft, and fometimes in the loweft Note of the
' Gamut. The fame Obfervation might be made on the
' Retailers of Small-coal, not to mention broken Glaffes
' or Brick-duft. In thefe therefore, and the like Cafes, it
' fhould be my Care to fweeten and mellow the Voices
' of thefe itinerant Tradefmen, before they make their
' Appearance in our Streets, as alfo to accommodate their
' Cries to their refpective Wares ; and to take care in
' particular, that thofe may not make the moft Noife who
' have the leaft to fell, which is very obfervable in the
' Venders of Card-matches, to whom I cannot but apply
' that old Proverb of *Much Cry but little Wooll.*

' SOME of thefe laft mentioned Muficians are fo
' very loud in the Sale of thefe trifling Manufactures,
' that an honeft fplenetick Gentleman of my Acquaintance
' bargained with one of them never to come into the Street
' where he lived: But what was the Effect of this Contract?
' Why, the whole Tribe of Card-match-makers which
' frequent that Quarter, paffed by his Door the very next
' Day, in hopes of being bought off after the fame manner.'

' IT

'IT is another great Imperfection in our *London* Cries,
'that there is no juft Time nor Meafure obferved in them.
'Our News fhould indeed be publifhed in a very quick
'Time, becaufe it is a Commodity that will not keep
'cold. It fhould not, however, be cried with the fame
'Precipitation as *Fire:* Yet this is generally the Cafe. A
'Bloody Battle alarms the Town from one End to ano-
'ther in an Inftant. Every Motion of the *French* is pub-
'lifhed in fo great a Hurry, that one would think the
'Enemy were at our Gates. This likewife I would take
'upon me to regulate in fuch a manner, that there fhould
'be fome Diftinction made between the fpreading of a
'Victory, a March, or an Incampment, a *Dutch*, a *Por-*
'*tugal*, or a *Spanifh* Mail. Nor muft I omit under this
'Head thofe exceffive Alarms with which feveral boifte-
'rous Rufticks infeft our Streets in Turnip-Seafon; and
'which are more inexcufable, becaufe thefe are Wares
'which are in no Danger of cooling upon their Hands.

'THERE are others who affect a very flow Time,
'and are, in my Opinion, much more tuneable than the
'former; the Cooper in particular fwells his laft Note
'in an hollow Voice, that is not without its Harmony;
'nor can I forbear being infpired with a moft agreeable
'Melancholy, when I hear that fad and folemn Air
'with which the Public are very often afked, if they
'have any Chairs to mend? Your own Memory may
'fuggeft to you many other lamentable Ditties of the
'fame Nature, in which the Mufick is wonderfully lan-
'guifhing and melodious.

'I am always pleafed with that particular Time of the
'Year which is proper for the pickling of Dill and Cu-
'cumbers; but alas, this Cry, like the Song of the Night-
'ingale, is not heard above two Months. It would there-
'fore be worth while to confider, whether the fame Air
'might not in fome Cafes be adapted to other Words.

'IT might likewife deferve our moft ferious Confi-
'deration, how far, in a well regulated City, thofe Hu-
'mourifts are to be tolerated, who, not contented with
'the traditional Cries of their Forefathers, have invented
'particular Songs and Tunes of their own: Such as was
'not many Years fince, the Paftry-man, commonly known
'by the Name of the Colly-Molly-Puff; and fuch as is

' at this Day the Vender of Powder and Wash-balls,
' who, if I am rightly informed, goes under the Name
' of *Powder-Wat.*

' I must not here omit one particular Absurdity which
' runs through this whole vociferous Generations, and
' which renders their Cries very often not only incom-
' modious, but altogether useless to the Public; I mean,
' that idle Accomplishment which they all of them aim
' at, of crying so as not to be understood. Whether or
' no they have learned this from several of our affected
' Singers, I will not take upon me to say; but most
' certain it is, that People know the Wares they deal in
' rather by their Tunes than by their Words; insomuch
' that I have sometimes seen a Country Boy run out to
' buy Apples of a Bellows-mender, and Ginger-bread
' from a Grinder of Knives and Scissars. Nay so strangely
' infatuated are some very eminent Artists of this parti-
' cular Grace in a Cry, that none but their Acquain-
' tance are able to guess at their Profession; for who else
' can know, that *Work if I had it,* should be the Signi-
' fication of a Corn-cutter?

' FORASMUCH therefore as Persons of this Rank
' are seldom Men of Genius or Capacity, I think it would
' be very proper, that some Man of good Sense and sound
' Judgment should preside over these public Cries who
' should permit none to lift up their Voices in our Streets,
' that have not tuneable Throats, and are not only able to
' overcome the Noise of the Croud, and the Rattling of
' Coaches, but also to vend their respective Merchandises
' in apt Phrases, and in the most distinct and agreeable
' Sounds. I do therefore humbly recommend myself as a
' Person rightly qualified for this Post; and if I meet with
' fitting Encouragement, shall communicate some other
' Projects which I have by me, that may no less conduce
' to the Emolument of the Public.

I am S I R, &c.

Ralph Crotchet.

THE INDEX.

A.

ABsence of Lovers, Death in Love, Number 241. How to be made easy, *ibid*.

Abstinence, the Benefits of it, N. 195.

Accompts, their great Usefulness, N. 174.

Acosta, his Answer to *Limborch* touching the Multiplicity of Ceremonies in the Jewish Religion, N. 213.

Action, a threefold Division of our Actions, N. 213. No right Judgment to be made of them, 174.

Admiration, one of the most pleasing Passions, N. 237.

Adversity, no Evil in itself, N. 237.

Advertisement from Mr. *Sly* the Haberdasher, N. 187. About the Lottery Ticket, 191.

Ambition, by what to be measured, N. 188. Many times as hurtful to the Princes who are led by it as the People, 200. Most Men subject to it, 219, 224. Of Use when rightly directed, 219.

Annihilation, by whom desired, N. 210. The most abject of Wishes, *ibid*.

Apes, what Women so called, and described, N. 244.

Apollo's Temple on the Top of *Leucate*, by whom frequented, and for what purpose, N. 223.

Apothecary, his Employment, N. 195.

Appetites, sooner moved than the Passions, N. 208.

Argument, Rules for the Management of one, N. 197. *Argumentum Basilinum*, what, 239. *Socrates* his way of arguing, *ibid*. In what manner managed by States and Communities, *ibid*.

Argus, his Qualifications and Employments under *Juno*, N. 250.

Aristænetus his Letters, some Account of them, N. 238.

Aristotle, the Inventor of Syllogism, N. 239.

Atheists great Zealots, N. 185. and Bigots, *ibid*. Their Opinions downright Nonsense, *ibid*.

B.

BAudy-houses frequented by wise Men, not out of Wantonness but Stratagem, N. 190.

Beggars, Sir *Andrew Freeport*'s Opinion of them, N. 232.

Boileau

The INDEX.

Boileau cenfured, and for what, N. 209.

Butts : the Adventure of a *Butt* on the Water, N. 175.

C.

Aprice often acts in the Place of Reafon, N. 191.
Caftilian. The Story of a *Caftilian* Hufband and his Wife, N. 198.

Charles the Great, his Behaviour to his Secretary, who had debauched his Daughter, N. 181.

Children, the Unnaturalnefs in Mothers of making them fuck a Stranger's Milk, N. 246.

Chinefe, the Punifhment among them for *Parricide,* N. 189.

Chriftian Religion, the clear Proof of its Articles, and Excellency of its Doctrines, N. 186, 213.

Club. The *She-Romp Club,* N. 217. Methods obferved by that Club, *ibid.*

Club Law, a convincing Argument, N. 239.

Coffee-houfe Difputes, N. 197.

Comfort, what, and where found, N. 196.

Conquefts, the Vanity of them, N. 180.

Conftancy in Sufferings, the Excellency of it, N. 237.

Cordeliers, their Story of St. *Francis* their Founder, N. 245.

Cornaro, Lewis, a remarkable Inftance of the Benefit of Temperance, N. 195.

Coverley, Sir *Roger de,* a Difpute between him and Sir *Andrew Freeport,* N. 174.

Cowards naturally impudent, N. 231.

Credulity in Women infamous, N. 190.

Cries of *London* require fome Regulation, N. 251.

Cunning, the Accomplifhment of whom, N. 225.

Curiofity, one of the ftrongeft and moft lafting of our Appetites, N. 237.

Cyneas, Pyrrhus's chief Minifter, his handfom Reproof to that Prince, N. 180.

D.

Ebauchee, his Pleafure is that of a Deftroyer, N. 199.
Dedications, the Abfurdity of them in general, N. 188.

Devotion, A Man is diftinguifh'd from Brutes by Devotion more than by Reafon, N. 201. The Errors into which it often leads us, *ibid.* The Notions the moft Refined among the Heathens had of it, 207. *Socrates's* Model of Devotions, *ibid.*

Difcontent to what often owing, N. 214.   Dif-

The INDEX.

Diſcretion an Under-Agent of Providence, N. 225. Diſtinguiſhed from Cunning, *ibid.*

Diſtinction, the Deſire of it implanted in our Natures, and why, N. 224.

Doctor in *Moorfields*, his Contrivance, N. 193.

Dorigny, Monſieur, his piece of the Transfiguration excellent in its kind, N. 226.

Drinking, a Rule preſcribed for it, N. 195.

Dutch, their Saying of a Man that happens to break, N. 174.

E.

EDucation, the Benefits of a good one, and Neceſſity of it, N. 215. The firſt thing to be taken care of in Education, 224.

Eginhart, Secretary to *Charles* the Great, his Adventure and Marriage, with that Emperor's Daughter, N. 181.

Euthuſiaſm, the Miſery of it, N. 201.

Epictetus, his Alluſion on human Life, N. 219.

Epitaph of a charitable Man, N. 177.

Eraſmus inſulted by a Parcel of *Trojans*, N. 239.

Eſtates generally purchaſed by the flower Part of Mankind, N. 222.

Eugenius, appropriates a tenth Part of his Eſtate to charitable Uſes, N. 177.

St. *Evremont*, his Endeavours to palliate the *Roman* Superſtitions, N. 213.

Exerciſe, the moſt effectual Phyſick, N. 195.

Expences, oftner proportioned to our Expectations than Poſſeſſions, N. 191.

Eyes, a Diſſertation on them. N. 250.

F.

FAble: of the Antiquity of Fables, N. 183. Fable of Pleaſure and Pain, *ibid.*

Face, a good one a Letter of Recommendation, N. 221.

Fame divided into three different Species, N. 218.

Faſhion: a Society propoſed to be erected for the Inſpection of Faſhions, N. 175.

Feaſts: the Gluttony of our modern Feaſts, N. 195.

Female Literature in want of a Regulation, N. 242.

Female Oratory, the Excellency of it, N. 247.

Foible, Sir *Jeoffry*, a kind Keeper, N. 190.

Forehead, eſteemed an Organ of Speech, N. 231.

Freeport, Sir *Andrew*, his Defence of Merchants, N. 174. Divides his Time betwixt his Buſineſs and Pleaſure, 232. His Opinion of Beggars, *ibid.*

O 3　　　　　G.

G.

GErmanicus, his Taſte of true Glory, N. 238.
Giving and *Forgiving*, two different Things, N. 189.
Glory how to be preſerved, N. 172, 218.
Good-nature, a Moral Virtue, N. 177. An endleſs Source
of Pleaſure, 196. Good-nature and Chearfulneſs, the
two great Ornaments of Virtue, 243.
Greeks, A Cuſtom practiſed by them, N. 189.
Greeks and *Trojans*, who ſo called, N. 239.
Grinning : A Grinning Prize, N. 137.

H.

HAbits, different, ariſing from different Profeſſions,
N. 197.
Hardneſs of Heart in Parents towards their Children moſt
inexcuſable, N. 181.
Henpeck'd : the Henpeck'd Huſband deſcribed, N. 179.
Herod and *Mariamne*, their Story from *Joſephus*, N. 171.
Heteroptick, who ſo to be called, N. 250.
Honours in this World under no Regulation, N. 219.
Hopes and Fears neceſſary Paſſions, N. 224.
Huſbands, an ill Cuſtom among them, N. 178.
Hypocriſy, the Honour and Juſtice done by it to Reli-
gion, N. 243.

I.

IDolatry, the Offspring of miſtaken Devotion, N. 211.
Jealouſy deſcribed, N. 170. How to be allay'd, 171.
An exquiſite Torment, 178.
Jezebels, who ſo called, N. 175.
Ill-nature an Imitator of Zeal, N. 185.
Jilts deſcribed, N. 187.
Imma, the Daughter of *Charles the Great*, her Story, N. 181.
Immortality of the Soul, the Benefits ariſing from a Con-
templation of it, N. 210.
Impudence recommended by ſome as Good-breeding,
N. 231.
Infidelity, another Term for Ignorance, N. 186.
Inquiſitive Tempers expoſed, N. 288.
Intereſt often a Promoter of Perſecution, N. 185.
Jupiter Ammon, an Anſwer of his Oracle to the *Athenians*,
N. 207.

K.

Kitty, a famous Town Girl, N. 187.

L. LA.

L.

Lacedæmonians, their Delicacies in their Senfe of Glory, N. 188. A Form of Prayer ufed by them, 207.

Lapirius, his great Generofity, N. 248.

Latin of great Ufe in a Country Auditory, N. 221.

Laughter a Counterpoife to the Spleen, N. 249. What fort of Perfons the moft accomplifh'd to raife it, *ibid.* A Poetical Figure of Laughter out of *Milton, ibid.*

Letters to the *Spectator*. From ——— with a Complaint againft a *Jezebel*, N. 175. from----who had been non-pluffed by a *Butt, ibid.* from *Jack Modifh* of *Exeter* about Fafhions, *ibid.* from *Nathaniel Henrooft*, a Hen-peck'd Hufband, 176; from *Celinda* about Jealoufy; 178; from *Martha Houfewife* to her Hufband, *ibid.* To the *Spectator* from---with an Account of a Whiftling-match at the *Bath*, 179; from *Philarithmus*, difplaying the Vanity of *Lewis* XIV's Conquefts, 180; from--who had married herfelf without her Father's Confent, 181; from *Alice Threadneedle* againft Wenching, 182; from--- in the *Round-houfe, ibid.* from----concerning *Nicholas Hart* the Annual Sleeper, 184; from *Charles Yellow* againft Jilts, 187; from a Gentleman to a Lady, to whom he had formerly been a Lover, and by whom he had been highly commended. 188; from a Father to his Son, 189. To the *Spectator*, from *Rebecca Nettletop*, a Town Lady, 190; from *Eve Afterday* who defires to be kept by the *Spectator, ibid.* from a Baudy-houfe In-habitant, complaining of fome of their Vifitors, *ibid.* from *George Gofling*, about a Ticket in the Lottery, 191. A Letter of Confolation to a young Gentleman who has lately loft his Father, *ibid.* To the *Spectator*, from an Hufband complaining of an heedlefs Wife, 194; from ----- complaining of a fantaftical Friend, *ibid.* from *J. B.* with Advice to the *Spectator*, 196; from *Biddy Lovelefs*, who is enamoured with two young Gentlemen at once, *ibid.* from *Statira* to the *Spectator*, with one to *Oroondates*, 199; from *Sufan Civil*, a Servant to another Lady, defiring the *Spectator's* Remarks upon voluntary Counfellors, 202; from *Thomas Smoky*, Servant to a paffionate Mafter, *ibid.* from a Baftard, complaining of his Condition as fuch, 203; from *Belinda* to the *Sothades*, 204; from *J. D.* to his Coquette Miftrefs, *ibid.* from a Lady to a Gentleman,

tleman, confessing her Love, N. 204. from angry *Phillis*, to her Lover, *ibid*. from a Lady to her Husband, an Officer in *Spain*, *ibid*. To the *Spectator* from *Belinda*, complaining of a Female Seducer, 205; from a Country Clergyman against an affected Singing of the *Psalms* in Church, *ibid*. from *Robin Goodfellow*, containing the Correction of an *Errata* in Sir *William Temple*'s Rule for Drinking, *ibid*. from *Mary Meanwell* about Visiting, 208; from a Shopkeeper with Thanks to the *Spectator*, *ibid*. from a Lover with an Hue and Cry after his Mistress's Heart, *ibid*. from *J. D.* concerning the Immortality of the Soul, 210; from *Melissa*, who has a Drone to her Husband, 211; from *Barnaby Brittle*, whose Wife is a Filly, *ibid*. from *Josiah Henpeck*, who is married to a Grimalkin, *ibid*. from *Martha Tempest*, complaining of her witty Husband, *ibid*. from *Anthony Freeman* the Henpeck'd, 212; from *Tom Meggot*, giving the *Spectator* an Account of the Success of Mr. *Freeman*'s Lecture, 216; from *Kitty Termagant*, giving an Account of the Romps Club, 217; from —— complaining of his *indelicate* Mistress, *ibid*. from *Susanna Frost*, an old Maid, *ibid*. from *A. B.* a Parson's Wife, *ibid*. from *Henrietta* to her ungracious Lover, 220. To the *Spectator* from—on false Wit, *ibid*. from *T. D.* concerning Salutation, *ibid*. from —— inquiring the Reason why Men of Parts are not the best Managers, 222; from *Æsculapius* about the Lover's Leap, 227; from *Athenais* and *Davyth ap Shenkyn* on the same Subject, *ibid*. from *W. B.* the Projector of the Pitch-Pipe, 228; from ——on Education, 230; from —— on the Awe which attends some Speakers in public Assemblies, 231; from *Philonous* on Free-Thinkers, 234; from—on Marriage, and the Husband's Conduct to his Wife, 236; from *Tristissa*, who is married to a Fool; *ibid*. from *T. S.* complaining of some People's Behaviour in Divine Service, *ibid*. from—with a Letter translated from *Aristænetus*, 238; from a Citizen in Praise of his Benefactor, 240; from *Rustick Sprightly*, a Country Gentleman, complaining of a Fashion introduced in the Country by a Courtier newly arrived; *ibid*. from *Charles Easy*, reflecting on the Behaviour of a Sort of Beau at *Philaster*, *ibid*. from *Asteria* on the Absence of Lovers, 241; from *Rebecca Ridinghood*, complaining

plaining of an ill-bred Fellow-Traveller, 242 ; from —— on a poor Weaver in *Spittal-Fields*, *ibid.* from *Abraham Thrifty*, Guardian to two learned Neices, *ibid.* from ——on *Raphael*'s Cartons, 244 ; from *Constantia Field* on the ninth Species of Women called Apes, *ibid.* from *Timothy Doodle* a great Lover of Blind-Man's Buff, 245 ; from *J. B.* on the several Ways of Confolation made use of by abfent Lovers, *ibid.* from *Troilus*, a declared Enemy to the *Greek*, *ibid.* from —on the Nursing of Children, N. 246 ; from *T. B.* being a Differtation on the Eye, 250 ; from *Abraham Spy* on a new Invention of Perfpective-Glaffes for the use of Starers, *ibid.*

Lovers of great Men, animadverted upon, N. 193.

Levity of Women, the Effects of it, N. 212.

Lye : feveral Sorts of Lies, N. 234.

Life to what compared in the Scriptures, and by the Heathen Philofophers, N. 219. The prefent Life a State of Probation, 237.

Logick of Kings, what, N. 239.

Lottery, fome Difcourfe on it, N. 191.

Love : the Tranfport of a Virtuous Love, N. 199.

Lover's-Leap, where fituated, N. 225. An effectual Cure for Love, 227. A fhort Hiftory of it, 233.

Luxury : the Luxury of our Modern Meals, N. 195.

M.

MAlvolio, his Character, N. 238. *Maple (Will)* an impudent Libertine, N. 203.

Man, the merrieft Species of the Creation, N. 249. The mercenary Practice of Men in the Choice of Wives, 196.

Merchants of great Benefit to the Public, N. 174.

Mill, to make Verfes, N. 220.

Mirth in a Man ought always to be accidental, N. 196.

Modefty and Self-denial frequently attended with unexpected Bleffings, N. 206. Modefty the contrary of Ambition, *ibid.* A due Proportion of Modefty requifite to an Orator, 231. The Excellency of Modefty, *ibid.* Vicious Modefty what, *ibid.* The Misfortunes to which the Modeft and Innocent are often expofed, 242.

Mothers juftly reproved for not nurfing their own Children, N, 246.

Motto, the Effects of an handfom one, N. 221.

Much Cry, but little Wooll, to whom apply'd, N. 251.

N.

N*Icholas-Hart,* the annual Sleeper, N. 184.
Nurfes. The frequent Inconveniences of hired Nurfes, N. 246.

O.

O Bedience of Children to their Parents the Bafis of all Government, N. 189.

Opportunities to be carefully avoided by the Fair Sex, N. 198.

Order neceffary to be kept up in the World, N. 219.

P.

P Arents naturally fond of their own Children, N. 192.
Paffions : the various Operations of the Paffions, N. 215. The ftrange Diforders bred by our Paffions when not regulated by Virtue, *ibid.* It is not fo much the Bufinefs of Religion to extinguifh, as to regulate our Paffions, 224.

Patrons and Clients, a Difcourfe of them, N. 214. Worthy Patrons compared to Guardian Angels, *ibid.*

People the only Riches of a Country, N. 200.

Perfians, their Notion of Parricide, N. 189.

Philofophers, why longer liv'd than other Men, N. 195.

Phocion, his Notion of Popular Applaufe, N. 188.

Phyfick, the Subftitute of Exercife or Temperance, N. 195.

Pictures, Witty, what Pieces fo called, N. 244.

Piety an Ornament to human Nature, N. 201.

Pitch-pipe, the Invention and Ufe of it, N. 228.

Plato, his Account of *Socrates* his Behaviour the Morning he was to die, N. 183.

Pleaders, few of them tolerable Company, N. 197.

Pleafure, Pleafure and Pain, a Marriage propofed between them and concluded, N. 183.

Poll, a Way of Arguing, N. 239.

Popular Applaufe, the Vanity of it, N. 188.

Praife, a generous Mind the moft fenfible of it, N. 238.

Pride : a Man crazed with Pride a mortifying Sight, N. 201.

Procurefs, her Trade, N. 205.

Prodicus, the firft Inventor of Fables, N. 183.

Profperity, to what compared by *Seneca,* N. 237.

Prti-

Providence, not to be fathom'd by Reason, N. 237.

Q.

QUALITY, is either of Fortune, Body, or Mind, N. 219.

R.

RACK, a knotty Syllogism, N. 239.
    Raphael's Cartons, their Effect upon the *Spectator,*
    N. 226, 244.
Readers divided by the *Spectator* into the *Mercurial* and
    Saturnine, N. 179.
Reputation, a Species of Fame, N. 218. The Stability
    of it, if well founded, *ibid.*
Ridicule the Talent of ungenerous Tempers, N. 249. The
    two great Branches of Ridicule in Writing, *ibid.*

S.

SAlamanders, an Order of Ladies described, N. 198.
    Sappho, an excellent Poetess, N. 223. Dies for Love
    of *Phaon, ibid.* Her Hymn to *Venus, ibid.* A Frag-
    ment of hers translated into three different Languages,
    229.
Satirists, best instruct us in the Manners of their respective
    Times, N. 209.
Schoolmen, their Ass Case, N. 191. How apply'd, *ibid.*
Self-Denial the great Foundation of Civil Virtue, N. 248.
Self-Love transplanted, what, N. 192.
Sentry, his Discourse with a young Wrangler in the Law,
    N. 197.
Shows and Diversions lie properly within the Province
    of the *Spectator,* N. 235.
Simonides, his Satire on Women, N. 209.
Sly, the Haberdasher, his Advertisement to young Tradef-
    men in their last Year of Apprenticeship, N. 187.
Socrates, his Notion of Pleasure and Pain, N. 183. The
    Effect of his Temperance, 195. His Instructions to his
    Pupil *Alcibiades* in relation to a Prayer, 207. a Catheche-
    tical Method of Arguing introduced first by him, 239.
    Instructed in Eloquence by a Woman, 247.
Sorites, what sort of Figure, N. 239.
Spectator, his Artifice to engage his different Readers, N.
    179. The Character given of him in his own Presence
    at a Coffee-house near *Aldgate,* 218.
Speech, the several Organs of it, N. 231.
Spy, the Mischief of one in a Family, N. 202.

State

State (future) the Refreshments a virtuous Person enjoys in Prospect and Contemplation of it, N. 186.

Stores of Providence, what, N. 248.

Strife, the Spirit of it, N. 197.

Sun, the first Eye of Consequence, N. 250.

Superiority reduced to the Notion of Quality, N. 219. To be founded only on Merit and Virtue, 202.

Superstition, an Error arising from a mistaken Devotion, N. 201. Superstition hath something in it destructive to Religion, 213.

T.

Talents ought to be valued according as they are apply'd, N. 172.

Taste (corrupt) of the Age, to what attributed, N. 208.

Temperance the best Preservative of Health, N. 195. what kind of Temperance the best, *ibid.*

Temple, (Sir *William*) his Rule for Drinking, N. 195.

Ten, call'd by the *Platonick* Writers the Complete Number, N. 221.

Thinking aloud, what, N. 211.

Trade, Trading and Landed Interest ever jarring, N. 174.

Tradition of the *Jews* concerning *Moses,* N. 237.

Transmigration, what, N. 211.

Trunk-maker, a great Man in the Upper-Gallery in the Play-house, N. 235.

V.

Virtue, the most reasonable and genuine Source of Honour, N. 219. Of a beautiful Nature, 243. The great Ornaments of it, *ibid.* To be esteemed in a Foe, *ibid.*

W.

Whistling Match described, N. 179.

Wife, how much preferable to a Mistress, N. 199.

Wise Men and Fools, the Difference between them, N. 225.

Wit; the many Artifices and Modes of false Wit, N. 220.

Women: deluding Women, their Practices exposed, N. 182. Women great Orators, 247.

Y.

Yawning, a *Christmas* Gambol, N. 179.

The End of the Third Volume.

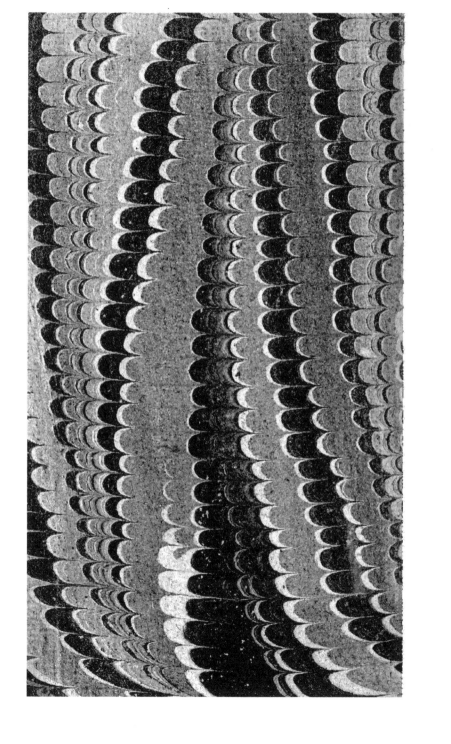

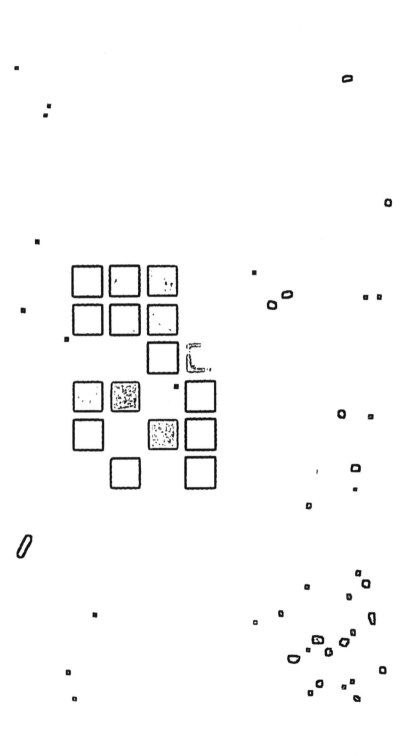